ACTIVEX™ FOR DUMMIES®

by Kurt D. Fenstermacher

Foreword by Don Crabb

IDG Books Worldwide, Inc.
An International Data Group Company

Foster City, CA ♦ Chicago, IL ♦ Indianapolis, IN ♦ Southlake, TX

ActiveX™ For Dummies®

Published by
IDG Books Worldwide, Inc.
An International Data Group Company
919 E. Hillsdale Blvd.
Suite 400
Foster City, CA 94404
http://www.idgbooks.com (IDG Books Worldwide Web site)
http://www.dummies.com (Dummies Press Web site)

Library of Congress Catalog Card No.: 96-79280

ISBN: 0-7645-0076-7

Printed in the United States of America

10 9 8 7 6 5 4 3 2 1

1E/QY/QR/ZX/IN

Distributed in the United States by IDG Books Worldwide, Inc.

Distributed by Macmillan Canada for Canada; by Transworld Publishers Limited in the United Kingdom and Europe; by WoodsLane Pty. Ltd. for Australia; by WoodsLane Enterprises Ltd. for New Zealand; by Longman Singapore Publishers Ltd. for Singapore, Malaysia, Thailand, and Indonesia; by Simron Pty. Ltd. for South Africa; by Toppan Company Ltd. for Japan; by Distribuidora Cuspide for Argentina; by Livraria Cultura for Brazil; by Ediciencia S.A. for Ecuador; by Addison-Wesley Publishing Company for Korea; by Ediciones ZETA S.C.R. Ltda. for Peru; by WS Computer Publishing Company, Inc., for the Philippines; by Unalis Corporation for Taiwan; by Contemporanea de Ediciones for Venezuela. Authorized Sales Agent: Anthony Rudkin Associates for the Middle East and North Africa.

For general information on IDG Books Worldwide's books in the U.S., please call our Consumer Customer Service department at 800-762-2974. For reseller information, including discounts and premium sales, please call our Reseller Customer Service department at 800-434-3422.

For information on where to purchase IDG Books Worldwide's books outside the U.S., please contact our International Sales department at 415-655-3172 or fax 415-655-3295.

For information on foreign language translations, please contact our Foreign & Subsidiary Rights department at 415-655-3021 or fax 415-655-3281.

For sales inquiries and special prices for bulk quantities, please contact our Sales department at 415-655-3200 or write to the address above.

For information on using IDG Books Worldwide's books in the classroom or for ordering examination copies, please contact our Educational Sales department at 800-434-2086 or fax 817-251-8174.

For press review copies, author interviews, or other publicity information, please contact our Public Relations department at 415-655-3000 or fax 415-655-3299.

For authorization to photocopy items for corporate, personal, or educational use, please contact Copyright Clearance Center, 222 Rosewood Drive, Danvers, MA 01923, or fax 508-750-4470.

 is a trademark under exclusive license to IDG Books Worldwide, Inc., from International Data Group, Inc.

About the Author

Kurt D. Fenstermacher has scaled Mt. Everest without oxygen, swum the English Channel, and perfected the fat-free potato chip. In addition to the 6,345 magazine articles and 872 books he has written, he has also translated several computer books from the original Babylonian script. (Those Babylonians were way ahead of their time.) Kurt used to refer to himself in the first person, but, after watching several Bob Dole campaign speeches on television, Kurt now refers to Kurt as Kurt.

Kurt has been programming since the early '80s, when he worked his way through *Compute!* magazine's *BASIC Computer Games*. (His experience with Visual Basic Scripting Edition, which is covered in this book, has brought him full circle — back to Basic.) He began work several years ago on his doctorate in artificial intelligence at the University of Chicago computer science department. As a member of the university's Intelligent Information Laboratory (the Info Lab), Kurt has been researching applications of artificial intelligence to problems of information management. Because of the Info Lab focus on building distributed information systems, he has been using and developing Internet and Web software for several years.

In addition to working on an MBA in finance at the University of Chicago Graduate School of Business, Kurt is studying ways to manage financial information more effectively from the computer side. In addition to research and software development, he has been writing about computers and software for several years. Most recently, he has authored the computer column in the University of Chicago campus newspaper. When he's not writing, studying finance, or researching information management, he likes to spend time outdoors (either cycling or camping) and in the kitchen (either cooking or eating).

ABOUT IDG BOOKS WORLDWIDE

Welcome to the world of IDG Books Worldwide.

IDG Books Worldwide, Inc., is a subsidiary of International Data Group, the world's largest publisher of computer-related information and the leading global provider of information services on information technology. IDG was founded more than 25 years ago and now employs more than 8,500 people worldwide. IDG publishes more than 275 computer publications in over 75 countries (see listing below). More than 60 million people read one or more IDG publications each month.

Launched in 1990, IDG Books Worldwide is today the #1 publisher of best-selling computer books in the United States. We are proud to have received eight awards from the Computer Press Association in recognition of editorial excellence and three from *Computer Currents'* First Annual Readers' Choice Awards. Our best-selling *...For Dummies*® series has more than 30 million copies in print with translations in 30 languages. IDG Books Worldwide, through a joint venture with IDG's Hi-Tech Beijing, became the first U.S. publisher to publish a computer book in the People's Republic of China. In record time, IDG Books Worldwide has become the first choice for millions of readers around the world who want to learn how to better manage their businesses.

Our mission is simple: Every one of our books is designed to bring extra value and skill-building instructions to the reader. Our books are written by experts who understand and care about our readers. The knowledge base of our editorial staff comes from years of experience in publishing, education, and journalism — experience we use to produce books for the '90s. In short, we care about books, so we attract the best people. We devote special attention to details such as audience, interior design, use of icons, and illustrations. And because we use an efficient process of authoring, editing, and desktop publishing our books electronically, we can spend more time ensuring superior content and spend less time on the technicalities of making books.

You can count on our commitment to deliver high-quality books at competitive prices on topics you want to read about. At IDG Books Worldwide, we continue in the IDG tradition of delivering quality for more than 25 years. You'll find no better book on a subject than one from IDG Books Worldwide.

John Kilcullen
President and CEO
IDG Books Worldwide, Inc.

Eighth Annual Computer Press Awards ≥1992

Ninth Annual Computer Press Awards ≥1993

Tenth Annual Computer Press Awards ≥1994

Eleventh Annual Computer Press Awards ≥1995

IDG Books Worldwide, Inc., is a subsidiary of International Data Group, the world's largest publisher of computer-related information and the leading global provider of information services on information technology. International Data Group publishes over 275 computer publications in over 75 countries. Sixty million people read one or more International Data Group publications each month. International Data Group's publications include: **ARGENTINA:** Buyer's Guide, Computerworld Argentina, PC World Argentina; **AUSTRALIA:** Australian Macworld, Australian PC World, Australian Reseller News, Computerworld, IT Casebook, Network World, Publish, Webmaster; **AUSTRIA:** Computerwelt Osterreich, Networks Austria, PC Tip Austria; **BANGLADESH:** PC World Bangladesh; **BELARUS:** PC World Belarus; **BELGIUM:** Data News; **BRAZIL:** Annuario de Informatica, Computerworld, Connections, Macworld, PC Player, PC World, Publish, Reseller News, Supergamepower; **BULGARIA:** Computerworld Bulgaria, Network World Bulgaria, PC & MacWorld Bulgaria; **CANADA:** CIO Canada, Client/Server World, ComputerWorld Canada, InfoWorld Canada, NetworkWorld Canada, WebWorld; **CHILE:** Computerworld Chile, PC World Chile; **COLOMBIA:** Computerworld Colombia, PC World Colombia; **COSTA RICA:** PC World Centro America; **THE CZECH AND SLOVAK REPUBLICS:** Computerworld Czechoslovakia, Macworld Czech Republic, PC World Czechoslovakia; **DENMARK:** Communications World Danmark, Computerworld Danmark, Macworld Danmark, PC World Danmark, Techworld Danmark; **DOMINICAN REPUBLIC:** PC World Republica Dominicana; **ECUADOR:** PC World Ecuador; **EGYPT:** Computerworld Middle East, PC World Middle East; **EL SALVADOR:** PC World Centro America; **FINLAND:** MikroPC, Tietoverkko, Tietoviikko; **FRANCE:** Distributique, Hebdo, Info PC, Le Monde Informatique, Macworld, Reseaux & Telecoms, WebMaster France; **GERMANY:** Computer Partner, Computerwoche, Computerwoche Extra, Computerwoche FOCUS, Global Online, Macwelt, PC Welt; **GREECE:** Amiga Computing, GamePro Greece, Multimedia World; **GUATEMALA:** PC World Centro America; **HONDURAS:** PC World Centro America; **HONG KONG:** Computerworld Hong Kong, PC World Hong Kong, Publish in Asia; **HUNGARY:** ABCD CD-ROM, Computerworld Szamitastechnika, Internetto online Magazine, PC World Hungary, PC-X Magazin Hungary; **ICELAND:** Tolvuheimur PC World Island; **INDIA:** Information Communications World, Information Systems Computerworld, PC World India, Publish in Asia; **INDONESIA:** InfoKomputer PC World, Komputek Computerworld, Publish in Asia; **IRELAND:** Computerscope, PC Live!; **ISRAEL:** Macworld Israel, People & Computers/Computerworld; **ITALY:** Computerworld Italia, Macworld Italia, Networking Italia, PC World Italia; **JAPAN:** DTP World, Macworld Japan, Nikkei Personal Computing, OS/2 World Japan, SunWorld Japan, Windows NT World, Windows World Japan; **KENYA:** PC World East African; **KOREA:** Hi-Tech Information, Macworld Korea, PC World Korea; **MACEDONIA:** PC World Macedonia; **MALAYSIA:** Computerworld Malaysia, PC World Malaysia, Publish in Asia; **MALTA:** PC World Malta; **MEXICO:** Computerworld Mexico, PC World Mexico; **MYANMAR:** PC World Myanmar; **NETHERLANDS:** Computer! Totaal, LAN Internetworking Magazine, LAN World Buyers Guide, Macworld Netherlands, Net, WebWereld; **NEW ZEALAND:** Absolute Beginners Guide and Plain & Simple Series, Computer Buyer, Computer Industry Directory, Computerworld New Zealand, MTB, Network World, PC World New Zealand; **NICARAGUA:** PC World Centro America; **NORWAY:** Computerworld Norge, CW Rapport, Datamagasinet, Financial Rapport, Kursguide Norge, Macworld Norge, Multimediaworld Norge, PC World Ekspress Norge, PC World Nettverk, PC World Norge, PC World ProduktGuide Norge; **PAKISTAN:** Computerworld Pakistan; **PANAMA:** PC World Panama; **PEOPLE'S REPUBLIC OF CHINA:** China Computer Users, China Computerworld, China InfoWorld, China Telecom World Weekly, Computer & Communication, Electronic Design China, Electronics Today, Electronics Weekly, Game Software, PC World China, Popular Computer Week, Software Weekly, Software World, Telecom World; **PERU:** Computerworld Peru, PC World Profesional Peru, PC World SoHo Peru; **PHILIPPINES:** Click!, Computerworld Philippines, PC World Philippines, Publish in Asia; **POLAND:** Computerworld Poland, Computerworld Special Report Poland, Cyber, Macworld Poland, Networld Poland, PC World Komputer; **PORTUGAL:** Cerebro/PC World, Computerworld/Correio Informatico, Dealer World Portugal, Mac*In/PC*In Portugal, Multimedia World; **PUERTO RICO:** PC World Puerto Rico; **ROMANIA:** Computerworld Romania, PC World Romania, Telecom Romania; **RUSSIA:** Computerworld Russia, Mir PK, Publish, Seti; **SINGAPORE:** Computerworld Singapore, PC World Singapore, Publish in Asia; **SLOVENIA:** Monitor; **SOUTH AFRICA:** Computing SA, Network World SA, Software World SA; **SPAIN:** Communicaciones World Espana, Computerworld Espana, Dealer World Espana, Macworld Espana, PC World Espana; **SRI LANKA:** Infolink PC World; **SWEDEN:** CAP&Design, Computer Sweden, Corporate Computing Sweden, Internetworld Sweden, it.branschen, Macworld Sweden, MaxiData Sweden, Natverk & Kommunikation, PC World Sweden, PCaktiv, Windows World Sweden; **SWITZERLAND:** Computerworld Schweiz, Macworld Schweiz, PCtip; **TAIWAN:** Computerworld Taiwan, Macworld Taiwan, NEW ViSiON/Publish, PC World Taiwan, Windows World Taiwan; **THAILAND:** Publish in Asia, Thai Computerworld; **TURKEY:** Computerworld Turkiye, Macworld Turkiye, Network World Turkiye, PC World Turkiye; **UKRAINE:** Computerworld Kiev, Multimedia World Ukraine, PC World Ukraine; **UNITED KINGDOM:** Acorn User UK, Amiga Action UK, Amiga Computing UK, Apple Talk UK, Computing, Macworld, Parents and Computers UK, PC Advisor, PC Home, PSX Pro, The WEB; **UNITED STATES:** Cable in the Classroom, CIO Magazine, Computerworld, DOS World, Federal Computer Week, GamePro Magazine, InfoWorld, I-Way, Macworld, Network World, PC Games, PC World, Publish, Video Event, THE WEB Magazine, and WebMaster; online webzines: JavaWorld, NetscapeWorld, and SunWorld Online; **URUGUAY:** InfoWorld Uruguay; **VENEZUELA:** Computerworld Venezuela, PC World Venezuela; and **VIETNAM:** PC World Vietnam. 10/22/96

Dedication

To my family, whose love has inspired me and whose support has encouraged me. And especially to my wife, Jeffie, who has suffered, better than anyone, the joys of writing.

Author's Acknowledgments

Authoring a book is a little like scoring the winning goal in a soccer game: It's *your* name up in lights, and most people forget about the rest of the team. Writing a book is a team sport (although it's usually a noncontact sport), and this page is my chance to give credit where credit is due.

If, after reading this book, you think that I should have stuck with my day job, you can blame Don Crabb. Don has encouraged my writing from the beginning and has been a wonderful guide to the world of computer book authoring. He also introduced me to his agent, David Rogelberg, and together they convinced the publisher of this book to give me my first shot. I owe both of them for their wisdom and patience with a first-time author.

The people at IDG Books Worldwide and Dummies Press have been extraordinary. In his role as acquisitions editor, Gareth Hancock has been helpful and tolerant of a newbie's questions and confusions. Darlene Wong has been a great source as well (and she's the one who sends out the checks). Mary Corder foolishly volunteered herself as the conduit for all my questions and problems and has worked very hard to help me. (She would make a great author of *Publishing For Dummies*.) Joyce Pepple has worked hard to make sure that the CD-ROM doesn't land me in jail, which I deeply appreciate. Mary Bednarek has been invaluable as well. The project editor, Rebecca Whitney, has tried hard to produce coherent text from my ramblings. Her experience and careful reading have balanced a tyro's writing.

Finally, I want to thank my family and friends. My parents, brothers, stepmother, and grandfather have encouraged me for many years, and their support has enabled me to write this book. My wife worked as hard on this book as anyone and has once again indulged my penchant for crazy projects. Our cat, BJ, deserves thanks for making sure that I don't take life too seriously — having her jump around on my keyboard really takes the pressure off. To my friends Grace and John Sawin, who seem to have as much invested in this book as I do, thanks. My academic advisor, Kristian Hammond, deserves credit for his understanding of a nontraditional graduate student.

Publisher's Acknowledgments

We're proud of this book; please send us your comments about it by using the Reader Response Card at the back of the book or by e-mailing us at feedback/dummies@idgbooks.com. Some of the people who helped bring this book to market include the following:

Acquisitions, Development, & Editorial

Project Editor: Rebecca Whitney

Acquisitions Editor: Gareth Hancock

Product Development Manager: Mary Bednarek

Permissions Editor: Joyce Pepple

Copy Editor: Michael Simsic

Technical Editor: Discovery Computing

Editorial Manager: Mary C. Corder

Editorial Assistant: Chris H. Collins

Production

Project Coordinator: Debbie Stailey

Layout and Graphics: E. Shawn Aylsworth, Theresa Sánchez-Baker, Theresa Ball, Brett Black, Cameron Booker, Maridee V. Ennis, Todd Klemme, Ruth Loiacano, Jane Martin, Drew R. Moore, Mark Owens, Laura Puranen

Proofreaders: Melissa D. Buddendeck, Henry Lazarek, Dwight Ramsey, Robert Springer, Carrie Voorhis, Ethel Winslow, Karen York

Indexer: Anne Leach

Special Help
Suzanne Packer

General and Administrative

IDG Books Worldwide, Inc.: John Kilcullen, CEO; Steven Berkowitz, President and Publisher

IDG Books Technology Publishing: Brenda McLaughlin, Senior Vice President and Group Publisher

Dummies Technology Press and Dummies Editorial: Diane Graves Steele, Vice President and Associate Publisher; Judith A. Taylor, Brand Manager; Kristin A. Cocks, Editorial Director

Dummies Trade Press: Kathleen A. Welton, Vice President and Publisher; Stacy S. Collins, Brand Manager

IDG Books Production for Dummies Press: Beth Jenkins, Production Director; Cindy L. Phipps, Supervisor of Project Coordination; Kathie S. Schutte, Supervisor of Page Layout; Shelley Lea, Supervisor of Graphics and Design; Debbie J. Gates, Production Systems Specialist; Tony Augsburger, Reprint Coordinator; Leslie Popplewell, Media Archive Coordinator

Dummies Packaging and Book Design: Patti Sandez, Packaging Specialist; Kavish+Kavish, Cover Design

◆

The publisher would like to give special thanks to Patrick J. McGovern, without whom this book would not have been possible.

◆

Contents at a Glance

Foreword xx

Introduction 1

Part I: The Beginning (A Very Good Place to Begin) 7
Chapter 1: What Is ActiveX? 9
Chapter 2: To ActiveX or Not to ActiveX? 17
Chapter 3: Teach Yourself HTML in 21 Minutes 25

Part II: ActiveX Components 51
Chapter 4: Birds of a Feather: The Building Blocks of ActiveX Controls 53
Chapter 5: Houston, We Have a Solution: The Microsoft Control Pad 67
Chapter 6: Laying It on the Line: Creating HTML Layouts 89
Chapter 7: "It's Better to Look Good than to Feel Good" 101
Chapter 8: The Sound of Music 155
Chapter 9: A Penny for Your Thoughts: Getting User Input 177

Part III: Scripting for ActiveX 235
Chapter 10: We Don't Need No Stinkin' Scripts 237
Chapter 11: The Basics of Scripting 245
Chapter 12: World Events and How to Handle Them 273
Chapter 13: The High-Fashion World of Object Modeling 299

Part IV: The Part of Tens 343
Chapter 14: Ten Cool ActiveX Controls 345
Chapter 15: Top Ten VBScript Tips 351

Appendix 359

Index 363

License Agreement 378

Installation Instructions 380

Reader Response Card .... Back of Book

Cartoons at a Glance

By Rich Tennant • Fax: 508-546-7747 • E-mail: the5wave@tiac.net

page 235

page 7

page 343

page 176

page 51

Table of Contents

Introduction 1

So What Is This ActiveX Thing, Anyway? 1
"Cover Me — I'm Going Intranet!" 2
Why Should You Buy This Book? 2
What's Inside? 3
    Part I: The Beginning (A Very Good Place to Begin) 3
    Part II: ActiveX Components 3
    Part III: Scripting for ActiveX 4
    Part IV: The Part of Tens 4
    About the CD-ROM 4
How This Book Works 4
Icons Used in This Book 5
What You Should Know before You Buy This Book 6
Don't Keep Me in Suspense 6
Ready, Set, Activate! 6

Part I: The Beginning (A Very Good Place to Begin) 7

Chapter 1: What Is ActiveX? 9

It's the Content, Stupid! 10
What Is ActiveX? 11
    ActiveX controls 11
    ActiveX documents 14
    ActiveX Scripting 15
    ActiveX Server Framework 15
    Java Virtual Machine 16
    Putting it all together 16

Chapter 2: To ActiveX or Not to ActiveX? 17

The Number-One Reason to Choose ActiveX: Microsoft 17
    Making the most of marketing muscle 18
    Remembering that variety is the spice of life 18
    Integrating beyond the network 19
    Reviewing Visual Basic 19
Handling Life without ActiveX 20
Going the Way of Java 21
Why Not ActiveX? 21
To ActiveX or Not to ActiveX: The Answer 22

Chapter 3: Teach Yourself HTML in 21 Minutes **25**

Oh, What a Tangled Web We Weave 26
  What's a Web? 26
  Do you know who your server is? 26
  The medium's the message 28
Skeletons in the HTML Closet: The Bare-Bones HTML File 30
What's in a Link? 31
  "Where's 123 Main Street?" (Web addresses) 31
  Understanding that links are relatively absolute 33
A Lightning-Quick Guide to HTML Tags 34
  Outlining your pages 35
  Brother, can you paragraph? 35
  Wishing for lists 36
  Adding a little style to your pages 36
Image Is Everything 40
  Getting in line with inline images 40
  Going outside with external images 42
  Getting a little background image on a browser 42
Turning the Tables on HTML 43
My HTML Has Been Framed! 45
  Building a frame 46
  Floating on a sea of frames 49

Part II: ActiveX Components *51*

**Chapter 4: Birds of a Feather: The Building Blocks
of ActiveX Controls** **53**

Who's in Control Here? 54
Handling Events Bigger Than the Oscars 54
Your Honor, I Object: The <OBJECT> Tag 55
  ALIGN 56
  BORDER 58
  CLASSID 58
  CODEBASE 59
  DATA 60
  DECLARE 60
  HEIGHT, WIDTH 60
  HSPACE, VSPACE 61
  ID 62
  NAME 62
  SHAPES 63
  STANDBY 63
  TYPE, CODETYPE 63
  USEMAP 64
Parameters: Do You Need to Know? 65
  NAME 66
  TYPE 66

Chapter 5: Houston, We Have a Solution: The Microsoft Control Pad **67**

Ground Zero: Starting Out with Control Pad 67
Changing Property Values (or, How to Make Money in Real Estate) 70
Using the Script Wizard to Link Controls 72
    What's a script? (Or, how to be a screenwriter) 72
    Knowing the proper incantations to start up the Script Wizard 73
    Ready for action: What to do for an event 75
    Taking your script out for a test drive 77
Exploring Script Wizard 78
    Redirecting the flow of traffic with Go To Page 78
    Traveling the world with VBScript (global variables) 79
    Using procedures: How to do something over and over 82
    Sorry — I don't do windows (but the Window object does!) 82
    Windows are objects too 83
    Documents are where it's at 84
    Where did you come from? (The Referrer property) 85
    Extra events 87

Chapter 6: Laying It on the Line: Creating HTML Layouts **89**

Getting into Position 89
Laying Out a Layout 90
    Adding a control 91
    Formatting a Layout 92
    Tooling around with the Toolbox 96
Taking Control of Your Layouts: The HTML Layout Control 97
    Inserting a Layout 98
    Properties 98
    Methods 100

Chapter 7: "It's Better to Look Good than to Feel Good" **101**

Understanding How to Read a Property Description 103
Letting Script Wizard Do the Work 104
Assigning Custom Values for Your Properties 104
    Accelerator 105
    AutoSize 106
    BackColor 106
    BackStyle 106
    BorderColor 108
    BorderStyle 108
    Caption 109
    CodeBase 109
    Enabled 109
    Font 110
    ForeColor 112
    Height 112
    ID 112
    Left 112
    MouseIcon 113

MousePointer 113
Picture 115
SpecialEffect 115
TabIndex 117
TabStop 117
Top 118
Value 118
Visible 118
Width 118
WordWrap 119
Introducing the Animated Button Control 119
Properties 120
Events 121
The United States of animated buttons 121
Methods 123
Chart 124
Properties 125
Events 133
Methods 133
Gauging Your Progress 133
Properties 134
Events 136
Methods 137
Making the Gradient 137
Properties 138
Events 140
Methods 140
Image Control 140
Getting inline 140
Taking control of images 141
Properties 141
Events 146
Methods 146
Label 147
Properties 148
Events 152
Methods 153
New 153
Properties 153
Events 154
Methods 154

Chapter 8: The Sound of Music **155**

Sound in the 'Ground: Background Sounds 156
Is It Live, or Is It RealAudio? 157
Serving Up a St(r)eaming Plate of RealAudio 157
Your RealAudio Toolbox 158
Serving audio for real 158
Cracking the RealAudio secret code 159

Eine kleine NachtRealAudio 159

Making Really Good RealAudio 160

The ActiveX RealAudio Player 160

Keeping it simple 162

Taking control of RealAudio Player 162

Naming names with Console 163

Being label-free 165

Making a fresh start 165

Should I stay or should I AUTOGO? 165

The Many Methods of the RealAudio ActiveX Control 166

Play until you stop 167

What's next? 167

Letting users have it their way 168

Lies, damn lies, and statistics 168

The RealAudio Control Hosts Some Major Events 169

When one clip closes, another opens
(OnClipOpened and OnClipClosed) 170

Giving your player some status (OnShowStatus) 171

Going to a URL 171

Intercepting URL events 172

Synchronize, Synchronize, Synchronize 173

Chapter 9: A Penny for Your Thoughts: Getting User Input 177

Form Controls and What They're Good For 178

On or off? 178

Listing lotsa lists 178

Great literature needs its own control 179

Round and round 179

Common Properties and Their Picky Little Details 180

Alignment 182

AutoTab 183

AutoWordSelect 184

DragBehavior 184

EnterFieldBehavior 185

HideSelection 186

IMEMode 186

IntegralHeight 186

Locked 186

MaxLength 187

PicturePosition 188

ScrollBars 189

SelLength 190

SelectionMargin 190

SelStart 190

SelText 191

TabKeyBehavior 192

Text 192

TextAlign 192

TripleState 193

Common Methods of Form Controls 194
    AboutBox() 194
    Clear() 195
    Copy() 195
    Cut() 195
    Paste() 195
    RemoveItem() 196
    SetFocus() 196
    ZOrder 196
Reading All about a Control 197
CheckBox: Understanding When a Simple Yes or No Will Do 198
    Much ado about null 199
    Properties 199
    Events 200
    Methods 200
ComboBox: Have Your List and Eat Your Text Too 200
    Properties 202
    Events 207
    Methods 207
Making a List Box and Checking It Twice 208
    Properties 209
    Events 218
    Methods 219
Knowing Your Option Buttons 219
    Properties 220
    Events 221
    Methods 221
Popup Goes the Menu! 221
    Reading the menu at the cybercafé 222
    Properties 224
    Events 224
    Methods 225
Putting a New Spin on Buttons 226
    Spinning your values 226
    Properties 227
    Events 229
    Methods 229
TextBox: Asking for User Input (And Showing That You Care) 230
    Properties 230
    Events 232
    Methods 233
Toggle This! 233
    Properties 233
    Events 234
    Methods 234

Part III: Scripting for ActiveX *235*

Chapter 10: We Don't Need No Stinkin' Scripts **237**

Why Write a Script? 237
Writing Scripts to Activate ActiveX 238
Choosing a Scripting Language (Speaking in Tongues) 240
What Can You Do With a Script? 241
  Acting and reacting 242
  Designing forms that talk back (interactive forms) 242
  Sharing your view of the world with broadcast news 244
  Playing a game 244

Chapter 11: The Basics of Scripting **245**

What's a Script? 245
Why Write a Script? 246
Writing Your First Script 246
  Introducing "Hello, world!" 246
  Understanding how "Hello, world!" works 247
  It's not a script — it's a comment 248
Working with Variables 249
  Naming variables 249
  Declaring the independence of variables 250
  Scopin' out variables 251
  Keeping things constant with constants 252
  Realizing that all variables are created equal (sort of) .. 253
  Declaring arrays 255
  Creating reference material 256
Stringing Your Data Along 257
Going with the Flow of Control 258
  Playing what-if? 258
  Looping 259
  Pick a case — any case 263
Smooth Operators 264
  The third R: 'rithmetic 266
  Compare and contrast 267
  Logically speaking 267
Procedural Anatomy 267
  "We all live in a yellow Sub procedure" 268
  Knowing how to argue with VBScript 268
  Proceeding with Function procedures 269
  Using Sub and Function procedures in code 270
  Knowing where to declare 271
"No Comment" Is No Good 272

Chapter 12: World Events and How to Handle Them **273**

Handling Events 274
  Living within the limitations of VBScript 275
  Writing an event handler 276

Common Events of ActiveX Controls 276
    Change events 276
    Drag 'til you drop 280
    The keys to the kingdom 285
    Mousin' around 287
    A miscellaneous event: Error 296

Chapter 13: The High-Fashion World of Object Modeling 299

Who Do Voodoo? You Do! 300
Objects for Peace, Love, and Understanding 300
Who's in Control Here? 301
The Door to the Object Model: The Window Object 305
    Properties 305
    Methods 310
Documenting the Document Object 316
    Properties 316
    Events 323
    Methods 323
Tying Things Together with a Link Object 326
    Properties 327
    Events 329
    Methods 331
Anchor Objects Aweigh! 331
The Object of My Form Desire 331
    Properties 332
    Events 335
    Methods 336
Sailing Away with the Navigator Object 336
    Properties 337
    Setting sail with a script 339
    Events 340
    Methods 340
Knowing Your History Object 340
    Properties 341
    Events 341
    Methods 341

Part IV: The Part of Tens *343*

Chapter 14: Ten Cool ActiveX Controls 345

Adobe Acrobat Reader 345
HotSpot in Town 345
MicroHelp Calendar (Mh3DCalendar) 346
MicroHelp Clock (MhClock) 347
MicroHelp Fax Plus 347
MicroHelp Wave (MhWave) 348
Microsoft Internet Control Pack 348

EarthTime (Starfish Software) 349
Envoy Viewer (Tumbleweed) 349
The VREAM WIRL (VRML) 350

Chapter 15: Top Ten VBScript Tips **351**

Get a Copy of the Documentation 351
Check Out Samples at the Microsoft Web Site 351
Join the Mailing List 352
Buy a Copy of Microsoft Visual Basic 352
Stop by VBPJ on the Web 353
Litter Your Scripts with Comments 353
Use the Option Explicit Statement 353
    Win the VBScript spelling bee 354
    Global or local? 354
Make Your Arrays As Dynamic As Your Pages 355
Run a Script When a User Clicks a Link 356
Write Fresh HTML in VBScript 357

Appendix *359*

Index *363*

License Agreement *378*

Installation Instructions *380*

Reader Response Card .... *Back of Book*

Foreword

· ·

Some months ago, Kurt Fenstermacher and I were sitting around my office and noodling some book ideas — predicting the future of the computer industry, if you will, as dangerous as that sounds! We kept coming back to the topic of the Internet, not too surprisingly. But what idea, what technology, in that domain would prove to be compelling over the next year? "How about ActiveX?" Kurt asked.

How about it, indeed. Here was a technology and a product that stood to change the way Web sites are created and used; yet, other than the Microsoft documentation, precious little has been written. If Web developers, Web administrators, and Web site gurus are going to take advantage of ActiveX, they need help. Kurt has provided it in spades with *ActiveX For Dummies*.

I've known Kurt Fenstermacher for quite a while now, ever since he matricu-lated into the Ph.D. program in my department. As the person tasked with riding herd over our polyglot student body, I always look for the extra-bright, the extra-sharp, the extra-talented among a student body that's one of the best in the country. Kurt easily showed himself superior in that competition. Long before *ActiveX For Dummies*, Kurt and I had spent many hours talking about what a computer journalist and author does. To hone his experience as a computer writer, Kurt convinced the skeptical editors of the University of Chicago student newspaper, *The Maroon*, that they needed a weekly computer review column from him. It's now one of the most popular weekly reads on campus. Lively, involved, but never cloying, Kurt's writing has moved from competent to charismatic, and that's not easy to do when you're explaining the technical details of software.

Kurt has deconstructed ActiveX to the point that he gets it. Totally. He gets its structure, its development — its soul, if software can have one. He reconstructs ActiveX into a format that anyone, even a dummy like me (and you, I surmise) can understand and apply. That's what a good computer book is all about.

Make no mistake then: This is a good computer book. It's one of the best to take a technical topic and simplify it successfully and with spirit. Although ActiveX can be daunting or even a little boring when you're cranking out the controls, *ActiveX For Dummies* never suffers either failure. Don't take my word for it. Read Kurt's book and tell us what you think. *ActiveX For Dummies* delivers the inside goods on what ActiveX is and how you can use it to improve any Web site. Let this book be your companion for finding and delivering the right ActiveX controls at the right time and place.

See you on the ether,

Don Crabb

decc@cs.uchicago.edu

URL: http://www.cs.uchicago.edu/~decc

November 1996
Chicago, Illinois

Introduction

• •

*A*long time ago I bought a book called *Calculus Made Easy,* by Silvanus P. Thompson; I figured that anyone who thought that calculus was easy had to be either a fool or a genius. From the beginning, Professor Thompson acknowledged that calculus involves some difficult material. He also said, however, that it had some easy stuff that virtually anyone could handle, as long as they knew a few tricks. His motto was, "What one fool can do, another can," and he insisted that anyone could learn the easy parts of calculus.

ActiveX is similar to calculus: Some parts are very difficult, and some parts are straightforward if you know the right tricks. This book focuses on the tricks for making ActiveX work for you. If you're ready to have some fun and discover the secrets of ActiveX, read on — and remember this: "What one dummy can do, another can."

So What Is This ActiveX Thing, Anyway?

After realizing that the Internet was really catching on, Microsoft decided that it was time to develop an Internet strategy. Luckily, all the pieces of an Internet were already lying around; they just had to be formed into a coherent whole. And so ActiveX was born. ActiveX is a set of technologies for designing and building software. Together, ActiveX technologies cover everything from software building blocks (called *controls*) to how to write a programming language. Because the term "ActiveX" encompasses so many different tools and specifications, talking about ActiveX can be a little confusing. This book focuses on two pieces of ActiveX: controls and scripting.

If you want to build a house, you have to start from scratch. You need someone to design and build the house, and, even if you want a bedroom just like the one in a hundred other houses, you still have to nail together boards and put up your own ceiling. House construction would be much simpler if you could choose from a few dozen already built bedrooms. When you wanted a living room, you could flip through a catalog of prebuilt living rooms and order your favorite. When you're building a Web page rather than a house, ActiveX controls are just like those prebuilt rooms. (A *page* is a file that is sent to a user's computer for display. A Web site is similar to a book, and each file at the site corresponds to a page in the book.)

Although you can't use an ActiveX control as your living room, controls exist for most common design tasks. If you want to display a banner across the top of your page, an ActiveX control was made just for you. If you want to enable visitors to your page to type comments, another ActiveX control can help you with that task. ActiveX controls are available to do most things you want to do, and a few may even do things you would never want to do.

Designing pages with ActiveX controls wouldn't be much fun if you couldn't force those controls to do your bidding — and that's what scripts are for. A *script* is a short computer program written to complete a specific task, and ActiveX has scripts too. One ActiveX technology, ActiveX scripting, tells language developers how to create a programming language that is guaranteed to work with the rest of ActiveX. Because few people enjoy developing a new computer language, Microsoft has done the hard work for you. VBScript is based on the popular Microsoft Visual Basic programming language, specially designed to work with ActiveX controls. Although it's possible to use ActiveX controls without writing any scripts, you can do much more with scripts than without them. With this book, you can begin by including pages in your controls and then adding scripts when you're ready.

"Cover Me — I'm Going Intranet!"

Although this book often talks about Web pages, ActiveX is also a great way to build intranet pages. (An *intranet* is a miniature version of the Internet, usually used within a company to provide information to corporate employees and customers.) ActiveX, which was designed by Microsoft, is built from the same technology as many other Microsoft applications. If you want to create pages for an intranet, this book can help. (Whenever you see the term "Web page," just think of it as "intranet page" with a spelling error.)

Why Should You Buy This Book?

Whether you're new to Web design or have been at it for a while, this book has something for you. If you have never created a Web page of your own, you can start with this book. Even though ActiveX has many powerful features, it's easier to begin designing your own pages. In this book, you begin with a brief HTML tutorial, which covers the basics you need to know in order to use ActiveX effectively. (*HTML*, which is short for HyperText Markup Language, is the language of the World Wide Web. An HTML file includes both content and instructions for how to display that content.)

After you're on speaking terms with HTML, you can move on to ActiveX controls. You can flip through the book right now, but you won't find a long list of ActiveX controls and their technical features. Instead, similar controls are grouped together, organized to correspond to the way you work. If you want to spruce up the look of your Web page, for example, check out Chapter 7. If you want visitors to your site to be able to tell you something, be sure to read

Chapter 9. When you're ready for scripting, you can turn to Part III, which shows you how to get the most from ActiveX controls. Even if you have never written a word of computer code, you can get started with scripting with a little help from the Microsoft Script Wizard.

If you have created your own Web site from nothing more than a handkerchief, a quart of oil, and two rubber bands, you can still find valuable information in this book. ActiveX is a hot technology. If you want to design Web sites and pages, you have to know about ActiveX. The problem is that there's much to know; the trick is to separate the wheat from the chaff. The Microsoft documentation is sometimes a good reference, but it's often incomplete (or even mistaken). Although ActiveX includes many technologies, this book tells you only the information you need in order to design better Web and intranet sites.

In this book, you get what you need, packed in a handy reference. If you're comfortable with HTML, you can dive right in to ActiveX controls and then scripting with VBScript. When you're ready for more, you can check out the Internet Explorer Object Model for Scripting, which enables you to control a user's browser through scripting.

What's Inside?

To make it easier to find what you need, this book is split into four parts.

Part 1: The Beginning (A Very Good Place to Begin)

The introductory material in Chapters 1 and 2 includes background information about ActiveX and why you should consider using ActiveX for Web and intranet development. Chapter 3 reviews HTML, including some new Internet Explorer features; if you have never used HTML, the chapter jump-starts your learning process and serves as a reference for later portions of this book. If you want to know about HTML in detail, take a look at *HTML For Dummies,* 2nd Edition, by Ed Tittel and Steven N. James (published by IDG Books Worldwide, Inc.).

Part II: ActiveX Components

Part II tells you all about the use of ActiveX controls for Web page development. After you get some background information about ActiveX controls in Chapter 4, you move on to tools for designing pages. The Microsoft Control Pad, described in depth in Chapter 5, is one of the best tools for working with ActiveX controls. The Control Pad incorporates a proposed addition to HTML: HTML layouts, which get the spotlight in Chapter 6. After you have mastered the tools, you can read about the controls that solve your problems: Chapter 7 offers suggestions for designing better-looking pages using ActiveX controls. If you want to add audio, it's no sweat for ActiveX — check out Chapter 8. When it's time to ask visitors to your site for information, turn to the ActiveX controls described in Chapter 9.

Part III: Scripting for ActiveX

Although ActiveX controls are a powerful addition to your bag of tricks for designing pages, with scripting you can do even more. Microsoft created VBScript to help you get more from ActiveX controls, and Part III shows you how. Chapters 10 and 11 give you an overview of scripting and VBScript, with examples to show you how to write scripts for ActiveX controls, and then Chapter 12 discusses events. Chapter 13 describes the Internet Explorer Object Model, which enables you to control a user's browser through scripts.

Part IV: The Part of Tens

The two chapters in this ultracool part of the book offer a quick rundown of some cool controls and a few tips for programming in VBScript.

About the CD-ROM

The CD-ROM in the back of the book is an integral part of the package. Because ActiveX is designed for creating dynamic, interactive software, you can't get the full effect from reading a book. The CD-ROM contains sample code you can (and should) try out for yourself. Because ActiveX is changing fast, you can also find links to Web sites with up-to-the-minute information. You should also visit the ActiveX pages at the ...*For Dummies* Web site (http://www.dummies.com), which has updated information about this book and ActiveX in general.

How This Book Works

If you're going to read this book, you should know a few things first.

All HTML tags in this book are shown in angle brackets, like this: <OBJECT>. Keep in mind that only HTML tags are in angle brackets — the attributes of a tag, such as HEIGHT and WIDTH, are not.

Some sample computer code is also shown in this book; you can easily recognize the code because it's in a monospace font:

```
object.Height = 200
```

(In this book, "computer code" refers to scripts in both VBScript and HTML files.) When you see some code written in monospace *and* italics, it's a placeholder. In the preceding line of code, you don't type the word *object* because it's just a placeholder to tell you that you put the name of an object there. Because most of the sample code you see in the text is on the CD-ROM in the back of the book, you don't have to do much typing. When I do want you to type something, it's in a special **boldface** font — just type *exactly* what you see.

Because the Web, the Internet, and ActiveX each have a language of their own, you may run across many new terms in this book. The first time I use a new term, I *italicize* it and briefly define it.

ActiveX and the Web (and intranets too) are changing continuously, and a great deal is going on in the background. Topics that are a little off course but that are still interesting or important are covered in separate boxed sidebars. You can usually skip them, but they often help put the main text in context. You may want to skip the sidebars on your first pass through a section and save them for later.

Icons Used in This Book

Throughout this book, icons in the margin highlight certain text:

You may know some of these things already, but they're still important. You will be a happier person later in life if you remember them.

Points out material that's more in-depth than the surrounding text. You can often find interesting tidbits in these paragraphs, but you can skip them if you want.

Marks suggestions to help you work smarter. In this book, tips include information about HTML style as well as ActiveX.

If this were Dante's book, he probably would write in the margin, "All hope abandon, ye who enter here." I think that it's easier to insert a Warning icon. It denotes material that could get you in trouble if you ignore it. Because ActiveX is a relatively new technology, you may encounter a few stumbling blocks — they're clearly marked with this icon.

What You Should Know before You Buy This Book

In writing this book, I have assumed that you already know a few things. You should already know where Jimmy Hoffa is buried and whether a second shooter was on the grassy knoll. (Okay, I'm kidding about the grassy knoll.) Although you don't already have to know about Web page design, you should be familiar with computers. If you think that "rebooting" means putting a fresh pair of sneakers on your computer, this is not the book for you. I also have assumed that you have already done some Web surfing of your own. Although you don't have to be a Web expert in order to understand what's in this book, it helps if you have already seen what's out there.

You need access to a computer that has a few programs installed on it. You need, at minimum, these two programs:

 ✔ Microsoft Internet Explorer (Version 3.0 or later)
 ✔ Microsoft Control Pad

(Both programs are available for free; if you look on the CD-ROM that accompanies this book, you can find directions for obtaining and installing them.)

For now, Internet Explorer 3.0 and Control Pad are available for only Windows 95 and Windows NT; versions for Apple computers are expected to be released soon. A plug-in for Netscape Navigator is available that enables Navigator to understand ActiveX pages, but it too is currently limited to Windows 95 and Windows NT.

Don't Keep Me in Suspense

If you're reading this book, let me know what you think. What's good? What's bad? What's missing? One of the advantages to having a Web site to accompany a book is that the Web site can change with your comments. If you want to see an example that's not in this book or if you want more details about a particular topic, let me know. You can reach me through IDG Books Worldwide, Inc., or through the company's Web site (`http://www.dummies.com`).

Ready, Set, Activate!

The purpose of ActiveX is to help you transform your imagination into reality with as little frustration as possible. (It doesn't always work that way, but it's something to strive for.) After you have read what's in this book, you will no longer be an ActiveX novice — you'll be an ActiveXpert!

Part I
The Beginning (A Very Good Place to Begin)

The 5th Wave   By Rich Tennant

KYLE AND TODDS SOFTWARE Co.

"THAT'S RIGHT, DADDY WILL DOUBLE YOUR SALARY IF YOU MAKE HIM MORE ACTIVEX APPLICATIONS."

In this part . . .

*I*f you can't tell an inactive *x* from an active *x,* you can find all the details here. ActiveX has been heralded (mostly by Microsoft) as the savior of the Web and labeled (mostly by anyone other than Microsoft) as the first step to world domination. In this part of the book, you find out what ActiveX really is and why you should care about it. You also get the lowdown on HTML, the language of the Web.

Chapter 1

What Is ActiveX?

In This Chapter

▶ What is ActiveX?

▶ Who uses ActiveX?

▶ Why does ActiveX matter to me?

*A*ctiveX is a new way to design Web page and intranet applications that stand out from the crowd. More than that, ActiveX is a set of technologies that work together to help you design attractive content for the Web and intranets and build better network applications. With ActiveX, you can easily add multimedia effects to your page; ActiveX technologies can make your Web pages sing and dance.

For example, a hospital's Web pages may include a video of a beating heart or animated procedures for home care instruction. News services may show live video of a breaking story and let you listen to the roar of a battle zone or the hush of a mountain stream. City symphonies can advertise the upcoming season with audio samples from planned performances. An electronics store can host a question-and-answer page on which befuddled customers can post common questions, and store employees can then respond with technical advice (VCRs would never flash 12:00 again).

The Web has been moving away from plain old text for a while, and many pages now include animations, sound, and video. ActiveX makes it much easier to add special effects to your pages, however, because it brings you prebuilt components. If you want to include a video on your page, for example, you simply add a video component and tell it which video to play. Visitors to your page can play, pause, or stop the video, and you don't have to worry about how that component works. (You can also make a little money by charging users a fee if they forget to rewind the video.) What's really important about ActiveX, though, is what it can do for *you*.

Caught in a Web of meaning

The Internet and the Web share their own lingo, which sounds a little odd if you haven't heard it. The *Internet* is a collection of computer networks that are interconnected. All the computers on the Internet, despite their various differences, are bound together by a common language (called TCP/IP). The *World Wide Web* (or just "the Web") is a bunch of documents bound together by links that lead users from one document to another. Most documents are linked to many other documents, which are linked to others, and so on. If you could see the Web, it would look like a cloud of points (the documents) connected by many lines (the links) running between the points, much like a horribly tangled spider web.

If you want to edit a word-processing document, you use a word-processing program. If you want to hear an audio clip, you start up a sound program. If you want to see a Web document, you use a Web browser. A *browser* is program designed for viewing files on the Web. Netscape Navigator and Microsoft Internet Explorer are both well-known Web browsers.

Documents on the Web are known as *pages,* which is a reflection of the Web's origins as a "web" of text documents. (The term *page* is no longer limited to the Web, though; any file that is intended to be viewed with a Web browser is generally called a page.) Each page is usually a single file stored on a computer. Most of (but not all) the computers that store Web pages are connected to the Internet. Many people confuse the Internet with the Web because of this close connection, but they're two different animals. The Internet is a collection of hardware — you can kick a part of the Internet and knock it over. The Web, however, is a group of documents and the links that bind them together.

It's the Content, Stupid!

The Web has evolved from a means for scientists to share research papers to an information source/entertainment provider/marketing behemoth, and the number of people "surfing" it has recently increased dramatically. As the number of Web surfers has risen, so have their expectations — people now expect to find Web sites packed with useful or entertaining information presented in a tantalizing way. No longer is it enough to publish written weather forecasts, culled from National Weather Service reports. Today's weather Web site must have graphic forecasts, videos showing the fury of a storm, and animations tracking a hurricane's progress. ActiveX technologies enable you to include all these types of elements easily in pages you design.

Corporations have also joined the Web stampede. Many corporations have public Web sites, but they have also created internal webs, known as intranets. (An *intranet* is a network whose design is based on Internet specifications but that is used within an organization and is generally not accessible from the outside.) Using an intranet, employees at some companies can check the balance in their retirement fund or switch their health-insurance plan. Other companies use intranets as sales tools, providing up-to-the-minute information to their sales force. Employees in the field can check inventory levels, verify pricing, and schedule shipments. Although many internal company sites lack the pizzazz of public sites, these internal sites often require sophisticated tools for accessing and presenting data. ActiveX technologies can help designers at these sites as well by offering advanced scripting and database tools.

What Is ActiveX?

ActiveX is a set of technologies Microsoft created to ease the development of network applications. Together, ActiveX technologies enable better design of Web and intranet pages, better server performance, and more-versatile documents. Some ActiveX technologies have been around for a while and have been dressed up for the Internet. Others have been developed specifically with the Internet in mind. Each technology offers tools for a common purpose: building better network applications. Because the specification is still young, Microsoft is still revising ActiveX technologies.

The current list of ActiveX technologies includes

- ✔ ActiveX controls
- ✔ ActiveX documents
- ✔ ActiveX Scripting
- ✔ Java Virtual Machine
- ✔ ActiveX Server Framework

Most of this book focuses on the ActiveX controls and scripts to link the controls. For now, the controls are the most mature piece of ActiveX because they are built on proven technology. As ActiveX evolves, however, the other components will fall into place.

ActiveX controls

ActiveX controls are similar to little elves that excel at doing one thing. Some elves hold up banners, others supervise animations, and a few can play music. If you were to go around saying that one of your showcase technologies depends entirely on elves, people in the computer industry would think that your company lacks a serious Internet strategy. (To make matters worse, it's tough for elves to get work permits.) Because Microsoft wants everyone to know that it does have an Internet strategy, it settled on "control" rather than "elf."

Controls are elves that are good at doing one thing and that don't need much guidance from a designer. (Not needing guidance is a big plus because elves don't take direction well anyway.) Here's the great thing about using elves: Whatever an elf does, you don't have to do.

Some controls/elves are specialized for many different tasks. (I'm sure that you're aware of elfin society's legendary specialization of labor — when is the last time you saw an elf in the role of a generalist?) One ActiveX control displays a flashy banner across the top of a Web page, and you can adjust the font and color and even decide what happens when a user moves the mouse pointer over the label. Another ActiveX control displays movies that have been recorded in any of several formats. Figure 1-1 shows several controls on a page. Read all about the Label and Image controls in Chapter 7, and the push button (a CommandButton control) in Chapter 9.

Although it's nice to have these types of controls, you can add these effects to Web pages in other ways. The advantage of using ActiveX controls is that they are part of a framework; by using pieces designed to work together, you can win big. If ActiveX controls sound good to you, you have the right book because I give you lots of information about which controls are available and how to use them to design the coolest Web page on your cyberblock.

Figure 1-1: ActiveX controls make adding impressive effects a snap. This page has two Label controls: an Image control and a push button.

Image control

Label control

Push-button control

We'll cross that platform when we come to it

The word *platform* is tossed around quite a bit these days, but its meaning is vague. Sometimes platform means the particular hardware from which a computer is built. At other times it means the operating system on which a computer runs. Every once in a while, platform means the combination of hardware and operating system. Because the Windows NT operating system isn't quite the same on a Pentium Pro as it is on a DEC Alpha workstation, for example, each one could be considered a separate platform. (If the possibility of confusion exists, you sometimes hear the more specific term *hardware platform,* which means just the computer itself.)

In the old days, computer programs were written for a specific platform and then ported to other platforms. (*Porting* is the act of converting a program from one platform to another.)

Microsoft might develop Word for Windows, for example, and then convert it to Word for the Macintosh. The problem is that porting is a pain and usually doesn't work too well.

In today's enlightened world of software development, developers try to create cross-platform solutions. (A *cross-platform* is a single system that works on many different platforms — adapting the single solution to a new platform should involve little or no work.) When Microsoft claims that ActiveX is a cross-platform solution, it's saying that you can design ActiveX applications and documents on a Pentium-based Windows 95 machine and it will work on an Apple System 7.5 PowerMac. When any company claims that it has a cross-platform development solution, let the buyer (that's you) beware.

ActiveX controls are designed as a cross-platform development tool. (If that last sentence sounds like gibberish, see the nearby sidebar, "We'll cross that platform when we come to it.") Microsoft has historically been known as a one-platform pony, despite creating software for several platforms. The software community's reaction to the company's cross-platform claim was quiet. Unlike earlier Microsoft claims of being committed to multiple platforms, it might not be kidding this time. Microsoft has handed over the job of maintaining ActiveX standards to an independent group. Although ActiveX is not yet a complete cross-platform solution, it's getting better.

ActiveX currently works well only with Windows (both 95 and NT). Microsoft has partnered with Metrowerks (a developer of Mac programming environments) to support ActiveX on the Macintosh platform. On the UNIX side, Microsoft is working with Bristol and Mainsoft to add ActiveX support. You will be able to write ActiveX controls and other ActiveX objects on any of these platforms, and your objects will work on the all other supported platforms.

ActiveX documents

Documents are hot. If you want to bluff a group of computer people at a cocktail party, you can use the word "document" frequently in conversation. If you think that someone is ready to call your bluff, you can pull out your big gun: Mention "document-centric computing." People who love this concept claim that users don't think in terms of applications — they think in terms of documents. They might be right: You rarely hear anyone say, "I mailed off a pen-and-paper file today." Instead, people talk about and work with documents, such as letters.

Because Web browsers must understand the many types of documents available on the Web, browsers are a good place to begin doing document-centric computing. The problem is that most Web browsers understand only Webspeak and few common file formats for images. After you follow a link to a Word document, for example, most browsers offer to download the file for you but don't display it. Microsoft isn't the first company to notice this problem, of course. Other companies have already developed ways to expand a browser's capabilities; some of the earlier technologies for building smarter browsers are discussed in this section.

"Help — I don't understand this file!"

The old standby for making browsers more capable uses *helper applications,* which are separate programs the browser calls on to display files in unknown formats. You can tell Navigator to start up Microsoft Word, for example, whenever it stumbles across a Word document. The problem is that users must install the correct helper applications and configure their browser to call the appropriate helper at the right time. After that's done, users still have to wait for a second program to start up whenever they encounter an unknown file type. As a designer, you lose the flow of a page and the integration of having everything in one place.

Plugging in to a browser

Netscape has created a plug-in standard that enables developers to build Navigator-friendly versions of applications. Because the plug-in adds to the browser's existing capabilities, users don't notice the difference between a plug-in–supported file and one the original browser supported.

Plug-ins have a few technical drawbacks, but the big one is that plug-ins must be platform-specific. (A *platform* is the combination of an operating system and particular hardware. Because different combinations require different software, most programs are platform-specific.) A plug-in for Windows 95, for example, doesn't work on a Macintosh. Plug-ins also create security issues because the plug-in specification doesn't include security features to stop a plug-in from playing games with a user's hard disk.

The ActiveX way

ActiveX documents are another approach for expanding a browser's capabilities. The ActiveX document specification tells developers how to integrate files with Web documents. ActiveX-enabled browsers then can display non-Web documents along with Web documents. ActiveX documents have two important advantages over other approaches:

- ✔ They are designed as part of the larger ActiveX framework.
- ✔ They are designed to be cross-platform.

For more info about ActiveX cross-platform issues, see the preceding sidebar, "We'll cross that platform when we come to it."

ActiveX Scripting

With ActiveX Scripting, you can write programs quickly and easily to link ActiveX controls or Java applets. (An *applet* is a cute little application — a small program focused on one task.) Scripting is an important part of ActiveX because that's how you customize your designs. Because each ActiveX control stands on its own, it's up to you, the designer, to make them work together. You can design layouts that are pleasing to the eye, but you want the controls to be more than an attractive mosaic; controls should work together too.

ActiveX Scripting includes both clients and servers. A *client* is a computer that requests service (usually a person with a Web browser lurching from one site to the next). A *server* is a computer that offers service, such as a Web server that sends out Web pages on request. The Toyota Web server, (`http://www.toyota.com`) for example, always stands ready to tell you all about Toyota cars and trucks. Sometimes it's more appropriate to write a script that runs on a client, and sometimes it's better to run a script from a server. Because ActiveX doesn't limit you to either method, you have the flexibility to choose the right solution for you.

ActiveX Server Framework

The Server Framework includes a bunch of services that are handy for creating Web sites or intranets. It has tools for security, which help protect data on your server and information in transit between users and your server. Database access tools offer an easy way to provide outside users with data from your system, without having to create a custom solution. You can even add to your Web site prebuilt search engines that enable visitors to your site to search for particular words or phrases. Don't worry about finding a family of server products that meets the ActiveX specification: Microsoft offers the Internet Information Server as its Web server product, which happens to fit the ActiveX Server Framework.

Java Virtual Machine

The ActiveX specifications incorporate a Java Virtual Machine (VM). (See the nearby sidebar, "Java is virtually a computer," for the scoop on the Java Virtual Machine.) Because ActiveX includes a Java VM, any ActiveX-enabled browser can work together with Java applications. As a designer, you benefit because you can mix and match Java and ActiveX solutions to your problems. You could create a form with some of the many ActiveX controls for input, for example, and then use a Java applet to graph the data from many users. (A *form* is an online version of forms in everyday life: You fill out the form and hand it in to someone.)

Putting it all together

The idea behind ActiveX is to create a group of technologies that work together to address network problems. Designers can build attractive pages by including ActiveX controls. The controls can then be linked together using any scripting language that conforms to the ActiveX Scripting specification. Designers can also incorporate Java applets and programs with ActiveX controls and know that the Java code will work with an ActiveX-enabled browser because the Java Virtual Machine is included in ActiveX.

Sometimes it's better to tackle a network problem from the server side rather than from the client side. The ActiveX Server Framework ensures that certain features are available to ActiveX-savvy designers. As the ActiveX standard grows, the integration will be even tighter, and the individual pieces will work better.

Java is virtually a computer

Java, from Sun Microsystems, is more than just a programming language — it's a system for writing and running software. One of the goals of the Java system is to enable developers to create cross-platform applications. (For more information about cross-platform issues, see the sidebar "We'll cross that platform when we come to it," earlier in this chapter.) The Sun solution to the thorny problem of many different platforms was to make all machines look exactly the same.

The Java Virtual Machine, or simply Java VM, is a computer in software. When you write a Java program, the program is written as though it were going to run on a Java VM. When a user with an Apple PowerMac runs your Java program, part of the Java system translates from the Java VM to the PowerMac, which then runs the program. Because your program was written for the Java VM and not specifically for the PowerMac, the same program runs on a Sun Solaris workstation. When a new computer or operating system is introduced, Sun (or someone else) can write a new translator from the Java VM to the new platform, and all Java programs will run on the new system.

Chapter 2

To ActiveX or Not to ActiveX?

· ·

In This Chapter

▶ Microsoft support for ActiveX

▶ ActiveX versus non-ActiveX solutions

▶ Why not ActiveX?

· ·

*W*hen you sit down to design a Web page, whether it's for fun or profit, you have lots of choices. As the World Wide Web has exploded, so have tools for Web development. HTML, the *lingua franca* of the Web, has become more sophisticated. (To find out more about HTML, see Chapter 3.) Java burst on the scene not long ago. Software companies are releasing new tools for page design and site management as fast as they can think up new product names.

Why should you bother with ActiveX when you have so many choices? ActiveX offers a powerful framework of many tools and techniques that are designed to work together; by using ActiveX, you have an integrated solution to the many problems of site design. Do you need a scripting language? ActiveX has it. How about tools for building sophisticated user interfaces? Many ActiveX controls that are ideal for designing user interfaces are available from many different companies. ActiveX brings together in one set of technologies designed to work together the solution to many problems.

If you're not sure whether ActiveX is right for you, this chapter should give you some perspective and some suggestions about why you might use ActiveX rather than another approach. If you're already convinced that ActiveX is the way to go, you can skip this chapter and begin developing ActiveX applications right away.

The Number-One Reason to Choose ActiveX: Microsoft

If you're reading this book, you probably have heard of Microsoft. (If you haven't, it's a medium-size software company that writes lots of software for IBM-compatible computers.)

Microsoft developed ActiveX, and ActiveX benefits from that association in several ways. Microsoft has tons of marketing muscle to tout the virtues of ActiveX design. Soon the company will use ActiveX technologies to integrate network computing into the Windows desktop. If you have written programs in the Microsoft Visual Basic programming language, you're already well prepared for working with ActiveX controls and scripts.

Making the most of marketing muscle

Many people in the computer industry complain about Microsoft, but it definitely knows how to market software. A year ago it was criticized for not having an Internet strategy, and now critics complain that the company is taking over the Internet. With the weight of Microsoft behind ActiveX, it's a standard that is gaining ground. Microsoft has solid business relationships with many third-party developers who have been developing ActiveX controls and other gizmos for many years.

Remembering that variety is the spice of life

Creating solutions from scratch is difficult; when other people have already solved the same problem you're experiencing, you shouldn't waste time reinventing the wheel. You're probably not the first person who ever wanted to include a pop-up calendar on an online form or who wanted Web site visitors to freely express their thoughts in prose. A primary advantage of ActiveX is that a stable of solutions to common (and uncommon) problems is already wrapped up in neat packages called ActiveX controls. Because these controls are based on Visual Basic controls (for the details, see the nearby sidebar "Don't know much about history"), thousands of these solutions exist.

 Because tool developers have been creating custom Visual Basic controls for a long time, many controls are available. Microsoft has recently been touting Visual Basic (Enterprise Edition) as *the* tool for corporate client/server development. Because client/server development has much in common with Web design, many controls can do double duty in Web design. Several controls that were originally developed for Visual Basic are shown on a Web page in Figure 2-1.

Client/server computing refers to the division of applications into two pieces:

- ✔ The client part runs on a user's computer and translates that person's actions into requests that are passed on to a server.
- ✔ The server part looks at requests, often from many clients at the same time, and sends back the requested information.

The server and clients are usually connected by a network and run on different machines.

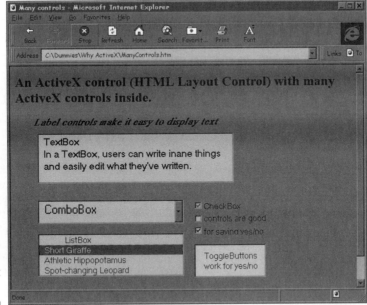

Figure 2-1:
Many
ActiveX
controls that
have been
developed
for Visual
Basic are
also handy
for creating
Web and
intranet
pages.

Integrating beyond the network

Microsoft has announced plans to integrate the Internet and the Windows desktop. Future versions of Windows will have a desktop that users navigate in the same way they follow links through the Web. ActiveX technology is at the heart of this integration, with most of the desktop built from ActiveX controls. If your Web site is well designed and built with ActiveX components, it should integrate seamlessly with the Windows desktop.

Reviewing Visual Basic

If you're already familiar with Microsoft Visual Basic, you have a big jump on the use of ActiveX controls and scripting. For example, using the Control Pad HTML Layout feature is similar to designing a form in Visual Basic. Also, Microsoft created a scripting language — VBScript — for use with ActiveX controls. Because the VBScript programming language is a subset of Visual Basic, Visual Basic programmers don't have to learn a new language. (Many Visual Basic features are disabled in VBScript, which can surprise programmers who expect the power of full-blown Visual Basic in VBScript. Part III discusses VBScript in more detail and how to use it with ActiveX controls.) An addition to the Microsoft Visual Basic family is on the way. Visual Basic 5.0 Control Creation Edition will make it easier to create ActiveX controls. Visual Basic developers soon will be able to construct ActiveX controls from scratch, customize existing ActiveX controls, or combine several ActiveX controls.

Don't know much about history

Some of the technologies Microsoft has bundled under the ActiveX name are brand-new, but others have been around the block. ActiveX controls are an outgrowth of controls used in Visual Basic. If you want to understand the role of controls, you have to know a little about how programming works in Visual Basic.

To create a Visual Basic program, you begin with a layout, which is a blank canvas you can draw on. You then add controls to the layout and position them on the layout. To build an application for storing addresses, for example, you place on the layout a text control for users to type a zip code. You don't have to write a program that lets users type and edit text because it has already been done for you in the control. After you have created a layout, you write code that ties together the various controls on the page.

Early versions of Visual Basic used Visual Basic controls, called *VBXs*, to make it easy for Visual Basic programmers to build programs. (The term VBX came from the control's file extension, .VBX.) Microsoft eventually made the (partial) leap to 32-bit computing. (Early computer

processors worked with 16 bits at a time; newer computers use 32 bits. Software for PCs has only recently caught up to hardware and is now labeled "32-bit.") Because VBXs weren't well suited to the new 32-bit world, Microsoft created a new control based on the OLE model.

OLE, which used to stand for *Object Linking and Embedding*, described anything built on the Microsoft COM specification. (OLE no longer stands for anything — it's just a term in itself.) The COM *(Component Object Model)* specification suggests a way for applications to communicate with one another. To make matters even more confusing, ActiveX has replaced OLE as the label for "anything built on the Microsoft COM specification."

OLE custom controls (also known as *OLE controls*, or *OCXs*) replaced VBXs. ActiveX controls are expanded versions of OCXs, with some extras tossed in to make them Internet-friendly. Some people still refer to ActiveX controls as OCXs, and ActiveX control files retain the extension .OCX.

Handling Life without ActiveX

Some of the things you can do with ActiveX you can also do without it. For example, you don't need ActiveX Scripting to write programs to run over a network: Java and JavaScript work well for writing network programs. *ActiveX Scripting,* one of several ActiveX technologies, tells language developers how to create a new scripting language. (VBScript, for example, is a language that conforms to the ActiveX Scripting specification.) You don't need ActiveX controls to create forms for users to fill out, because most browsers support forms in HTML using the <FORM> tag.

Why bother with ActiveX at all? ActiveX and Java are both competitors and complements. Java and ActiveX were designed from different perspectives, and the two visions clash. ActiveX and Java can work together, however, although neither one really needs the other.

Going the Way of Java

Although Java is a programming language, it is designed to support a particular style of developing and distributing applications. In the Java approach, applets reside on computers all over the network. (An *applet* is a small program focused on a specific task.) Users all over the network then build applications for themselves by assembling their favorite applets for each task. In a Java world, for example, you wouldn't buy Microsoft Word for word processing. Instead, you would find the best spell-checking applet, the best text-editing applet, and the best applet for creating bibliographies and use them together for word processing. If you never used a word processor's picture-editing features, you wouldn't bother to find a picture-editing applet. Although this vision sounds like a good idea, it turned out to be optimistic — the average user doesn't have the time, energy, or expertise to assemble powerful applications. ActiveX isn't currently targeted toward enabling users to build their own applications. Designers use ActiveX technologies to jump-start their own development, but users benefit from designers having produced a better product.

Comparing ActiveX to Java is similar in some ways to comparing apples and oranges, but the comparison is inevitable. Java is a programming language designed for writing networked applications over unsecured networks. ActiveX is a set of technologies for distributing content across the Web. In some ways, Java is more fundamental than ActiveX because you could write programs to implement ActiveX in the Java language. One shortcoming of Java, however, is that it's so low-level that you do have to write programs. If you want to do something that hasn't been done, it's probably just as easy to do it in Java as it is in ActiveX. If it has already been done, you can probably find an ActiveX way to do it. The bottom line on ActiveX and Java is that you don't have to choose one over the other because they can work together.

Many Web sites ask visitors to fill out forms and send them in electronically. Forms are so widespread that the HTML standard includes a <FORM> tag to build online HTML forms. ActiveX has many controls that let designers create friendly forms that users are happy to fill out. The <FORM> tag is no bed of roses, though, because you have to process the form data after it gets to the server. The processing is usually performed with CGI scripts, which are difficult to work with. (CGI stands for *Common Gateway Interface,* a method of interacting with a Web server.) ActiveX has the advantage of including a compatible scripting language that integrates well with the ActiveX controls from which forms are built.

Why Not ActiveX?

Although ActiveX offers many advantages for Web designers, it has some weaknesses too — primarily a lack of tools for designing with ActiveX. Also, despite promises of cross-platform support, ActiveX doesn't work equally well on all systems. (*Cross-platform* refers to the capability of one version to run on many different computers and operating systems.) Both problems can be fixed, however, and better solutions are on the way.

Creating stunning Web pages can be a little tricky with the tools available today. The Microsoft Control Pad works well with ActiveX controls and HTML layouts, but not for writing straight HTML sans ActiveX. Several companies sell excellent HTML editors, but the products don't yet include ActiveX support. (*HTML editors* are programs designed specifically for working with HTML; they're word processors for HTML.) Because HTML editing and ActiveX control insertion are so closely linked, the lack of an editor that does both is a pain. Rather than work with one document in one program, you have to switch between two different programs. (The Microsoft FrontPage editor is particularly a disappointment. Although FrontPage is a great tool for visual editing of HTML, working directly with the HTML code is difficult.) Because the software companies that develop HTML editors are aware of ActiveX, though, better tools are on the way.

Microsoft presents ActiveX as a cross-platform solution for designing network applications. That goal is an ambitious one, and Microsoft has trouble meeting it. The Windows roots of ActiveX show through in some places, and those roots often clash with other computer environments. For example, ActiveX lets you choose from several predefined styles for the mouse pointer, but the styles are Windows styles. Furthermore, to be able to use most ActiveX controls, you have to install Internet Explorer Version 3.0. If you're using Windows 95 or Windows NT 4.0, you're in luck; if you use another operating system, however, you may have some trouble. Microsoft has recently released a beta version of Internet Explorer 3.0 for Windows 3.1. Although Macintosh users must still use Internet Explorer 2.1, which lacks many Version 3.0 features, a beta version of Internet Explorer 3.0 has been released. Microsoft has also released a development kit for creating ActiveX controls on the Macintosh, but the Windows controls don't yet work with the Mac version of Internet Explorer 3.0. The lack-of-support situation is getting better; as ActiveX gains a stronger foothold in the marketplace, more companies will design ActiveX-enabled tools for people outside the Windows camp.

To ActiveX or Not to ActiveX: The Answer

Whether ActiveX is right for you depends on who you are and why you're designing Web pages. If you expect Windows users to visit the pages you design, ActiveX can offer you a powerful solution today. You can design pages with sophisticated layouts that include multimedia effects and interact with users. Although ActiveX is mostly a Windows phenomenon, that situation is changing quickly. Because Microsoft has ceded control of the ActiveX specification to an independent group, other companies can develop browsers that support ActiveX. As these browsers become available on other platforms, more and more users will benefit from ActiveX-designed pages.

Don't forget that because ActiveX can be used on the server as well as on the client, you can benefit from ActiveX server technologies even if your users don't have ActiveX capability themselves. You can use an ActiveX Web server and add the capability to search without ever telling your users that ActiveX is doing all the work. In short, ActiveX is a new way to design network applications, and nothing else is quite like it.

Testing your newfound knowledge

1. **Comparing ActiveX to Java is similar to comparing apples with oranges because:**

   A. ActiveX comes in a red box, and Java comes in an orange box.

   B. ActiveX is a set of technologies, and Java is network programming language.

   C. ActiveX doesn't have anything to do with coffee.

   D. You can't make orange juice with Java.

2. **ActiveX form controls are better than the <FORM> tag for designing online forms because:**

   A. ActiveX includes a handy, easy-to-use scripting language.

   B. "ActiveX" sounds cooler.

   C. The <FORM> tag is old news.

   D. There's a <FORM> tag?

Chapter 3

Teach Yourself HTML in 21 Minutes

• •

In This Chapter

▶ Looking at what the Web is and how it works

▶ Creating an HTML file from scratch

▶ Linking up with links and Web addresses

▶ Adding common HTML tags to your documents

▶ Introducing images

▶ Using HTML tables to display tabular data

▶ Splitting up a browser window by using frames

• •

*I*f you think that an anchor is something to keep boats from drifting away and that a link is just one piece of a chain, you probably should read this chapter. It gives you a brief introduction to the bare essentials of HTML and jump-starts your ActiveX experience even if you have never created a Web page.

If you're already familiar with HTML, you might want to at least glance at the sections about tables and frames. This chapter is a quick overview of HTML; if you want the whole story, you can find all the details in *HTML For Dummies,* 2nd Edition, by Ed Tittel and Steve James, and *MORE HTML For Dummies,* by Ed Tittel (both published by IDG Books Worldwide, Inc.).

If you're up on the latest advances, you'll notice that style sheets are discussed in this chapter. (*Style sheets,* also called *cascading style sheets* or *CSSs,* enable Web designers to use text styles just as they're used in word processors. You can create a Title style, for example, and then apply the style to titles on all your pages, which will then have a consistent appearance. If you decide to change the appearance of your titles, you simply change the style sheet and the change is reflected in all your pages.) Although style sheets are important for HTML designers, they're not crucial to ActiveX design, so I don't discuss them in this book. If you plan to design Web pages extensively, you should become familiar with style sheets.

Oh, What a Tangled Web We Weave

You probably have noticed that the World Wide Web (or WWW) is everywhere. Many television commercials now display Web addresses, and trading tips about hot new Web sites has become acceptable cocktail-party conversation. Although more and more people have surfed the Web wave to newfound information, few people have created their own Web pages. Will Rogers might have said, "Everybody talks about the Web, but nobody does anything about it." Although you might be one of the many people who haven't created their own site, that's about to change.

What's a Web?

The World Wide Web is a strange creature that looks much like another odd animal — the Internet. The resemblance is so striking that the Web beast is often confused with the Internet beast, even though the two are different creatures. The *Internet* is the name of a collection of computers that are linked together and that all speak the same language. All it takes to add a computer to the Internet is to connect it to another computer that's already connected to the Internet. That's the reason the Internet is expanding so rapidly: It's easy to be connected to it.

The language of the Internet is *TCP/IP,* which is short for Transmission Control Protocol/Internet Protocol. If you have set up a computer to connect to the Internet, you probably have had to adjust some TCP/IP settings on your machine. TCP/IP is just a convention for sending and receiving information. Because all the computers on the Internet use it, any computer can communicate with any other computer.

The Web is similar to the Internet because the Web is also a collection of machines that speak a common language. Computers on the Web use this common language to send out documents you can view on your computer. Web documents are written in *HyperText Markup Language (HTML)* and then shared among computers.

Do you know who your server is?

The Web is much like a restaurant. When you sit down in a restaurant, you look over the menu and then place an order describing the food you want. The kitchen receives this order and prepares the food. The Web also has kitchens, menus, and customers. While you're surfing the Web, you play the role of customer, choosing from among the various links you see and then getting more information as you follow each one.

The primary difference between the Web and real-life kitchens is that Web customers are called "clients" rather than "customers" because the former term sounds more impressive. The computers in a Web kitchen, called *servers,* store Web pages and send them out on request.

Figure 3-1 illustrates the relationship between clients and servers and shows what goes on between them. First, a client computer places an order with one of the Web's many kitchens, or individual servers. The order is sent in HTTP, and a piping-hot, freshly served document is sent back using HTTP. *HTTP* is the HyperText Transfer Protocol, a convention for communication between Web servers and clients. When the order is ready, you get a heaping helping of HTML, which the client (your computer) can munch on.

Because the Web has its own language and customs, you need a special program to make sense of it. *Web browsers,* or just *browsers,* are the waiters of the Web. Microsoft Internet Explorer and Netscape Navigator are the two most popular Web browsers. Your browser places your order with a Web kitchen

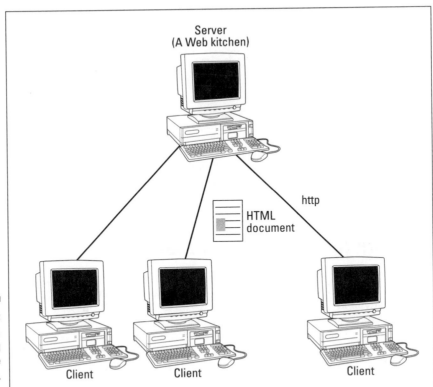

Figure 3-1:
Get a
satisfying
meal at the
Web diner.

(a server) and then nicely formats your order on-screen after the kitchen has prepared your document. A document displayed in the browser window is often called a *page* (see Figure 3-2). A page usually corresponds to a single HTML file, which is shown near the top of the browser window. Microsoft plans to incorporate browser technology directly into the Windows desktop so that a browser won't be a separate program; instead, it will be just an extension of your operating system.

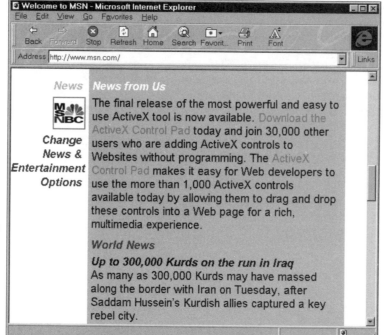

Figure 3-2:
You use a browser to view documents on the Web.

The medium's the message

If you're a news junkie, you can choose how you want to get your news fix: Some radio stations broadcast nonstop news, and you can watch your local television affiliate or pick up a newspaper. For every one of these types of media, you can choose in which language you want your news delivered: Arabic, English, French — whatever. On the Web, though, both these choices are already made for you. Rather than beam information over radio waves, the Web transfers information through *HTTP*, as described in the preceding section. Just as you don't have to know how frequency modulation works in order to listen to your favorite FM station, you don't have to know how HTTP works in order to use the Web.

Although information is sent back and forth using HTTP, the information is phrased in *HTML:* This HyperText Markup Language is handy for describing how documents should look, which makes it a good choice for Web documents. A *markup language* is an agreed-on set of codes that are added to a document; each code is called a *tag.* (Most of the time, codes come in pairs: one for the beginning and one for the end of the text being marked, and each pair is known as a single tag.) To emphasize a piece of text, for example, you "mark it up" by adding codes for emphasis, like this:

```
[Emphasize]This is really important![Stop emphasizing].
```

You don't see markup languages often in everyday life. Rather than add some sort of markup to a language, people who speak and write usually change the way their words sound or alter the appearance of text, like this: THIS IS REALLY IMPORTANT! Imagine going to see your favorite play and hearing an actor say, "For these next few lines, I'm going to be really sad, but I'll cheer up toward the end" and then delivering the next few lines in a monotone. If you're just surfing the Web, you never see the markup because your computer translates it into something you can see and hear. If you're planning to create your own pages, however, you'll be reading and writing HTML.

Wouldn't you know it? — there's a markup language for specifying markup languages: Standardized General Markup Language (SGML). Because the rules for HTML are specified in SGML, if you don't like HTML, you can specify your own language in SGML. If you're ambitious, try creating a markup language for defining markup languages that specify markup languages.

Skinny mocha or tall latté? (The flavors of HTML)

Like everything else, HTML is evolving — and it's evolving very fast. In the beginning, the Web was a means for scientists to share research papers with each other. Because most scientists didn't worry much about the appearance of their papers, the first version of HTML (1.0) was lean and mean but didn't give designers much control over how a document looked. As the Web began to catch on, page designers wanted more control over how a page was displayed on a Web surfer's computer. The second version of HTML (2.0) added new ways to control the display of information and allowed the use of interactive forms that users could fill out. Designing the Web was becoming more complicated, but designers wanted even more control.

The HTML specification is determined by a committee that isn't much different from any other group. Everyone wanted to add something to HTML 2.0 to make it better. After everyone had thrown in their favorite addition, HTML 3.0 was, unfortunately, a mess. Because HTML 3.0 was complicated, the current, streamlined version (HTML 3.2) was drafted. It features all sorts of fancy additions: interactive forms, tables, and more. If you're just starting out designing Web pages, you don't have to use all the fancy additions — but they're there when you need them. If you want a feature that isn't in HTML, just wait, and someone else will probably add it — or you can find an ActiveX control to do the job for you.

Skeletons in the HTML Closet: The Bare-Bones HTML File

Like all good specifications, the HTML specification is very specific. You can't simply toss in a few HTML tags and some well-written prose and expect to create an HTML file. Every HTML file starts from the same basic template, which marks the file as being HTML and divides it into two sections: the head and the body:

```
<HTML>
    <HEAD>
        <TITLE>...</TITLE>
        :
    </HEAD>

    <BODY>
        :
    </BODY>
</HTML>
```

In addition to this template, all HTML files must have the extension .html (or .htm, for systems that allow only three-letter extensions).

The HEAD section of an HTML document begins with the <HEAD> tag and stores information about the document. Every HEAD section must include a <TITLE> element, which specifies the page title. (Most browsers display the <TITLE> element in the browser window's title bar.) The HEAD section also often includes details about how the document was created. Most HTML editors credit themselves as the creator of a document, for example, by including a tag in the HEAD section. Following the HEAD section, the BODY section is the "meat" of an HTML document. The BODY section includes all the text, all the images, and most scripts.

Web browsers can be either very strict about HTML or play fast and loose with the HTML specification. A <TITLE> element is required by the specification, for example, but most browsers display pages that don't have a <TITLE>. Just because your browser tolerates lapses in correct HTML doesn't mean that all browsers do. If you want to be sure that your pages conform to the specification, you can use an HTML *validation service,* which reads your HTML files and then reports any problems with your HTML. Most validation services let you decide how strict the checking should be. You can find a listing of these services on Yahoo! at this address:

```
http://www.yahoo.com/Computers_and_Internet/Software/
        Data_Formats/HTML/Validation_Checkers/
```

Many companies sell HTML editors you can use just like word processors, except that they create HTML files for you. If you plan to do a great deal of HTML editing, these programs make it easy to link pages, style text, and add images. Netscape Navigator Gold has an editor built-in to a Web browser. FrontPage, from Microsoft, and HoTMetaL Pro, from SoftQuad, are two of the many stand-alone editors you can use.

You don't need a fancy HTML editor to produce great-looking HTML files. More and more programs are beginning to feature options for creating Web versions of their own files. Many Microsoft programs (Word and PowerPoint, for example) have Internet Assistants that produce HTML versions of their regular (non-Web) files. If you're using Windows, you can create HTML files from scratch with the lowly Notepad program (which just might be the world's most popular HTML editor). On a Macintosh, the shareware programs Alpha and BBEdit both have excellent add-ons for creating HTML. If you're using UNIX, you can use GNU emacs, which has many HTML extensions. (If you're a UNIX masochist, you can use vi.)

What's in a Link?

Hypertext is the foundation of the Web. Everywhere you turn on the Web, you see it. *Hypertext* is text that is linked to other, related text. If you have ever read a dictionary definition full of unfamiliar words, you have already found a great use for hypertext: If every word in the definition were linked to its own definition, you would spend less time flipping pages.

No application process exists for making regular text become hypertext — you transform ordinary text into hypertext through HTML. The HTML *anchor tag* lets you build links to related material. An anchor tag has an address and two markers: a beginning and an end. The address tells the browser where to look for the linked material, and the markers set off the linked text from ordinary, lesser text.

"Where's 123 Main Street?"
(Web addresses)

Trying to find an unfamiliar address while driving at night in a new city can be a frustrating experience. Imagine how your Web browser would feel if you told it, "I know it's on the Web somewhere, but I don't know the exact location." To keep browsers from wandering around in the dark (because you know that browsers never stop to ask for directions), the Web has a rigid address system. Web addresses don't look like 235 South Bartholomew Road; instead, they look like this:

```
http://www.microsoft.com/ie/default.htm
```

Most Web addresses are presented as a *URL,* or Uniform Resource Locator. If you need to say URL, you can pick your favorite pronunciation: "ural" (rhymes with "earl") or (spelled out) "U-R-L." A URL has all the information the browser needs in order to find what you're looking for.

A URL can have as many as five parts. When you put all these pieces together, a URL looks like this:

```
protocol://server-address/pathname/page-name#page-section
```

Here's an explanation:

- ✔ `protocol`: On the Web, the protocol is usually HTTP, although browsers understand other protocols too (FTP and news, for example).
- ✔ `server-address`: The server address is the name of the computer, which, because it's often on the Internet, has an Internet address. Most Web server addresses begin with `www`, but they're not required.
- ✔ `pathname`: The pathname tells the Web server where to find the file within the server's directories. Because directories are labeled in many different ways, the UNIX style is used as the common standard.
- ✔ `page-name`: Because a directory may have many pages within it, a URL includes the name of a page, which is usually an ordinary filename.
- ✔ `#` (number sign): Some pages are so jam-packed with stuff that you will want to go straight to a particular section. The # symbol tells the browser where the page-name stops and the page-section begins.
- ✔ `page-section`: This portion of the URL identifies a particular location within a page. A hypertext glossary, for example, often includes hundreds of terms on a single page. You usually find an index sorted by letter at the top of the page; clicking the *H,* for example, at the top takes you directly to words that begin with *h.* The *h* in the index works by including a reference to the "h" section of the page, using the `page-section` part of the URL.

Although most people aren't familiar with UNIX, pathnames in UNIX are similar to DOS and Windows, except that the backslashes (\) used in DOS and Windows directory names are reversed (/). For Macintosh users, the colons in pathnames are also replaced by forward slashes (/). Table 3-1 summarizes the characters used in UNIX pathnames.

Some Web addresses include a *port number,* which selects a specific port to which the browser should connect. To understand ports, imagine yourself on a sandy beach along a coastline, with ships floating past you. Each coastline has many ports where ships dock; some ports are specialized for one kind of cargo. Suppose that coffee beans usually go to port 13, which becomes known as the coffee port. It's the same way with Web servers, which are similar to coastlines: All Web traffic usually goes in and out the same port. Because it's usually the same port, no one bothers to use the port number. Because some Web servers want to be different, though, they use a different port for Web traffic, and then you have to specify a different port number. The port number, which is part of the server address, follows immediately after the name of the server, separated by a colon. Here's the general form:

```
www.different-server.edu:port-number
```

To make it easy to remember, the anchor tag is <A>, as shown in this example:

```
<A HREF="http://www.microsoft.com/">Microsoft</A>
```

The <A>...</A> is the anchor tag, which marks the beginning and end of the text link. The other piece of an anchor is the address (given as a URL) that tells a browser where to find the related material. Browsers often display links so that they stand out — for example, by showing links in a different color, underlining links, or both. After you have figured out anchors, you're well on your way because the rest of HTML looks very similar.

Table 3-1	Pathname Characters on the Web	
Character(s)	*What It Does*	*Example*
/	Separates levels	`/building/top-floor/bed room`
..	Moves up one level	`../bedroom` (the directory one level up is `/building/top-floor`)
.	Changes to current directory	`./`

Understanding that links are relatively absolute

When you're creating a link, you can use either relative or absolute pathnames. A *relative pathname* specifies the location of a document in relation to the current document. If you create on the Web an atlas of all the known planets in the universe, you can organize the universe into directories. At the top level are galaxies and then planets, continents, countries, and so on. All your Canadian maps are then in this directory:

```
/milkyWay/earth/northAmerica/canada
```

To provide a link to Canada's southern neighbor on one of the Canadian maps, you could use a shorter pathname that gives the location relative to the Canadian maps:

```
../unitedStates
```

An *absolute pathname* is one that includes the entire path regardless of whether it's necessary. If you use the absolute pathname to provide a link from one of your Canadian maps to the United States, you have to write out the entire pathname instead:

```
/milkyWay/earth/northAmerica/unitedStates
```

If you're linking together several related pages, you should use relative links. Relative links work well because you can easily move all related pages to another location without having to update the links. They're also faster for people who use your site. If you're creating links outside a group of related pages, though, you should use absolute pathnames instead.

A Lightning-Quick Guide to HTML Tags

Now that you have cut your teeth on the anchor tag, you're ready to chow down on the rest of HTML (okay, maybe not the rest of it, but enough to get you started building pages with ActiveX). In this section, I discuss structure tags, which provide the framework for a Web page (as described in Table 3-2), describe style tags that can add a touch of class to your pages, and then tell you about images.

Table 3-2 Structure Tags for Organizing HTML Documents

Style	*Tags*	*Description*
Heading	<H#>...</H#>	Outline structure of a document; includes six levels (level 1 is most significant, and level 6 is least). You specify the heading level by replacing # with a number from 1 to 6.
Paragraph	<P>...</P>	Beginning of paragraph.
Unnumbered list	<UL> <LI>item : <LI>item </UL>	Each item marked by its own <LI> tag is marked separately, usually by a bullet.

Style	Tags	Description
Numbered list	\<OL\> \<LI\>*item* : \<LI\>*item* \</OL\>	Each item marked by its own \<LI\> tag is numbered consecutively when displayed.
Definition list	\<DL\> \<DT\>*term* \<DD\>*definition* : \<DT\>*term* \<DD\>*definition* \</DL\>	Dictionary entry is a \<DT\>, \<DD\> pair that can be repeated within a dictionary list.

When you're dealing with ActiveX, you also need one more tag that isn't discussed in this chapter. Because the OBJECT tag is so important in ActiveX and is more complicated than most other HTML tags, it gets its own breakdown in Chapter 4.

Outlining your pages

HTML has several tags for outlining a document's logical structure. You usually don't see an actual outline in the browser window, but different parts of the outline look distinctive to set them apart. Heading tags create the outline, and you can have as many as six levels. (You probably won't need that many levels unless you're very detail-oriented.) Figure 3-3 shows an example of each of the heading tags, with normal text inserted (between levels 3 and 4) for comparison.

Don't use heading tags as a shortcut to change the appearance of text; use them only to outline the structure.

Brother, can you paragraph?

Because HTML specifically tells browsers to ignore line breaks and spacing on a page, if you want text to show up in separate paragraphs, you have to insert paragraph tags yourself. If you want just a blank line, you can use a \<BR\> tag, which tells the browser, "I'm not saying that I want a new paragraph, but add a blank line anyway."

You don't have to insert the closing paragraph tag (\</P\>) because the browser creates a new paragraph when it sees the next \<P\> tag. It's a good idea to add the \</P\> tag anyway because future browsers may require it. Many programs that write HTML for you (FrontPage and HotMetaL Pro, for example) do include the tag.

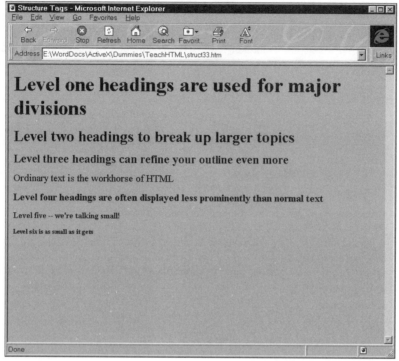

Level one headings are used for major divisions

Level two headings to break up larger topics

Level three headings can refine your outline even more

Ordinary text is the workhorse of HTML

Level four headings are often displayed less prominently than normal text

Level five -- we're talking small!

Level six is as small as it gets

Done

Figure 3-3:
Structure tags help sort out heading levels in a document.

Wishing for lists

Lists show up frequently in page design, and you can format them in lots of ways. If you want to present just a list of items, you can use the unnumbered list, which displays all list items in the same way. If the order of items is important, you can emphasize the order by using a numbered list, which inserts a number next to each item. Definitions use a special kind of list, which works well if you're creating a glossary page. A single dictionary list can have as many term–definition pairs as you want. Figure 3-4 shows numbered, unnumbered, and definition lists as they appear in Internet Explorer.

Because many browsers put a bullet in front of each item in an unnumbered list, it's often called a *bulleted list.*

Adding a little style to your pages

Because all structure and no style makes Jack a dull boy, HTML has several tags that change the way text is displayed in a browser. You can emphasize text, mark an item to be defined, or format a section of text as computer code. Style tags are either *logical* or *physical.* Logical tags don't specify the appearance of

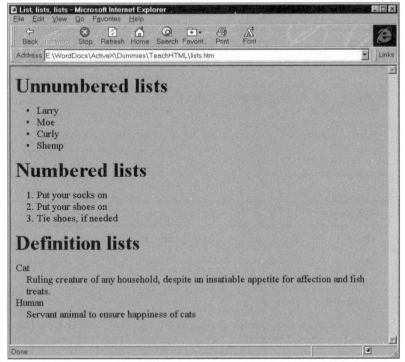

Figure 3-4:
Lists, lists, and more lists. The numerous list styles in HTML can fulfill all your list needs.

text — they simply indicate that the text has a special meaning. Physical styles are particular about the appearance of the text — they tell the browser, "Format this text just the way I want it." The most common logical styles are listed in Table 3-3; the physical tags are listed in Table 3-4.

Table 3-3	Logical HTML Style Tags	
Style	*Tag*	*Description*
Citation	<CITE>...</CITE>	Cites a source as a reference and is usually shown in *italics*
Computer code	<CODE>...</CODE>	Code from a computer program that's usually shown in a `fixed-width font`
Definition	<DFN>...</DFN>	Marks a term to be defined and is usually shown in *italics*
Emphasis	<EM>...</EM>	Emphasizes important text and is usually shown in *italics*
Keyboard	<KBD>...</KBD>	Text typed on a computer and usually shown in a plain, `fixed-width font`

(continued)

Table 3-3 *(continued)*

Style	Tag	Description
Literal sequence	<SAMP>...</SAMP>	Literal sequence of characters that are shown in a `fixed-width font`
Strong emphasis	<STRONG>...</STRONG>	Strongly emphasizes text and is usually shown in **bold**
Variable value	<VAR>...</VAR>	Indicates a placeholder for a value to be named later and is typically displayed in *italics*

Table 3-4 — Physical HTML Style Tags

Style	Tag	How It's Displayed
Bold	<BOLD>...</BOLD>	In **bold**
Italic	<I>...</I>	In *italics*
Typewriter	<TT>...</TT>	As a "typewriter" font (usually a plain, `fixed-width font`)

In HTML, you can mark text as special by adding emphasis or noting a term to be defined, for example. The browser then displays the special text differently to set it apart from normal text. Don't expect logical styles to be displayed in the same way for every user, though.

Figure 3-5 gives you an idea of how various logical styles typically look, but different browsers may display the same style differently. Because many browsers let users customize the display of logical styles, you can never be sure how your HTML will be formatted — so don't depend on any particular appearance.

Stick with logical (rather than physical) styles whenever you can. Because users can often control the display of logical styles, they may have already customized the way their browser displays text. If you use physical styles, though (see Figure 3-6), *you* are controlling the way things appear instead of leaving it up to users.

If you want to display a large block of text that has already been formatted, but not in HTML, you can use the preformatted tag <PRE>. The <PRE> tag tells the browser to display the text between <PRE> and </PRE> just as it appears in the file, including multiple spaces, line breaks, and everything else that's usually ignored. This tag is handy if you feature poetry by e. e. cummings in your Web pages.

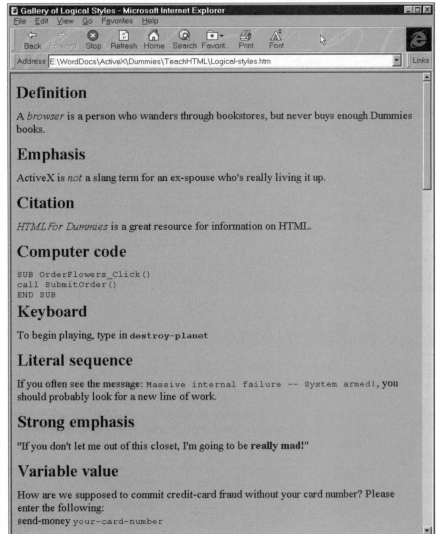

Figure 3-5:
What's
logical
about
styles?

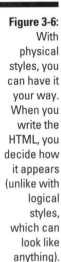

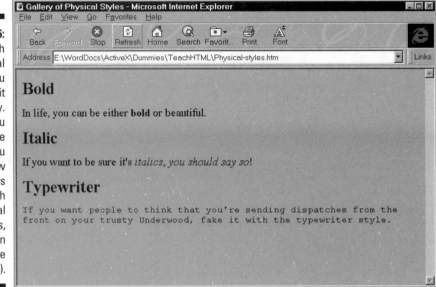

Figure 3-6: With physical styles, you can have it your way. When you write the HTML, you decide how it appears (unlike with logical styles, which can look like anything).

Image Is Everything

You can easily turn plain text into hypertext with HTML, but even hypertext can get a little dry. A hypertext version of an insurance policy is still an insurance policy. With images, you can make Web pages more attractive and more informative. Because images are so important, HTML has special tags for displaying them. Images fall into three categories, and each one uses a different tag, as described in Table 3-5.

Table 3-5	Images and Their Tags	
Image Type	*Tag*	*Example*
Inline	<IMG SRC>	<IMG SRC="ocean-breeze.gif">
External	<A HREF>	<A HREF="kids.gif">kids</A>
Background	<BODY BACKGROUND>	<BODY BACKGROUND="bground.gif">

Getting in line with inline images

Inline images are displayed right along with text in the browser window. Most browsers understand the XBM (*X bitm*ap), GIF, and JPEG formats. Although the <IMG> tag has many attributes, the most common are ALT, ALIGN, HEIGHT, and WIDTH. Here's the syntax for the <IMG> tag:

```
<IMG
    SRC="..."
    ALT="..."
    ALIGN=alignment
    HEIGHT=value
    WIDTH=value>
```

The ALT attribute should include a brief text description of what's in the image, in case users can't see the image.

You can use the ALIGN attribute to control how the image is aligned with its surroundings. The HEIGHT and WIDTH attributes tell the browser the size of the image. (Get more details about the ALIGN, HEIGHT, and WIDTH attributes in Chapter 4, in the section "Your Honor, I Object: The OBJECT Tag.") Figure 3-7 shows Internet Explorer with an inline image of Internet Explorer. (The technique for including background images, like the one shown in this figure, is discussed later in this chapter, in the section "Getting a little background image on a browser.")

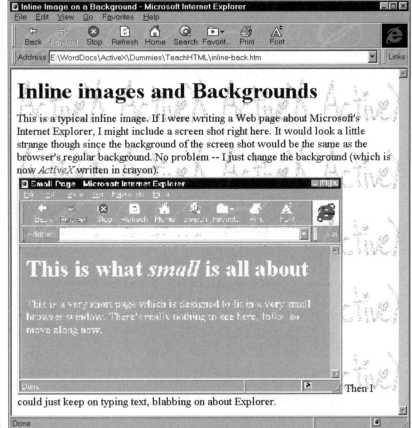

Figure 3-7: Tired of gray? You can liven up a browser's background by replacing it with an image. The image is repeated until it fills the window.

If the browser knows in advance how much room an image takes up on a page, it can lay out the page at the same time an image is being downloaded. If you specify the HEIGHT and WIDTH as attributes of the <IMG> tag, the page is displayed faster than if the browser has to wait for the entire image to download.

If the height and width of the image are different from the HEIGHT and WIDTH specified in the <IMG> tag, the browser scales the image to fit within the area defined by HEIGHT and WIDTH. You can use this scaling to speed up the down-loading of your page by including small images on your page (which download quickly) and then specifying a larger HEIGHT and WIDTH to force the browser to scale the image to a larger size.

Going outside with external images

External images are images that either can't be shown inline or that you want to be viewed separately. Because Web browsers don't understand many graphics formats, users often have to use another program in order to view graphics. (As a page designer, you might avoid the use of inline images, which slow the loading of a page.) To use an external image, simply create a link to the image file by using the trusty (but never rusty) anchor tag, <A>.

To avoid overloading pages with many large, inline images, you can display a smaller version of each image inline and create a link to a larger image. For example, you could insert the following chunk of HTML on your page:

```
<A HREF="BigExternal.gif">
    <IMG SRC="SmallInline.gif">
</A>
```

Users see the smaller image on the page and can click it to view the larger version.

Getting a little background image on a browser

Although most browsers display a gray background by default, you can often change the background to an image. An airline Web site, for example, may use an image of blue sky as a background, and a consulting company may use the company logo as a background image. You specify the background image by using the BACKGROUND attribute of the <BODY> tag.

A background image doesn't have to be large because most browsers automati-cally *tile* a small background image. When you *tile* an image, you repeat the same image over and over until it fills the available space. In addition to using small images, which are faster to download, tiling automatically adjusts the background when the browser window is resized. Figure 3-7 shows Internet Explorer with a tiled background image, which is repeated throughout the browser's background. (The background image is the word *ActiveX* written in gray crayon on a white background.)

 Background images can enhance a Web site, but you must design them carefully. If a background is very large, it slows the downloading of every page that uses the image. Be sure that users can clearly see any text and images against your background.

Turning the Tables on HTML

A *table* in HTML is an easy way to format columns of text. In the dark days of the World Wide Web, table tags didn't exist and creating tables was tricky; more recent versions of HTML support tables. Tables consist of a title, headers, and data. Table 3-6 lists the HTML tags for tables.

Table 3-6	A Table of Table Tags
Tag	*What It Does*
<TABLE>	Identifies a table in HTML; to create a border, add the BORDER attribute
<CAPTION>	Sets the title of the table
<TR>	Marks a row within a table
<TH>	Marks a table cell as a header cell; text is bold and centered by default
<TD>	Marks a cell within a table as a data cell; text is left-aligned and centered vertically by default

Newer versions of HTML enable you to control the formatting within tables as well as build them. Table 3-7 lists the special attributes used for tables.

Table 3-7	Table Attributes	
Tag	*Values*	*What It Does*
ALIGN	LEFT, RIGHT, CENTER	Identifies a table in HTML
VALIGN	TOP, MIDDLE, BOTTOM	Sets the title of the table
COLSPAN	*n*	Specifies number of columns (*n*) a cell spans
ROWSPAN	*n*	Specifies number of rows (*n*) a cell spans
NOWRAP	No value needed	Turns off word wrapping within a cell

Figure 3-8 shows a table that was built using table tags.

Figure 3-8:
Don't use
this table to
make
choices
about
personal
nutrition; it
expands to
fill the
available
width of the
browser
window.

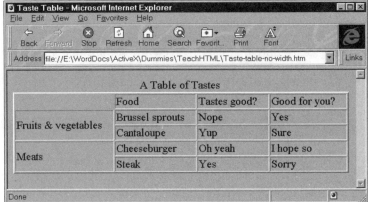

Here's the HTML code for building the table:

```
<table border=2 width=100%>
    <caption align=top>A Table of Tastes</caption>
    <tr>
        <td></td>
        <td>Food</td>
        <td>Tastes good?</td>
        <td>Good for you?</td>
    </tr>
    <tr>
        <td rowspan=2>Fruits & vegetables</td>
        <td>Brussel sprouts</td>
        <td>Nope</td>
        <td>Yes</td>
    </tr>
    <tr>
        <td>Cantaloupe</td>
        <td>Yup</td>
        <td>Sure</td>
    </tr>
    <tr>
        <td rowspan=2>Meats</td>
        <td>Cheeseburger</td>
        <td>Oh yeah</td>
        <td>I hope so</td>
    </tr>
```

```
   <tr>
      <td>Steak</td>
      <td>Yes</td>
      <td>Sorry</td>
   </tr>
</table>
```

As you glance through the HTML code for the table, you should notice a few things. The <TABLE> tag has a WIDTH attribute set to 100 percent so that the table automatically fills the browser window. Each row is bracketed by a <TR>...</TR> pair and has three data cells, each marked with <TD>...</TD>. The first row is used as the header row and contains the labels Food, Tastes good?, and Good for you?. Two of the cells (Meats and Fruits & vegetables) span two columns apiece, using the ROWSPAN attribute.

My HTML Has Been Framed!

Sometimes one window isn't enough. With frames, you can split the one large browser window into panes; each pane then can display its own page. The tags for building frames are listed in Table 3-8. Frames enable you to display related content all at one time. Frames are commonly used, for example, to show simultaneously a table of contents and the content. You can put a frame on the left side of the browser, which has the contents, and the right side then displays specific pages. By clicking within the table of contents frame, you can change the document shown in the frame on the right. Figure 3-9 shows a variation of this approach, which adds a banner at the top of the browser window. The lower part of the window is then split into two panes: a table of contents and a chart.

Table 3-8   Framing a Window with the HTML Frame Tags

Tag	What It Does
<FRAMESET>	Creates a new group of frames and can be nested
<FRAME>	Creates a new frame and must appear inside a <FRAMESET>
<IFRAME>	Floating frame that can be embedded within a page (only in Internet Explorer)

Frames are not part of the official HTML specification, but both Internet Explorer and Netscape Navigator support them. The syntax for frames described in the following section follows the Microsoft frame specification for Internet Explorer.

Figure 3-9:
Using
frames, you
can divide
a browser
window into
several
independent
windows
called
frames.
Each frame
can display
its own
page, and
one frame
can change
while the
others
remain the
same.

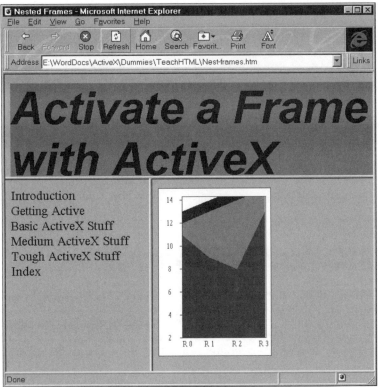

Building a frame

Each of the panes shown in Figure 3-9 is a frame, and each frame belongs to a frameset. You can't create a frame within a frame, but you can create a frameset within a frameset (called a *nested frameset*). The panes in the figure were created using nested framesets; Figure 3-10 shows the structure of the frames shown in Figure 3-9. In Figure 3-10, one frameset splits the browser window into a top and bottom pane: frameset A and frameset B, respectively. Frameset A contains a frame (frame 1) and a frameset (frameset B); frameset B is nested inside frameset A. Frameset B is then split into frames 2 and 3.

Four files were necessary to create the frames shown in Figure 3-9. One file lists the framesets and frames, and the other three are the HTML files, which fill each of the three panes. The frame file for Figure 3-9 looks like this:

```
<HTML>
<HEAD>
    <TITLE>Nested Frames</TITLE>
</HEAD>
```

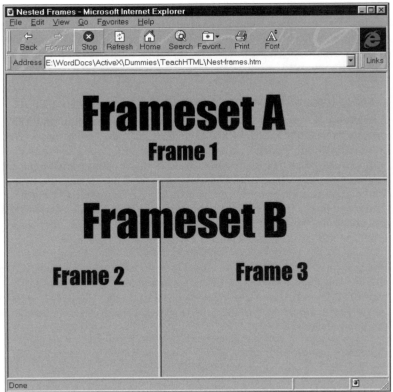

Figure 3-10:
Framesets
can nest
inside one
another:
Frameset B
nests inside
frameset A.

```
<FRAMESET ROWS="35%,*">
   <FRAME SCROLLING=NO SRC=banner.htm>
   <FRAMESET COLS="40%,*">
      <FRAME SRC=ToC.htm>
      <FRAME SRC=main-contents.htm NAME="main">
   </FRAMESET>
</FRAMESET>
</HTML>
```

Unlike most HTML files, no <BODY> tag is included in the HTML for the frame
file. Instead, the </HEAD> tag is followed immediately by a <FRAMESET> tag.
The reason is that a frame file has no content of its own — it simply organizes
content in other files.

The HTML uses only a few of the many attributes for the <FRAME> and
<FRAMESET> tags, but they are the most common attributes. The ROWS
attribute of the first FRAMESET tag splits the browser window into two rows:
The first row is 35 percent of the window's height, and the second row is the
remainder of the window (indicated by the *). The second frameset splits the

second row of the first frameset into two columns: The leftmost column is 40 percent of the browser window's width, and the second column takes up the remainder of the width. Each frame has its own HTML file, which is specified by the SRC attribute. The topmost frame, for example, is filled with the contents of the file banner.htm.

Playing the name game with frames

Suppose that you want to create a table of contents within one frame and display in an adjacent frame the page chosen from the contents. You create the table of contents and provide from each section in the table a link to the appropriate page. There's a catch, though: If you insert an ordinary link, the browser dutifully loads the selected page, but loads it into the table of contents frame and erases the contents from the frame. You have to tell the browser, "Sure, the link is in the table of contents, but I want to display the linked page in the adjacent frame, not in the contents frame." HTML has, fortunately, a way to label the individual frames within a window and then refer to frames by name.

You use the NAME attribute of the <FRAME> tag and the TARGET attribute of the <A> tag together to label and refer to frames. When you create a frame with the <FRAME> tag, name the frame by setting the NAME attribute to the chosen name. For example, you might give the name "main" to the frame in which you display pages:

```
<FRAME SRC=main-contents.htm NAME="main">
```

Now you can refer to the frame as "main" and create links in the table of contents frame, which loads pages into the frame named "main." To target another frame, include the TARGET attribute in the link:

```
<A HREF="basic.htm" TARGET="main">Basic ActiveX Stuff</A>
```

When a user follows a link from the table of contents, the linked file is displayed in the frame called "main" (where the rain falls mainly on the plain).

No scrolling allowed

When Internet Explorer loads a page, Explorer automatically includes scroll bars if the contents of the page don't fit within the window. The same is true for frames: If a frame has more content than will fit within the frame, scroll bars appear automatically. If you know that you never will want to use scroll bars, you can prevent Internet Explorer from displaying them for a frame by setting the SCROLLING attribute to No. Scrolling has been turned off for the first frame shown in Figure 3-9. (Scrollbars are enabled by default for the other two frames, but they aren't necessary.)

Floating on a sea of frames

Microsoft Internet Explorer adds a unique twist to frames: floating frames. A *floating frame* is a rectangular frame that can appear anywhere within a window, just as an inline image can. Figure 3-11 shows a floating frame embedded in a page.

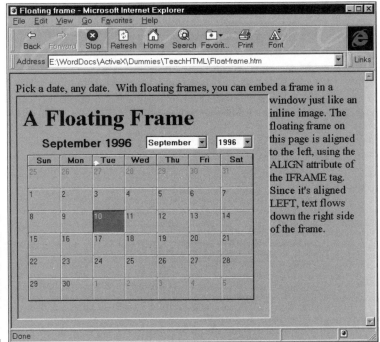

Figure 3-11: The floating frame displays an ActiveX calendar control.

Floating frames are similar to regular frames, but floating frames use the <IFRAME> tag rather than the usual <FRAME> tag. As you can see in the following HTML code, the <IFRAME> is included directly in the middle of a paragraph of text, just like an inline image:

```
<HTML>
<HEAD>
    <TITLE>Floating frame</TITLE>
</HEAD>
<BODY>
    <P>Pick a date, any date.
    <IFRAME
        HEIGHT=400
        WIDTH=450
        SRC="calendar.htm"
        ALIGN=LEFT>
```

(continued)

(continued)

```
   </IFRAME>
   With floating frames, you can embed a frame in a
   window just as you can do with an inline image.
   The floating frame on this page is aligned to the
   left, using the ALIGN attribute of the IFRAME tag.
   Because it's aligned LEFT, text flows down the
   right side of the frame.
   </P>
</BODY>
</HTML>
```

Unlike typical frame files, which have no <BODY> tag (see the section "Building a frame," earlier in this chapter), files with an <IFRAME> tag should have a <BODY> tag. Because you use an <IFRAME> tag to create a frame floating within a page, you have to add a <BODY> tag to include the surrounding content.

Today, only Microsoft Internet Explorer understands the <IFRAME> tag, which creates a floating frame within a browser window. The floating frame can display an HTML file that's different from the one in the main window, as shown in Figure 3-11.

Testing your newfound knowledge

1. What is a URL?

A. An unusually rotten lemon.

B. A phrase from that old song that goes "... thought I was the Duke of URL."

C. A universal address used to specify files on the Web.

D. Just the Southern pronunciation of Earl.

2. Why are frames useful in HTML?

A. Because there are lots of images but no good place to hang them.

B. To make an embarrassing page you have designed look as though someone else de-signed it.

C. Because without good, sturdy frames, HTML would fall down.

D. They make it (sort of) easy to show several related files simultaneously.

Part II
ActiveX
Components

The 5th Wave   By Rich Tennant

"EXCUSE ME - IS ANYONE HERE NOT TALKING ABOUT ACTIVEX?"

In this part . . .

If you have always wanted to be in control, this is your chance. ActiveX controls are only one of the many facets of ActiveX technologies, but they certainly are useful for jazzing up Web pages. This part of the book presents a sampling of the many available controls and some suggestions for how to use them to design better Web pages.

Chapter 4

Birds of a Feather: The Building Blocks of ActiveX Controls

In This Chapter

▶ Understanding controls

▶ Handling events

▶ Using the <OBJECT> tag

▶ Working with the <PARAM> tag

*T*he ActiveX specification includes standards for building custom controls (still called OCXs by veteran programmers) that are intended as self-contained modules. If you want users to send mail commenting on a particular Web page, for example, you should include a mailer control on the page. No muss, no fuss. Need a combination mousetrap–dishwasher–typewriter? No problem — just drop in a prebuilt control, and you're done. One advantage ActiveX has over other approaches is that it has a vast selection of ready-made controls from which to choose.

When you design a Web page using ActiveX, much of the work has been done already by developers who have written the thousands of available controls. You still have the tricky task, however, of choosing and assembling the appropriate components. You also have to ensure that the controls you have chosen work together: If some chosen controls generate data and others receive data, they have to be compatible. If controls are written to the ActiveX specification, they should, of course, interoperate flawlessly. It's a cruel world, though, so some controls are less cooperative than others. When control developers promise interoperability, always remember the phrase "Trust, but verify."

ActiveX controls are objects in the object-oriented sense. To understand ActiveX controls, you have to know something about object-oriented technology. In the object-oriented paradigm, objects are self-contained and autonomous: They know who they are and what they can do. Objects are generally divided into two parts:

✔ Information

✔ Actions

A graph object, for example, may include the value of data points to be graphed and a variable to determine the style of the graph. The graph object would also include instructions for different graph styles. That's the crux of an object: It has data, and it also has instructions for using the data. In the past, software developers have viewed information and action as separate. Object-oriented programming, however, bundles them into one package: the object.

Who's in Control Here?

ActiveX controls can have as many as four attributes, although not all controls have all four:

- ✔ **State:** The internal condition of an object. My cat, for example, has two states: asleep and hungry.

- ✔ **Property:** Used to specify the parameters of an object. Color, size, and location are all common properties.

- ✔ **Method:** The things an object knows how to do. One of my cat's methods, for example, is apparently "Awaken servants for 6 A.M. feeding."

- ✔ **Event:** A signal from the world that an object generates. A button object, for example, might generate the event "Someone clicked the mouse over me." My cat reacts to the event "box of cat treats being shaken loudly" but not to the event "Servant said, 'Get off the keyboard!'"

ActiveX controls are designed as objects themselves; information (states and properties) and actions (methods) are built-in to each control. So what good are events? Events support another common technique in software design: event-driven programming. Years ago, software was designed to lead users around by the nose (although few packages included the necessary nose ring and rope, which had to be purchased separately). A user's purpose was to "fill in the blanks" by answering questions posed by the program, which eventually churned out an answer. To the surprise and consternation of many developers, few users enjoyed this process.

Handling Events Bigger Than the Oscars

Event-driven programming was developed to make programs responsive to users. The basic principle was that *users* (rather than programs) should determine what they want to do and when they want to do it. In event-driven programming, programmers write *event handlers,* which are procedures triggered by a particular event, and then take appropriate action.

Who's driving this thing?

Although event-driven programming is designed to free users to do what they want, that's not always a good thing. Most event-driven systems, therefore, allow for *modal* dialog boxes, in which users can't do anything else until they have dealt with a particular dialog box. Suppose that your program has detected that a user's hard disk is on fire and you notify her with a dialog box that says, "Hey, your hard disk is on fire. You had better get a fire extinguisher." You don't want the user to ignore your message and spell-check a document instead. Therefore, a dialog box that

displays a critical error message should be modal, and most other dialog boxes should be *nonmodal*.

Users can ignore nonmodal dialog boxes by avoiding them. An e-mail program might notify you that new mail has arrived, for example, by popping up a dialog box. If you're writing an e-mail message, you might not want to stop to check out the new mail. If the notification were a nonmodal dialog box, you could continue your correspondence.

The event "spent the last dollar in my wallet," for example, might trigger an event handler whose first step is "find an automatic teller machine." After you begin writing scripts, you spend most of your time writing event-handling procedures for events generated by the controls you're using. You may even occasionally become enraged at the control developers who failed to anticipate the particular event you want to respond to, but that's part of the allure of programming.

Your Honor, I Object: The <OBJECT> Tag

The ability to design ActiveX controls is all well and good, but your genius goes unrecognized unless you can insert controls into a Web page. Because the original specification of HTML predates ActiveX, there was no way to insert an ActiveX control. (For the details about HTML and HTML tags, refer to Chapter 3.) The goal of HTML was to make the structure of a document explicit; tags were created to mark headings, emphasize important points, and incorporate other documents. In early versions of HTML, only one medium could be embedded in a document: images, by using the IMG tag. No means existed for inserting other types of media, such as sound, and including dynamic objects was out of the question. (Although HTML has always allowed *linking* to any type of media, you couldn't include an object as an integral part of a page. You could create a link to a sound file, for example, which would be downloaded and played when a user followed the link, but you couldn't embed a radio in a page and have it play sounds independently of the browser.)

People want more than images, though, which the authors of the HTML specification recognized. A new tag (<OBJECT>) has been added recently to enable designers to incorporate many types of media directly into HTML documents, including dynamic objects, such as ActiveX controls. Because the <OBJECT> tag specification is flexible enough to encompass many media types, it is also complicated. It's the only way to include ActiveX controls in your pages, however, so it's important to understand it.

The complexity of the <OBJECT> tag is necessary because you're specifying the information the browser needs to incorporate the included object. An <OBJECT> tag has two parts: one for the browser (a clue to the object's implementation) and one for the object (any parameters or properties the object needs). The two parts are both described by the tag's attributes. Because the <OBJECT> tag contains information about an object's implementation, you can even insert an ActiveX control the browser has never seen.

This list shows the valid attributes for <OBJECT> tags:

ALIGN	DECLARE	STANDBY
BORDER	HEIGHT	TYPE
CLASSID	HSPACE	USEMAP
CODEBASE	ID	VSPACE
CODETYPE	NAME	WIDTH
DATA	SHAPES	

If you insert a Chart control object into an HTML page, the first part of the <OBJECT> tag looks something like this:

```
<<OBJECT>
   classid = "clsid:FC25B780-75BE-11CF-8B01-444553540000"
   CODEBASE = "http://www.microsoft.com/ie/download/activex/
           iechart.ocx#version=4,70,0,1086"
   id = chart1
   width = 400
   height = 200
   align = left
   hspace = 0
   vspace = 0>
```

ALIGN

```
ALIGN=TEXTMIDDLE
```

There comes a time in every object's life when it has to choose a side (or a middle). That time comes when you set the ALIGN attribute. Using ALIGN, you can line up an object with the current line of text or as a distinct object. Because the current line of text is displayed in the current font, many values for the ALIGN attribute are related to the current font. The height of the current line, for example, depends on the height of the characters on that line, which is an attribute of the current font. Table 4-1 summarizes the alignment values that anchor an object to the current line; Table 4-2 describes the alignment values that enable an object to float on the page rather than be treated as part of the current line.

Don't be confused by the similarity of ALIGN and Alignment. The ALIGN attribute for an <OBJECT> tag is different from the Alignment property of a particular control.

Table 4-1	Fifty (Okay, Six) Ways to Anchor Objects to a Line
ALIGN Value	**Object Position**
TEXTTOP	Top of object is aligned with top of current font.
MIDDLE	Middle of object is aligned with baseline of current font.
TEXTMIDDLE	Middle of object is aligned with a line halfway between baseline and x-height of current font. (The *x-height* is the distance from the baseline of a font to the top of a lowercase *x* in Western character sets. If the text font is an uppercase-only style, the x-height is the height of an uppercase *X*. For other writing systems, TEXTMIDDLE aligns the middle of the object with the middle of the text.)
BASELINE	Bottom of object is aligned along baseline of text line.
TEXTBOTTOM	Bottom of object is aligned with bottom of current font.
TOP	Top of image is aligned with tallest item on line containing the image.

Table 4-2	How to Float an Object without Any Water
ALIGN Value	**Object Position**
LEFT	Floats down and over to current left margin; subsequent text flows past right side of visible area of the object.
CENTER	Floats after end of current line and is then centered between left and right margins; text following the object begins at left margin of next line.
RIGHT	Floats down and over to the right margin; following text flows past left side of visible area of the object.

BORDER

```
BORDER = 10
```

You often use an object as a link to somewhere else by enclosing it in an anchor element (<A>...</A>). (You can read about links and anchor elements in Chapter 3.) If you do so, you can set off the object by specifying a border around it. You use standard units to specify a border's thickness. (The details about standard units are discussed in the "HEIGHT, WIDTH" section, later in this chapter.) Although the default is to use no border, you can specify BORDER = 0 to make clear that you intended no border — rather than you simply forgot to include one.

CLASSID

A typical CLASSID parameter is a really long number that uniquely identifies a class, as shown in this example:

```
CLASSID = "clsid:FC25B780-75BE-11CF-8B01-444553540000"
```

Despite the myriad of features included in browser software, most browsers still aren't very smart. If you refer to an object that wasn't built-in to a browser, the browser wants to know every little detail about that object. (Browsers generally don't like being kept in the dark.) You don't have to supply the details yourself — you only have to tell the browser where it can find the details. As a little twist to keep things interesting (this stuff is interesting, isn't it?), several schemes exist for specifying the location of an object's implementation. Each addressing scheme has a slightly different syntax, any of which can be used as the CLASSID value.

The addressing scheme used for ActiveX controls treats the CLASSID as a class identifier. The CLASSID identifies the *class*, not the object. All objects created from the same class (all ActiveX Label controls, for example), therefore, have the same CLASSID.

The CLASSID attribute was created to enable designers and programmers to refer to COM (Component Object Model) classes. COM classes are identified by the initial sequence clsid (it's short for *class id*entifier); the clsid sequence has been carried over to the <OBJECT> tag. (Because the curly braces traditionally used in clsids have been deemed unsafe for use in URLs, the braces were dropped in the <OBJECT> tag.)

Here's a typical CLASSID attribute:

```
clsid:FC25B780-75BE-11CF-8B01-444553540000
```

I can never remember the last four digits, so I always have to look it up. You don't have to struggle with never-ending clsid numbers, though, because tools such as Microsoft Control Pad and HoTMetaL Pro (from SoftQuad) insert these values for you.

CODEBASE

The CLASSID uniquely identifies a particular class of objects, but that doesn't help if a user's system has never seen a similar object. Suppose that you have created a nifty new control called SlicerDicer. It slices and dices and is in a Web page you have created. When a user visits your Web page, the <OBJECT> tag's CLASSID distinguishes the object on your page as a SlicerDicer from a TextBox control, for example. The user's system has, unfortunately, never seen the marvelous SlicerDicer you have created and has no idea how it works.

CODEBASE to the rescue! If a user's system doesn't know how a particular control works, the CODEBASE attribute tells the system where to go for more information. After the user's system realizes that SlicerDicer is a new control, it checks the CODEBASE attribute, which is a URL that points to the code for the control. The user's system then can download a copy of the control, and your Web page then slices and dices like an old pro, after the new SlicerDicer object has been installed. The next time the user visits your page, that person's system checks the control's CLASSID against the list of installed controls. The system discovers that the control has been downloaded before, and the CODEBASE attribute isn't necessary.

The following HTML code shows an example that uses the CODEBASE attribute:

```
CODEBASE = "http://www.microsoft.com/ie/download/activex
            iechart.ocx#version=4,70,0,1086"
```

In the frenzied world of the Web, there's no time for civility, and sometimes a shoving match ensues. On the Web, though, it's a technical shoving match of *pushes* and *pulls*. If a Web client asks for a document from a Web server, it is pulling that document from the server. If the server sends a document without having been asked to send it, however, it's a push. The CODEBASE attribute doesn't just tell the client where to find the control — it also pushes the control onto a user's machine. If you set the CODEBASE attribute for an object, the server reads it and sends the appropriate control without the user's asking for it. (Most browsers check with users to see whether they want the control and then give them the chance to cancel the download.)

The preceding CODEBASE value has a URL that points to the Microsoft Web server, where a downloadable version of the control is available. Some version information is also tagged on to the end of the URL to ensure that the browser is always using the most up-to-date version. If a user has an outdated version of a control, the browser downloads the updated version.

DATA

```
DATA = "http://www.microsoft.com/data/stock-market/
              june12.dat"
```

The DATA attribute is a URL, which points to the object's data. If the object were an animation, the DATA attribute might point to an AVI file. To insert a Shockwave movie into a page, for example, you have to use the DATA attribute:

```
<<OBJECT>
   data=shocknew.dcr
   type="application/director"
   width=288
   height=200>
   <img src=shocknew.gif
        alt="Best with Shockwave">
</<OBJECT>>
```

DECLARE

```
DECLARE
```

The DECLARE attribute tells the browser, "Don't bother to create this object yet — I just want a placeholder for it." You can achieve some sophisticated effects by using DECLARE, but it's generally not necessary. If you need more information about the use of DECLARE, you can get details at the Web site for the World Wide Web Consortium (http://www.w3.org).

HEIGHT, WIDTH

```
HEIGHT = 40.0pi
```

The HEIGHT and WIDTH attributes tell the browser the size of the box that encloses an object. Although you don't always see a box drawn on the page, the browser uses the HEIGHT and WIDTH attributes to aid in page layout. Because HEIGHT and WIDTH are already specified, the browser doesn't have to wait for the object to be downloaded to determine the object's size. If HEIGHT and WIDTH aren't specified, the browser must wait until the object is downloaded to lay out the page. When the browser has to wait, an icon appears within a box while an image is being downloaded. Then the icon is suddenly replaced by the object, and the small box mushrooms to encompass the entire object.

You can specify HEIGHT and WIDTH in any of the *standard units* listed in Table 4-3. Because measurements are often needed for page layout, a standard set of measurement units has been defined by the World Wide Web Consortium

(W3C). The standard set of units is broad enough that each designer can use familiar units but narrow enough that all browsers can support them. The table also indicates how to mark a number with a particular unit of measure.

Table 4-3	Standard Units of Measurements	
Unit	*Specified By*	*Example*
Pixel		300
Percentage of available window space	%	60%
Inch	in	0.5in
Pica	pi	3.0pi
Point	pt	36pt
Centimeter	cm	5cm

In case you have forgotten the metric system and various publishing measures, 1 inch is equal to 6 picas, and 72 points is equal to 2.54 centimeters.

If the visible portion of an object doesn't match the HEIGHT x WIDTH box size, the browser should scale the object to fit. You can use this scaling feature to save download time: Create a reduced-size version of your image, and then specify the HEIGHT and WIDTH of the full-size image. The smaller image takes less time to download but is displayed in the appropriate size by the browser. You can also reduce the image size by creating an image with fewer colors (from 24-bit to 8-bit color, for example), but a smaller image that's scaled up usually looks better than a larger image with fewer colors.

If you have rented a movie video, you may have seen the notice indicating that the movie has been formatted to fit your screen. The formatting is necessary because movie screens are much wider than they are high, and television screens are usually square. If the movie were simply scaled down to fit your television, the image would look too short. To avoid this problem with your images, be sure to maintain the same ratio of HEIGHT to WIDTH as the actual image. Otherwise, images appear distorted.

HSPACE, VSPACE

```
VSPACE = 5%
```

Whenever you insert a visible object on a page, it has two "boxes": the *inner box* and the *outer box* (their relationship is shown in Figure 4-1).

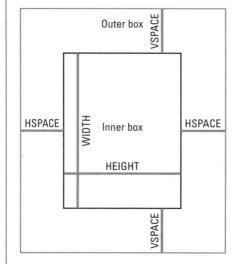

Figure 4-1:
Every object
is drawn
inside two
boxes: an
inner box
and an
outer box.

✔ **Inner box:** Encloses an object, whose size is specified by the HEIGHT and WIDTH attributes. The HSPACE and VSPACE attributes determine the empty space around the inner box, which sets it off from the rest of the page. HSPACE is the length on the left and right sides; VSPACE is the padding along the top and bottom. Both are given in standard units (refer to Table 4-3).

✔ **Outer box:** The size of the inner box plus the padding specified by HSPACE and VSPACE. The additional padding gives your objects some breathing room so that they're not crowded by other elements on the same page. As the browser lays out the page, it treats your object as though it were in the larger, outer box, although the object itself is only the size of the inner box.

ID

```
ID = "Big-n-Hairy-Gorilla"
```

The ID attribute is an object's nickname, which can be used throughout a document. You can set the ID for an object to "Big-n-Hairy-Gorilla," for example, and then refer to it using that name throughout the page.

NAME

```
NAME = "http://www.somwehere-over-rainbow.org/form/"
```

If you're not using forms on your pages, you can forget about using the NAME attribute. If you do use forms, you will recognize this attribute as the data sent to the server when the form is submitted.

Don't be confused by the many uses of NAME. If you have used Visual Basic controls, you might recall using the NAME property to label the control for later reference (in code, for example). The role previously played by NAME in older Visual Basic controls (VBX and OCX) has been replaced by the ID attribute of the <OBJECT> tag; NAME is now used only with forms. To keep things interesting, NAME is also used to identify the property being set within a PARAM tag. (For more information about the PARAM tag, see the section "Parameters: Do You Need to Know?" later in this chapter.)

SHAPES

```
SHAPE = CIRCLE COORDS = "0, 0, 100"
```

Although image maps are often rectangular with rectangular regions, there's no reason to stifle your creativity. The sample values shown here create a circular region with a radius of 100 pixels. With the SHAPES attribute, you can specify any polygonal shape. You don't have to use the SHAPES attribute for ActiveX controls, however, so you can forget about it for now.

STANDBY

```
STANDBY = "I know it seems like forever, but you just have to
          be patient."
```

Sometimes large objects take a long time to load into a user's browser; at other times, small objects take a long time to load. You can entertain users while they're waiting by displaying a short bit of text until the object is loaded. (You can even include special accented characters!) To use STANDBY, pick a brief spot of text and assign it to the STANDBY attribute of the object.

TYPE, CODETYPE

```
TYPE = "text/plain"
```

In an unusual display of commonsense naming, the TYPE attribute is used to denote the type of media that's referenced, which is a handy thing for the browser to know. The TYPE attribute can save time for users because the browser can decide whether it can handle the object *before* it downloads the object. If the browser doesn't have the faintest idea about media of that type, it can just call the whole thing off. The TYPE attribute isn't always necessary because it is sometimes implied by other attributes. With ActiveX controls, a separate TYPE attribute usually isn't necessary because the class (determined from the CLASSID) uniquely identifies the media type as well.

The TYPE system wouldn't be useful unless everyone agreed on what the valid types are. For example, if Microsoft wants the type of a Word document to be "document/ms-word" and I think that it should be of type "data/that-crazy-word-processor," we would be in trouble. Because no one wants that kind of confusion, there are agreed-on types, known as Internet Media Types, and a standard process for registering new types. (To see what some of those types are, choose View⇨Options from within Internet Explorer and then click the File Types tab. Netscape Navigator also supports many of the same types.)

Almost identical to TYPE, the CODETYPE attribute instead specifies the media type for the code that implements an object. Like other applications, ActiveX objects are written by programmers, and computer code is created; a user's system interprets the code as a series of instructions. Sometimes a user's system has to download the control's computer code (for more details about when the code must be downloaded, see the "CODEBASE" section, earlier in this chapter). If the control does have to be downloaded, the browser must know which format the code is in. The CODETYPE attribute tells the browser the format of the code rather than the format of data associated with a control (which the browser knows from the TYPE attribute).

USEMAP

```
USEMAP = "http://www.slow-server.com/img_maps.html#demobar"
```

The USEMAP attribute lets you treat an image as a road map to the Web; users can click an image and be transported to a different location. (Imagine how easy it would be to take the kids on a summer vacation if you could unfold a map of the world and just point to your vacation destination!) Although image maps don't cut your driving time, they can ease the process of navigating around your Web site. The USEMAP attribute lets you create client-side image maps, which offer faster response for users than do the older, server-side image maps. (For more information about server- versus client-side image maps, see the following sidebar, "Server or client — whose side are you on?")

Using a URL doesn't necessarily imply that the map isn't on the current page, because you can use the NAME attribute of an anchor to specify a section within the current page. You can get the details about client-side maps by using the USEMAP attribute, at the Spyglass Web site: http://www.spyglass.com/techspec/tutorial/img_maps.html.

Server or client — whose side are you on?

Image maps fall into two categories: *server-side* and *client-side.* (Remember that *server* in this context refers to the Web server that sends out pages. The pages are then displayed by a *client,* which is the Web browser on the user's machine.) With a server-side image map, a user clicks the mouse on an image (the map) displayed by the browser, and then the browser transmits to the server the location of the mouse click within the image. The server has a file that tells it the address each portion of the map points to, and the server returns the appropriate address to the browser. The browser then goes to the new address. The problem with this approach is that because Web traffic is heavy these days, going back and forth to the server takes time.

Client-side image maps work differently and reduce the traffic over the network. With client-side maps, the file that lists addresses for each map location is stored on the client machine. When a user clicks an image map, the browser looks up the correct address to jump to, and nothing is sent to the server. Client-side image maps are faster because they eliminate what's typically the weakest link: the network connection between client and server.

Parameters: Do You Need to Know?

You can pack a great deal of information into the <OBJECT> tag, but it's not the whole story. The attributes of the <OBJECT> tag tell the browser about the object, but the object needs information too. You tell the object (in this book, usually an ActiveX control) what it needs to know by using the PARAM attributes. The <PARAM> tag has its own attributes, which include NAME, VALUE, VALUETYPE, and TYPE.

The Chart control included with Microsoft Control Pad is typical of many ActiveX controls. The appearance and behavior of the control is determined by control properties you can set and modify through scripting. Chart controls are embedded in a page by using an <OBJECT> tag, and the control's properties are set by using a <PARAM> tag.

The following snippet of HTML code, which is used throughout this section, was yanked from an <OBJECT> tag to illustrate the use of the PARAM attribute:

```
<PARAM NAME="ChartType" VALUE="12">
<PARAM NAME="hgridStyle" VALUE="0">
<PARAM NAME="vgridStyle" VALUE="0">
<PARAM NAME="colorscheme" VALUE="0">
<PARAM NAME="rows" VALUE="4">
<PARAM NAME="columns" VALUE="4">
```

Each <PARAM> has a NAME attribute associated with it, which identifies the property being set. A VALUE attribute follows each NAME and sets the initial value for the property. The Chart control has many more properties than are listed in this example, but most of them simply use the default value built into the control. (Don't worry if <PARAM> tags look messy — you usually use a program to insert and edit controls rather than do so by hand.)

NAME

Most objects have so many properties that it has gotten to the point that you can't tell one property from another. The only way to keep properties straight is to use the NAME attribute to call them by name. In the preceding example, the Chart control has many properties that determine such things as the type of chart, color scheme, number of rows, and number of columns. What's a valid value for a NAME attribute? That depends on the object because the PARAM tag specifies properties for a particular object. In the ActiveX world, each control property is a valid name.

TYPE

If the VALUE is a URL and the VALUETYPE is set to REF, you use the TYPE attribute to specify the type of data pointed to by the URL. In other words, forget the TYPE attribute — you probably won't need it.

Testing your newfound knowledge

1. What does the CLASSID parameter do?

A. Adds a touch of class to an otherwise dull object.

B. Uniquely identifies a particular object, such as a version of an ActiveX control.

C. Nothing — it's just a really long number.

D. Substitutes for objects that never finished school.

2. What does NAME do?

A. Specifies form data that should be submitted to a server.

B. Identifies the property being set inside a PARAM tag.

C. It was used to label controls before the days of ActiveX.

D. I know that this sounds crazy, but it's all of the above.

Chapter 5

Houston, We Have a Solution: The Microsoft Control Pad

· ·

In This Chapter

▶ Inserting ActiveX controls into HTML

▶ Adjusting the properties of ActiveX controls

▶ Using Script Wizard to link controls

· ·

*I*f you have designed a Web page from scratch in HTML, you have undoubtedly experienced true frustration. Forgotten quotation marks swallow up unsuspecting links, and normally sedate browsers run wild when you feed them unruly HTML files. What you need is something that handles the details for you so that you can work on the big picture. Hey, wait — that's what computers are supposed to do! If you're creating Web pages, you can choose from many products to handle the details for you. If you want to insert and edit ActiveX controls, though, you don't have many choices yet. One of the few available ActiveX editors is Microsoft Control Pad, which is free.

With Control Pad, you can insert ActiveX controls into an HTML page and adjust the controls to your liking. You can use Control Pad to change the size, color, font, and many other properties of an HTML page. Control Pad then generates HTML for you and even enables you to link controls with scripts. If you have never written a script, you can use the Script Wizard to link events in one control to actions in another. You can change the color of a Label control, for example, after a user clicks a button.

Ground Zero: Starting Out with Control Pad

If you don't have Control Pad installed on your system, you can download it from the Microsoft Web site (at http://www.microsoft.com) or follow the links on the CD-ROM in the back of this book. After you start up Control Pad, you see the template of an HTML page in which you can begin inserting controls. You also see a toolbar above the file, as shown in Figure 5-1.

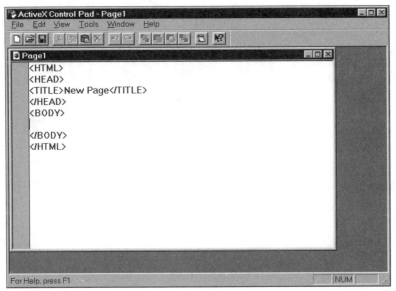

Page1

```
<HTML>
<HEAD>
<TITLE>New Page</TITLE>
</HEAD>
<BODY>

</BODY>
</HTML>
```

For Help, press F1   NUM

Figure 5-1:
Blasting off
with Control
Pad.

If you have already begun creating your own HTML page, you can click File⇨Open to open that file instead. After you have opened the file, you can get to work inserting and editing objects.

ActiveX controls can't help you win friends or advance your career unless you include them in your Web pages — an easy task with Control Pad. The following instructions describe how to insert a control into an HTML file (not into an HTML layout — for those instructions, see Chapter 6):

1. **Choose Edit⇨Insert ActiveX Control.**

   A list is displayed of all the controls installed on your machine.

2. **Choose a control from the list and click the OK button.**

   For this example, I have inserted a button (the Microsoft Forms 2.0 Command button on the list).

   Two additional windows appear on-screen: Edit ActiveX Control and Properties. The Control Pad window resembles Figure 5-2.

3. **Now you can change a control's property values by choosing a property from the Properties dialog box or by resizing and moving the control in the Edit ActiveX Control window.**

   For more information about changing property values, see the following section.

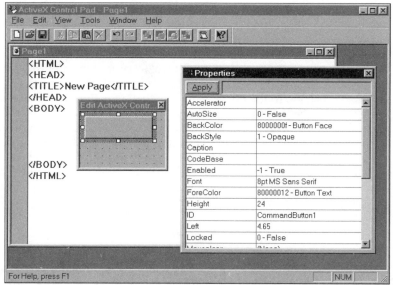

Figure 5-2:
Using
Control Pad
to insert an
ActiveX
control.

4. **After you have finished adjusting properties by using the Properties menu and moving or resizing the control in the Edit ActiveX Control window, close both the Properties and Edit ActiveX Control windows by clicking their respective close boxes.**

After you have closed both windows, Control Pad inserts the HTML code for your control directly into your HTML file. Here's the HTML code Control Pad inserted for the command button I created:

```
<OBJECT ID="CommandButton1" WIDTH=213 HEIGHT=52
 CLASSID="CLSID:D7053240-CE69-11CD-A777-00DD01143C57">
    <PARAM NAME="VariousPropertyBits" VALUE="268435483">
    <PARAM NAME="Caption" VALUE="Press me now!">
    <PARAM NAME="Size" VALUE="4509;1079">
    <PARAM NAME="FontName" VALUE="Arial">
    <PARAM NAME="FontHeight" VALUE="360">
    <PARAM NAME="FontCharSet" VALUE="0">
    <PARAM NAME="FontPitchAndFamily" VALUE="2">
    <PARAM NAME="ParagraphAlign" VALUE="3">
    <PARAM NAME="FontWeight" VALUE="0">
</OBJECT>
```

That's the beauty of Control Pad — you don't have to write down all that stuff between the <OBJECT> tags. You don't even have to know what it means! (You should thank your lucky stars that Control Pad is here to help. Previously, you had to look up those long CLASSID numbers in the System Registry. Believe me — you don't wanna go there.)

After you have finished adjusting a control to your liking, Control Pad creates the HTML code for you (using the <OBJECT> tag), but it replaces any changes you made by hand to the HTML. Suppose that after Control Pad has inserted the HTML for the button in the preceding example, you decide to change the caption to "Click here." If you do so by editing the HTML directly, everything is fine unless you use the Properties window again. Every time you close the Properties window, Control Pad creates a new <OBJECT> tag for your control. If you have edited an <OBJECT> tag by hand since you last used the Properties window, the Control Pad overwrites any changes you have made. Until this problem is (hopefully) fixed in a later release of Control Pad, be careful about changing the HTML directly.

Changing Property Values (Or, How to Make Money in Real Estate)

You can't call a control truly your own until you have customized it by adjusting its properties. Because a control's properties determine its size, shape, color, and behavior, after you can change properties, the world is your oyster. (To prove my point, later versions of Control Pad may include a coupon you can use at your neighborhood raw oyster bar.)

Using Control Pad to change properties is easy: Open the Properties dialog box for the control, pick a property, and enter a new value. You can open the Properties menu for a control in three ways; which method you use depends on whether you're editing raw HTML or an HTML layout and whether you just inserted the control. Table 5-1 summarizes these methods.

Table 5-1	Getting to the Properties Menu	
File Type	*Just Inserted a Control?*	*What to Do*
HTML	Yes	Nothing (Properties menu pops up automatically)
HTML	No	Click control's icon in the left margin, and then click the Properties menu title bar
HTML Layout	Yes	Double-click the control
HTML Layout	No	Double-click the control

After the Properties menu for the control is displayed, you see a list of all the control's properties and their current values. To change a property, click the property in the list and enter the new value in the text box at the top of the Properties menu.

Figure 5-2 shows a command button I've inserted that doesn't yet have a caption. Because buttons become lonely without a caption, I added the caption "Press me now!" After clicking the Caption property, I clicked in the text box at the top of the menu and typed the new caption so that the Properties menu looks like Figure 5-3.

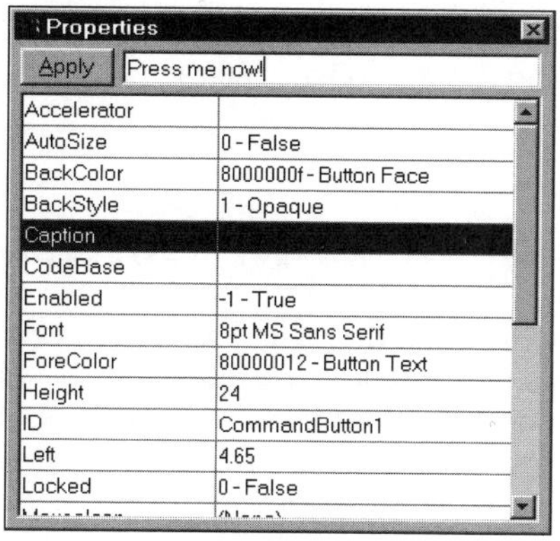

Figure 5-3:
Lonely
button
meets
caption.

Properties	
Apply	Press me now!
Accelerator	
AutoSize	0 - False
BackColor	8000000f - Button Face
BackStyle	1 - Opaque
Caption	
CodeBase	
Enabled	-1 - True
Font	8pt MS Sans Serif
ForeColor	80000012 - Button Text
Height	24
ID	CommandButton1
Left	4.65
Locked	0 - False

Clicking the Apply button on the Properties menu updates the button in the Edit dialog box with the new caption. If you look closely (*very* closely), you see that the caption appears on the button in a very small font. Although an 8-point sans serif font is a great choice for an eye chart, switch to a larger font so that people with less-than-perfect vision can see your pages.

To change the Font property, click Font on the Properties pop-up menu. Unlike with the Caption property, the text box at the top of the Properties menu is grayed out. You can type new font names in that box until you're blue in the face, and the font won't change.

What madness is this? Is ActiveX nothing but a fast track to eyestrain, where only the smallest fonts can be used? Nay, for if you look closely at the text box, you see a square with three small dots on the right side of the Properties menu. As you may already know, three small dots are the international menu symbol for "click here for more options."

If you click the magic three-dot box, a typical font dialog box is displayed that lets you choose an appropriate font. For my button, I've chosen a stunning Gothic font in an outlandish point size, but you can choose your own favorites. The trick to changing properties is to know your options. Some properties offer drop-down menus (marked by a down arrow on the right), from which you can choose an appropriate value. Others offer the "three-dot box," and still others offer a combination of these techniques. (If you want some practice with one of the combination choices, try changing the ForeColor or BackColor for a control.)

You often can skip a step by double-clicking the property within the Properties menu. If you double-click Caption, for example, you immediately see a text cursor in the text box instead of having to click in the text box a second time. If you double-click the Font property, you go directly to the Font dialog box. Double-clicking a color property brings up the Color dialog box, in which you choose from many existing colors or create custom colors. For a Boolean property (one that can be only true or false, such as the Visible property), double-clicking changes the value from true to false and vice versa. Try double-clicking *your* favorite property. (If you double-click the person next to you, go directly to jail, do not pass "Go," and do not collect $200.)

Using the Script Wizard to Link Controls

ActiveX controls can breathe new life into a dull page, but scripts can really liven up your controls. With scripts, you can link together controls on your page so that pressing a button changes the font in another control. Users can fill out forms, and your scripts can adjust the form as it's filled out. Scripts are so important to ActiveX that I've devoted an entire part of this book to scripting (see Part III). Although I don't give you any scripting details until then, you can get started with scripting right now: With Script Wizard, you have to know only *what* you want to do, not *how* to do it. The rest of this chapter tells you how you can put Script Wizard to work for you.

What's a script? (or, how to be a screenwriter)

You're probably thrilled to know that Script Wizard can lend a hand, but you still may wonder: What is a script? A *script* is a set of instructions to do something at a particular time. There's more to that definition than is obvious at first glance. "Something" can range from changing a background color to creating a new employee record in a corporate database. "A particular time" may mean Tuesday at 3 a.m., but it may also mean whenever a user presses a certain button or looks at a particular Web page. You write scripts so that a computer does the same thing over and over, but you have to tell it only one time what you want. (Try that with a four-year-old kid and you can appreciate the power of scripting.)

If you have used Microsoft programs other than Control Pad, you may have already used wizards. *Wizard* is Microsoft-speak for a guide designed for a specific task. The wizard knows what's necessary to accomplish a task and asks you to simply fill in some blanks. After you have finished using a wizard, you have created a brand-new thingamajig. The Script Wizard looks a little different from other wizards, but the idea is the same.

Knowing the proper incantations to start up the Script Wizard

If you're in Control Pad, you can start up the Script Wizard by choosing Tools⇨ScriptWizard from the menu bar. For this example, I have created two objects that will be linked together using Script Wizard. The first object is a colorful label; the second is a command button. After you're done with the Script Wizard, pushing the command button changes the label colors. If you want to follow along at your computer, you can either create your own label and button or load the file chlblcol.htm from the CD-ROM in the back of this book. Starting Script Wizard displays a window similar to the one shown in Figure 5-4.

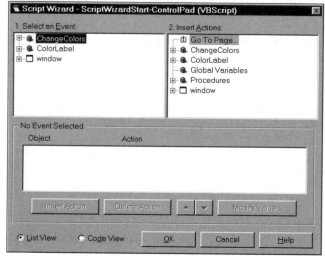

Figure 5-4:
Starting the
Script
Wizard.

Before you begin linking the button and label by using the Script Wizard, a little explanation is necessary. As mentioned, a script is a set of instructions to do something at a particular time. In ActiveX scripting lingo (which is used by the Script Wizard), the "something" is an action and the "particular time" is an event. That explains why the two numbered panes in the top half of the Script Wizard window are labeled Select an Event (the events pane) and Insert Actions (the actions pane). First, you tell the Script Wizard *when* you want something done (the event), and then you tell it *what* to do (the action).

The events and actions are organized by using a scheme that's familiar to Explorer users. (That's Explorer the Windows 95 replacement for File Manager, not Explorer the Internet browser. Rumors abound that eventually *all* Microsoft software programs will be named something-Explorer: Internet Explorer, Word Explorer, Number Explorer. . . .) The top-level objects are displayed, and each has next to it a small plus sign (+) within a square. When you click the plus sign, the components of the top-level object are displayed. In the events pane, the ChangeColors button is initially highlighted. If you click the plus sign next to the button name, you see all the events generated by that button (ChangeColors).

The example shows a button (ChangeColors) and a label (ColorLabel); the goal is to have the label change colors when the button is pressed. You want to know when a user presses the button, which is an event. Unfortunately, you can't just make up your own events — you're limited to the events that have already been defined for the control you're using:

1. **In the Script Wizard's events pane, click the plus-sign symbol just to the left of the ChangeColors button object.**

   The Script Wizard lists all the events defined for the ChangeColors button. The plus sign switches to a minus (–) to let you know that you're looking at the expanded view, and you'll move to the top of the event list. (The entire list of events is too long to display on-screen, and you can't resize the Script Wizard window.)

   Knowing which events are defined for a control is only half the battle, though, because you have to decide which event is the right one for you. Remember that you're looking for the event that corresponds to a user's clicking the ChangeColors button. You have three options for deciding which event is the one you want:

   - Look at the list of events and guess.

   - Read the online Help description of every event the control has, and pick one.

   - Read through Chapter 12, which describes the most common events.

   In this case, the Click event does just what you want when the user clicks the button: The Click event fires.

2. **To choose the ChangeColors button's Click event (which should be displayed after Step 1), simply click the word *Click* (the third event in the ChangeColors list).**

   Click is mouse-talk for "press once." How do I know that? I just do — so there.

   Selecting the event tells the Script Wizard *when* you want something to happen, but you still have to tell the Script Wizard *what* to do. The following section continues this example by discussing how to choose the action for the Click event.

Ready for action: What to do for an event

After choosing the Click event on the left side of the Script Wizard, the bottom pane's label changes from No Event Selected to On ChangeColors Click Perform the following Actions. That's fine and dandy, except that no actions are listed and it therefore won't be much of a performance. Now is the time to add the action.

Remember that the goal is to have the label (ColorLabel) change colors when a user clicks the button (ChangeColors). In the preceding section, you took care of the "when the user clicks the button" part; now you must add the "change colors" part:

1. **Because you want the action to affect the ColorLabel object, click the plus symbol next to the ColorLabel object in the actions pane.**

   If you skim through the list of actions for the ColorLabel object, you don't see anything that sounds like "change color." Instead, you see what looks like a list of properties for a Label control: Accelerator, AutoSize, and BackColor, for example. (You also see some objects, indicated by a box with another plus-sign symbol to the left. That symbol tells you that you can glance at the innards of those objects too, by clicking the plus sign.)

   Although the Actions pane invites you to insert an action, you're really choosing the properties you want to modify. To change the colors of the label, for example, modify the foreground and background colors. The current ColorLabel is yellow on blue, and you can change it to red on black.

2. **Click the BackColor property in the actions pane, and then click the Insert Action button (you can also double-click the BackColor property).**

   Inserting a BackColor "action" brings up a dialog box for choosing a new color (you can't do much with a color other than change it).

3. **Choose black and press OK.**

   Script Wizard lists a new action in the bottom pane; the pane is labeled On ChangeColors Click Perform the following Actions.

   The Object column now includes a row labeled ColorLabel, and the Action column to the right says "Change BackColor to &H00000000." The Script Wizard window should look like the one shown in Figure 5-5.

   (If you see instead a line that begins with "Sub ChangeColors_Click( )," it means that you're in code view rather than list view. To switch back to list view, click the List View option in the lower-left corner of the screen.)

Follow this procedure for changing the ForeColor (it's similar to the preceding set of steps):

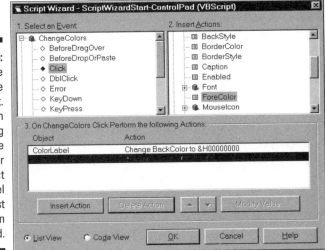

Figure 5-5:
A glimpse
into the life
of a script.
The action
for changing
the
BackColor
of the object
ColorLabel
has just
been
inserted.

1. **Scroll down to the ForeColor property in the actions pane and double-click ForeColor.**

   A dialog box (labeled ColorLabel ForeColor) pops up.

2. **Click any of the red squares and press the OK button.**

   After clicking the OK button, the ColorLabel ForeColor disappears, and you should see a new action added to the bottom pane of the Script Wizard. In the Object column of the bottom pane, you see the ColorLabel object, but now the Action column lists the ForeColor property.

3. **After you have inserted the second action, click the Script Wizard's OK button.**

   The Script Wizard vanishes, and you see the HTML code again.

If you scroll through the HTML file, you see a new chunk of text:

```
<SCRIPT LANGUAGE="VBScript">
<!--
Sub ChangeColors_Click()
    ColorLabel.BackColor = &H00000000
    ColorLabel.ForeColor = &H000000FF
end sub
-->
</SCRIPT>
```

The Script Wizard has done its work: After you choose the events and actions, it writes the script for you.

Although the beginning of the script tells the browser that the language used is VBScript, Script Wizard can also produce JavaScript. (*JavaScript* is a scripting language designed by Netscape to enable Web developers to write scripts to control Navigator. JavaScript has nothing to do with Java, but their similar names often confuse people.)

The new script does just what you want. When a user clicks the ChangeColors button, the button generates a Click event. The Click event causes the script that you (and the Script Wizard) wrote to run; the script then changes the background and foreground colors of the ColorLabel object. (Now is a good time to save the HTML file, in case you suffer one of those extremely rare crashes in Windows; choose File⇨Save to save the file.)

As you glance down the left margin of your HTML file, you see two little icons. Control Pad uses icons to help you quickly find objects (such as buttons and text boxes) and scripts within your HTML files. Now that you have inserted a script, you see a scroll icon, which is aligned with a <SCRIPT> tag. The second icon is a three-dimensional box, which is the icon for an object. The box is lined up with an <OBJECT> tag, which defines the object. You can see the properties for the object by double-clicking the box.

Taking your script out for a test drive

Although you have created a little script magic, you won't realize your own brilliance until you load up your new page in Microsoft Internet Explorer (you can use any ActiveX-enabled browser, but Internet Explorer is currently the only reliable ActiveX browser):

1. **Start up Internet Explorer and choose File⇨Open.**

   The Open dialog box appears.

2. **Enter the filename (including the full path) of the sample file.**

   If you created your own file from scratch to follow along with the example, enter the name of your file. If you want to check out the sample file from the CD-ROM in the back of this book, use the name chlblcol.htm.

   You can click the Browse button to look at the files in a directory and choose the file by clicking the filename. (The Browse button shows the same view that Windows 95 Explorer does.)

   After you have entered the filename and clicked the OK button, Internet Explorer loads the page. You should see a button (the ChangeColors button in your HTML file) just below a label (the ColorLabel label in the example you have been working on) with yellow writing on a blue background.

3. **When you're ready for a thrill, click the button and watch the label's colors change to red on black.**

Exploring Script Wizard

The Script Wizard window has a few extras tossed in on the side, which you may have noticed while building your script. For the file with the button and the label (chlblcol.htm on the CD-ROM in the back of this book), the Script Wizard appears, as shown in Figure 5-6.

Even if only two objects (the button and the label) are in the HTML file, you have a bevy of choices for inserting actions. If you look at the items listed in the actions pane, you see, in addition to the original two objects, Go To Page, Global Variables, Procedures, and window. The Script Wizard gives you lots of flexibility while still making it easy to create scripts.

Figure 5-6:
Script
Wizard has
a few bells
and a
couple of
whistles you
can use.

Redirecting the flow of traffic with Go To Page

The Go To Page action pops up all the time when you use the Script Wizard. A Go To Page action forces the browser to jump to a new page (just as though the browser's user had clicked to follow a link). As an ActiveX designer, you can use the Go To Page action to cause a user's browser to jump to any page you choose. Because Go To Page is an action that's built-in to the Script Wizard, you can choose to associate the Go To Page action with any event. In short, you can turn any event for any object into a link.

Most links in HTML are created by using an anchor tag:

```
<A HREF="URL for new page">link</A>
```

In scripting parlance, this anchor is equivalent to "perform a Go To Page action on a Click event." With scripting, however, you can create links based on *any* event for *any* object. In an image linked to another page, for example, you could associate a MouseOver event (generated by an ActiveX Image control) with a Go To Page action. Then, as soon as a user moves the mouse pointer over that image, the browser jumps to the new page.

To use Go To Page, choose an event from the event pane and then double-click Go To Page. A dialog box pops up, and you can enter as a URL the address of the new page. Remember that URLs aren't limited to http; you can also use news, ftp, and others. If you don't remember, take a look at the section "'Where's 123 Main Street?' (Web addresses)" in Chapter 3.

Using Go To Page is usually a straightforward process, but keep these two caveats in mind:

- ✔ **When a dialog box pops up and offers a Color button to click, don't do it.** Because of a bug in the Script Wizard design, the same dialog box is displayed for every action you choose, even though it's not appropriate for every action. (You *could* choose a color if you really wanted to, but you would wind up jumping to a page like #FF683C — and nobody wants that.)

- ✔ **Watch out for the infinite loop, in which a user can cycle endlessly between two (or more) pages.** Suppose that you create page A and page B. If you have a Go To Page action from A to B and another action from B to A, make sure that users don't wind up going from A to B to A to B to. . . . It's easy to fall into this trap if the Go To Page action is linked to one of the mouse events rather than to a Click or DblClick event. Someone browsing your pages may not realize that she has moved the mouse and triggered the Go To Page action.

Traveling the world with VBScript (global variables)

Usually when you (or the Script Wizard) create a script, you use variables to temporarily store values. Most variables are created inside a procedure and disappear when the procedure ends. These variables, known as *local variables,* are the scratch paper of procedures: They exist only as long as the procedure that defines them.

The first two lines of the following script don't do much — but they do use a local variable, and you can't ask for more than that:

```
Sub ChangeColors_Click ()
   localBackColor = ChangeColors.BackColor
   ColorLabel.BackColor = localBackColor
         :
         :
end sub
```

In this script, the variable localBackColor is created just before it is assigned the button's background color. The next line uses the variable to set the background color of the label. After `end sub` is reached, though, all trace of localBackColor vanishes. That's fine if you don't need the value anymore, but sometimes you want values to hang around longer than the procedure in which they're defined.

Global variables exist independently of any procedure; global variables hang around until the browser moves on to a new page. (For more information about global and local variables, see Chapter 11.)

To create a global variable using the Script Wizard, follow these steps:

1. **Move the mouse pointer anywhere within the actions pane.**
2. **Right-click the mouse button.**

   The right mouse button brings up a *context menu,* which is a menu whose items change depending on the context. In Windows 95 and Windows NT, right-clicking usually calls up a context menu.
3. **From the context menu, choose New Global Variable.**

   A dialog box pops up on-screen.
4. **Type a name for your new variable in the dialog box and click OK.**

If you want to check your handiwork, you can see a list of global variables by expanding the Global Variables label in the actions pane (just click the plus symbol to its left).

Being able to create global variables is a great thing, but you also have to assign values to them. Choose from these two methods:

- Use the equal sign (=) in scripts you write yourself.
- Assign a value by using the Script Wizard.

Assigning a value to a global variable is similar to using the Script Wizard to associate an action with an event:

1. **Decide when you want to assign the new value.**

   With Script Wizard, *when* means deciding which object and which event for the object should trigger the assignment. If you have a particular object in mind, the Window object and its onLoad event are good choices.

Global, shmobal — who needs global variables anyway?

Global variables are handy if you have to use the same variable in many procedures — create it just once and use it over and over again. Suppose that you have set up your own color scheme and have chosen colors for everything from button backgrounds to pop-up menu text. You could create global variables for each color value so that you have a list of global variables: myButtonForeColor, myTextBoxBackColor, and myTextForeColor, for example. All you have to do is assign each component's colors to the appropriate global variable.

Why bother to create global variables for all your colors? Imagine that after ignoring the many warnings plastered on the side of every step ladder, you stand on the top step. Like all top-steppers, you fall and bang your head on the wall. Suddenly you see colors in a whole new light and realize that the color scheme you had previously used was all wrong. Do you have to edit every control to change its colors? No, you just change the global variables, and you're

done. (Too bad you're not as good at climbing ladders as you are at writing scripts.)

In the preceding example (using global variables for colors in a color scheme), global variables are used as *constants,* which are variables whose values cannot be changed while a script is running. (Because VBScript doesn't let you create your own constants, there's no guarantee that the variables' values won't be changed. Instead, you have to promise yourself not to change a variable's value.) You could also use global variables not as constants but as just regular variables. You could refer to them in many different scripts and change their values all the time, but this idea is so bad that it ranks up there with standing on the top step of a stepladder.

Changing global variables all the time can only lead to trouble. Sooner or later, you forget about one procedure that changes a global variable and then don't understand why all your text is printed in three-point Gothic. If you want the whole story, turn to Part III and read all about scripting.

The Window object represents the browser, and the onLoad event represents the browser's loading of the page. Choosing the Window object and its onLoad event ensures that your global variable gets its new value as soon as the page loads into the browser.

2. **Click the plus-sign symbol next to the object you have chosen in the events pane, and then choose an event by clicking the event name.**

3. **In the actions pane, expand the Global Variables object by clicking the plus-sign symbol next to it.**

4. **In the actions pane, click the global variable whose value you want to set.**

5. **Click the Insert Action button (you can also double-click the name of the global variable).**

6. **In the dialog box that pops up, enter a value or the name of another variable and press OK.**

    Script Wizard lists a new action in the bottom pane.

The new action has a row of its own in the bottom pane. Although the object column is blank, the Action column shows that your global variable is assigned a new value.

Using procedures: How to do something over and over

A good reason to write a procedure is when you realize that you're repeatedly performing the same task. (I would love to create a procedure to take out the trash, but the trash cans are too heavy for my computer to lift. Everybody says that computers are becoming more powerful all the time, but they still can't pick up a week's worth of trash.) When you're using the Script Wizard, you will likely often want to do the same things over and over. Rather than go through the same motions to create each step from scratch, you can call on another procedure you have already written — or one that the Script Wizard has written for you.

In the actions pane is an object labeled Procedures, which contains all the procedures in the current file. If you expand the Procedures object (by clicking the plus-sign symbol to its left), you see the list and can choose one by double-clicking it (or clicking the Insert Action button in the lower left corner). You can reuse procedures by clicking an event in the events pane and then double-clicking a procedure in the actions pane. Then, whenever the event fires, the procedure also runs.

Sorry — I don't do windows (but the Window object does!)

The Window object (represented by a small window icon) represents the browser window in which your page is loaded. Think of the browser window as the frame for art you create. The HTML and scripts you write are brush strokes on canvas, but eventually your work is framed. The frame itself has some attributes, which are represented in the Script Wizard as the events and actions of the Window object. (To find out all about the Window object, see Chapter 13.)

The Window object is handy for creating special effects, such as changing the background color. Although you should try to design your Web pages so that they can be displayed in any environment (various background colors or font sizes, for example), sometimes you have to adjust the background to suit your tastes; the Window object gives you entry into the inner sanctum to modify attributes of the user's browser.

The Window object has two events associated with it: onLoad and onUnload, which correspond to when your page is first loaded and just before it's unloaded, respectively. If you want to change the background color, for example, the onLoad event is a good time to do so. The Window object doesn't generate many events, but it has plenty of properties to adjust and methods to invoke.

You can feast on the Window object in all its complexity in Chapter 13; the rest of this chapter provides a quick summary. You should experiment by using the Script Wizard to link different events with different actions, just to see what happens. Because most of the properties you can change have descriptive names, you can usually guess what they are. Don't worry — you can't break anything by playing with scripts.

Windows are objects too

Notice in the two top Script Wizard panes that the Window object is marked by a small icon, although it's a window icon rather than the box icon you see for other objects. Despite the different icon, windows are objects too. Just as the labels and buttons you create have properties, so do Window objects. The only difference is that the window's properties are usually other objects rather than just numbers or strings.

Although you may not have realized it, you have already created objects that have object properties themselves. The Font property, used by many controls, is an object — that's why it's displayed next to a box icon rather than the usual property icon.

A Window object is nothing more than the sum of its parts. If you understand the parts, you understand windows. Table 5-2 summarizes the objects that every window contains.

Table 5-2	Window Objects
Table Object	*Description*
Frame	A list of frames collected under the top-level window. Frames are similar to panes in a window: You can split a window into different independent sections.
History	Like Hansel and Gretel, every browser leaves a trail indicating where it has been. (You can see all your browser's bread crumbs by looking at its history. In Internet Explorer, choose Go⇨Open History Folder.) Within a script, you can access the history list by using the History object.
Navigator	Tells you about the browser application (name and version, for example). Doesn't it seem odd that part of the Internet Explorer model would be named for Explorer's biggest competitor?

(continued)

Table 5-2 *(continued)*

Table Object	Description
Location	The key to profiting from real estate (just kidding). This object has information about the location of the current window. The URL for a window and many other interesting tidbits are available by using this object.
Script	Stores all the procedures defined in the currently loaded HTML file. (Even though every Script object is part of a Window object, you don't see the Script object listed in the actions pane, so you can forget about the Script object until Chapter 13.)
Document	Represents all the stuff in the current HTML file (for example, links, anchors, and ActiveX objects.)

Documents are where it's at

Although you can do lots of things with Window objects, a Document object has many useful properties to play with. Want to change the background color? How about a new shade for links? Do you want to know which of the many Web pages brought a user to the current document? All these tasks are wrapped up in the Document object.

You can create documents in a rainbow of colors by changing properties of the Document object. If the standard gray background of most browsers looks lifeless to you, you can easily change the background to a color you like. When you change it, however, you're just getting started: To ensure compatibility, you should also change the link and foreground colors. If you inadvertently set the background color to match a user's link color, for example, the links will fade into obscurity even faster than disco.

Changing the colors used in documents is a kinder, gentler way to enforce a new color scheme because the new scheme lasts only as long as the document you have created is displayed in the user's browser. After a user moves on to another page, that person's original color choices are restored. Because the best time to make color changes is when a page is loading, you should use the Script Wizard to link the changes to the window onLoad event (see the section "Extra events," later in this chapter). Figure 5-7 shows the Script Wizard window after three actions (all color changes) have been tied to the onLoad event.

Thanks to the wizard of scripting, the colors of the browser's background, link, visited link, and foreground change as the page is loaded. (A *visited link* is one that leads to a page a user has already visited. By using a different color for pages that have already been visited, the browser prevents a user from going in virtual circles.) You should, therefore, always choose different colors for link (linkColor) and visited links (vlinkColor).

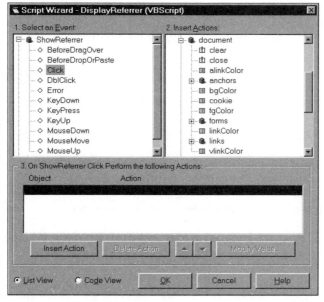

If you look closely at the properties for the Document object, you will notice also the alinkColor property. It sets the color for an *active link* — a link becomes active when a user moves the mouse pointer over the link but doesn't click the link. Although this idea sounds neat-o, Internet Explorer 3.0 doesn't support this feature.

Don't forget that when you change the display colors for a browser, you may be interfering with the user's carefully chosen combination. For example, you might think that red links on a green background lend a touch of Christmas spirit to a holiday page. Unfortunately, you may have just rendered the links invisible to people who have red-green color-blindness. Sometimes you must change the color scheme of a page to mesh with design elements on the page; before you do so, however, be sure to weigh the costs.

Where did you come from? (the Referrer property)

Sometimes it's not enough to know where you are — you have to know where you have been. If you have designed a Web page, you may want to know which site your visitors have just visited to get to your page. If you're tracking Web advertising, for example, in order to measure the effectiveness of different ad locations, you will want to know how people arrived at your site. Maybe you just want to ask each visitor, "Where did you come from?" If a user has followed a link to reach your page, the Window object can tell you the URL for the page with the link that was followed.

The Document object (which is part of the Window object) has a Referrer property, which holds the URL for the referring document. If a user followed a link to your site from the following location, for example:

```
http://www.cool-site.com/ego-booster.html
```

the Referrer property of the Document object would contain this string:

```
http://www.cool-site.com/ego-booster.html
```

The Script Wizard doesn't list "referrer" among the document's properties, so you have to work a little script magic of your own.

If you want to use the Referrer property, follow these steps:

1. **Open an HTML file in Control Pad and start the Script Wizard.**

2. **Choose an event from the event pane.**

   In Figure 5-8, I have created a button that, when clicked, displays the referring page; therefore, I have chosen the Click event for the button. The document property has been expanded in the actions pane so that you can see that no Referrer property is listed.

Because no Referrer property is listed, you have to create your own action from scratch. After choosing the Click event for the button (ShowReferrer), switch to code view without selecting any action. The bottom pane changes to show the first line of the procedure.

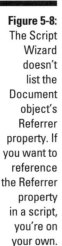

Figure 5-8: The Script Wizard doesn't list the Document object's Referrer property. If you want to reference the Referrer property in a script, you're on your own.

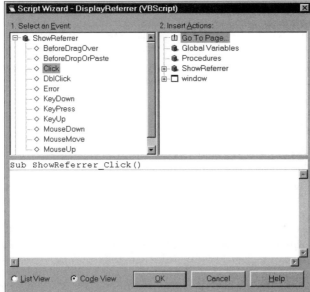

The bottom pane is now split into two parts: the line with the procedure name on it and a scrollable part below the light gray line. To create a little action of your own, click in the bottom pane, below the gray line. Now you can type your own procedure. For now, just enter the following single line:

alert "The referring page was: " + document.referrer

When you're done, you can switch back to list view if you want to use Script Wizard to create other procedures. In list view, however, you can't see your procedure — you see only a message to remind you that you have created a custom action. Don't panic — you can always switch back to code view to view or change your procedure. Click OK, and the Script Wizard inserts the script into your file for you. Don't forget to save the HTML file and make a note of the name you choose (DisplayReferrer is a good choice for this example).

Next, create another HTML page (call it ReferringPage) and include a link to the page DisplayReferrer. Now you're ready to go. Fire up Internet Explorer, and load the file ReferringPage. Follow the link you created to DisplayReferrer, and then click the ShowReferrer button. If a message pops up and says that the referring page was ReferringPage, it worked! You can celebrate any way you want, but I recommend doing a little jig.

There's lots more you can do by linking events and actions with Script Wizard. Feel free to mix and match events and actions and even include a few actions of your own. The online Help feature gives you details about all the properties and events, some of which don't appear in the Script Wizard window, even though you can use them.

Extra events

You probably have seen the Script Wizard window enough times to notice that the Window object has not only actions but also events. You see, in addition to any objects you have created, the Window object in the event pane. Window objects aren't very eventful, though — you choose from only two events: onLoad and onUnload. The onLoad event fires up when the page is being loaded, which makes it a good time for changing display attributes, such as colors.

The Window object is displayed in the events pane only if you're editing an HTML file. If you're working with an HTML layout file, you can't use the Script Wizard with window events. You could insert your own window onLoad procedure into the text file for the layout — you just can't use the Script Wizard to do it. (Why not? Who knows what evil lurks in the heart of Microsoft?) You don't have to worry, though, because the HTML layout has its own onLoad event, which you *can* access through the Script Wizard.

The Window object also has an onUnload event, which fires up when a window is unloaded. A window is unloaded on two occasions: when a user jumps to a new page or quits the browser. The onUnload event is your chance to wave good-bye as a user leaves your page. If you have changed any of the window's parameters during the onLoad event, it's a good time to clean up after yourself and put everything back the way you found it.

Testing your newfound knowledge

1. Control Pad makes it easy to:

A. Launch rockets into low Earth orbit.

B. Change the channel on your space-age television.

C. Insert and edit ActiveX controls.

D. Control other peoples' thoughts through Internet Explorer.

2. Using Script Wizard, you can:

A. Create blockbuster Hollywood scripts with an ordinary word processor.

B. Link ActiveX events and actions to do cool stuff.

C. Conjure up ActiveX minions to do your bidding, except that they don't do windows.

D. Easily write directions for any card trick.

Chapter 6

Laying It on the Line: Creating HTML Layouts

· ·

In This Chapter

▶ Inserting objects into a Layout

▶ Adjusting Layouts by moving and resizing objects

▶ Inserting Layouts into existing HTML pages

· ·

*W*hen you design Web pages with Microsoft Control Pad, you can do so in one of two ways. First, you can create a traditional page that contains HTML to tell the browser what the page should look like. (Chapter 5 tells you how to use Control Pad to create pages using only HTML tags.) The problem with the straight HTML method is that you can't control exactly where objects appear on the page because HTML doesn't include tags that say, "This object has to go four pixels below the top of the Layout and four pixels to the right of the left side." With ActiveX, you can control object positioning. The other method for page design uses the HTML Layout control. You can design HTML Layouts in Control Pad and then include them in your pages by inserting an HTML Layout control into an HTML file.

Getting into Position

If you look closely at some Web pages, you see a mishmash of items packed in so tightly that you can barely tell the GIFs from the JPEGs. Many times, these pages have been designed with that most common of Web-design tools (for Windows): Notepad. The problem is that although Notepad lets you edit raw HTML just fine, you have no idea what the finished product will look like: As a page designer, you're flying blind. If you're like most people, you prefer to design pages visually, just as you imagine them. Several tools can help you do just that: FrontPage (from Microsoft), HoTMetaL Pro (SoftQuad), and other products generate HTML based on your design. Each of these tools lacks something, however: exact control over the position of objects displayed in a browser window.

The HTML standard is missing some useful features, but one of the biggies is *positional control.* Current versions of HTML offer no way to specify the locations of objects on an absolute coordinate grid. Although most designers want to *know* that the label for a text control is, for example, exactly 23 points from the right edge of the control, there's no way to specify that measurement. Microsoft is working to address this problem (at least for ActiveX mavens) with the HTML Layout control. This control reads an HTML Layout file (with the .alx extension) and then positions the objects exactly as specified in the Layout. Imagine that as you casually saunter down the street, a small child stops you and asks that most awkward of questions: "Where do HTML Layouts come from?" As an old ActiveX hand, you have a ready answer, "Why, they come from the ActiveX Control Pad."

Laying Out a Layout

If you want the positional control of an HTML Layout, you have to follow a two-step process. First you create a Layout by using the Microsoft Control Pad, which is covered in this section. Next, you insert the layout into an HTML file by using the Control Pad Edit⇨Insert HTML Layout command. (For information about the HTML Layout control, see the section "Taking Control of Your Layouts: The HTML Layout Control," later in this chapter.)

To build an HTML Layout, fire up Control Pad and choose File⇨New HTML Layout from the menu bar (or press Ctrl+E). A blank Layout is displayed.

You don't have to be a positional control freak to love HTML Layouts. You can also use HTML Layouts to give all your pages a consistent look. By creating a single Layout (.alx) file and inserting it into many different pages, you can reuse the work you have already done. If you later change the HTML Layout file, all the pages that include the Layout show the updated Layout. You could create a signature with your logo and e-mail address, for example, and store it in a Layout. If you insert the signature in all your pages, it's easy to change them all when you get a new e-mail address — just update the Layout file.

The process of using Control Pad to design a Layout consists of two tasks:

- ✔ Inserting controls
- ✔ Adjusting the position of controls in the Layout

You can read about how to insert controls in the following section; the section after that, "Formatting a Layout," tells you how to adjust the position of controls.

Adding a control

Adding a control to an HTML Layout is a little different from adding a control directly to an HTML file. Rather than use the Edit⇨Insert ActiveX Control command, as you would with an HTML file, you insert controls on Layouts by using the Toolbox.

To place a control on the page, follow these steps:

1. **Click the control's icon on the Toolbox.**

2. **To fix the control's position, move the mouse pointer over the Layout grid.**

   Clicking on the grid inserts the control, with the control's upper left corner fixed at the mouse pointer's location.

3. **Drag the mouse pointer to size the control and then click to mark the lower right corner.**

   Hey, this isn't rocket science — you have to follow only three steps.

Now you can right-click a control to display a context menu, drag the control around in the Layout, and do all the other things that seem good and proper. A *context menu* is one on which the options change depending on the context. In Windows 95 and NT, right-clicking the mouse usually brings up a context menu. Because an HTML Layout has a different context than a plain old HTML file, a control's context menu is different as well. On an HTML Layout, a control's context menu contains several options for positioning the control. (For more information about your positioning options, see the following section, "Formatting a Layout.") The beauty of this system is that you have absolutely positioned the controls within the Layout. *Absolute positioning* means that each object on an HTML Layout always appears in the same location on the HTML Layout. You get the convenience of visual design of your pages, and you can rest assured that your creations will be rendered just as you have envisioned them.

Absolute positioning is a double-edged sword. You're guaranteed that two objects that are next to one another in your Layout are always displayed side by side. You're also guaranteed that the Layout won't adapt to a user's browser. If your Layout is 500 pixels wide and a user's browser window is only 420 pixels wide, for example, the user doesn't see the right side of your Layout. You should try to build compact Layouts to make it easy for users to view the entire Layout within their browser windows. (The most common screen resolution is 640 pixels wide x 480 pixels high, which doesn't leave much room for big Layouts.)

Control Pad shows a grid of dots by default. The dots don't appear when the Layout is displayed — they're just there to help you align controls on the Layout.

If you're using Control Pad to create your HTML Layouts, you can adjust the options to your taste, by choosing the Tools⇨Options⇨HTML Layout command from the menu bar. Then you can change the grid spacing (both horizontal and vertical), decide whether you want the grid to appear, and even choose to have Layout items snap to the grid. (*Snap to grid* means that although you can insert a control anywhere within the Layout, the control's corner is automatically aligned to the nearest grid intersection.)

Because every browser shows things a little differently, the only way to be sure that you have achieved the effect you want is to test your creation on *every* browser. If you have time and money to burn, you can adjust each page for the subtle nuances of those quirky browsers and then write a script that detects the browser and sends out custom pages. (For more information about browser detection, see the description of the Navigator object, which is part of the Internet Explorer Object Model, in Chapter 13.)

Formatting a Layout

An extra menu option is squeezed between the View and Tools options. The Format menu gives you control over the positioning of controls embedded in an HTML Layout. Although you can click an object in a Layout and drag the object around, Control Pad has sophisticated tools for formatting the objects on a page. Most of these tools are listed on the Format menu, which is displayed whenever you're working on an HTML Layout file. Each of the menu items on the Format menu (see Table 6-1) deserves a brief explanation; in this section, I see that they get it.

Table 6-1	Format Menu Commands for Positioning Objects
Command	*What It Does*
Align	Aligns any part of all selected objects
Make Same Size	Redraws selected objects to same size (horizontal, vertical, or both)
Size	Resizes an object within a Layout
Horizontal Spacing	Changes horizontal spacing among selected items
Vertical Spacing	Changes vertical spacing among selected items
Snap To Grid	Turns grid snapping on or off
Send To Back	Sends an object to the back of the line
Move Backward	Moves an object back one place in line
Move Forward	Moves an object forward one place in line
Bring To Front	Sends an object to the front of the line

Align

To align several items in the Layout, follow these steps:

1. **Select all the controls you want to align.**

2. **Click within a control's selection rectangle to make it the dominant control.**

   The dominant control is simply the control that was most recently clicked, so if you change your mind, simply click the new dominant control.

   The *dominant control* is the control to which all the other controls are aligned. You can tell which control is dominant because its selection box has white rather than black *sizing handles,* those little boxes that appear at the corners and middles of selected objects; clicking and dragging a sizing handle resizes the selection. Figure 6-1 shows the dominant control in a group.

Figure 6-1:
The Dominant label (indicated by the white sizing handles) represents the dominant object in this group of three labels.

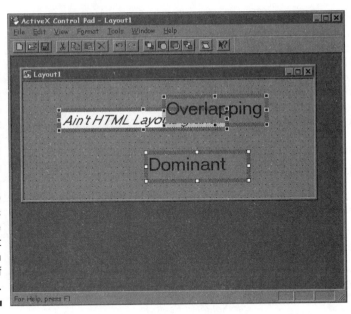

3. **Choose Format⇨Align and then one of the alignment options listed in Table 6-2.**

Table 6-2	HTML Layout-Alignment Commands
Command	**What It Aligns**
Lefts	Left edges of all selected items
Centers	Center of all controls in a single vertical line
Rights	Right edges of all selected items
Tops	Top of all items
Middles	All items so that a horizontal line passes through the middle of all selected items
Bottoms	Bottoms of selected items
To Grid	Ignores the dominant control and aligns the upper left corner of each selected control with its nearest grid point

Make Same Size

Sometimes, as you're creating a Layout, you get swept up in the moment and litter the Layout with objects of many different shapes and sizes. Don't worry: Control Pad can help you clean up the mess. Often you have several objects of similar sizes, but you want them to be exactly the same size. The Make Same Size option on the Control Pad Format menu can resize controls for you.

To make several controls the same size, follow these steps:

1. **Select all the controls you want to align.**

2. **Click a control to make it the dominant control.**

   The dominant control is described in the preceding section. Figure 6-1 shows the dominant control in a group.

3. **Choose Format⇨Make Same Size from the menu bar and choose one of the options listed in Table 6-3.**

Table 6-3	Commands for Making Multiple Objects the Same Size
Command	**Resizes Selected Controls**
Width	To same width as dominant control
Height	To same height as dominant control
Both	To same height and width as dominant control

Size

From the Format menu, you can choose Size, which has two choices: Size To Fit and Size To Grid. Size To Fit sizes an object to be just large enough to show the object's picture and any text on the object. The Size To Grid choice redraws an object so that each corner of the object falls on a grid point.

Horizontal Spacing and Vertical Spacing

The Format menu lets you control the vertical and horizontal spacing between controls. After you have chosen either Format⇨Horizontal Spacing or Format⇨Vertical Spacing, you can choose from the options listed in Table 6-4.

Table 6-4	Commands for Spacing Controls in a Layout
Command	**What It Does**
Make Equal	Makes uniform all horizontal and vertical spaces between controls of the same size
Increase	Widens by a grid block the space between controls
Decrease	Reduces by a grid block the space between controls
Remove	Removes the space between controls so that they just touch

When you're using the Make Equal option, the amount of horizontal and vertical space depends on the size of the area for displaying controls and the combined width of all controls.

You can change the width and height of a grid block (independently) by choosing Tools⇨Options⇨HTML Layout from the menu bar.

Snap To Grid

Snap to grid means that you can drag a control anywhere on the Layout except that when you drop it on the Layout, it "snaps" to the nearest grid intersection. Putting a check mark next to this item turns on the Snap To Grid feature; clicking to remove the check mark turns off the option.

You can also turn the Snap To Grid option on or off by choosing Tools⇨Options⇨HTML Layout from the menu bar.

Send To Back, Move Backward, Move Forward, and Bring To Front

In an HTML Layout, you can pile objects on top of one another so that they overlap. If you imagine a line that begins at the top of the Layout and stretches to the bottom of a pile, you can understand where "front" and "back" come from. To move an object to the front of the line (on top of the heap), select the item and then choose Bring To Front. To move an object to the back, select the item and then choose Send To Back. If you want to move an item just one place in line, you can move it back one place with Move Backward; to move an item closer to the front of the line, choose Move Forward.

Tooling around with the Toolbox

The Toolbox, which is displayed whenever you're working on an HTML Layout file, enables you to place controls in the Layout. The most common tools are on the Standard tab, and you might have some on a tab marked Additional. (Although it's called a Toolbox, the tools are really just the same ActiveX controls you've already seen. I use the term "tool" in this section, but a tool is really just a control.) You're not limited to the tools or pages included in the Toolbox by default, because you can add your own.

Adding a new tool

If you have acquired ActiveX controls other than those distributed with Internet Explorer or Control Pad, you probably will want to include those controls in pages you design. You might want to use a Gauge control, for example, to design a progress bar. A *progress bar* is initially displayed as an outline, but is filled in to show the completed percentage of an operation. Most browsers show a progress bar, for example, while downloading a file. Microsoft includes a Gauge control with Visual Basic, and many control developers offer Gauge controls.

To add a Gauge control (or any other control) to the Toolbox, follow these steps:

1. **Click the Toolbox tab for the page on which you want to add a control.**

2. **Right-click the mouse on the Toolbox page.**

   The Toolbox shortcut menu pops up.

3. **Choose Additional Controls from the shortcut menu.**

   An Additional Controls dialog box pops up. It lists all the controls that Control Pad knows about. When you add controls to the Toolbox, you see a menu that lets you check off the controls you want to add to a page.

4. **Place a check mark next to the controls you want on the page and click the OK button.**

   Icons for the new tools appear on the page.

Adding a new page

If you have lots of controls in your Toolbox, you can add more pages to better organize them. Here are the steps for adding a new page to the Toolbox:

1. **Right-click the mouse on the tab for any page.**

   A menu pops up; the first item is New Page.

2. **Choose New Page and enter a name for the page.**

3. **Add controls by using the procedure described in the preceding section, "Adding a new tool."**

Other Toolbox tricks aren't frequently used, but they're still useful. For more information about the Toolbox, look under "toolbox" in the Control Pad online Help index.

Taking Control of Your Layouts: The HTML Layout Control

Creating an HTML Layout is great, but no one will ever see your genius without the HTML Layout control. Because browsers understand only HTML documents and not Layout files, you have to insert the Layout into an HTML file. To insert a Layout file into the current HTML file, choose Edit⇨Insert HTML Layout while you're working on an HTML (.htm) file. You can insert as many HTML Layouts into an HTML file as you want, and they are drawn in the order the browser encounters them in the HTML file.

If you want to use HTML Layouts just to get more control over the placement of controls, you're finished. Design an HTML Layout, save it, and insert it into an HTML file with Control Pad; when you load the HTML file that includes your Layout, you see the fruits of your labor.

If you crave even more control, though, you can tinker with the HTML Layout control. The remainder of this section focuses on the control itself instead of on designing an HTML Layout.

Although the HTML Layout control is one of the first controls described in this book, it's not the simplest. You may want to read about other controls in Chapter 7 and experiment with them before tackling the HTML Layout control.

Inserting a Layout

When you insert an HTML Layout into an HTML file, Control Pad inserts an HTML Layout control. The HTML Layout control then points to the Layout file (with the .alx extension) that you have just created with Control Pad. After inserting an HTML Layout control into the page, for example, you might see the following HTML code:

```
<OBJECT
   CLASSID="CLSID:812AE312-8B8E-11CF-93C8-00AA00C08FDF"
   ID = "Example_alx"
   STYLE = "LEFT:0;TOP:0">
   <PARAM NAME = "ALXPATH"
      REF
      VALUE = "file:C:\HTML-Layouts\example.alx">
</OBJECT>
```

Now when the browser loads the HTML code on your page, it reaches the <OBJECT> tag and finds the HTML Layout control. The Layout control then takes over and displays the HTML Layout (.alx) file that is named in the VALUE attribute of the NAME parameter. Because the HTML Layout control knows how to read a Layout file, it positions everything on the page just as you had designed it. Using the HTML Layout control is a straightforward process because all the real work lies in setting up a Layout. You have to adjust a few options, however, which are outlined in the following section.

Properties

Although the HTML Layout control works a little differently from other controls, it has properties, events, and methods, just like other controls do. The following list shows all the Layout control's properties (the DrawBuffer property is marked in bold because it is described in the following section; the other properties are discussed in Chapter 7, in the section "Common Properties of Display Controls"):

BackColor	**DrawBuffer**	ID
CodeBase	Height	Width

To set the properties of the HTML Layout:

1. **For a Layout you have already inserted in an HTML file, you can click the Layout object's icons in the left margin to open the Layout file.**

2. **After the HTML Layout file is open, right-click the mouse over a blank spot on the Layout, and then choose Properties from the context menu that pops up.**

DrawBuffer

Most of the properties for the HTML Layout control you have seen before, but DrawBuffer is a little different. An explanation of how to use it is somewhat technical, so you can probably ignore it unless you have problems loading complicated HTML Layouts (most likely with a number of overlapping controls).

You can set DrawBuffer to any value between 16,000 and 1,048,576, but deciding on a value is only half the battle. You also have to set the DrawBuffer property to your chosen value — which is more difficult than it sounds because you can't use the Properties dialog box for your Layout. Instead, you can change the value only at run time through a script. The trick is that because you have to set the DrawBuffer before the browser can begin drawing anything, you have to set the value early in the process of loading the Layout.

Events

The HTML Layout control has just one supported event, onLoad.

onLoad

```
sub object.onLoad = function-name
```

To use the HTML Layout control's onLoad event, you first have to write a function that does whatever you want done when onLoad fires. Next, write a script and include a line in which you assign the function name to the HTML Layout object's onLoad event. When the script runs, the function you've written starts as soon as the onLoad event fires.

The HTML Layout control has to chew on the HTML Layout file before it can spit it out. (In polite society, chewing is called *parsing,* or the process of reading a file and deciding what it means.) The onLoad event occurs after the chewing is done but before the spitting out. Incidentally, the Window object also has some chewing and spitting of its own to do, but they both happen *after* the HTML Layout control has finished eating.

In case you're curious, the HTML Layout control lacks an onUnload event. If you want to do something when the HTML Layout is unloaded, try the Window object's onUnload event instead. (The Window object's onUnload event fires when the window itself is unloaded; you can read all about the Window object in Chapter 13.)

You can script the Window onLoad event from HTML but not from within the Layout (.alx) file. When you're editing a Layout file, therefore, the Script Wizard does not display the Window onLoad and onUnload events. If you want to use the Script Wizard to write a script for the onLoad event, wait until after you have inserted the Layout into an HTML (.htm) file, and then start up the Script Wizard.

Methods

The HTML Layout control has only the Item() method, which lets you pick an item (by either name or index) from a collection of items.

Item

```
Set Object = object.Item(collectionindex)
```

A *collection* is just a bunch of objects that are usually related in some way. For example, all the controls in an HTML Layout form a collection. Collections are handy if you want to treat a group of objects as a single object, but sometimes you want to pick out individual items (the squeaky wheel from a collection of wheels, for example). The Item method does just that: Give it the name or number of the particular item, and you get just what you want. (Or, as the Rolling Stones sang, you don't always get what you want, but at least sometimes you get what you need.)

Before you can get anything, you have to tell the Item() method which item you want. You specify the item with the `collectionindex` parameter, which can be either a string or an integer. If you want to select a member by name, you use a string. If you prefer to select a member by index, you can use an integer — don't forget that the collection is zero based: The first item is item 0, and the last of *n* items is item *n–1*.

An error occurs if you use an invalid index or name for `collectionindex`.

Testing your newfound knowledge

1. **HTML Layouts are handy because they fill which gap in the HTML standard?**

   A. The standard method for ordering pizza over the Web for home delivery.

   B. The lack of control over the exact positioning of objects displayed by a browser.

   C. HTML doesn't include a good recipe for marinara sauce.

   D. There's no way to add smell to a Web page.

2. **If you want to display an HTML Layout, you have to first create the Layout and then:**

   A. Spread butter liberally over the disk with the HTML Layout file and toast it to a golden brown.

   B. Dance around the computer while chanting, "O Great One, please display my Layout!"

   C. Insert the Layout into an HTML file using the Control Pad Edit menu.

   D. Ask a browser very nicely to show you the Layout.

Chapter 7

"It's Better to Look Good than to Feel Good"

. . . .

In This Chapter

▶ Adding animated buttons for that cartoon look

▶ Displaying data with charts

▶ Tracking progress with gauges

▶ Adding a splash of color with gradients

▶ Polishing your image with the Image control

▶ Labeling your work with fancy text

▶ Showing off what's new on your site

. . . .

*B*ecause ActiveX controls evolved from custom controls used in Visual Basic programming, many controls are available. Visual Basic is marketed by Microsoft as a tool for developing applications quickly, by first designing their appearance and then linking the visual objects with code written by the programmer. The same approach has carried over to Web design with ActiveX: You use tools such as Control Pad to lay out the pages and then write some scripts to tie it all together.

If you buy an ActiveX control off the rack, it probably won't fit quite right — you will have to make a few alterations. By adjusting the properties of a control, you can create a perfect fit. Although every ActiveX control has its own set of properties, many controls share some of the same properties. Rather than list the many common properties of display controls under the description of each control (which would make this book extremely heavy), I provide a summary of the most common properties that determine a control's appearance. Each of the properties in Table 7-1 is discussed in more detail later in this chapter, in the section "Assigning Custom Values for Your Properties."

Table 7-1   Common Properties of ActiveX Display Controls

Property	Description
Accelerator	Enables a shortcut key (hot key) that enables users to jump to the control using the keyboard
AutoSize	Automatically resizes a control to display the entire caption
BackColor	Controls the background color, which is usually the predominant color for the control; text is shown in the foreground color
BackStyle	Background style can be either transparent or opaque; if it's transparent, you can see through the control to what's underneath
BorderColor	Specifies the color of a control's (optional) border only if the border is created with BorderStyle rather than with SpecialEffect
BorderStyle	One of two ways to add a border (SpecialEffect is the other)
Caption	A control's text, sometimes used as a label for the control
CodeBase	Address of code that implements control
Enabled	Ready and able? Some controls can be disabled to prevent their use but still remain visible to the user
Font	Font object that determines font characteristics for text; unlike most properties, the font property is an object and not simply a single value
ForeColor	Foreground color, most commonly used to set the text color
Height	Height of the control in pixels
ID	Name used to identify an object (in Visual Basic, it's the Name property)
Left	Distance of a control's upper left corner from the left edge of the HTML layout that contains the control
MouseIcon	Custom icon used as the mouse pointer; used with the MousePointer property
MousePointer	Determines the style of the mouse pointer and can be used with the MouseIcon property to create custom mouse pointers
Picture	Bitmap image to display on an object
SpecialEffect	Specifies visual appearance of an object (flat, raised, or sunken, for example)
TabIndex	Position of a single object in the HTML Layout's tab order
TabStop	Determines whether user can press Tab to move to the object

Property	Description
Top	Vertical distance from the top of a control to the top of the containing HTML layout
Value	Content of a control (text in a text box, for example)
Visible	Control is hidden if Visible is FALSE; control is shown if Visible is TRUE
Width	Control's width in pixels
WordWrap	Determines whether words that cross a line break are moved to next line

Understanding How to Read a Property Description

The entries for the common properties listed in this chapter are organized for easy reference. Each description lists the property name, the syntax, and the controls to which the property applies. How you read an entry depends on how you work with controls. To insert ActiveX controls in your pages, you can either use Control Pad or type the HTML tags yourself. Using Control Pad is simpler because you adjust properties by using pop-up menus, and then the HTML code is inserted automatically. If you like to do things the old-fashioned way, you have to use the syntax for the HTML <OBJECT> tag.

The <OBJECT> tag includes parameters, which are used to adjust the properties. (For more information about the <OBJECT> tag, see Chapter 4.) The control itself is the <OBJECT>, and the control's properties are given as PARAM values. Each property gets its own PARAM tag (there's less squabbling that way): The property is given as the NAME attribute, and the property's value is specified with the VALUE attribute. The following chunk of HTML creates a label; the label's properties are specified through the PARAM, VALUE pairs:

```
<OBJECT ID="BigLabel" WIDTH=253 HEIGHT=37
 CLASSID="CLSID:978C9E23-D4B0-11CE-BF2D-00AA003F40D0">
   <PARAM NAME="Caption" VALUE="I've Got Properties!">
   <PARAM NAME="Size" VALUE="5376;762">
   <PARAM NAME="Accelerator" VALUE="76">
   <PARAM NAME="FontHeight" VALUE="360">
   <PARAM NAME="FontCharSet" VALUE="0">
   <PARAM NAME="FontPitchAndFamily" VALUE="2">
   <PARAM NAME="FontWeight" VALUE="0">
</OBJECT>
```

Letting Script Wizard Do the Work

If you use Script Wizard to insert and edit scripts, you don't have to worry about the syntax because it's already taken care of. (All the magical details about the Script Wizard are in Chapter 5, which discusses the Microsoft Control Pad.) If you do your own scripting, however, you need the syntax to tell you how to modify properties. Most syntax entries include straight brackets ([ ]) to mark optional material. In the Alignment property's syntax, for example:

```
object.Alignment [= AlignValue]
```

the brackets tell you that you can take it or leave it. Remember, however, that it's an all-or-nothing deal.

The Alignment property has two acceptable forms:

```
object.Alignment
object.Alignment = AlignValue
```

Saying that both forms are acceptable is somewhat deceptive because you use one form to get the Alignment value (the first form) and the other to set it (the second form). Because the ActiveX specifications and online help use this form, however, you should be familiar with it.

Assigning Custom Values for Your Properties

In assigning the Alignment value, notice that the value on the right side is AlignValue. The reason is that the Alignment property, like many others, has its own defined constants you can use to set the property's value. The constants are just nicknames for the allowable values. Although it doesn't make any difference to the computer whether you use the actual values or the nicknames, you should stick with nicknames. If you're reading a script and you see this line:

```
ToggleTwo.Alignment = 1
```

you may not remember that an AlignValue of 1 means that text is aligned to the right of the control. If the same line instead reads this way, however:

```
ToggleTwo.Alignment = fmAlignmentRight
```

you would have no trouble remembering whether it was left or right. When you're ready to use properties such as Alignment, look in the control descriptions to find out about the constant values and their meanings.

When you use properties that have predefined constants, such as the Alignment property, you should use those constants. If you stick with the constants, you don't have to rewrite scripts when Microsoft redefines an Alignment of 1 to be centered rather than right. Although the meaning of 1 might change, fmAlignmentRight always means aligned on the right. If you use a property without predefined constants, you should define the constants yourself. That way, when *you* decide to make a change, you have to change the value of a constant in only one place rather than look through every script you wrote.

Accelerator

```
object.Accelerator [= string]
```

The Accelerator property lets you assign a key as a shortcut key for an ActiveX control. Rather than drag that furry mouse around, you can press the accelerator key for a control and switch to that control. The keys can also be a little disorienting because you don't have any visual feedback to confirm that the focus has shifted.

Focus is the capability of a control to accept input from a user. When you choose File⇨Open in most programs, a dialog box appears, and the focus switches to the dialog box so that you can type the name of the file you want to open. Clicking an object usually switches the focus to that object.

When you click a button, the button is redrawn to make it look as though you're pressing a button, and then something happens. When you use accelerator keys, however, you go directly to "something happens."

Accelerator keys are handy for designing larger forms, on which users might want to skip around frequently without dragging a mouse along.

The accelerator property only activates the chosen key as a hot key — it doesn't tell users what that key is. Unless you want to keep your users guessing, be sure to tell them which key to use.

In the preceding example, notice that even though you're only specifying an accelerator *key,* you can set the property to any value, including "supercalifragilistic," which has many keys. If you specify a string of more than one character, the control just ignores everything except the first character.

AutoSize

```
object.AutoSize [= Boolean]
```

Computers are supposed to make our lives easier by handling the details for us, and that's the purpose of AutoSize. If you're too busy to figure out how big a control has to be to contain its entire caption, just set AutoSize to TRUE. As the size of the caption text changes, so too does the size of the control. (AutoSize doesn't do much, but it's the little things in life that matter.) For controls without captions, the control is resized to display the information in the control. ComboBox has no caption, for example, but it does resize itself so that it displays all the text.

 Be careful with the AutoSize property because it's not clever about resizing captions. For example, the AutoSize property often resizes a control by changing the control's width to accommodate the widest character in the text and then stretches the control's height until it's tall enough to contain all the text characters stacked on top of one another. For now, it's okay to use AutoSize at design-time (as you're designing pages); don't use AutoSize at run-time, however (when users are viewing the pages you have designed). AutoSize eventually may be smart enough to avoid distorting text beyond readability, but don't count on it today.

BackColor

```
object.BackColor [= Long]
```

Objects that are displayed on-screen have at least two color attributes: foreground and background color. The background color is the color of the stuff in back (hence, the name BackColor). The background color tends to predominate because most controls visually consist of nothing (empty space) more than something (text and borders, for example). Although setting the BackColor property is easy, determining what to set it to is tricky.

If you use the BackStyle property to make the control transparent, it doesn't matter how you set BackColor — the background color is "clear."

BackStyle

```
object.BackStyle [= fmBackStyle]
```

Everyone has a little style, and that goes for ActiveX controls as well. Although the BackStyle property doesn't add that elusive touch of class to your controls, you can see right through them.

A horse of another color

If you could simply use the name of the color, it would be too easy and just anybody could do it. People everywhere would simply write:

```
MyControl.BackColor = Teal
```

(Although Internet Explorer does let you use some common colors, only a few colors are defined.) To hide the true meaning from the uninitiated, you must use cryptic codes rather than color names. If you want teal, for example, you write

```
MyControl.BackColor = 4966415
```

What's special about 4966415?

Computers are color-impaired: They understand only red, green, and blue. As it turns out, those three colors are all you need in order to produce any other color. Colors are usually specified by giving the amount of red, green, and blue on a scale of 0 to 255. If you mix 15 units of red with 200 units of green and 75 units of blue, you get a lovely shade of teal. Because computers aren't

good at arithmetic in base 10, these numbers usually are converted to hexadecimal (base 16). The following table shows the combination that produces teal:

Color	Decimal	Hexadecimal
Red	15	0F
Green	200	C8
Blue	75	4B

Even though computers prefer hexadecimal, people don't. Because people build computers, though, we usually get our way. Rather than set the BackColor property to a bunch of hexadecimal numbers, we just use one big decimal number. The big hexadecimal number 4BC80F is equal to the decimal number 4966415.

In polite society, hexadecimal numbers are prefaced with 0x so that they're easy to distinguish from decimal numbers. Therefore, I should have written 4966415 as 0x4BC80F.

Table 7-2 lists the two defined constants used with BackStyle. The BackStyle property should be called the CantSeeThrough property because when you set it to fmBackStyleOpaque (which is equal to 1), you can't see what's behind the control. If you set BackStyle to 0, you can see right through the control.

Table 7-2   BackStyle Values: Oh, Say Can You See through It

Constant	Can You See through It?	Value
fmBackStyleTransparent	Yes	0
fmBackStyleOpaque	No (control background is opaque)	1

The default value is opaque, which is why you usually can't see through the controls in a layout.

The BackStyle applies to only the *control,* not to images displayed by the control. If you use an Image control to show off a bitmapped image, you can make the control transparent, but you can't see through the image. (A *bitmapped image* is the computer equivalent of pointillism: Images are created by specifying colors for many individual dots, which the human eye blends together to form a picture.)

If you want to make a bitmapped image transparent, consider using a transparent GIF. Most image-editing programs can create *transparent* GIFs, which take on the background color of the window in which they're displayed.

BorderColor

```
object.BorderColor [= Long]
```

Because the BorderColor property doesn't do much for you unless you have a border, you must set the property to a value other than fmBorderStyleNone.

You specify the BorderColor by using a color number with the same scheme you use for BackColor. (For more information about color numbers, see the preceding sidebar, "A horse of another color.")

Only borders drawn with BorderStyle (rather than borders created by the SpecialEffect property) use BorderColor as the border color.

The SpecialEffects property uses system colors defined for borders instead. (For Windows operating systems, system color settings are stored in the Control Panel, in either the Desktop folder or the Color folder.)

BorderStyle

```
object.BorderStyle [= fmBorderStyle]
```

You can create a border around a control in two ways: BorderStyle and SpecialEffect. Although the SpecialEffect property lets you add effects that are fancier than plain borders, you can't change the color of the border, which is determined by the system colors. If you use BorderStyle to create a border, however, you can then set the BorderColor property to a color of your choosing.

For your convenience, the BorderStyle property has its own predefined constants, as shown in Table 7-3.

Table 7-3	Bordering with Style	
Constant	*Value*	*Description*
fmBorderStyleNone	0	No visible border line
fmBorderStyleSingle	1	Single-line border

Caption

```
object.Caption [= String]
```

If you have something to say, say it with a Caption property. Use the Caption property to identify controls to the user. Set the Caption property to a descriptive label, and away you go. If you can't think of a Caption, you're stuck, of course, with the functional but uninspired default value. The first Label object in a layout, for example, gets the default caption Label1.

If you have a long caption but a short control, something has to give. It's usually the caption, which is truncated to fit inside the control. If you set the AutoSize property, however, the control expands to fit the caption.

CodeBase

```
object.CodeBase [= URL]
```

Despite the best efforts of Microsoft, some people roaming the Web don't have every available ActiveX control installed on their computer. What happens when you include a control on your page but the person browsing your site doesn't have that control installed? CodeBase comes to the rescue! The CodeBase property is a URL that has the address of the control's implementation. An ActiveX-enabled browser knows that it can go to the address listed in the CodeBase property and find the code needed for the control. The browser then can download the control, install it, and flawlessly display your page.

Enabled

```
object.Enabled [= Boolean]
```

Sometimes you want to render a control powerless but want it to remain visible as a warning to other controls that might challenge your authority. If this situation happens often, you probably should seek counseling; if it happens only occasionally, you can satisfy your lust for power with the Enabled property.

By setting the Enabled property to FALSE, you prevent users from interacting with the control. (Technically, you prevent a control from receiving the focus and responding to user-generated events.) Because the control appears dimmed, users know that that particular control is out of commission. Although you can still manipulate the control through scripting, users can't click it or change it.

The Enabled property interacts with the Locked property to produce different effects, as listed in Table 7-4. Depending on the values of Enabled and Locked, a control may or may not be able to receive the focus. If a user is prevented from entering information or choosing a control, it can be dimmed so that the user knows that the control cannot receive the focus. (Many programs' dimmed menu choices don't apply in the program's current context for the same reason.) The Enabled and Locked properties also determine whether users can copy or change text in a text control.

Table 7-4	The Subtle Interplay between the Enabled and Locked Properties				
Enabled	*Locked*	*Get Focus?*	*Dimmed?*	*Copy Data?*	*Edit Data?*
True	True	Yes	No	Yes	No
True	False	Yes	No	Yes	Yes
False	True	No	Yes	No	No
False	False	No	Yes	Yes	Yes

Font

Although no Font property really exists, this seems like a good place to discuss Font *objects*. Every control — and every layout — has its own Font object to tag along. The Font object has its own properties you can set to display the font you want. Font objects have several properties that are unique to fonts, as listed in Table 7-5.

Table 7-5	Variations on a Font	
Attribute	*Values*	*What It Does*
Bold	Boolean	Increases the stroke weight of the font
Italic	Boolean	Angles the text from upright to slanted
Size	Currency	Specifies the size of the font in points (72 points equal one inch)
~~Strikethrough~~	Boolean	Prints a horizontal line through the middle of each character

Attribute	Values	What It Does
Underline	Boolean	Draws a cute little line under each letter
Weight	Integer	Indicates the stroke weight of the font on a scale from 0 to 1000

What most people call a font is really a *typeface* (Arial or Courier, for example). A font includes a typeface, point size, stroke weight, and a few other attributes. Most attributes, except perhaps stroke weight, are familiar to anyone who has used a word processor. *Stroke weight* is the thickness of the lines used to draw characters. (The text that adorns every parent's refrigerator has a heavy stroke weight.) As mentioned, the stroke weight ranges from 0 to 1000; a stroke weight of 0 uses the system's default stroke weight. The Bold property and the stroke weight are closely related, as shown in Table 7-6.

Table 7-6	The Bold and Weight Properties Together Again		
If You Set	To	Then	Is Set To
Bold	True	Weight	700
Bold	False	Weight	400
Weight	> 550	Bold	True
Weight	<= 550	Bold	False

With all this flexibility, it's easy to request a font that doesn't exist on the client system. If that happens under Windows, Windows simply uses the closest font it can find.

Because controls are associated with Font objects, which have their own properties, you have to do a little extra work to set the Font properties for a control. In the following example, a ToggleBox control is set to display 12-point italic Arial.

```
Sub ToggleButton1_Click()
   If ToggleButton1.Value = True Then
      ToggleButton1.Font.Name = "Arial"
      ToggleButton1.Font.Italic = True
      ToggleButton1.Font.Size = 12
   Else
      ToggleButton1.Font.Name = "Arial"
      ToggleButton1.Font.Italic = False
      ToggleButton1.Font.Bold = True
      ToggleButton1.Font.Size = 12
   End If
End sub
```

ForeColor

```
object.ForeColor [= Long]
```

Objects displayed on-screen have at least two color attributes: foreground and background color. The background color is the color of the stuff in back, and the foreground is what's up front. If you think of pen and paper, the background color is the color of the paper, and the color of the ink is the foreground.

Height

```
object.Height [= Single]
```

Height sets the height of the control in pixels. If the control is resized, the Height property is updated to the new value, and the preceding height is stored in the property OldHeight. You can therefore resize a control by using a script and then easily return the control to its original size.

ID

```
object.ID [= String]
```

The ID property assigns to the object a nickname you can use to reference the object later. You might assign a control the name "Pat," for example, and then later refer to the control as "Pat." When you want to write a script to handle a mouse click on the control named Pat, you (or the Script Wizard, as described in Chapter 4) write a procedure called Pat_Click( ).

If you have used Visual Basic (VB) in the past, you should recognize the ID property as the Name property in Visual Basic; the property's name has been changed to protect the innocent. The real reason for the name change is that because the Name property now uses the <OBJECT> tag, the Name was changed to the ID property to avoid confusion.

Left

```
object.Left [= Single]
```

Although Height and Width determine a control's size, you still have to tell the container where to position the control. The Left property sets the control's distance from the left edge of the container. A value of 0, therefore, positions the control flush against the left edge; negative values obscure the leftmost part of the control. On most systems, any value between –32,768 and 32,766 is valid.

The Left property of a ComboBox control affects only the text portion of the control, not the list portion.

MouseIcon

```
object.MouseIcon = picture
object.MouseIcon = LoadPicture(pathname)
```

The mouse icon of an object is the image used for the mouse pointer whenever a user moves the mouse over that object. To assign an image for the mouse pointer, you can either assign a picture directly to the MouseIcon property or use the LoadPicture( ) method to load a picture from a file. If you choose to use the LoadPicture( ) method, you must specify the pathname to the file as a string expression.

You might want to create a custom mouse pointer to maintain a theme. You might create a golf game, for example, and use a picture of a golf club for the mouse pointer. Or you might create a virtual sewing application and turn the mouse pointer into a sewing needle.

The MouseIcon property is valid only when the MousePointer property (described next) is set to 99.

MousePointer

```
object.MousePointer [= fmMousePointer]
```

A *mouse pointer* is the small image that tracks mouse movements to show you the mouse's current location on-screen. Although Windows users usually see either an arrow pointing northwest or a cursor in the shape of an I (called the *I-beam cursor*), Windows has many different images for the mouse pointer to remind users of how the mouse is being used. If you want to show the appropriate mouse pointer for an action, it's up to you to change the pointer.

Table 7-7 lists the many different mouse pointers and the values for the MousePointer property.

Table 7-7   The Many Faces of the MousePointer

Constant	Value	Description
fmMousePointerDefault	0	Standard pointer
fmMousePointerArrow	1	Arrow
fmMousePointerCross	2	Cross-hair pointer; usually used for defining selections
fmMousePointerIBeam	3	I-beam; commonly used when inserting text to show the location of the next insertion
fmMousePointerSizeNESW	6	Double arrow pointing northeast–southwest
fmMousePointerSizeNS	7	Double arrow pointing north–south
fmMousePointerSizeNWSE	8	Double arrow pointing northwest–southeast
fmMousePointerSizeWE	9	Double arrow pointing east–west
fmMousePointerUpArrow	10	Up arrow
fmMousePointerHourglass	11	Hourglass; used to show that Windows is busy and is momentarily ignoring the user
fmMousePointerNoDrop	12	"Not" symbol (circle with a diagonal line through it) on top of the object being dragged; used to indicate that what's being dragged cannot be dropped at its current location
fmMousePointerAppStarting	13	Arrow with an hourglass; usually means that the current application is busy but the user can switch to another application
fmMousePointerHelp	14	Arrow with a question mark (used as the Help pointer); clicking an item displays Help information about that item
fmMousePointerSizeAll	15	Sizes all cursor (arrows pointing north, south, east, and west)
fmMousePointerCustom	99	Uses the icon specified by the MouseIcon property

If you want to use a custom mouse pointer, you have to set the MousePointer property to 99.

Although ActiveX is intended to be cross-platform, the MousePointer property is one of several based solely on the Microsoft Windows interface. Other platforms use different mouse pointers; Apple computers, for example, use an image of a watch as the "Don't bother me, I'm busy" pointer. Microsoft *should* have created constants such as fmMousePointerBusy and then enabled the operating system to display its own mouse pointers.

Picture

```
object.Picture = LoadPicture(pathname)
```

By setting the Picture property, you can draw a bitmapped image on an object, which makes it easy to create a customized appearance for your controls. You can create several images and then use the Picture property to display the images on various controls.

While designing an HTML layout, you can use the control's property page to assign a bitmap to the Picture property. While running an HTML layout, you must use the LoadPicture function to assign a bitmap to Picture.

To remove a picture that is assigned to a control, click the value of the Picture property on the property page and then press the Delete key (pressing the Backspace key does not remove the picture).

For controls with captions, the PicturePosition property specifies where to display the picture within the object; the PictureSizeMode property determines how the picture fills the object.

Transparent pictures sometimes have a hazy appearance. If you do not like this appearance, display the picture on an Image control. Image controls support opaque images.

SpecialEffect

```
object.SpecialEffect [= fmSpecialEffect]
```

The SpecialEffect property enables you to enhance the appearance of an object, using one of several defined styles. Each of the special effects adds a 3-D look to an object — you choose the look by picking a value for the SpecialEffect property.

The numerous constants used with the SpecialEffect property are shown in Table 7-8. Each of the special effects in the table is shown in Figure 7-1.

Figure 7-1:
Add a 3-D
look to
objects on
your page
by using the
SpecialEffects
property.
Here,
Internet
Explorer
displays
several
labels, each
with a
different
special
effect.

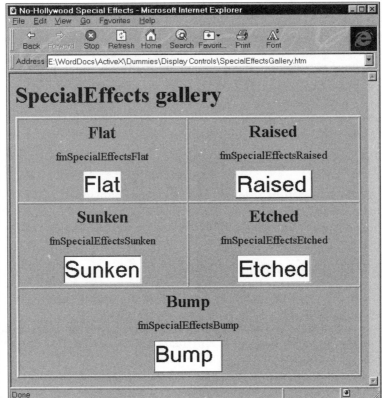

Table 7-8   Creating Special Effects with No Hollywood Help

Constant	Value	Description
fmSpecialEffectFlat	0	Sets off object by a change of color, a border, or both (default value for Image and Label)
fmSpecialEffectRaised	1	Highlights object on the top and left and a shadow on the bottom and right
fmSpecialEffectSunken	2	Makes control and its border appear to be carved into the form that contains them
fmSpecialEffectEtched	3	Makes border appear to be carved around the edge of the control
fmSpecialEffectBump	6	Produces ridge on the bottom and right and appears flat on the top and left

Although both the SpecialEffect and BorderStyle properties can create borders around an object, they don't play well together: If you use one of these properties to create a border, the other property is wiped out. If you set SpecialEffect to fmSpecialEffectRaised, for example (which implies a border), the system sets BorderStyle to fmBorderStyleNone (which means no border). If you set the SpecialEffect property to fmSpecialEffectFlat, however (which does not include a border), you can specify a border with the BorderStyle property.

Because SpecialEffect uses the system colors to define its borders, borders may be rendered in different colors on different computers. In the Windows operating system, system color settings are stored in the Control Panel, either in the Desktop folder or the Color folder.

If you want to set the color used for borders and you're willing to give up the 3-D effects of the SpecialEffects property, you can use the BorderStyle property to draw a border. With BorderStyle, you control the border color through the BorderColor property.

By adding a 3-D look to your objects, the SpecialEffects property makes your pages look more polished.

TabIndex

```
object.TabIndex [= Integer]
```

The objects on a page have an order to them, called the *tab order,* or the order in which users step from object to object by pressing the Tab key on the keyboard. An object's place in the tab order is specified by the TabIndex property; the first object's index is 0. You can change an object's place in the tab order by assigning it a different TabIndex.

The TabOrder isn't related to the order in which objects appear on-screen, so don't be fooled.

TabStop

```
object.TabStop [= Boolean]
```

Just because an item is in the tab order doesn't mean that you want users to be able to press Tab to move to the object. Because users probably don't need to be able to tab to a Label object, for example, you can force the Tab key to skip over objects in the tab order by setting the object's TabStop property to FALSE. The default value for TabStop is TRUE, which means that the Tab key stops at the object as a user tabs through the objects on a page.

The TabStop property can be set only while you are designing the page — you can't change the TabStop through a script.

Top

```
object.Top [= Single]
```

Although the Height and Width determine a control's size, you still have to tell the container where to position the control. The Top property sets the control's distance from the top edge of the container. A value of 0, therefore, positions the control flush against the top edge; negative values obscure the topmost part of the control. On most systems, any value between –32,768 and 32,766 is valid.

Value

```
intrinsicObject.value [=string]
```

The Value property lets you either read or assign the value for an *intrinsic control* (one that's part of Internet Explorer rather than a third-party control added separately).

Visible

```
object.Visible [= Boolean]
```

Now you see it, now you don't. By using the Visible property, you control whether an object is visible or hidden. If the object is hidden, it's still there but users don't see it. If you can set an object's Visible property to FALSE when you design the page, the page doesn't show when a user loads the page. You can then change the Visible property to TRUE by using a script so that the object is displayed. When you're ready to hide the object again, just set the Visible property to FALSE.

Objects are always visible while you're designing a page. Don't worry if you set an object's Visible property to FALSE and you can still see the object — it doesn't appear after the browser loads the page.

Width

```
object.Width [= Single]
```

The Width property represents an object's width in pixels. If you change the size of a control, the Height or Width property stores the new height or width. If you specify a negative setting for the Left property, the object has the correct width, but the leftmost strip of the object is hidden.

WordWrap

```
object.WordWrap [= Boolean]
```

If a line of text ends in the middle of a word, you can display the line in two ways:

- ✔ The line can simply break in the middle of the word, with the remainder of the letters in that word beginning on the next line.

- ✔ The text can be wrapped. In *wrapped* text, line breaks always fall between words; if a line would break in the middle of a word, then the entire word moves to the next line.

Controls that display text check the WordWrap property to decide whether to use the first or second method. The default value for the WordWrap property is TRUE, which means that the text is wrapped. If you set WordWrap to FALSE, a line may break in the middle of a word if the word is at the end of the line.

Although WordWrap is most commonly used with text controls, it applies to the Label control as well, which is why it's mentioned in this chapter. You might need WordWrap for a Label object if you have a very long label or a large font but limited width.

Introducing the Animated Button Control

The Animated Button control can jazz up Web pages by adding color and motion. This control displays a button and includes an animation. The animation be can silly and fun, or it can be related to the button's task. If you have used Windows Explorer (with Windows 95) to copy files between directories, for example, you have seen the animation that shows pages flying from one folder to another folder. The animation reinforces the action by showing users what's going on.

The Animated Button object works by displaying different sequences from the same Audio Video Interleave (AVI) file at different times. When the control has the focus but before a mouse button is clicked, for example, the Animated Button object might show frames 7 through 13 of its associated AVI file. After the left mouse button is clicked, the Animated Button object might show frames 7 through 20 of the AVI file. You use the control's properties to control which sequences are displayed at different times.

The most difficult part of using the button control is creating the animation to be displayed. Rather than automatically step through a series of image files, as many other animation widgets do, the Animated Button control displays an AVI file.

Don't spend too much time tweaking AVI files for your Web pages. They're fine for animating buttons but have otherwise been replaced by the ActiveMovie ASF format. (You can find more information about the ActiveMovie control on the CD-ROM in the back of this book.)

You can't use just any AVI file with the Animated Button control — it must meet several conditions regarding compression, start frames, and color palette:

✔ The AVI must have been either RLE or 8-bit compressed. You have to either work with files already compressed in this way or open the file with an AVI editing program and save it again with either of these two compression schemes.

✔ Because the Windows Animation Common Control states that the start frame of any sequence must be a keyframe, you have to either limit yourself to sequences with this property or edit the file yourself.

✔ The file's palette must match that of the Internet Explorer. In other words, the file can use only the colors that Internet Explorer uses.

Properties

The properties of the Animated Button control are straightforward, as you can see in Table 7-9. Except for the file location (given by the URL property), each property specifies either the starting or ending frame for a particular state. (For information about the states of the Animated Button control, see the section "The United States of animated buttons," later in this chapter.)

Table 7-9	**The Not-So-Animated Button Control Properties**
Property	**Description**
URL	URL location of the AVI file to be used
DefaultFrStart	Start frame for the Default state
DefaultFrEnd	End frame for the Default state
MouseOverFrStart	Start frame for the MouseOver state
MouseOverFrEnd	End frame for the MouseOver state
FocusFrStart	Start frame for the Focus state
FocusFrEnd	End frame for the Focus state
DownFrStart	Start frame for the Down state
DownFrEnd	End frame for the Down state

Events

Most Animated Button controls, despite their flashy appearance, lead a dull existence. Even animated buttons have a few significant events in their lives (**boldfaced** events in the list are described in this section; other events are described in Chapter 9):

Click	**Enter**	**Leave**
DblClick	**Focus**	

When a user double-clicks the mouse, three events are fired: two Click events and the DblClick event.

Enter, Leave

```
Sub object_Enter()
Sub object_Leave()
```

The Animated Button object resembles a cat: It's territorial and wants to know the comings and goings of the local mouse. An Animated Button object's territory is the region of the page covered by the control. Two events let you know when the Animated Button object has spotted a mouse in its territory:

- ✔ Enter
- ✔ Leave

After the mouse pointer crosses the boundary of an Animated Button object, the object fires off an Enter event. When the mouse is on its way out, an animated button generates a Leave event.

Focus

```
Sub object_Focus(FocusState)
```

The Focus event occurs whenever the Animated Button control receives or loses the focus. Although the Microsoft documentation doesn't mention the possible values for the FocusState parameter, testing shows that when the button control receives the focus, the FocusState is set to 1. When the button control loses the focus to another control on the same layout, the FocusState is set to 0.

The United States of animated buttons

Although most ActiveX controls don't have states, the Animated Button control does. A *state* represents the internal condition of an object. An automobile object, for example, might have these states: off, idle, forward, and reverse.

Driving the car changes its internal condition, and you see the change as it moves among the states.

The Animated Button control uses its internal state to control the animation. The various states of the Animated Button control are listed in Table 7-10.

Table 7-10 The Few but Proud States of the Animated Button Control

State	What It Means
Down	Left mouse button has been clicked while positioned over the object
Focus	Control receives the focus
MouseOver	Mouse cursor moves over the control
Default	Mouse cursor is not over the control, and the control does not have the focus

The chicken or the egg: Precedence of state

The states of the Animated Button control are mutually exclusive — a control cannot possibly be in two different states at the same time. The catch is that the definitions of the states aren't mutually exclusive: The mouse cursor could be positioned over a control (the MouseOver state) while the control has the focus (the Focus state).

To avoid any confusion, the states have a pecking order, and each state has its own precedence. Whenever two states both can apply (when the mouse is positioned over the Animated Button control and the control has the focus, for example), the control breaks the tie by switching to the state with higher precedence. Table 7-10 lists the states by their precedence. The Down state has precedence over all other states, and the Default state is at the bottom of the pecking order.

Getting in focus

If the control has focus, the control state is set to Focus (unless a mouse click occurs, as described in the preceding section). What is focus? If you have ever been around a small child who wants to be the focus of attention, you already know. Although every window, button, and control on-screen wants to be the one to receive your input, only one of them can be handling your input at any time: That one has the focus. A window or button usually gets the focus because someone moves the mouse over it and then clicks.

Just remember that focus is similar to a weird game of hot potato, in which a user is always throwing the potato. When a user moves the mouse and clicks, the new object catches the potato, and the preceding object loses it. In this game, the potato is the focus.

Feeling a little out of focus?

The description of how focus changes (a user moves the mouse pointer and then clicks) really applies only to Windows (including 3.x, 95, and NT). Many UNIX systems have different rules for changing focus. Under the X Windows system, for example, users don't have to click: If a user moves the mouse pointer over another window, that window gains the focus after a short time, without a mouse click.

Hang on — it gets even more confusing. In Windows (and on the Mac), an object with focus generally comes to the front. That's not necessarily true in the UNIX world, however. Instead, you can often type in an editor without being able to see what you have typed because another window obscures what you're typing.

If you never use a UNIX system, why should you care? The answer is because ActiveX is intended to be cross-platform, which means that someone running a Web browser under the Sun Solaris system (a UNIX variant) might be browsing pages you have designed. If you have made assumptions about the state of a control based on Windows, UNIX users might become confused or even upset. (The last thing you want is a herd of upset UNIX users.)

If a user moves the mouse pointer over the Animated Button object, the object switches to the MouseOver state. Don't forget, though, that each state has its own place in the pecking order of states, and MouseOver is near the bottom.

As mentioned in the preceding section, the Default state is at the bottom of the pecking order: If there's no reason for the AnimatedButton control to be in another state, it's in the Default state. If it's not in another state, it implies that the mouse cursor isn't positioned over the control and that some other object has the focus.

Methods

The Animated Button control has only one method: AboutBox( ). This method is relatively standard among ActiveX controls: It simply displays copyright information about the control. The AboutBox( ) method takes no arguments and returns nothing.

Although the copyright might not seem exciting (unless you're the copyright holder, of course), it often contains a control's version information, which can be useful for troubleshooting control problems. If a user complains that a control isn't working as it should, that person may have a version that's different from the one the designer used.

The following HTML code from the Microsoft Web site demonstrates the typical code for an Animated Button control:

```
<OBJECT
    ID="anbtn"
    CLASSID="clsid:0482B100-739C-11CF-A3A9-00A0C9034920"
    TYPE="application/x-oleobject"
    CODEBASE = "http://activex.microsoft.com/controls/
            iexplorer/ieanbtn.ocx#version=4,70,0,1161"
    ALIGN="left"
    WIDTH=300
    HEIGHT=100>

    <PARAM NAME="URL" value = "http://www.microsoft.com/ie/
            download/activex/win95.avi">
    <PARAM NAME="defaultfrstart" value="0">
    <PARAM NAME="defaultfrend" value="7">
    <PARAM NAME="MouseOverfrstart" value="8">
    <PARAM NAME="MouseOverfrend" value="15">
    <PARAM NAME="focusfrstart" value="16">
    <PARAM NAME="focusfrend" value="23">
    <PARAM NAME="downfrstart" value="24">
    <PARAM NAME="downfrend" value="34">

</OBJECT>
```

In this example, you can see that you set the frame sequences for each state's animation by using the properties, such as FocusFrStart. FocusFrStart specifies the frame number for the first frame shown while the control is in the Focus state. The frames are given as numbers, which you can enter in the Properties dialog box for the control using the ActiveX Control Pad.

Chart

If a picture is worth a thousand words, a chart should be good for at least a few hundred. The Chart control achieves one of the goals of ActiveX by enabling Web developers to create better dynamic content. The Chart control enables you to build many kinds of charts, including pie, point, line, area, bar, column, and high/low/close charts, as shown in Figure 7-2.

More and more Web sites are using the Web as a front end for back-office operations, by displaying information such as prices or order histories. Unfortunately, users are getting socked with a fistful of data. Because the data is often generated on the fly (perhaps as the result of a database query), showing the numbers in a graphic format hasn't been possible.

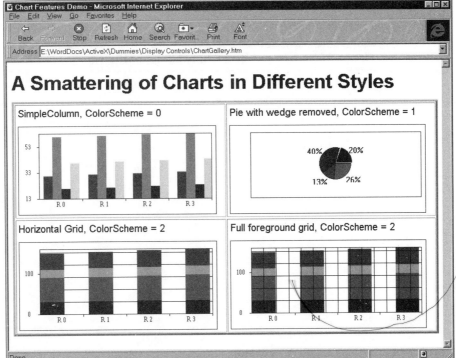

Figure 7-2:
The Chart
control
gives you
the freedom
to design
charts that
suit your
page-design
needs.

Properties

The Chart control is flexible; you can use more than 20 preset chart styles to display data. You can add gridlines, legends, labels, and other features to find just the chart you want. The BackStyle property is described earlier in this chapter, in the section "Assigning Custom Values for Your Properties"; the rest of the Chart controls' many properties (shown in **boldface** in the following list) are described in more detail in this section:

BackStyle	**Data**	**RowName**
ChartType	**DataItem**	**Rows**
ColorScheme	**DisplayLegend**	**Scale**
ColumnIndex	**GridPlacement**	**URL**
ColumnName	**HorizontalGrid**	**VerticalGrid**
Columns	**RowIndex**	

ChartType

```
object.ChartType [= integer]
```

The ChartType property lets you choose the chart style from a list of available types (see Table 7-11).

Table 7-11	The Many Faces of Charts	
Value	**Chart Type**	**Variation**
0	Pie	Simple
1		Wedge removed
2	Point	Simple
3		Stacked
4		Full
5	Line	Simple
6		Stacked
7		Full
8	Area	Simple
9		Stacked
10		Full
11	Column	Simple
12		Stacked
13		Full
14	Bar	Simple
15		Stacked
16		Full
17	High/low/close	Simple
18		Wall Street Journal
19	Open/high/low/close	Simple
20		Wall Street Journal

Most chart types are self-explanatory, except perhaps for the high/low/close chart (also known as a "stocks" chart), as shown in Figure 7-3. High/low/close charts were developed to show the fluctuation in stock prices over time. Each stock has a high and a low trading price for the day; the close is the stock price at the end of the day. Open/high/low/close charts are similar, but include the price of the day's first trade (the *opening* price). Figure 7-3 shows an open/high/low/close chart — a bunch of vertical bars that stretch from the low price to the high price, with marks across each one to indicate opening and closing prices.

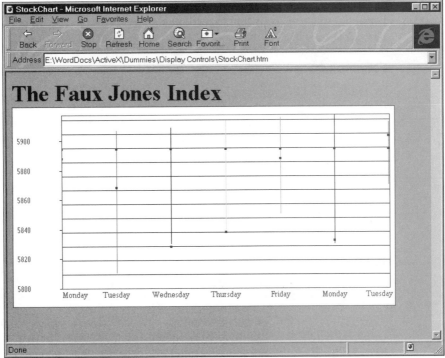

Just because it's *called* a stock chart doesn't mean that you have to use it for stock prices. The water temperature in a hotel shower, for example, can swing from scorching hot to bone-chilling cold. You eventually lunge for the control and cut it off; the last temperature is the closing temperature. (Keep this handy tip in mind if you ever design a hotel Web site!)

Buy low, sell high.

ColorScheme

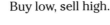

```
object.ColorScheme [= integer]
```

A *color scheme* is a set of colors used to fill regions within a chart. The three predefined color schemes are numbered 0, 1, and 2. Unfortunately, you can't create new color schemes; because you have no other way to set the colors of filled regions, you should experiment with each of the three schemes.

Because colors vary dramatically among monitors, make sure that your color choices are reasonable for a variety of monitors. Colors that look stunning on a 24-bit high-end graphics card on a PowerMac may be lifeless on a 256-color PC desktop. If you have important data (and whose data isn't important?), you should offer users a choice of color schemes, perhaps through a Popup menu control.

Not all people can see all color combinations. Because red-green colorblindness is not uncommon, for example, avoid using red lines on a green background. (This example is another good reason to offer users a choice of color schemes.)

ColumnIndex

```
object.ColumnIndex [= integer]
```

The ColumnIndex property is used to mark a particular column for later operations. To set the name for a particular column, for example, you choose the column by setting the ColumnIndex property and then use the ColumnName property to assign its name. To name the third column "Gallons sold," for example, you use the following code fragment:

```
ColumnIndex = 3
ColumnName = "Gallons sold"
```

ColumnName

```
object.ColumnName [= integer]
```

You use the ColumnName property to assign a label to a data column. The name is then used in legends and labels for the chart. The column being named is determined by the current value of the ColumnIndex property.

Columns

```
object.Columns [= integer]
```

You determine the number of columns in a chart by setting the Columns property.

Data

```
object.Data[row] [= value_1 value_2 ... value_n]

object.Data[row][column] [= value]
```

The Data property enables you to add data with fewer hassles than with the DataItem property. The syntax listing for the Data property is a little different from syntax listings for other controls. The square brackets around the *row* and *column* items do not mean that those items are optional. Instead, you can choose from either of the two forms listed (with and without *column*), but you must enclose the *row* and *column* numbers in square brackets.

If you're using the Microsoft Control Pad, you don't see a Data property listed when you edit a Chart control, but you can still use the Data attribute of the <PARAM> tag. Although the use of the Data attribute is faster than specifying values individually by using DataItem (see the following "DataItem" section), it's probably not as fast as using a URL (see the "URL" section, later in this chapter) to create an entire chart.

When you design a page with a chart (or any ActiveX control), an <OBJECT> tag is created. The <OBJECT> tag will have its own <PARAM> tags to assign various properties. You can use these <PARAM> tags to assign properties without any help from Microsoft Control Pad — just use a text editor to edit the HTML file.

Here's the general format for the Data attribute:

```
<param name="data[x]" value="num1 num2 num3">
```

Don't forget that the first row and column are both 0, not 1.

You could create a chart with three columns and six rows, for example, by using the following HTML code:

```
<param name="data[0]" value="37 75 100">
<param name="data[1]" value="31 113 200">
<param name="data[2]" value="91 64 165">
<param name="data[3]" value="37 75 100">
<param name="data[4]" value="87 37 93">
<param name="data[5]" value="91 64 67">
```

With the Data property, you can specify individual items as well as entire rows, by adding a column number. You can assign the fifth row, one column at a time, for example, by adding the following <PARAM> tags to your chart object:

```
<param name="data[5][0]" value="91">
<param name="data[5][1]" value="64">
<param name="data[5][2]" value="67">
```

DataItem

```
object.DataItem [= value]
```

A chart without data is, of course, like Fred without Ginger (or chicken breast without ginger, which adds more than you might think). You provide chart data in one of two ways:

- ✔ Use the RowIndex, ColumnIndex, and DataItem properties.

- ✔ Specify a URL. (For more information about using a URL to provide chart data, see the "URL" section, later in this chapter.)

To use the first method, use RowIndex and ColumnIndex to choose the point you want. To set the value for the second column of the third row (3,2) to 37, for example, set RowIndex equal to 3 and ColumnIndex equal to 2. Next, assign the value 37 to the DataItem property.

If you have a large chart or one that changes frequently, you should use the URL method for supplying data (described later in this chapter, in the "URL" section) because you don't have to specify individual data points with the URL method.

DisplayLegend

```
object.DisplayLegend [= Boolean]
```

The Chart control automatically creates a legend for you if you set DisplayLegend equal to TRUE. The legend shows each data series and how it appears on the graph. If you set DisplayLegend to FALSE, no legend is shown. If you write a script to change this property, you can let users choose whether they want to see a legend.

GridPlacement

```
object. GridPlacement [= Boolean]
```

If users need to read values accurately from a chart you display, you can help them by drawing gridlines on the chart. Users can then follow a gridline across or from top to bottom and read values. You can draw gridlines in the horizontal and vertical directions independently by setting the HorizontalGrid and VerticalGrid properties.

As the page designer, you can choose whether to draw gridlines on top of the chart (in the foreground) or behind the chart (in the background). If you have seen charts drawn on graph paper, you have seen gridlines drawn in the background. To draw foreground gridlines, set GridPlacement = 1; for background lines, set GridPlacement = 0.

If your chart is densely packed with many data points, you may want to display the gridlines in the foreground to prevent the many data values from obscuring the gridlines.

HorizontalGrid

```
object. HorizontalGrid [= Boolean]
```

If you want gridlines drawn across the width of a chart, set HorizontalGrid to TRUE. You can also specify whether gridlines should be drawn in the foreground or background of the chart by setting the GridPlacement property.

RowIndex

```
object.RowIndex [= integer]
```

You can use the RowIndex property to mark a particular row for later operations. To set the name for a particular row, for example, you choose the row by setting the RowIndex property, and then you use the RowName property to assign its name. To name the third row "Month," for example, you use the following code fragment:

```
RowIndex = 2
RowName = "Month"
```

RowName

```
object.Rows [= integer]
```

You use the RowName property to assign a label to a data row. The name is then used in legends and labels for the chart. The current value of the RowIndex property determines which row RowName names.

Rows

```
object.Rows [= integer]
```

You set the number of rows in a chart by setting the Rows property.

Scale

```
object.Scale [= percent]
```

Use the Scale factor to reduce the value of data points uniformly; the allowable values range from 1 to 100, with 100 percent scaling as the default. If a data point is invalid, it is automatically scaled to 100 percent (no change).

URL

```
object.URL [= URL]
```

The URL property offers an alternative to the DataItem property for specifying values for data points. The URL property specifies the address of a data file. The only hitch is that the data must be in a particular (but not too complicated) format. The advantage of using a URL rather than the DataItem method is that you can easily add the Chart control if you already have Web pages that have been displaying numeric data.

If you want to use the URL method, you need a data file (whose address is then given by the URL property) that supplies the data for the chart. The Chart control is picky about the format of its data files:

```
ChartType
NumRows
NumColumns[TAB]ColumnName_0[TAB]ColumnName_1[TAB]ColumnName_2
          ...
RowName_1[TAB]DataValue_0[TAB]DataValue_1[TAB]DataValue_2
          ...DataValueN
RowName_2[TAB]DataValue_0[TAB]DataValue_1[TAB]DataValue_2
          ...DataValueN
...
RowName_m[TAB]DataValue_0[TAB]DataValue_1[TAB]DataValue_2
          ...DataValue_N
```

The first line in the file indicates the chart type, which you specify using the values of the ChartType property (refer to Table 7-11). The next line in the data file shows the number of rows in the chart. The third line specifies the number of columns, optionally followed by the name of each column. The column names should be separated by tab characters. Each successive line supplies data for a different row. The row lines begin with an optional row name followed by one number for each column. If you plan to include a row name, make sure that it's followed by a tab.

The data for the stock chart shown in Figure 7-3, for example, looks like this:

```
19
7
4          Open      High      Low       Last
Monday     5888.46   5901.24   5800.39   5894.74
Tuesday    5868.46   5907.24   5810.39   5894.74
Wednesday  5828.46   5909.24   5830.39   5894.74
Thursday   5838.46   5914.24   5840.39   5894.74
Friday     5888.46   5916.24   5850.39   5894.74
Monday     5832.46   5918.24   5830.39   5894.74
Tuesday    5903.46   5913.24   5870.39   5894.74
```

This data file tells the chart control to create a simple open/high/low/close chart (ChartType = 19) with seven rows and four columns and with the week-days as column labels.

Because the Chart control is picky about the data and its format, you have to watch out for problems if you use a URL to point to a data file. If you include commas in your numbers, for example, the control reads only the digits before the first comma for each value. If you plan to use a Chart control to display data that's generated on the fly, you should triple-check to ensure that a file is always created in the correct format.

The Microsoft Control Pad often plays tricks when you're editing objects. Some versions of Control Pad let you enter a URL property, for example, but then delete the URL entry and create an <OBJECT> that uses the Data attribute to supply the data. This bug is a serious one because even if the data in the file were updated, the chart remains the same (because the chart data comes from the Data attribute rather than from the data file). To add insult to injury, Control Pad also forgets the row and column labels that were included in the data file.

VerticalGrid

```
object.VerticalGrid [= Boolean]
```

If you want gridlines drawn from the bottom to the top of the chart, set VerticalGrid to TRUE. (You can specify whether the gridlines should be drawn in the foreground or background of the chart by setting the GridPlacement property.)

Events

Chart controls don't generate any events.

If they bring back the game show "To Tell the Truth" and you want to pick out the *real* ActiveX expert, you might ask, "Which events does the Chart control generate?" Only an ActiveX whiz remembers that the answer is none.

Methods

Like many other controls, Chart controls have only the AboutBox( ) method. When this method is invoked, it displays the About box, which displays information about the control.

Gauging Your Progress

Imagine driving a car without a gas gauge, speedometer, or odometer: You would never know how fast you were going or whether you had any gas left — and you would probably be a little on edge as you cruised around town. Although visitors to your Web site don't want to be surfing blindly either, few designers keep users informed about what's going on. With a gauge object, however, you can perform this service. Many vendors offer ActiveX gauge controls you can include on your page.

Gauge controls have many potential uses. A weather site might build a thermometer from a gauge control. Space games can track fuel levels with a gauge. You can also create progress bars with a gauge control. (A *progress bar* is a visual representation of the portion of a task that has finished. For example, most browsers show a progress bar during a file download.)

Properties

The Gauge control described in this section has many properties, which are described earlier in this chapter, in the section "Assigning Custom Values for Your Properties." The properties of the Gauge control include the ones in the following list (properties in **boldface** are discussed in this section):

AutoSize	**InnerLeft**	**NeedleWidth**
BackColor	**InnerRight**	**Picture**
CodeBase	**InnerTop**	**Style**
Enabled	Left	TabIndex
ForeColor	**Max**	Top
Height	**Min**	Value
ID	MouseIcon	Visible
InnerBottom	MousePointer	Width

BackColor, ForeColor

```
object.BackColor [=colorNumber]
object.ForeColor [=colorNumber]
```

If you have created a linear gauge (either the horizontal or vertical style), ForeColor is used to fill the gauge as the value of the gauge increases. Figure 7-4 shows how ForeColor replaces BackColor as the value of a horizontal gauge increases. (You can read all about colors and their numeric values earlier in this chapter, in the sidebar "A horse of another color.")

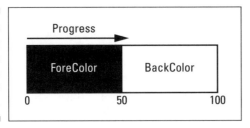

Figure 7-4: Marking progress with a gauge control.

InnerBottom, InnerLeft, InnerRight, InnerTop

```
object.InnerBottom [= numPixels]
object.InnerLeft [= numPixels]
object.InnerRight [= numPixels]
object.InnerTop [= numPixels]
```

A gauge control is really a box within a box. The inner box includes the needle (if it's a needle-style gauge) or the fill area (if it's a linear gauge style). Each of the Inner*XXX* properties sets the distance in pixels from the outer box to the inner box. The InnerBottom property, for example, sets the distance from the bottom of the outer box to the bottom of the inner box.

Figure 7-5 shows the relationship between the inner and outer boxes and values for InnerBottom, InnerLeft, InnerRight, and InnerTop. The inner box (where the action is) is defined relative to the outer box by using the values for InnerBottom, InnerLeft, InnerRight, and InnerTop.

Max, Min

```
object.Max [= integer]
object.Min [= integer]
```

The Max and Min properties set the maximum and minimum values for the gauge, respectively. If the value of the gauge is set higher than the maximum, it is reset to the value Max. Likewise, if the value is set lower than the minimum, it is reset to the value Min.

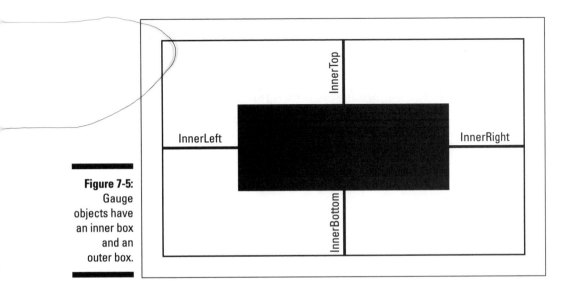

Figure 7-5:
Gauge objects have an inner box and an outer box.

NeedleWidth

```
object.NeedleWidth [= numPixels]
```

For gauge styles that use a needle, this property sets the width of the needle in pixels. Don't forget that the needle must fit within the inner box defined by the InnerBottom, InnerLeft, InnerRight, and InnerTop properties. If you create a small inner box, you have to use a small needle.

Picture

The Gauge control's Picture property is the same as the Picture property discussed earlier in this chapter (in the section "Assigning Custom Values for Your Properties"), with one exception: The portion of the Picture image that falls within the inner box (see the section "InnerBottom, InnerLeft, InnerRight, InnerTop") is not drawn — only the outside edges of the picture appear. Pictures can still enhance your gauges, though: You can draw a thermometer, for example, with an inner box that fills the thermometer's "glass" as the temperature rises.

Style

```
object.Style [= fmGaugeStyle]
```

The Gauge control supports several different kinds of needles, including linear, semicircular, and full-circle styles. The styles are summarized in Table 7-12 and are shown in Figure 7-6.

Table 7-12	Gauge Types
Value	**What the Gauge Looks Like**
0	Horizontal; gauge fills from left to right as values increase
1	Vertical; gauge fills from bottom to top with increasing values
2	Semicircular; needle moves from left to right — looks like a speedometer
3	Full circle; needle moves clockwise in a circle, starting (value = Min) and ending (value = Max) at 9 o'clock

Events

The Gauge control has several common events, as listed here. The only non-standard event is the Change event, which fires whenever a Gauge object's Value property changes (for detailed information about the Gauge control's events, see Chapter 12):

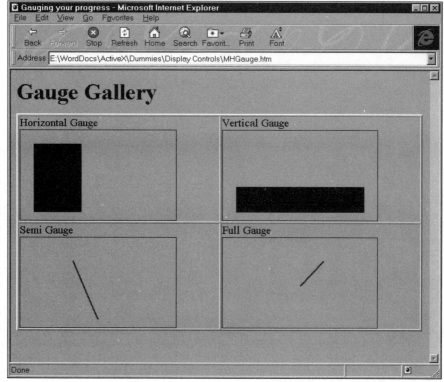

Figure 7-6:
The Gauge
control has
several
styles you
can use to
achieve
different
effects. The
Gauge Style
property
determines
which style
is used.

Change	KeyDown	MouseDown
Click	KeyPress	MouseMove
DblClick	KeyUp	MouseUp

Methods

Although the Gauge control supports several methods when used with Visual
Basic, you're limited to the Refresh( ) method when the control is included on a
Web page. The Refresh( ) method takes no arguments and simply updates the
control's appearance. Because a Gauge object updates its display when the
Value property changes, you rarely need the Refresh( ) method.

Making the Gradient

If your Web pages are dull and lifeless, you can liven them up with a splash of
color. The Gradient control adds a sophisticated touch by creating a transition
from one color to another. One part of a Gradient object is one color, and

another region is a second color. The colors flow from one region to the other, changing from one color to another. Gradient controls are easy to use because there are few parameters to set and they look nice (see Figure 7-7).

Figure 7-7: This control lets you create a transition among different regions of color. The lovely violet on the left (it used to be violet) blends into black on the right.

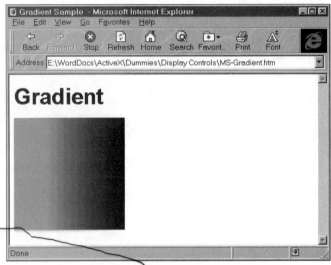

A narrow horizontal (or vertical) Gradient makes an excellent divider for major sections within a Web page, when a plain horizontal rule won't do. (You can create a plain horizontal rule with the <HR> tag.)

Properties

A Gradient object is simply two colored regions with a transition between them. Here's a list of the properties needed to specify the regions and transition (**boldfaced** properties are described in this section):

CodeBase	Height	**StartPoint**
Direction	ID	Top
EndColor	Left	Visible Width
EndPoint	**StartColor**	Visible Width

Direction

```
object.Direction [= integer]
```

The Direction property determines the direction in which the transition is made. The property can take any value from 0 through 7, as shown in Table 7-13.

Table 7-13	Transition Directions for the Gradient Control
Value	**Direction**
0	Horizontal (from StartColor on the left to EndColor on the right)
1	Vertical (from StartColor on top to EndColor at the bottom)
2	Toward the center (from StartColor around the outside to EndColor at the center)
3	Toward the corner (from StartColor in the north–northwest quadrant to EndColor in the south–southeast quadrant)
4	Diagonal down (from the upper left to the lower right)
5	Diagonal up (from the lower left to the upper right)
6	Around the StartPoint (specified by the StartPoint property)
7	Along the line from the StartPoint to the EndPoint

EndColor, StartColor

```
object.EndColor [= colorNumber]
object.StartColor [= colorNumber]
```

The Gradient control creates a transition between two colors: StartColor and EndColor. ("Start" and "end" are determined relative to the direction chosen for the transition.) The Gradient object displays a gradual transition from one color to another, and the EndColor property sets the ending color. You specify the EndColor by using a number that represents a particular color.

EndPoint, StartPoint

```
object.EndPoint [= (x, y)]
object.StartPoint [= (x, y)]
```

For some transition directions, each region revolves around a point. For those transitions (Direction = 6 or 7), the StartPoint is the point at the beginning of the transition. If you specify the direction as 6, StartPoint specifies the location of the point to be displayed in StartColor, with the transition to EndColor radiating outward. If you set the Direction property to 7, StartPoint determines the beginning of the line along which the color transition occurs. EndPoint, which is the end of the line along which the transition occurs, is shown in EndColor.

The parameters x and y, which you specify in pixels, are screen coordinates of the points EndPoint and StartPoint.

Events

Gradient controls do not generate events.

Methods

Like many other controls, Gradient controls have only the AboutBox( ) method. When the method is invoked, it displays the About box, which displays information about the control.

Image Control

Sometimes it seems that as many image formats are available as images; most browsers understand only a handful of image file formats. In the past, you could display images with a browser in one of two ways:

- With an external viewer
- As an inline image

If a browser encounters an image in an unrecognized format, the browser often tries to start another program (the external viewer) that can display the foreign format. Although a user can see the image, the flow of your page is interrupted, and you can't integrate the image with the rest of the page. As though that weren't enough injustice to heap on unsuspecting Web surfers, visitors to your page have to wait for yet another program to start up on their system.

Getting inline

Fortunately, most browsers (including Netscape Navigator and Internet Explorer) can display images inline. An *inline image* is one that a browser can display on its own, without help from any other application. The term *inline* is used because the image is shown in the browser's window, in line with other elements on the page. Most browsers currently show GIF and JPEG images inline. The problem with inline images is that the design isn't modular: If a hot new image format hits the Web scene, you can't add the format as an inline without upgrading to a new version of the browser. If you're developing for multiple browsers, you can't guarantee that each one can display the same image formats inline.

Taking control of images

Thanks to ActiveX, you can have the flexibility of external viewers with the convenience of inline images. The ActiveX Image control displays images inline, in any of several formats, with any ActiveX-enabled browser. With an Image control, you can showcase your favorite pictures. In addition, the Image control lets you customize the display of your images.

The Image control can scale and crop several common graphics file formats, including GIF (both '87 and '89 versions), JPEG, WMF, and Windows bitmap (.bmp) formats.

The Image control doesn't contain the image itself; instead, you set the PicturePath property, which is a URL for the image to display. Because the control doesn't contain the image, you cannot edit the picture by using the control — you can change only how the image is displayed. You can't, therefore, change the colors in an image or make an image transparent with this control; you have to use an image-editing program (such as Adobe Photoshop or Paintbrush).

If you're building an HTML layout, you can use the Image control to create a background image for your page by setting the control's size to the size of your layout.

Properties

The Image control has the following properties (this section discusses the **boldface** properties in detail):

AutoSize	Enabled	**PictureSizeMode**
BackColor	Height	**PictureTiling**
BackStyle	ID	SpecialEffect
BorderColor	Left	Top
BorderStyle	**PictureAlignment**	Visible
CodeBase	**PicturePath**	Width

PictureAlignment

```
object.PictureAlignment [= fmPictureAlignment]
```

The PictureAlignment property determines how an Image is aligned with its container. You can position the image at any of the four corners or in the center of the container; the position depends on the value of fmPictureAlignment. The many ways to align a picture are shown in Table 7-14.

Table 7-14	Aligning a Picture within an Image Control	
Constant	**Value**	**Description**
fmPictureAlignmentTopLeft	0	Top left corner
fmPictureAlignmentTopRight	1	Top right corner
fmPictureAlignmentCenter	2	Center
fmPictureAlignmentBottomLeft	3	Bottom left corner
fmPictureAlignmentBottomRight	4	Bottom right corner

If you tile an image using the PictureTiling property, PictureAlignment determines the placement of the first "tile." If you set PictureAlignment to fmPictureAlignmentCenter, the image is centered and successive images are tiled around it.

If you set the PictureSizeMode property to fmSizeModeStretch, you can forget about PictureAlignment: The image is scaled up to fill the entire container.

PicturePath

```
object.PicturePath = URL
```

The PicturePath property tells the Image control where to find the image for display. If you had an appropriate picture of an elephant, you might specify the path with the following:

```
elephant.PicturePath = http://www.elephant-pix.com/african-
                       bull.bmp
```

The PicturePath must be a URL, not a UNC specification. What is a *UNC spec?* It's either the basic plan for building a Carolina Tarheel or a means for specifying addresses across networks. In this case, it's the latter. A typical UNC address is in the form `//servername/dirname`, which looks vaguely like a URL. Don't be fooled by the similarity, though — stick to URLs for your PicturePath properties.

PictureSizeMode

```
object.PictureSizeMode [= fmPictureSizeMode]
```

Embedding images in Web pages can be tricky because you know the size of the image but don't know the size of the window on a viewer's computer. The Image control includes the PictureSizeMode property to control how the image is adjusted to fit on the displayed HTML page. You have two choices: Maintain or increase the image size. If you choose to increase the image size, you can either stretch or zoom it. Table 7-15 summarizes the possible values of fmPictureSizeMode and their effects.

Table 7-15		PictureSizeModes
Constant	**Value**	**What It Does**
fmPictureSizeModeClip	0	If image is smaller than the container, nothing happens; if image is larger than the container, image is cropped
fmPictureSizeModeStretch	1	Stretches picture to fill the container and might distort the picture in either the horizontal or vertical direction
fmPictureSizeModeZoom	3	Scales the picture and maintains the aspect ratio

Snip, snip

It's a fact of life that some images scale poorly. If you have an image of text (rather than text itself), scaling the image to fit a window can make it unreadable. If you use an image to highlight detail, distorting the image may render it useless. In these cases, you should set PictureSizeMode to fmPictureSizeModeClip, which doesn't increase the image size. If the window is too small to display the entire image, the image is cropped. (A *cropped image* is one in which part of the image is cut and not displayed.)

S t r e t c h i n g an image

If you prefer to have your images fill the browser window when they're displayed, you can set PictureSizeMode to either fmPictureModeStretch or fmPictureSizeModeZoom. Stretching the image causes it to expand both vertically and horizontally, until it reaches an outer edge. After the image reaches an outer edge, it begins stretching in the other direction until it fills the entire container. In Figure 7-8, the original image measures 100 x 125 pixels, and the browser window measures 250 x 200 pixels. The image is therefore scaled up by a factor of 200/125 (or 1.6) to be 160 x 200 pixels. Because the image still does not fill the window, it is stretched in the horizontal direction from 160 pixels to the full 250-pixel width of the browser.

Who's zooming who?

If you set PictureSizeMode to fmPictureSizeModeZoom, the image is scaled up but the aspect ratio is maintained, as shown in the lower left corner of Figure 7-8. The *aspect ratio* is the ratio of an object's width to its height (see the nearby sidebar, "Image controls on the big screen.") The aspect ratio for the window usually differs from the image's aspect ratio. Zooming an image, therefore, usually leaves some blank space at either the top or bottom of the browser window. If you want the image to be as large as possible for a container but have the same ratio of height to width, use the zoom setting.

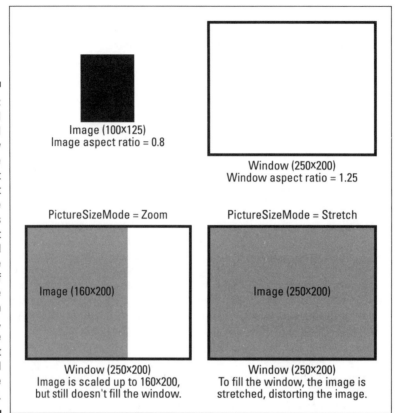

Figure 7-8:
The original image and the window have different aspect ratios. If the image is zoomed, it does not fill the entire window. If the image is then stretched, it fills the window but is distorted by the stretching.

Image (100×125)
Image aspect ratio = 0.8

Window (250×200)
Window aspect ratio = 1.25

PictureSizeMode = Zoom

PictureSizeMode = Stretch

Image (160×200)

Image (250×200)

Window (250×200)
Image is scaled up to 160×200, but still doesn't fill the window.

Window (250×200)
To fill the window, the image is stretched, distorting the image.

Image controls on the big screen

The *aspect ratio* of an object is the ratio of its width to its height. If you change the aspect ratio of an image, it usually appears distorted. That's why movies have to be "formatted to fit your screen" when they're shown on television: The aspect ratio of movie theater screens and televisions is different. (Movie theater screens are wider than they are high, and television screens are square.) If you try to fill a TV screen with a movie theater film, the movie appears distorted. Because no one wants to watch a squished movie, TV people chop the sides of each movie frame so that the image fits within a television screen.

When you use an Image control to display an image, you display the image within the control's visible area. If your image has one aspect ratio but the Image control has a different aspect ratio, you have the same problem as television movies: If you try to shoehorn the image into the control, your image appears distorted. You should either make sure that your Image controls have the same aspect ratio as your images or clip your image to fit within the control.

PictureTiling

```
object.PictureTiling [= Boolean]
```

If you want to tile the floor of your container with an image, you can save a trip to the hardware store: Just set the PictureTiling property to TRUE. The tiling effect depends on other properties of the Image object. You control where the first tile is laid by setting the PictureAlignment property.

If you align the center of the picture with the center of the container (by setting PictureAlignment to fmPictureAlignmentCenter), that's where the first tile is laid. Tiles (made up of your image) are laid around the center until the entire container is covered. You control where the last tile is laid by setting the PictureSizeMode. If you set PictureSizeMode to fmPictureSizeModeClip, for example, the last tile laid is clipped if it doesn't fit in the remaining space. Figure 7-9 shows several tiling styles, each using a different value for fmPictureAlignment.

Figure 7-9:
The Image control can tile images by repeating a small image to fill a larger space. The Picture-Alignment property determines where the first tile is laid. Each Image object in the figure uses a different value for the Picture-Alignment property.

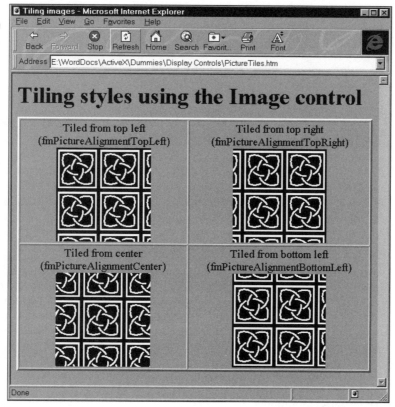

You can create an attractive background from a small image by using the PictureTiling property. Rather than create a background image large enough to fill the browser's window, the Image control (with the PictureTiling property set to TRUE) repeats the smaller image until it fills the window.

When you use the PictureTiling property of the Image control, the tiling is done on the user's computer (the client side) rather than at the Web server (the server side). By tiling with a small image, you retain the aesthetic value of a custom background without paying the price of long download times for a large background image.

Events

Although an image event sounds like a convention for political spin doctors, the Image control has its share of events. (For more information about each of these events and event programming, see Chapter 12.) The events of the Image control are listed here for reference:

BeforeDragOver	MouseDown
BeforeDropOrPaste	MouseUp
Enter	MouseMove
Exit	

Methods

The Image control has two built-in methods: Move( ) and ZOrder( ). (The ZOrder( ) method is described in detail in Chapter 9, so only the Move( ) method is discussed in this section.)

Making the move

```
object.Move( [Left [,  Top [,  Width [,  Height ]]]])
```

Although moving can be a pain if you have to pack a moving van and drive cross-country, it's no problem when you move with ActiveX. The Move( ) method handles the packing and shipping of both large and small controls for you. You can move an HTML layout, a collection of controls, or a single control to any location.

The Move( ) method has two ways for you to specify the destination:

  ✔ Ordered arguments
  ✔ Named arguments

If you use ordered arguments to specify the destination, you list each of the arguments in order, separated by commas. If you want to skip an argument between two arguments, you still include the comma.

Suppose that you want to move a control but want to specify only the left coordinate and that you want to change the width but not the height. You invoke the Move( ) method with the following:

```
objectOnTheMove.Move(newLeft, ,newWidth)
```

Because the Top argument was skipped between the Left and Width arguments, the comma was included as a placeholder. Even though the Height argument (which normally follows the Width parameter) was omitted, no comma follows the Width argument because the missing Height argument didn't fall between two arguments.

Named arguments are arguments labeled as part of the call to the method that enables you to list the arguments in any order. You can change the left, top, and height properties, for example, with the following call to Move:

```
objectOnTheMove.Move Left := 4, Height := 5, Top := 20
```

Notice that the arguments don't have to appear in their normal positional order.

Label

Label controls provide a flexible way to display text, as shown in Figure 7-10. Several controls enable you to format text in many ways. Two of the most common Label controls have their own capabilities:

- ✔ **Label Object:** The Label control described in the Microsoft documentation for ActiveX controls (although this control, also known as ieLabel, can rotate text at any angle and wrap text along any curve, it cannot display a picture)
- ✔ **Microsoft Forms Label 2.0:** Can display background pictures but cannot rotate text or render letters along a curve

Because the Label Object is more flexible, it is discussed in this section; for the remainder of this section, the term "Label control" refers to the control listed as the Label Object.

Using the Label control, you can create headings and titles that stand out from regular text. In the old days of Web design (about six weeks ago), you could use HTML formatting tags to set the typeface, foreground color, background color, and other text attributes. The Label control extends these earlier tags to enable you to control alignment, rotate text, and even render text along a line.

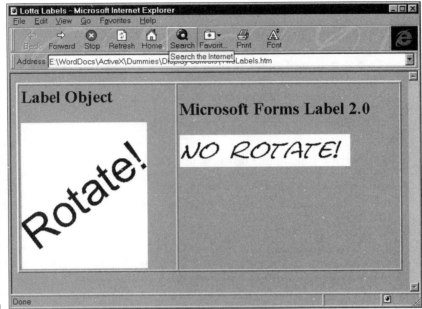

Figure 7-10:
Two
common
Label
controls are
available,
both of
which give
you more
flexibility
than
traditional
HTML tags.

Labels offer lots of control, which might tempt you to experiment with many styles, colors, and sizes. Although you should try out many styles to gauge various effects, keep in mind that a little Label goes a long way. Think of Label as sugar for your Web pages: Sprinkle a little of it around to sweeten your pages (and remember that too much promotes page decay).

Properties

The Label control gives you three ways to spice up your text:

- ✔ You can use all the usual Windows font attributes to set the alignment, size, and style of your text.
- ✔ You can rotate text at any angle you specify.
- ✔ You can fill the area between two lines with text and shape the letters to fit the area between the lines.

This list shows the properties of the Label control (properties described in this section are in **boldface**):

Alignment	**FontBold**	ID
Angle	**FontItalic**	Left
BackColor	**FontName**	**Mode**

BackStyle	**FontSize**	Top
BotPoints	**FontStrikeout**	**TopPoints**
BotXY	**FontUnderline**	**TopXY**
Caption	ForeColor	Visible
CodeBase	Height	Width
FillStyle		

Alignment

```
object.Alignment [= fmAlignment]
```

How do you want your text justified? You specify the alignment by setting the Alignment property to one of the values listed in Table 7-16.

Table 7-16	The Many Possible Ways to Align a Label	
fmAlignment	*Vertical*	*Horizontal*
0	Top	Left
1	Top	Centered
2	Top	Right
3	Centered	Left
4	Centered	Centered
5	Centered	Right
6	Bottom	Left
7	Bottom	Centered
8	Bottom	Right

Angle

```
object.Angle [= integer]
```

Text within a label can be rotated about a point. You can spin text so that it reads from right to left or even from top to bottom. The Angle property specifies the degrees of counterclockwise rotation. If you want your text to read from the bottom up, for example, you set the Angle to 90°.

BotPoints, BotXY, TopPoints, TopXY

```
object.BotPoints [= integer]
object.TopPoints [= integer]
```

With Label controls, you're not limited to rendering text along straight lines. As shown in Figure 7-11, you can curve text along arbitrary lines. Because some curves require many points in order to be drawn smoothly, ActiveX programmers created the PageGen tool to enable you to design curved text graphically rather than numerically. You give the Label control two lines (a top and a bottom), and the text fills the space between them.

As you probably remember from high school geometry class, it takes only two points to make a straight line. Unfortunately, arbitrary curves are a little trickier.

One technique for specifying wavy lines is to simply list lots of points that lie along the line. If the points are close enough, they trace a smooth line when joined together. It probably has been a while since you played "connect the dots," so here's a chance to brush up on your rusty skills. (Web design is really all about awakening your inner child. After you have constructed your first label, feel free to play in the sandbox.)

Although you need lots of points to make a smooth line, no one wants to list hundreds of points for each label. With a graphical label-making tool, you could simply draw the curves and then have someone else figure out the points. PageGen is that label-making tool: You draw the top and bottom lines, and it automatically calculates the numerous points.

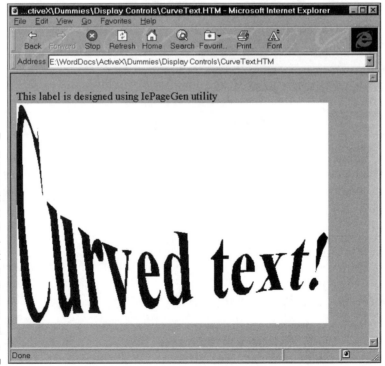

Figure 7-11:
The Label Object can fill text between any two curves — you give it the points on the curves and the text, and Label does the rest.

Figure 7-12 shows the PageGen program in action; the curves shown were later filled in to create the label shown in the figure. The Settings menu lets you control the appearance of the text in your Label control. Using the mouse, you draw two lines, and then PageGen creates a label that fills the area between the two lines.

The four properties (TopPoints, TopXY, BotPoints, BotXY) specify the lists of points for the top and bottom lines, respectively. The TopPoints property tells the Label control how many points are in the top line. The TopXY property then lists the two-dimensional coordinates of each point. The list of points is passed to the control as an array.

A single point might be given as

```
<param name="TopXY[1]" value="(86, 490)">
```

This line tells the Label control that the second point (most arrays begin with the 0 element) on the top line is located at (86, 490). You specify the bottom line in the same way.

FillStyle

```
object.FillStyle [= Boolean]
```

You can choose whether you want your text to print in outline (FillStyle = 1) or solid (FillStyle = 0) characters.

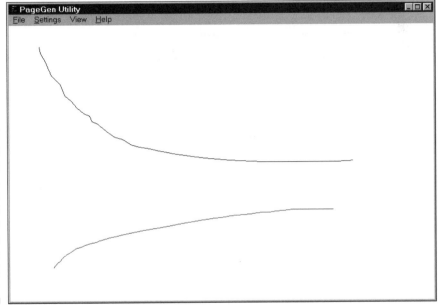

Figure 7-12:
With PageGen, you can create snazzy labels as easily as drawing two lines.

If you edit the Label control with the Microsoft Control Pad, be sure to double-check the FillStyle property. The Control Pad generates HTML that includes the FillStyle property twice; it's always set to 0 (solid characters) at least one of those two times. The PageGen utility (mentioned earlier in this chapter, in the section "BotPoints, BotXY, TopPoints, TopXY") doesn't have this problem and generates Label objects correctly.

FontBold, FontItalic, FontName, FontSize, FontStrikeout, FontUnderline

```
object.Bold [= Boolean]
object.Italic [= Boolean]
object.Size [= Integer]
object.StrikeThrough [= Boolean]
object.Underline [= Boolean]
object.Weight [= Integer]
```

These properties are the usual font-specification suspects: They let you adjust a typeface for just the look you want. If you happen to specify a font that doesn't exist on a user's system, users see the closest substitute instead.

Mode

```
object.Mode [= fmMode]
```

The Mode property determines how the text is drawn on the Label control. The first two modes are for regular text, and the second two are for text rendered between lines. The various modes are listed in Table 7-17. If you use the PageGen utility to create curved text, you have to use either mode 2 or 3.

Table 7-17	Text-Rendering Modes
fmMode	*Description*
0	Normal (same as Visual Basic Label control)
1	Normal text with rotation
2	User-specified lines, rendered without rotation
3	User-specified lines, rendered with rotation

Events

The Label control has events for common mouse actions and an event that fires whenever the label text is changed. (For details about mouse action events, see Chapter 12.) The events supported by the Label control are listed in Table 7-18.

Table 7-18	Events in the Life of a Label
Event	*When It's Generated*
Click	When mouse is clicked while positioned over the Label control
Change	When Caption (label text) has changed
MouseDown	When a user holds down the mouse button while mouse is positioned over the label
MouseOver	When mouse is positioned over the Label control
MouseUp	When mouse button is released with mouse pointer positioned over the label

Methods

The Label control is lean on methods — you can use only the About( ) method. When this method is invoked, it displays the About box for the associated Label control. The About box provides information about the Label control (such as copyright information for the control).

New

In the fast-paced world of Web design, new items are regularly added to Web sites. Unfortunately, a Web site often has so much that separating the wheat from the chaff is difficult. Users frequently miss the latest and greatest addition to your Web site if you don't point it out. You don't want to have items marked as new, however, when they have been on your site for three months. The New Item control is designed to help you solve both problems: You can highlight an item and fix an expiration date for the "new" marker.

Properties

The New control has several properties (properties described in this section are shown in **boldface**):

CodeBase	ID	TabIndex	Visible
Date	**Image**	TabStop	Width
Height	Left	Top	

Date

```
object.Date [= date]
```

The Date property sets the expiration date for the New control: After this date, the New control no longer appears. You should specify the date in the American style: month/day/year (9/1/1996, for example).

Image

```
object.Image [= image]
```

If you don't set the Image property, the control displays a small tag with "New!" printed in black in a yellow background. You can use the Image property to specify any image you want; the image is specified by the URL for a Windows bitmap image (.BMP).

Events

New controls don't generate any events.

Methods

The New Item control has only a single method: the lowly AboutBox( ) method. Calling AboutBox( ) pops up a description of the New Item control.

Testing your newfound knowledge

1. What can an Image control do for you?

A. Make you more popular by improving how others see you.

B. Polish your public persona.

C. Display image files in any of several formats.

D. Image controls can't do anything for you.

2. Gradient controls are useful because you can:

A. Easily find the steepest part of a hill.

B. Create attractive horizontal dividers for splitting up large Web pages.

C. Assign yourself any grade you want.

D. Whiten your teeth by brushing with the rough side of a gradient.

Chapter 8

The Sound of Music

● ●

In This Chapter

▶ Understanding sound and the Web

▶ Adding background sounds to Internet Explorer pages

▶ Playing audio with the RealAudio ActiveX control

▶ Creating multimedia slide shows based on RealAudio clips

● ●

*O*ne of the most important things you can do to spice up your Web site is to add multiple media. Sound, animations, and video set your site apart from text-laden pages with all the spark of rotting wood. Adding sound is a challenge for any Web page designer, though. You gotta have a sound file, and that's just the beginning. Because not all sound formats are equal in the eyes of Web surfers, you have to use a common format. You also have to consider how the sound gets from your server to the browser and what happens when the sound arrives. ActiveX has many features for handling sound, and several controls are available for playing sound on a user's machine. This chapter begins with a brief overview of the issues to consider and then describes several common controls you can use to add sound to your site.

When it comes to the people who visit your page, you want to give them only the best: CD-quality sound beamed straight to their browsers in real-time. (*Real-time* means that listeners hear the sound live instead of playing back a sound that was recorded previously.) The problem is that sound is big: One minute of CD-quality, stereo sound is more than 10MB! That's why sending audio over the Web involves compromise. Because lots of software is available to help you provide sound from your Web site, you don't have to worry about the technical aspects. None of the software avoids compromise, however: It just hides the details from you. When you choose software for your site, be sure to weigh the trade-offs and decide what's right for you.

Unlike images, which are widely supported in many formats, most browsers don't include built-in support for sound. Users then have to spend a little time adding sound capabilities to their browsers, and you can't be sure that all users have tools for sound playback. Many excellent third-party tools are available, however, which can act as viewers. In browser lingo, a *viewer* is an external program that is started to handle a file for which a browser lacks built-in support.

Squeezing a sound

Quality sound takes lots of space. Although CD-ROMs hold hundreds of megabytes of information, they have room for only a little more than an hour of music. If you don't need CD-quality sound, you can dramatically decrease the amount of data that's needed, but still not enough to make audio practical over slow Web connections. Another way to reduce the resources necessary for sound is to compress it. Most sounds have lots of repetition, and you can eliminate that repetition (and save a great deal of space) by using a compression algorithm.

Several compression procedures are widely used. You don't have to know how any of the compression algorithms work because the tools you use for serving audio do their compression automatically. Most tools dramatically reduce

the amount of data that's necessary, but there's a catch: The most effective procedures for compressing sound are *lossy compression algorithms,* which are algorithms that destroy some of the original data. Lossy algorithms trade reduced quality for better compression. Most users who hear compressed audio don't notice a difference, but you should consider the trade-offs that different products offer.

The dark side to compression is decompression. Audio is transmitted in compressed form to save download time, but it then must be decompressed. Decompressing a file is similar to untying a large but well-tied knot. Because most computer processors struggle during decompression, the process can create a noticeable slowdown on all except the fastest machines.

If you expect users to have a particular program to play back sounds at your site, include a link to the page where the program can be downloaded.

Sound in the 'Ground: Background Sounds

Internet Explorer 3.0 is one browser that does include support for *background sounds,* or sounds that are played as a page is loading and that can continue to play after the page is finished loading. You can see the <BGSOUND> tag in action at The Microsoft Network (MSN) home page. Users can customize the MSN home page (http://www.msn.com/) to suit their own tastes; then, whenever they point their browser to http://www.msn.com/, they see the home page they have designed. Users can also choose the music that plays while the MSN home page is loaded. After they do that, a new home page is created with the <BGSOUND> tag.

Using the <BGSOUND> attribute, you can embed background sounds in pages. Here's the syntax:

```
<BGSOUND
    SRC = "url"
    LOOP = n>
```

Specify the location of the sound file using a URL; the <BGSOUND> accepts WAV and AU samples and sounds in MIDI format. You must include, at minimum, the SRC attribute; the LOOP attribute is optional.

The <BGSOUND> tag doesn't need a closing tag (</BGSOUND>) — everything the browser needs is included in <BGSOUND>.

The WAV format is Windows own sound format, which can be played on computers running Windows 3.1 and later by the Media Player included in every version of Windows. The AU format, developed by Sun Microsystems, is also commonly used, especially among UNIX users. The MIDI format, widely used for music, is not as commonly used on the Web as the other two formats.

The LOOP attribute of the <BGSOUND> tag specifies the number of times you want a selection played. If you set LOOP to either 1 or INFINITE, the sound repeats endlessly until the user leaves the page or presses the Internet Explorer Stop button.

Is It Live, or Is It RealAudio?

With the Progressive Networks RealAudio tools, you can serve real-time audio from your Web site. RealAudio uses a proprietary compression technique to encode recorded audio or live broadcasts. If a RealAudio Server is installed at your site, you can offer streaming audio to anyone with a RealAudio Player. *Streaming* means that a continuous stream of data is sent, and the audio is played as it arrives at the user's browser instead of the user having to download the audio and play it back in separate steps. With RealAudio Player Version 2.0, you can offer users streamed audio of the same quality as a monophonic (not stereo) FM broadcast. The newer player, Version 3.0, offers enhanced quality, but it's still not as good as a compact disc player.

RealAudio Player is available as a stand-alone player, a Netscape plug-in, and an ActiveX control. Progressive Networks has also recently introduced *synchronized multimedia,* in which you can create an audio slide show by stepping through Web pages in time with the audio.

Serving Up a St(r)eaming Plate of RealAudio

Although you can embed an ActiveX RealAudio Player control in pages you design, visitors to your site don't benefit from having the player unless you supply RealAudio to it. To offer users RealAudio from your site, you have to do some extra work. The Progressive Networks RealAudio site (you can find it at `http://www.realaudio.com/`) has mounds of documentation on how to prepare and serve RealAudio files.

Here's a brief outline of the steps to serving RealAudio:

1. **Install a RealAudio Server if you want to provide streaming audio.**

   If you're not interested in offering streaming audio, you can skip this step. Without streaming audio, visitors to your site must wait for an entire Real Audio file to download before playing any part of it.

2. **Get a sound source — either prerecorded or live.**

3. **Create a RealAudio format file by using the RealAudio Encoder to encode the original source.**

   Encoding a live broadcast is more complicated than encoding a prerecorded file and requires some additional software.

4. **Create a *RealAudio metafile.***

   It's a link between the Web server, which serves HTML pages, and the RealAudio Server, which serves RealAudio streams.

5. **Include a link in an HTML page to the RealAudio metafile on the Web server.**

You can encode and play RealAudio files without anyone else's assistance. If your site doesn't have a RealAudio Server, however (see the upcoming section "Serving audio for real"), you need help from the Web server's administrator to install the server. If you're the administrator, you're home free. If you're not the administrator, you probably should start shopping for a nice gift. (If you want to add RealAudio streams to your own personal pages, you can install the RealAudio Personal Server without access to your Web server.)

Your RealAudio Toolbox

If you want to play back RealAudio files, you have to have only a version of the RealAudio Player. *Serving* RealAudio files, however, requires three tools: RealAudio Server, RealAudio Encoder, and RealAudio Player.

Serving audio for real

The RealAudio Server works much like a Web server: Users request RealAudio files from the server, which are then sent to the user's browser and played. (If you don't have a RealAudio Server, you can't serve RealAudio, but users can still download RealAudio files from your Web server and play them back by using a RealAudio Player.) You must have a RealAudio Server, however, installed and accessible from your Web server, to offer streaming audio. Progressive Networks offers two RealAudio servers: RealAudio Server and RealAudio Personal Server. The Personal Server is free, but it's limited to two concurrent streams: Either one person can listen to two streams, or two people can each listen to one. If you expect numerous users to listen to audio, you have to purchase a RealAudio Server.

Even if you don't have a RealAudio Server (and therefore can't stream audio to your users), you can still benefit from RealAudio. Using the RealAudio Encoder, you can dramatically compress audio sources and save your users some download time by sending a much smaller file. Because the RealAudio Player is widely available, you can be sure that almost any user can download and install one. You can use the RealAudio format for all your audio rather than try to maintain a different file format for each platform.

Cracking the RealAudio secret code

Although a RealAudio Server serves RealAudio streams, you still have to transform your audio source into RealAudio format. The RealAudio Encoder transforms both prerecorded and live audio into the RealAudio format, which users can then play back on a RealAudio Player. The RealAudio Encoder is free, and you can use it (even without a RealAudio Server) to encode audio files that users can then download and play back. Encoding live audio for broadcast is a little more complicated than using an existing source, but the *RealAudio Content Creation Guide* (available from the RealAudio Web site) contains detailed instructions.

Eine kleine NachtRealAudio

RealAudio Player plays back audio that has been encoded in the RealAudio format (and *only* that format). RealAudio Players are available for all make and manner of Windows, OS/2, Macintosh, and the most common UNIX flavors. A RealAudio Player plug-in is available for browsers that support the Netscape *plug-in architecture,* which is a specification that enables programmers to extend a browser's built-in capabilities. For example, the RealAudio Player plug-in handles the playback of RealAudio files, but it appears to users as though the browser is doing it alone. The RealAudio Player is also available as an ActiveX control, although the software is still in the beta stage. *Beta* software isn't available for commercial release, but companies make it available for evaluation purposes. By embedding the ActiveX control in pages you create, you ensure that any user with an ActiveX-enabled browser can listen to RealAudio streams from your site.

Making Really Good RealAudio

When it comes to producing RealAudio, there's a right way and a wrong way. Because you want to do everything right (you bought a ...*For Dummies* book, didn't you?), here are a few tips for creating great RealAudio files:

- ✔ **Start with good audio.** Your audio will never be better than the original, but that's no reason to start off with a poor audio source. Don't record a live concert over a telephone in a thunderstorm and then encode it as a RealAudio file.

- ✔ **Make your audio easier for users to digest.** I'm not saying that you can offer only soothing Barry Manilow recordings — just divide your audio into bite-size pieces. With RealAudio, you can split recordings into clips by creating separate files for each clip. Users then can choose the clips they want without listening to lots of sappy stuff.

- ✔ **Make it easy to play your audio.** If you use the RealAudio ActiveX control, people with ActiveX-enabled browsers can easily play back RealAudio files. You don't have to exclude less enlightened folks, however: Just add a link from your page to the RealAudio download page (which you can find on the RealAudio home page, at `http://www.realaudio.com/`).

- ✔ **Don't stop at audio.** Using ActiveX, you can easily add images and animations to go along with your audio. You could write a script, for example, that lets users move the mouse over an image and play different audio clips depending on the mouse location.

- ✔ **Old audio gets stale.** Change frequently the audio you offer, and users will always wonder what new clip you might have added. Even if you're working on your own personal Web pages, it doesn't hurt to keep people coming back.

The ActiveX RealAudio Player

The RealAudio ActiveX control enables you to embed a RealAudio Player inline. The player is displayed within the page just like an inline image (Chapter 3 has the goods on inline images) and gives users the same control as the stand-alone RealAudio Player 2.0 does. Figure 8-1 shows a RealAudio Player embedded within a page. As a page designer, you control the appearance and functions of the Real Audio Player control by changing its properties, which are listed in Table 8-1. You can set the property values either through Microsoft Control Pad or directly in the PARAM attribute of the <OBJECT> tag.

The control also includes several handy events and methods.

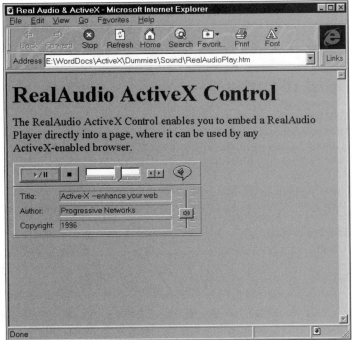

Table 8-1   Properties of the RealAudio ActiveX Control

Property	Value Type	Description
AutoGotoURL	*boolean*	Specifies how a URL event is handled: TRUE indicates that the control forwards the URL event to the browser, and FALSE sends the event OnGotoURL instead
AutoStart	*boolean*	Determines whether the control automatically begins playing after the source data is available
Console	*string*	Console name used to link multiple control instances
Controls	ControlsValue	Visible components of the control
NoLabels	*boolean*	Removes the Title, Author, and Copyright labels from the window, even though the title, author, and copyright are still shown
Reset	*boolean*	Removes all URLs from the playlist
SRC	*URL*	(Required) Sets the source of the RealAudio clip; the protocol must be either pnm, http, or file

The Microsoft Control Pad Properties dialog box shows slightly different names for each of the properties (Source rather than SRC, for example), but the correspondence between Table 8-1 and Control Pad is clear.

Keeping it simple

If you want to use the player, you must have something to play, so the SRC property is required. Everything else is up to you. The SRC property is a URL, but it's limited to one of three protocols: `pnm`, `http`, and `file`. (The `pnm` protocol is the Progressive Networks protocol for accessing RealAudio servers.)

Another basic property is AutoStart, which begins playing a clip as soon as the source data is available, if it's set to TRUE. If AutoStart is FALSE, the player begins loading clips for playback, but the player doesn't start up until a user clicks the Play button.

Taking control of RealAudio Player

Although you can use the RealAudio Player by specifying only a source (using the SRC attribute), you can add a few twists as well. The Controls property determines which controls are displayed by the player. If Controls is left unspecified or is set to ALL, a full-blown player is displayed. Valid values for Controls include the ones in this list:

All	PlayButton	StopButton
ControlPanel	PositionField	StatusField
InfoPanel	PositionSlider	VolumeSlider
InfoVolumePanel	StatusBar	

Figure 8-2 shows several players, each with a different Controls value. Only a few of the many choices are shown in Figure 8-2; be sure to experiment with some of the other values.

You might want to limit the size of controls displayed on-screen to save space within a Web page. A single Play/Pause button is much smaller than the entire player. You could also assemble a custom player from individual pieces by using the Console parameter, which is described in the following section.

Figure 8-2:
At design time, you can specify which parts of the Player control are visible by setting the Controls property of the RealAudio Player.

Naming names with Console

Sometimes you want to have more than one instance of the player on the same page. Throughout a long page, for example, you might include several Play/Pause buttons so that a user can scroll through the page and always have a Play/Pause button in view. Or you might want to place the Play button in one area and the Stop button in another. The Console property lets you assign a name to an object and then use the name to link separate instances: All instances with the same Console name work as one unit.

If you look closely at Figure 8-2, you can see that the sliders on the ControlPanel instance and the All instance are in the same relative position. All the players shown in the figure are linked together because they all share the same Console value ("Dummies"), as shown in the HTML for the first three instances (All, ControlPanel, and PlayButton):

```
<H2>All</h2>
<br>
<OBJECT
```

(continued)

(continued)

```
    CLASSID="clsid:CFCDAA03-8BE4-11CF-B84B-0020AFBBCCFA"
    HEIGHT=134
    WIDTH=300>
    <PARAM NAME="SRC" VALUE="ferdinand.ra">
    <PARAM NAME="Controls" VALUE="all">
    <PARAM NAME="Console" VALUE="Dummies">
</OBJECT>

<br>
<H2>ControlPanel</h2>
<br>
<OBJECT
    CLASSID="clsid:CFCDAA03-8BE4-11cf-B84B-0020AFBBCCFA"
    HEIGHT=40
    WIDTH=350>
    <PARAM NAME="Controls" VALUE="ControlPanel">
    <PARAM NAME="Console" VALUE="Dummies">
</OBJECT>

<br>
<H2>PlayButton:    </h2>
<OBJECT
    CLASSID="clsid:CFCDAA03-8BE4-11cf-B84B-0020AFBBCCFA"
    HEIGHT=20
    WIDTH=40>
    <PARAM NAME="Controls" VALUE="PlayButton">
    <PARAM NAME="Console" VALUE="Dummies">
</OBJECT>
```

All three instances (in addition to those not shown) are linked together by the common Console value. In addition to any Console name you can dream up on your own, you see two special Console values: master and unique. A Console value of master links to all instances. If you have two different console names (rock and easy-listening, for example) and then add an instance whose Console property is set to master, the last instance links to both rock and easy-listening.

All the players on the page share one source (given by the SRC property for the first instance, labeled "All"). Because all the components shown in Figure 8-2 are linked together, you don't have to specify the source a multiple number of times.

Sometimes you want to link to all other instances using master, and at other times you want to be sure that you don't link to any other instances. You can't guarantee that you won't accidentally link your instance to an existing instance, however, because you might happen to choose an existing Console name. If you set the Console property to unique, however, you're guaranteed that your instance isn't linked to any other instance (not even another instance with the name unique).

If you want to create a custom RealAudio Player with only some of the components available (the Play button and the Volume Slider, for example), you can mix and match two instances of the player and then link the two together with a common Console name.

Being label-free

If you're trying to squeeze a few more items on a page, you can trim down the RealAudio Player with the NoLabels property. By default, every player instance shows the title, author, and copyright (which are embedded in the clip by the RealAudio format). Each of these fields is also labeled (Title, Author, and Copyright) by default. If you set NoLabels to TRUE, however, the title, author, and copyright fields are still shown, but without the labels. Your player instance isn't any shorter, but it is narrower (and less cluttered) without the labels.

If you remove the labeling for author, title, and copyright, users won't know which field is which. It's unlikely, of course, that an author would be mistaken for a copyright or that what looks like an author could be a title. If the artist formerly known as Prince changed his symbol to © 1997 and then released a song called "Elvis Presley," for example, things could get a little confusing.

Making a fresh start

If you want more than one file to play when a user clicks a link, you can create a metafile that contains several URLs on separate lines (with no blank lines), as shown in this example:

```
pnm://www.server.com/hello.ra
pnm://www.server.com/its-been-nice.ra
pnm://www.server.com/goodbye.ra
```

(A *metafile* is a file that lists the URLs of sound clips. The metafile is stored on the Web server, but points to files on a RealAudio Server. For more information about metafiles and configuring RealAudio, see the *Content Creation Guide* at the RealAudio Web site.)

When you specify more than one URL to play, the player creates a playlist. You can erase the playlist and start from scratch by setting the Reset property to TRUE.

Should I stay or should I AUTOGO?

The AutoGotoURL property determines how a URL event is handled. If AutoGotoURL is TRUE, the event is passed on to the browser, which probably follows the link. If AutoGotoURL is FALSE, however, the URL event triggers an

OnGotoURL event. If you don't care what happens when a URL fires, you don't have to change AutoGotoURL (whose default value is TRUE). If you have big plans for URLs, though, you can write a script that's triggered by the OnGotoURL event and then set AutoGotoURL to FALSE.

The Many Methods of the RealAudio ActiveX Control

The RealAudio control has methods that mimic the controls on a RealAudio Player, as listed in Table 8-2. A user can stop the clip that's playing, for example, by clicking the Stop button on the control; the page designer can stop a clip by calling the DoStop( ) method, which has the same effect.

Table 8-2	The RealAudio Control Methods
Method	*What It Does*
AboutBox( )	Displays copyright information for the control (not a clip)
CanPlayPause( )	Detects whether the Play/Pause function is available and returns either TRUE or FALSE
CanStop( )	Is there a Stop function in the house? No shades of gray here: either TRUE or FALSE
DoGotoURL( )	Causes the control to attempt a navigation to the specified URL in the specified frame target; the container must support URL browsing
DoPlayPause( )	Plays or pauses the current clip (the same as clicking the Play/Pause button)
DoNextItem( )	Skips to the next clip in a metafile
DoPrevItem( )	Jumps back to the preceding clip in a metafile
DoStop( )	Stops the current clip (just like clicking the Stop button)
EditPreferences( )	Opens the Preferences dialog box so that users can set their RealAudio preferences
HasNextItem( )	Tests whether the source has a next item; either it does (TRUE) or it doesn't (FALSE)
HasPrevItem( )	Returns TRUE if there's a clip before the current clip; otherwise, returns FALSE
HideShowStatistics( )	Shows or hides the Connection Statistics dialog box
IsStatisticsVisible( )	Tests whether the Connection Statistics dialog box is displayed and returns either TRUE or FALSE

None of the methods accepts any parameters, except for DoGotoURL( ), which takes two arguments: a URL and a target (given as a string). None of the methods returns anything, except where noted.

Play until you stop

Most of the RealAudio control's methods duplicate functions on the RealAudio Player buttons. You probably can't be there to push the buttons for your users, so you can do it through scripting. You could let users do all the button-pushing for you; with the scripting methods, however, you can control RealAudio playback without even showing a player. You can display an image using the Image control, for example, and then map different regions of the image to different RealAudio clips. The Image control then triggers an event, which you can handle by playing a clip.

The DoPlayPause( ) and DoStop( ) methods mimic the Play and Stop buttons, respectively. Unfortunately, you can't know in advance (that is, when you design the page) whether either method will be applicable at *run-time*, or when a user runs your script. If you want to call either DoPlayPause( ) or DoStop( ) from a script, you should check to make sure that it's even possible to play, pause, or stop a clip. (If no clip is playing, for example, there's nothing to stop, so CanStop( ) returns FALSE.) The CanPlayPause( ) and CanStop( ) methods each return TRUE if their respective capabilities are present. If you want the RealAudio Player to stop playing the current clip, you write a line like this (as in VBScript):

```
If RA-Player.CanStop() Then RA-Player.DoStop()
```

For more information about VBScript and scripting, see Chapter 10.

What's next?

The DoNextItem( ) and DoPrevItem( ) methods skip to the next clip and previous clips in a series, respectively. (You can create a series of clips by specifying multiple URLs in a metafile; the clips are then stored on a playlist and played successively.) As with the Play/Pause and Stop methods, you have to be sure that a next item exists (or a previous one, in the case of the DoPrevItem( ) method). The HasNextItem( ) and HasPrevItem( ) methods report TRUE if the appropriate items exist. The HasNextItem( ) returns TRUE if multiple clips exist and the current clip is not the last in the series; HasPrevItem( ) returns TRUE if multiple clips exist and the clip that's playing is not the first one in the series.

Letting users have it their way

Every user who has installed a RealAudio Player (including those with ActiveX-enabled browsers who received the control automatically) has a RealAudio preferences file. The preferences stored in the file affect RealAudio Players on the same machine because they all share the same file. Users can edit the file by using the RealAudio Preferences dialog box, which you can display by calling the EditPreferences( ) method (see Figure 8-3). (To find out more about methods and how to call them, see Chapter 10.)

Figure 8-3:
Users can adjust the options for RealAudio Players installed on their machines.

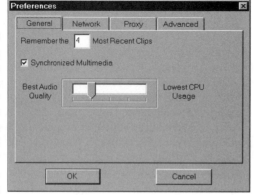

The Synchronized Multimedia box must be checked for users to be able to view and hear pages designed with RealAudio synchronized multimedia.

Lies, damn lies, and statistics

Just as the best-laid plans go awry, so too do RealAudio transmissions. The Connection Statistics box gives users a picture of how smoothly they're receiving a RealAudio signal, as shown in Figure 8-4. The statistics that are displayed summarize the reliability of the connection between the RealAudio server and a user's machine. If the sound quality is poor, it may be because much of the sound is lost on the way to a user's computer — the Statistics window can tell you whether that's the case.

If the Connection Statistics box isn't already on-screen, you can display it by calling the HideShowStatistics( ) method. You don't have to look at a user's screen to know whether the window is already displayed because the IsStatisticsVisible( ) tells you. If the Connection Statistics box is already displayed on-screen, the IsStatisticsVisible( ) method returns TRUE. You can hide the Statistics window from view by calling HideShowStatistics( ). (If you want to find out more about methods and calling them, see Chapter 10.)

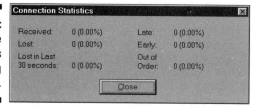

Figure 8-4:
Making sure
that things
are going
well.

At a low level, the Internet and similar networks exchange packets of data. A *packet* is a small bundle of information sent as a discrete unit. Sometimes a packet that is sent never arrives at its destination — the packet gets lost. Also, because packets have no set route to follow to travel from one computer to another across the Internet, one packet may be sent immediately following another and yet follow a much different path to reach its destination. Because different packets follow different paths, packets can arrive out of order because some paths are faster than others. The statistics that RealAudio displays reflect these problems.

The RealAudio Control Hosts Some Major Events

The RealAudio control includes events to let you know what's going on in the control's world. If a new clip is opened or a clip is closed, for example, the control notifies your script by firing an event. The control's events are listed in Table 8-3. If you want to use events, you have to know about some basic scripting (covered in Chapter 10) and a few things about events (discussed in Chapter 11).

Table 8-3	Events in the Life of a RealAudio Control
Event	**What It Means**
OnClipOpened	A clip has been opened by the control.
OnClipClosed	Fires just before the first clip plays and after a clip has closed and no clip is currently open.
OnShowStatus	The text in the Status window (which may or may not be visible) is changing.
OnGotoURL	A URL event has been encountered for the RealAudio clip that's playing (occurs only if the AutoGotoURL property is FALSE).

Although the word *frame* is usually used to describe windows that consist of several panes, every browser window has at least one frame. The single window displayed by most browsers is a frame, even if it's not split into panes.

When one clip closes, another opens (OnClipOpened and OnClipClosed)

```
Sub ObjectName_OnClipOpened(shortClipname, url)
Sub ObjectName_OnClipClosed()
```

When an audio clip is opened for play, it's a significant event in the life of a RealAudio Player. To celebrate, the player triggers an OnClipOpened event and offers the name of the clip and the clip's URL to anyone who is listening. You can use scripting to link actions with clip openings. In Figure 8-5, you can see the result of the following script fragment (EOL is a global variable I defined to insert a new line):

```
Sub RealAudioPlayer_OnClipOpened(shortClipName, url)
    ClipOpenMsg = "OnClipOpen has fired!" & EOL & EOL & "The
            clip name is: " & shortClipname & EOL & "The URL
            is: " & url
    MsgBox(ClipOpenMsg)
end sub
```

The OnClipOpen event fires before the clip is loaded — even before the player's display is updated. In Figure 8-5, you see that the player in the background is blank because the clip hasn't yet been loaded.

The other side of opening is closing, which is also a big deal to a RealAudio Player, so it has a complementary event: OnClipClosed. If a clip has just closed and no current clip is playing, an OnClipClosed event is fired. If you have just loaded a page with a RealAudio Player, the following sequence of events is generated after a user presses the Play button:

```
OnClipClosed
OnClipOpen
OnClipClosed
```

If you load a page with a player that starts up automatically (because the AutoStart property is TRUE), the initial OnClipClosed and OnClipOpen events do not occur: The player just begins playing the first clip.

Figure 8-5:
It's opening
night for
the hot
new clip.
Whenever
a clip is
opened, the
player fires
off an
OnClipOpen
event that
carries with
it the short
name for the
clip and the
clip's URL.

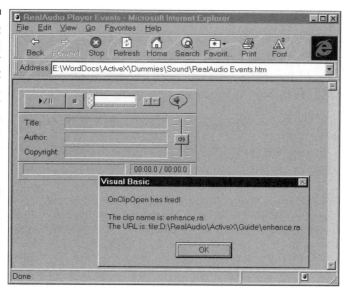

Giving your player some status (OnShowStatus)

```
Sub ObjectName_OnShowStatus(statusText)
```

The RealAudio ActiveX control lets you know when the text in the Status window is changing, by triggering an OnShowStatus event. The status text appears in the Status window, as shown in Figure 8-6. The event tells you not only that the status text has changed but also even what the new text is. The OnShowStatus event includes a parameter called statusText, which is a string with the new status text. This event is handy if you want to display your own Status window. You might want to "dress up" a RealAudio Player, for example, by creating your own components and then using scripts to duplicate the original components. You might display only a Play/Pause button and then use a Label control to show the status text in different colors or fonts.

Depending on the player's Controls property, the Status window might not be displayed. (Refer to Table 8-1 for more information about Controls.)

Going to a URL

```
Sub ObjectName_OnGotoURL(url,target)
```

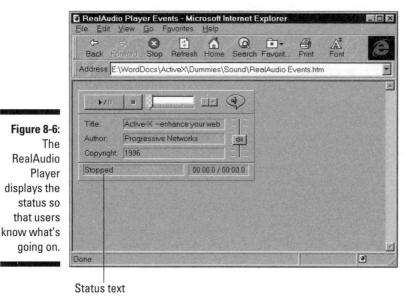

Figure 8-6:
The
RealAudio
Player
displays the
status so
that users
know what's
going on.

Status text

The OnGotoURL event enables you to respond to URL events through scripts you write rather than through a user's browser. The event is used together with the AUTOGOTO property and the DoGotoURL() method. The following section talks about the OnGotoURL event.

Intercepting URL events

The RealAudio control lets you specify how URL events are handled, but you usually don't need this flexibility. A *URL event* is an event inserted into an audio clip to enable synchronized multimedia presentations. The URL event tells the RealAudio Player to ask the browser to load a new page. (For more information about URL events, see the following section.) If you're not using synchronized multimedia to create slide shows, you can probably skip both this section and the following one. Shoot, you can even forget about AutoGotoURL, DoGotoURL(), and OnGotoURL. If you're looking to complicate your life by using synchronized multimedia, this short section explains AutoGotoURL, DoGotoURL(), and OnGotoURL in detail.

As a page designer, you decide what happens when a URL event occurs while an audio clip is playing. A URL event can be either passed on to the browser or handled through scripts you write. If a URL event is passed on to the browser (the typical situation), the browser most likely will load the new page specified by the URL. With the RealAudio ActiveX control, however, you can handle URL events on your own — but only ones that occur while the control is playing an audio clip.

The RealAudio control has three elements for handling URL events: a property (AutoGotoURL), a method (DoGotoURL()), and an event (OnGotoURL). (The RealAudio control's events are listed back in Table 8-3.) If you want to handle URL events in your own script, you must set the AutoGotoURL property to TRUE. This action forces the control to trigger an OnGotoURL event, which you can handle in a script. If you then want to load the URL in your script, you must call the DoGotoURL() method. The method DoGotoURL() takes two parameters: a URL and a target. The URL is the address of the page to load, and the target is where the page is loaded; you should specify a frame as the target.

Synchronize, Synchronize, Synchronize

The RealAudio Player's strength is audio, but you can use RealAudio tools to combine audio with Web pages to create a multimedia slide show for visitors to your site. Using RealAudio *synchronized multimedia,* you can link successive Web pages with an audio track, and the RealAudio Player keeps the audio and pages in step with each other. The audio serves as a timeline; as a user moves through the audio, the timeline is also advanced.

For people who live outside the world of ActiveX, the RealAudio plug-in also works with synchronized multimedia events, as does the stand-alone player.

Although synchronized multimedia works with a RealAudio plug-in, sending the Web browser to a new URL loads the new page and unloads the RealAudio plug-in. To avoid this problem, you should use frames: one frame for the RealAudio Player and a second frame for slides in your slide show. (For more information about frames, see Chapter 3.)

Because RealAudio is an audio tool at heart, synchronized multimedia starts with the audio. After you have created (and encoded) the audio clips, the Timeline Editor enables you to play the clip and insert events at any point in the audio clip, as shown in Figure 8-7. (RealAudio does not support synchronized multimedia events with live audio.) The events are incorporated into the audio clip, and the RealAudio Player triggers the events during playback. Some events change the author, title, or copyright text that's displayed, and others load a new page into the browser (a URL event). The URL events enable you to create slide show presentations by causing the browser to load a specified page as the audio clip plays — users can sit back as the audio is played and new text and images are loaded into the browser window, in time with the audio.

Although the term *event* is used for both control events (such as Click or MouseMove) and events for synchronized multimedia, they are different kinds of events. You can use events that are built in to controls to write scripts that perform actions, but synchronized multimedia events are used only by the RealAudio Player. (You can write scripts that respond to the URL event; refer to the preceding section.)

The RealAudio system stores the information for the synchronized events in a file with a .rae filename extension. The RealAudio Server automatically locates this file when the listener opens the .ra file. The RealAudio Server then streams audio and event information to the player. As the event information is streamed to the RealAudio Player, the player sends information to the Web browser to tell it when to update the page's content.

If you want to prepare a presentation using synchronized multimedia, follow these steps:

1. **Round up the RealAudio clips you plan to use.**

   You can either encode sound files into the RealAudio format or use existing RealAudio clips. You encode clips by using the RealAudio Encoder, which is available for free from the RealAudio Web site (just hop on over to http://www.realaudio.com/).

2. **Create the Web pages (the slides in the slide show).**

Figure 8-7:
The RealAudio Timeline Editor lets you weave slide shows by adding links to Web pages in step with audio. Users can listen to the audio as update images are displayed.

3. **Start the Timeline Editor. A dialog box asks you to select the initial audio track box. Click the radio button labeled Select audio for new file and then click OK.**

4. **From the Add Audio Clip dialog box that appears, open the first RealAudio clip for the presentation. Play the clip by pressing the Play button on the toolbar.**

   After the clip is playing, you can click the toolbar event buttons to add events at different points in the clip. You can add events to force a jump to a new URL or an event to change the title, author, or copyright. Each type of event has its own button, and you can insert an event by clicking the matching button. As you add events, bars appear on the Timeline Graph to show the starting time and duration of each event.

   After the clip has finished playing, you can drag the bars (which represent events) on the Timeline Graph to adjust their starting times. To change the duration of an event, click the bar and then click in the edit window (in the lower right corner of the Timeline Editor window). You can also change the starting times in the edit window.

5. **Double-click each event's bar in the Timeline Graph or the entry in the Event List.**

   Double-clicking takes you to the edit window, in which you can enter URLs for the URL events or change the text displayed for Title, Author, or Copyright events.

6. **Save the project file by choosing File⇨Save.**

7. **Test the presentation by using the RealAudio Player and a browser, and then reopen the project to fix any problems.**

8. **Build an HTML page, and include a link to the .ram (RealAudio metafile) file created by the Timeline Editor.**

   Following the link from the HTML page should start the presentation so that you can sit back and relax.

After you have created your slide show presentation, users can view it by following the link to the RealAudio metafile. The link takes them to the metafile, which points to the RealAudio clip (a file with the extension .ra). The RealAudio Player loads the audio and displays the first page, and away the user goes.

Don't forget that the pages you display are an integral part of the slide show. You can add images, text, and anything else you would link from a Web page. Users can pause the RealAudio Player to pause the presentation and then follow links or study images on your pages.

Testing your newfound knowledge

1. What is streaming audio?

A. A recording of a babbling brook with animal noises in the background

B. Audio that has boiled over

C. Audio that listeners can hear as it's sent instead of waiting for a file to download and then playing the file back later

D. Audio that runs naked through public places, usually as part of a fraternity initiation

2. RealAudio synchronized multimedia enables you to:

A. Tap your foot in time with music, even if you have no rhythm

B. Create a slide show by linking Web pages that are updated in time with a RealAudio clip

C. Set two multimedia watches to the same time, down to the second

D. Watch a group of seasoned competitors splash around in a pool while doing the same thing at the same time

Try to make the audio *complement* your pages rather than repeat what's on them. If you have built a slide show to sell something, for example, don't record yourself reading the text of the slides and then add that to your presentation. Instead, if you want to sell a hot new product, accompany your slides with fast-paced, upbeat music. (Be careful about whose music you use — long dead composers are much less likely to sue for copyright infringement than current artists.)

The 5th Wave

TESTING THE ™686 CHIP

"IT'S FAST ENOUGH FOR ME.'

Chapter 9

A Penny for Your Thoughts: Getting User Input

· ·

In This Chapter

▶ Making forms for user input

▶ Understanding common properties and methods of form controls

▶ Building check boxes, combo boxes, list boxes, and text boxes for text display and input

▶ Creating option buttons and spin buttons

▶ Setting up pop-up menus for selecting items

· ·

*A*lthough the Web is an excellent forum for presenting information, it's also an effective way to gather information. Most people will talk about anything — you just have to get them started. On the Web, you start users talking by asking them to fill out an online form. Because people spend lots of time filling out forms and standing in line, it's no surprise that they're very good at both. On-line forms range from a few snippets of personal information (name, e-mail address, and telephone number, for example) to online subscription forms for free periodicals that require more information than you could find in a typical medieval monastery.

Many Web sites want to gather information from the site's visitors. The reasons for collecting information are as varied as the people collecting it. Some companies want demographic data about site visitors. Other sites offer services and need information to tailor responses to users' needs. Often forms ask for contact information for follow-ups. Regardless of the reason for soliciting information from users, there's one common thread: Users are being asked to spend time doing something they wouldn't ordinarily do.

When was the last time you were eager to fill out a form? You never hear someone exclaim, "The best part of health insurance is the mountain of forms I have to fill out!" As a page designer, your mission (should you decide to accept it) is to make filling out online forms as painless as possible. Because no one will want to fill out your forms, you also should know users' incentive for completing your form. Sometimes a form is a gateway to downloading free software or accessing additional information. The Goodyear site, for example, offers a tire-selector service: by completing several short forms, you can find just the right tire (Goodyear, of course) for your car.

The tough part of writing about form design is that no good terms describe the people who fill out the forms. Although "form fillers" leaps to mind, it sounds like the additives in a cheap hot dog. "Users" doesn't quite capture it either, because they're filling out forms but not really using anything. In this chapter, I refer to the people who fill out forms as "form filler-outters," or FFOs, for short. Remember that all we do, we do for the good of the FFO.

Form Controls and What They're Good For

The process of building online forms can be tricky because you have to gather many kinds of information. It also must be easy for FFOs everywhere to fill out your forms. As an official ActiveX aficionado, you have access to a wide array of sophisticated controls for creating forms. Making a discussion of all the controls fit in this chapter would be impossible, so the rest of this section is a short guide to the controls in this chapter and their uses, organized by category.

On or off?

Often you want to pose yes–no questions on a form. Do you want green peppers on that? Can we send you e-mail? Do you know how to drive a stick shift? Several controls can be used to ask yes–no or true–false questions. Although each of these controls can be used for the same purpose, each has a slightly different appearance. You can see the lot of them in Figure 9-1. Check boxes let FFOs answer yes–no questions, and check boxes use a check mark to remind FFOs that they have answered yes. OptionButton controls appear as small circles; when an FFO sets an option button to TRUE, a dot appears within the circle. OptionButton controls can also be grouped together so that selecting one deselects all other option buttons in the same group. ToggleButton controls also offer yet another way to say yes or no.

Listing lotsa lists

If you already know what your FFOs will say, you can save them the trouble of writing out the information by presenting a list of choices. Several ActiveX controls make it easy for you to present a list of choices. The ListBox control can offer FFOs many choices from which they can select one or more items, depending on how you have configured the ListBox object. If you know what most FFOs will say but can't cover all the possibilities, you can use a combo box, which combines a list box and text box. With a combo box, FFOs choose from your list or type their own items.

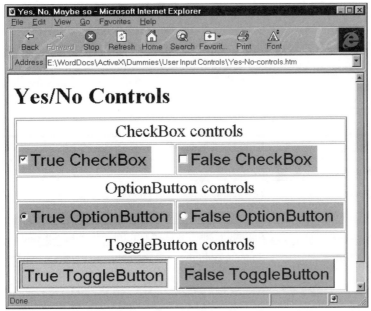

Figure 9-1:
Each of the
ActiveX
controls that
can be used
for yes–no
questions
has a
slightly
different
appearance.

If you want to offer a list of choices but are pressed for space on-screen, you can use a Popup Menu control. A pop-up menu is hidden until an FFO activates it, usually by clicking a button. The menu pops up and then disappears after a choice has been made.

Great literature needs its own control

If you're soliciting free-form responses from visitors to your site, you want to use a text box. FFOs then can type fresh text or edit existing text. Text boxes offer basic editing capabilities, including cut-and-paste and even drag-and-drop. A password feature even hides sensitive text from prying eyes!

Round and round

The SpinButton control doesn't do much on its own; instead, FFOs can use it to change the value of other controls. You can tie a spin button to a text box that displays the name of a month, for example, so that clicking the spin button steps to the next or preceding month, without FFOs having to type the name of the month. (This feature is especially useful for FFOs who can't remember the order of months.) Although this control doesn't sound like much, it gives your pages a professional look.

Common Properties and Their Picky Little Details

You can adapt most form-building controls to different needs by changing the control's properties. Table 9-1 lists the most common properties for form-building controls.

Table 9-1	Common Form Control Properties
Property	*Description*
Accelerator	Sets a shortcut key for an object
Alignment	Sets position of control relative to its caption
AutoSize	Automatically resizes a control to display the entire caption
AutoTab	Specifies whether an automatic tab occurs when the maximum allowable number of characters is entered in a text box
AutoWordSelect	Determines whether words or characters are selected
BackColor	Controls background color, which is usually the predominant color for the control; text is shown in the foreground color
BackStyle	Sets background style to either transparent or opaque (if it's transparent, you can see through the control to what is underneath)
BorderColor	Specifies the color of a control's (optional) border, but only if the border is created with BorderStyle rather than with SpecialEffect
BorderStyle	One of two ways to add a border (SpecialEffect is the other)
Caption	A control's text, sometimes used as a label for the control
Codebase	Address of code that implements control
DragBehavior	Turns drag-and-drop on or off (for controls that support drag-and-drop)
Enabled	Ready and able? Some controls can be disabled to prevent their use but still remain visible
EnterFieldBehavior	Determines what is automatically selected when FFO enters a text field
Font	Font object that determines font characteristics for text; unlike most properties, the font property is an object and not simply a single value
ForeColor	Foreground color, most commonly used to set the text color
Height	Height of the control, in pixels

Property	Description
HideSelection	Determines whether selected text remains highlighted when a control does not have the focus
ID	Name used to identify an object (in Visual Basic, this is the Name property)
IMEMode	Controls mode of the Input Method Editor (IME); applies only to applications written for the Far East
IntegralHeight	Chooses between full lines or partial lines of text, such as AutoSize for height
Left	Distance of a control's upper left corner from the left edge of the HTML Layout that contains the control
Locked	If TRUE, prevents FFOs from altering contents
MaxLength	Maximum number of characters that can be entered in a text box
MouseIcon	Custom icon used as the mouse pointer; used with the MousePointer property
MousePointer	Determines the style of the mouse pointer and can be used with the MouseIcon property to create custom mouse pointers
Picture	Picture (in a bitmap file) to display on an object
PicturePosition	Location of a control's picture relative to the control's caption
ScrollBars	Specifies vertical scroll bars, horizontal scroll bars, both, or none
SelectionMargin	Determines whether a line of text can be selected by clicking in the margin
SelLength	Number of characters selected in a text box
SelStart	Either the starting point of selected text or the insertion point if no text is selected
SelText	Selected text of a control
SpecialEffect	Specifies the visual appearance of an object (flat, raised, or sunken, for example)
TabIndex	Location within an HTML Layout's tab order
TabKeyBehavior	Determines whether pressing Tab key inserts a tab character or jumps to next field
TabStop	Determines whether pressing Tab key stops on an object or passes right on by
Text	Sets the text in a text box or changes the selected row in a list box
TextAlign	Sets the alignment for text within a control

(continued)

Table 9-1 *(continued)*

Property	Description
Top	Vertical distance from the top of a control to the top of the containing HTML Layout
TripleState	Determines whether the NULL state can be chosen for buttons or check boxes
Value	Object's current content
Visible	Determines whether control is hidden or visible (if FALSE, control is hidden; if TRUE, control is visible)
Width	Control's width in pixels
WordWrap	Determines whether text within a control wraps at the end of a line

Many properties that apply to form controls apply also to display controls. They're discussed in Chapter 7 and listed here:

Accelerator	Font	SpecialEffect
AutoSize	ForeColor	TabIndex
BackColor	Height	TabStop
BackStyle	ID	Top
BorderColor	Left	Value
BorderStyle	MousePointer	Visible
Caption	Picture	Width
Codebase	PicturePosition	WordWrap
Enabled		

The property descriptions in this chapter follow the same conventions used in Chapter 7. For a refresher on the format, check out the section "How to Read a Property Description" in Chapter 7.

Alignment

```
object.Alignment [= fmAlignment]
```

Although most form elements include captions to label each item, you can decide which side of the object is labeled. You can choose to place the caption to the right or left of the object (both positions are shown in Figure 9-2). Regardless of which value you choose for the Alignment property (see Table 9-2), the caption is always left-aligned.

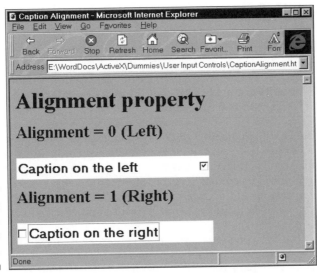

Figure 9-2:
The Alignment property determines how an object's caption is aligned relative to the rest of the object (the caption is always left-aligned).

Table 9-2   Left-Winged and Right-Winged Captions

Constant	Value	Position of Caption
fmAlignmentLeft	0	To the left of the control
fmAlignmentRight	1	To the right of the control (default)

Although the Alignment property exists on the ToggleButton, the property is disabled. You cannot set or return a value for this property on the toggle button.

AutoTab

```
object.AutoTab [= Boolean]
```

For text boxes, the MaxLength property specifies the maximum number of characters that can be entered in the box. After the maximum number of characters is reached, the AutoTab property determines whether FFOs are automatically bumped to the next field.

On a form that accepts zip codes (only the five-digit version) followed by a telephone number, for example, you can use the MaxLength property to set the maximum number of characters for the zip code field to five and then set AutoTab to TRUE. After the fifth digit is entered, the cursor jumps automatically to the telephone field.

Although many controls support the AutoTab property, many do not, so double-check before you use it.

AutoWordSelect

```
object.AutoWordSelect [= Boolean]
```

If you want to select individual characters within words, this property must be set to FALSE; if AutoWordSelect is TRUE, selecting a block of text, even from within a word, always selects entire words.

While testing the TextBox control, I discovered that with AutoWordSelect set to TRUE, using the mouse to select text does indeed select only entire words. From the keyboard (using the Shift and arrow keys), however, I could select individual characters. This contradicts the Microsoft documentation, so it may change in future versions of the control. If you don't like the AutoWordSelect property and you're visiting someone else's TextBox object, it's handy to know.

Imagine that every time you step on the gas in your car, it lurches to the next stoplight — no stopping in the middle of a block. Need to pick up some groceries? You can walk back to the store from the nearest light; that's AutoStoplightSelection. Personally, I despise automatic word selection; if I want to select an entire word, I drag the cursor a few extra characters. Perhaps I'm odd, but I often combine parts of different words by deleting the end of one and the beginning of another. It doesn't matter what you (or I) prefer, of course. You have to design your page based on the preferences of the people who visit your page.

DragBehavior

```
object.DragBehavior [= fmDragBehavior]
```

If you do a great deal of word processing, you're probably already familiar with dragging and dropping text. After you have selected a block of text, you click the mouse within the selection and begin dragging, and an insertion point appears. When you release the mouse (drop the text), the selected text is inserted at the insertion point. Although "drag and drop" is a common buzzword, with text it's really just good ol' "cut and paste" with a couple of steps removed. DragBehavior has its own predefined constants, as listed in Table 9-3.

Table 9-3	**Behavior That's a Drag**	
Constant	*Value*	*Description*
fmDragBehaviorDisabled	0	Prohibits dragging and dropping text (default)
fmDragBehaviorEnabled	1	Drag-and-drop until you drop

There's really no harm in enabling drag-and-drop for text. FFOs who are aware of drag-and-drop can use it without hindering those who haven't been initiated into the sacred rites of text movement.

EnterFieldBehavior

```
object.EnterFieldBehavior [= fmEnterFieldBehavior]
```

Although EnterFieldBehavior sounds like it might control how baseball players take the field, it's not nearly as interesting. Instead, this property determines how selected text is handled when an FFO tabs into a field.

The values for EnterFieldBehavior are listed in Table 9-4. You can either have all the text in the field selected or restore the last selection.

Table 9-4	Selecting Text on Entry	
Constant	*Value*	*What It Does*
fmEnterFieldBehaviorSelectAll	0	Selects every last bit of text upon entry
fmEnterFieldBehaviorRecallSelection	1	Maintains the last selection

When you're designing a form, you often anticipate some responses and supply default values for them. In these cases, you want to select all the text in the field in order to make it easy for FFOs to enter an entirely new, unanticipated response. If you're designing a Web site for the Royal High Order of the Much Maligned Weasel, you might assume that visitors who fill out an online survey are associate members and fill in their affiliation for them. Perhaps the Order's long tradition of defending rodents attracts a cyberpasserby who tackles the survey questions with gusto, in which case you will have misjudged the affiliation. After an FFO tabs to the field, though, the entire text describing the affiliation ("Right Honorable Associate Member of the Royal High Order of the Much Maligned Weasel") is selected, and the FFO's first keystroke replaces the whole bloody thing.

If just a little text is in a field, such as a zip code or telephone number, you should set the EnterFieldBehavior property to select all the text in the control (fmEnterFieldBehaviorSelectAll). If the text control is larger, you should let only a part of the text be selected and retain that selection when the FFO returns to the field.

The EnterFieldBehavior property controls the way text is selected only when an FFO tabs to the control, not when the control receives the focus as a result of the SetFocus( ) method. After a call to SetFocus( ), the contents of the control are not selected and the insertion point appears after the last character in the control's edit region.

HideSelection

```
object.HideSelection [= Boolean]
```

The HideSelection property determines whether text that's selected in a control stays highlighted when the focus moves elsewhere.

If HideSelection is TRUE, the highlighting disappears from the selected text when the focus moves to another field. Don't confuse highlighting with the actual selection, though. If HideSelection is TRUE, the highlighting disappears, but the text is still marked as selected. When an FFO returns to the control (when the control regains the focus), the highlighting returns. The highlighting of the selected text remains, however, if HideSelection is FALSE.

IMEMode

```
object.IMEMode [= fmIMEMode]
```

The World Wide Web lives up to its name as a global phenomenon: People from all over the world browse sites in countries they have never physically visited. When you design pages, you have to remember that people visiting your site may not use the same character set, much less speak the same language. The languages of the Far East in particular use much different characters that are difficult to create with English keyboards. The Input Method Editor (IME) is designed to address this problem. Using the IMEMode property, you can specify which IME mode is used at run time.

If it's important that your forms support hirigana or katakana, you should read the detailed Microsoft reference information about the IME for text controls.

IntegralHeight

```
object.IntegralHeight [= Boolean]
```

Some lines of text are taller than others. If you want a list box to resize itself so that each line is tall enough to show all the text on the line, set this property to TRUE (the default). If you're concerned that the list box may grow beyond the dimensions you have set, you can set IntegralHeight to FALSE — but taller lines of text might be clipped from above.

Locked

```
object.Locked [= Boolean]
```

The Locked property determines whether FFOs can change the data in a field. If Locked is TRUE, the field cannot be changed. A locked text box still displays text, for example, but the FFO cannot edit the text.

Sometimes you want to fill in a field on a form, but you don't want to allow FFOs to change what is in the field. You might create an order form that displays an FFO's customer number, for example, and then want to prevent that person from changing the customer number and placing an order for someone else. You can prevent FFOs from fiddling with the customer number by setting a TextBox control to the customer number and then locking the text box by setting its Locked property to TRUE.

Filling out a form should be a dynamic process: The form itself may change as a result of entries by an FFO. If a customer chooses to pay by check, you have no need to ask for a credit card number. Using the Locked property for the credit card fields, you can prevent anything from being entered in those fields. To do so, you write a script that locks the credit card fields after another form of payment is selected. (For more information about writing scripts for forms, see Chapter 10.)

Even when a control is locked and enabled, it can still initiate events and receive the focus.

MaxLength

```
object.MaxLength [= Long]
```

As Clint Eastwood might say, "A control's gotta know its limitations." One of those limitations, the maximum number of characters accepted by a text control, is set by the object's MaxLength property. No connection exists between the MaxLength setting of a text object and the object's size: If it has more characters than will fit within the object's dimensions, the characters just aren't displayed.

Although a MaxLength of 0 seems short, doing so means that there's no limit on the number of characters, except for the available memory.

Although you might use the MaxLength property to rein in verbose FFOs, you have another reason for setting the maximum length: It acts as a check on FFOs who may mistakenly try to enter more characters than necessary. By setting MaxLength, you ensure that extra characters can't be entered. If you want to include a field for a Social Security number, for example, you have no reason to create a field that's 30 characters long.

The MaxLength and AutoTab properties can work together. If AutoTab is set to TRUE and the maximum number of characters is reached, the FFO automatically jumps to the next field.

PicturePosition

```
object.PicturePosition [= fmPicturePosition]
```

The PicturePosition property sets the location of the picture relative to the picture's caption. The myriad of possibilities are shown in Table 9-5. This property is ignored if no picture is specified by the Picture property.

Table 9-5	Possible Picture Positions		
Constant Relative to Picture	*Value Relative to Caption*	*Picture*	*Caption*
fmPicturePositionLeftTop	0	Left	Aligned with top of picture
fmPicturePositionLeftCenter	1	Left	Centered relative to picture
fmPicturePositionLeftBottom	2	Left	Aligned with bottom
fmPicturePositionRightTop	3	Right	Aligned with top
fmPicturePositionRightCenter	4	Right	Centered relative
fmPicturePositionRightBottom	5	Right	Aligned with bottom
fmPicturePositionAboveLeft	6	Above	Aligned with left edge
fmPicturePositionAboveCenter	7	Above	Centered below picture (default)
fmPicturePositionAboveRight	8	Above	Aligned with right edge
fmPicturePositionBelowLeft	9	Below	Aligned with left edge
fmPicturePositionBelowCenter	10	Below	Centered above picture
fmPicturePositionBelowRight	11	Below	Aligned with right edge
fmPicturePositionCenter	12	Center of control	Centered horizontally and vertically on top

The picture and the caption as a unit are centered on the control. If no caption exists, the picture's location is relative to the center of the control.

ScrollBars

```
object.ScrollBars [= fmScrollBars]
```

If you have used a computer for more than a few minutes, you probably have seen a scroll bar. Although computers give you the power to imagine vast canvases of words and images, most computer monitors are small, and an individual program window is even smaller. With scroll bars, you can move the viewing area so that you can see an area larger than can be displayed.

You control which dimensions can have scroll bars by setting the ScrollBars property to one of the values listed in Table 9-6.

Table 9-6		ScrollBars Possibilities
Constant	*Value*	*Description*
fmScrollBarsNone	0	No scroll bars (default)
fmScrollBarsHorizontal	1	Horizontal scroll bar
fmScrollBarsVertical	2	Vertical scroll bar
fmScrollBarsBoth	3	Both horizontal and vertical scroll bars

If a scroll bar is visible, its scroll box is limited to the visible region of the scroll bar. The *scroll box* is the box drawn within the scroll bar that indicates the relative position of the current viewing area. If a scroll bar is not visible, you can set its scroll position to any value. Negative values and values greater than the scroll size are both valid.

If the ScrollBars property is either fmScrollBarsHorizontal or fmScrollBarsBoth for a single-line control, the control displays a horizontal scroll bar if two conditions are met:

- ✔ The text must be longer than the edit region (otherwise, a scroll bar wouldn't be necessary).
- ✔ Enough room must be available on-screen to display the scroll bar beneath the control's edit region.

A multiline control shows a horizontal scroll bar only if all the following conditions are true:

- ✔ The edit region contains a word longer than the edit region's width.
- ✔ The control has enabled horizontal scroll bars.
- ✔ The control has enough room to include the scroll bar under the edit region.
- ✔ The WordWrap property is set to FALSE.

SelLength

```
object.SelLength [= Long]
```

Where there's text, there's selection. *Selected text* is text that has been marked by either an FFO (using the mouse or keyboard) or through a script. After text is selected, it can be used for any of several operations (cutting and copying, for example). The SelLength property exists to tell a programmer (that's you) how many characters are selected within a text object.

If SelLength is 0, no text is selected. If you set the value of SelLength to less than 0, that's an error. If you set the SelLength property to a value greater than the current number of characters in a text object, however, the SelLength is reset to the actual number of characters. If a text box has 32 characters and you set the SelLength property to 57, for example, the SelLength property is reset to 32.

The SelLength property is *always* valid, even when the text object's selection isn't visible or the object does not have the focus.

If you set the SelStart property in a script (see the following section), any existing selection is canceled, the SelLength is set to 0, and an insertion point is placed in the text.

SelectionMargin

```
object.SelectionMargin [= Boolean]
```

When the SelectionMargin property is TRUE, a small gap (the selection margin) appears beside the text. Clicking within the selection margin selects the current line. When SelectionMargin is FALSE, no margin appears and clicking in the margin simply moves the insertion point. Two text boxes, with and without a selection margin, are shown in Figure 9-3.

If the SelectionMargin property is TRUE when a control is printed, the selection margin is also printed.

SelStart

```
object.SelStart [= Long]
```

The value of the SelStart property is either the number of the character at the starting point of selected text or the location of the insertion point if no text is selected. If you set the value of SelLength to less than 0, that's an error. If you set the value of the SelStart property to a value greater than the current number of characters in a text object, however, the property's value is reset to the actual number of characters.

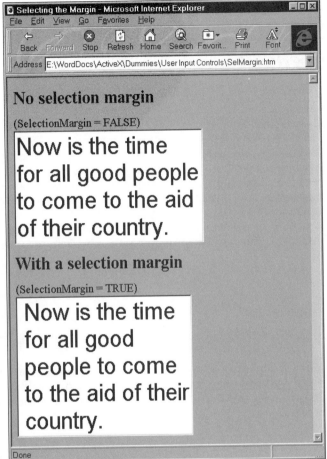

Figure 9-3:
If Selection
Margin is
TRUE, a
gap (the
selection
margin)
appears
beside the
text, and
clicking in
the margin
selects the
current line.

If you change the value of the SelStart property in a script, any existing selection is canceled, SelLength is set to 0, and an insertion point is placed in the text.

The SelStart property is always valid, even when the control does not have focus.

SelText

```
object.SelText [= String]
```

Unlike the SelLength and SelStart properties, which tell you only about the selected text, the SelText property is the real McCoy. If selected text is in a text object, you can retrieve it by using the SelText property.

You can also change the selected text within a text object by setting the SelText property to a new value. (If no text is selected and you set SelText to a new value, the new text is inserted at the insertion point, but no text is selected.)

TabKeyBehavior

```
object.TabKeyBehavior [= Boolean]
```

Tab keys lead a busy life because they have to do double-duty: Sometimes, pressing Tab inserts a Tab character; at other times, pressing Tab jumps to the next field in a form. You can determine just how the Tab key works by setting the TabKeyBehavior property for a control. If TabKeyBehavior is TRUE, pressing Tab inserts a tab character in the edit region; if TabKeyBehavior is FALSE, pressing Tab moves the focus to the next object in the tab order (default).

The TabKeyBehavior property involves a twist, however. If the MultiLine property is FALSE, the Tab key always jumps to the next field regardless of TabKeyBehavior.

Text

```
object.Text [= String]
```

The Text property is the heart of a text control. You can use this property to either get the current text in a control or set the text to a new value. If you set either the Value property or the Text property of a text control, the other is also set to the new value.

TextAlign

```
object.TextAlign [= fmTextAlign]
```

The TextAlign property determines how text within a control is aligned within the control. You can choose to have text left-justified, centered, or right-justified. The values for each alignment are shows in Table 9-7.

Table 9-7		Justify Your Text
Constant	*Value*	*What It Does*
fmTextAlignLeft	1	Aligns first character of text with left edge of control (default)
fmTextAlignCenter	2	Centers text
fmTextAlignRight	3	Aligns last character of text with right edge of control

TripleState

```
object.TripleState [= Boolean]
```

The TripleState property determines whether FFOs can choose the NULL state of a button or check box. A button or check box is shaded when it is set to NULL to distinguish it from TRUE and FALSE. Sample check boxes are shown in each of the three states in Figure 9-4.

Although you can always set a button or check box to NULL by using a script, FFOs can choose only checked (TRUE) or unchecked (FALSE) unless you set TripleState to TRUE. If TripleState is FALSE, FFOs can set a button or check box to only TRUE or FALSE.

Figure 9-4:
Check boxes
and buttons
can have a
third state
(NULL);
buttons
and boxes
that are
currently
NULL are
shaded to
distinguish
them from
TRUE or
FALSE.

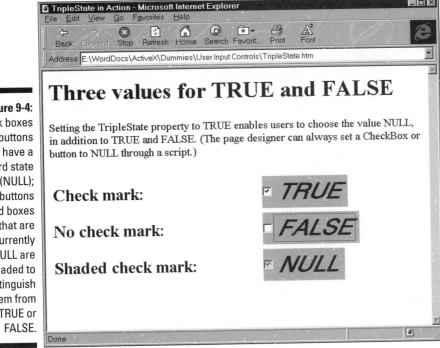

Common Methods of Form Controls

Just as most form controls have similar properties, they have similar methods. The most common methods are listed in Table 9-8.

Table 9-8	Common Methods of Form Controls
Method	*What It Does*
AboutBox()	Displays information about a control's implementation
AddItem()	Adds an item (or row) to a list
Clear()	Removes all items in a list
Copy()	Places selected text in the Clipboard and leaves original selected text
Cut()	Removes selected text and places it in the Clipboard
Paste()	Stuffs Clipboard text into an object
RemoveItem()	Yanks a row of items from a list
SetFocus()	Switches focus to the object invoking SetFocus()
ZOrder()	Moves an object's window to either front or back of the z-order

AboutBox ( )

```
object.AboutBox()AddItem()
```

The AboutBox() method displays a dialog box that provides information about the control's implementation (copyright date and author, for example). For a single-column list box or combo box, AboutBox() adds an item to the list; for a multicolumn list box or combo box, it adds a row to the list:

```
Variant = object.AddItem([ item [, varIndex]])
```

If you supply a valid value for varIndex, the AddItem() method places the item or row at that position within the list. If you omit varIndex, the method adds the item or row to the end of the list. The value of varIndex must not be greater than the value of the ListCount property.

For a multicolumn list box or combo box, AddItem() inserts an entire row; that is, it inserts an item for each column of the control. To assign values to an item beyond the first column, use the List or Column property and specify the row and column of the item.

You can add more than one row at a time to a combo box or list box by using List.

AddItem( ) is the best way to insert items into a single-column list box or combo box. If you have to add columns to a multicolumn list box or combo box, use the List or Column properties rather than AddItem( ).

Clear ( )

```
object.Clear
```

Proceed with caution: For a list box or combo box, Clear( ) removes everything from the list.

Copy ( )

```
object.Copy
```

The Copy( ) method places a copy of the selected content (as defined by the current selection) into the Clipboard. For a text box or combo box, the Copy( ) method copies the currently selected text.

Cut ( )

```
object.Cut
```

The Cut( ) method removes the selected content from an object and places it on the Clipboard. For a combo box or text box, the Cut( ) method moves the selected text to the Clipboard. The object invoking Cut( ) does not have to have the focus. If it does not a current selection, however, nothing happens.

Paste ( )

```
object.Paste
```

The Paste( ) method copies whatever is on the Clipboard into the current object. The TextBox and ComboBox controls interpret everything pasted into them as text.

RemoveItem ( )

```
Boolean = object.RemoveItem(rowIndex)
```

Removes a row from the array of items in a list box (or the list box part of a combo box). Because the row numbering begins with 0, an index of 1 indicates the second row.

SetFocus ( )

```
object.SetFocus
```

The SetFocus( ) method switches the focus to the object that invoked the SetFocus method. Although FFOs typically shift the focus by clicking the mouse on a new object or by pressing the Tab key on a form, you can use the SetFocus( ) method to switch the focus from a script. It's possible that the object that's supposed to receive the focus can't do so. If you attempt to set the focus to an object that can't receive it, the focus reverts to the preceding object and an error is generated.

Setting the focus to a control usually does not activate the control's window or place it on top of other controls. You should be careful that the FFO is expecting a change of focus and that it's obvious where the new focus is. You can switch the focus to a TextBox object that's covered by other windows so that FFOs can type text in the text box without seeing anything change.

ZOrder

```
object.ZOrder( [ zPosition])
```

Although *z-order* sounds like an instruction to a French waiter, it's really the order in which overlapping windows are displayed on-screen. Windows at the top of the z-order are shown in the foreground; windows farther back in the z-order are shown in the background, as shown in Figure 9-5.

Using the ZOrder( ) method, you can send a window to the front of the z-order or to the back. You specify either the front or back by setting the zPosition parameter when you call the ZOrder( ) method; the values for zPosition are shown in Table 9-9.

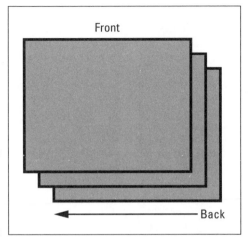

Figure 9-5:
Windows
stacked in
z-order.

Front

Back

Table 9-9		Changing a Control's Place in Line with ZOrder( )
zPosition	*Value*	*Where the Window Appears*
fmTop	0	At the front of the z-order (by default), on top of other controls
fmBottom	1	At the back of the z-order, underneath other controls

Reading All about a Control

Many ActiveX controls are useful for designing forms, and several are described in this chapter. Each control is presented in a similar format. The control descriptions begin with an overview of the control, which focuses on what the control does and how it can be useful to you. Next, the properties of the control are listed. The property listing shows all the properties for a given control so that you know which properties are available. Within the property listing, some properties are shown in boldface. These properties are either unique to a particular control or work differently from the same property in other controls. Only the marked properties are discussed in detail; unmarked properties have already been described earlier in this chapter, in the section "Common Properties and Their Picky Little Details."

A listing and description of the events the control supports follow the property listing. The event listing is similar to the property listing: All events supported are listed, but only the special events are marked and discussed. Unlike the unmarked properties (which are discussed in this chapter), the unmarked events are discussed in Chapter 11. Because the events are more complicated and their use requires some familiarity with scripting, you have to hang on until Chapter 12.

Each control description ends with a listing and discussion of the control's methods. As with properties, only the marked methods are described under each control. The methods most commonly found in form controls are discussed earlier in this chapter, in the section "Common Methods of Form Controls."

CheckBox: Understanding When a Simple Yes or No Will Do

We all have choices to make in life, and yes–no choices are among the best — you have a 50-50 chance of picking the right one. When you want to offer one of these simple choices, you can limit the discussion by using a CheckBox control. Although this control isn't much to look at, it's invaluable for creating forms. Figure 9-6 shows several CheckBox controls in action.

The list box also lets you put a check mark by selected options so that you can use the list box rather than a group of CheckBox controls.

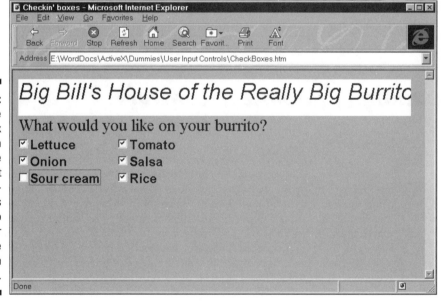

Figure 9-6: The CheckBox objects on this page indicate that this fat-conscious burrito consumer leaves the sour cream in the fridge.

Much ado about null

When you add a check box to a form you're working on, you usually have to decide whether you want the check box to start in the TRUE or FALSE state. The catch is that you may set a check box to TRUE when an FFO wants FALSE. "No problem," you say, "the esteemed FFO can simply click the check box, and it's FALSE." What if the FFO slips right past that check box? If you only had a way to tell whether the check box was clicked, you could rest more easily at night.

The solution to this problem is nothing — or more specifically, the NULL state. The NULL state is an "extra" state along with TRUE (checked) and FALSE (unchecked). You can use a short script to initialize your form and then use the script to set all your check boxes to NULL. If you add the NULL state to your check boxes, you can wait until an FFO completes the form and then use a script to check whether any of your check boxes is still NULL. If you find a check box that is NULL, you can pop up a brief message to inform the kindly FFO to choose between truth and falsity.

Properties

Although check boxes have many properties, most are common to form controls:

Accelerator	ForeColor	SpecialEffect
Alignment	Height	TabIndex
AutoSize	ID	TabStop
BackColor	Left	Top
BackStyle	Locked	TripleState
Caption	MouseIcon	Value
Codebase	MousePointer	Visible
Enabled	Picture	Width
Font	PicturePosition	WordWrap

Enabled

```
object.Enabled [= Boolean]
```

A disabled check box shows the current value but is dimmed and does not allow changes to the value from the user interface.

Events

All the CheckBox events are discussed in Chapter 11, along with examples of their use:

BeforeDragOver	Enter	MouseDown
BeforeDropOrPaste	Error	MouseMove
Change	Exit	MouseUp
Click	KeyDown	
DblClick	KeyUp	

The Microsoft Control Pad Help file also lists the AfterUpdate and BeforeUpdate events as applying to several form controls, including CheckBox. After some research, however, I have not been able to use either of these events with any control embedded in a Web page.

If you want to know when an object's data has changed, use the Change event. Although the Change event is easy to use, you should remember that it fires whenever an FFO does anything with the data in an object, regardless of whether the data actually changes. If an FFO clicks on a check box to change it from checked to unchecked, for example, and then clicks again to change it back, two Change events are generated — even though the check box has returned to its original, checked state.

Methods

You can find a description of both methods for CheckBox controls, SetFocus( ) and ZOrder( ), earlier in this chapter, in the section "Common Methods of Form Controls."

ComboBox: Have Your List and Eat Your Text Too

The ComboBox control combines the text capabilities of a single-line text box with the list capabilities of a list box. Using the text box portion, an FFO can enter a new value or choose an existing value, as with a list box. In Figure 9-7, the FFO is using one of four ComboBox objects to enter a new animal (ferret) that isn't on the drop-down list. ComboBox controls are wonderful if you think that FFOs will probably choose from a prepared list and occasionally enter a new item.

Entering a new item in the text box portion of a combo box doesn't add the item to the drop-down list — it simply sets the combo box's Value property to the entered item (although if you want to add the typed-in item to the list, you can do so with a script).

The list in a combo box consists of rows of text. Each row can have one or more columns, which can appear with or without headings. Some applications do not support column headings; others provide only limited support.

A combo box shows only a single line of text (unless the FFO is actively selecting an item from the drop-down list). If you want more than a single line to be visible at all times, you should use a ListBox control. If you want to use a combo box and limit values to those in the list, you can set the Style property of the combo box so that the control looks like a drop-down list box.

Properties

The properties of a ComboBox control are listed here, with the special properties of combo boxes shown in **boldface;** because a combo box is a combination of a list box and a text box, the combo box shares many properties with each of these controls:

AutoSize	ForeColor	SelLength
AutoTab	Height	SelStart
AutoWordSelect	HideSelection	SelectionMargin
BackColor	ID	SelText
BackStyle	IMEMode	**ShowDropButtonWhen**
BorderColor	Left	SpecialEffect
BorderStyle	List	**Style**
BoundColumn	ListCount	TabIndex
CodeBase	ListIndex	TabStop
Column	**ListRows**	Text
ColumnCount	ListStyle	TextAlign
ColumnHeads	**ListWidth**	TextColumn
ColumnWidths	Locked	Top
DragBehavior	MatchEntry	TopIndex
DropButtonStyle	**MatchRequired**	Value
Enabled	MaxLength	Visible
EnterFieldBehavior	MouseIcon	Width
Font	MousePointer	

Rather than duplicate descriptions of properties discussed elsewhere, Table 9-10 shows in which major section of this chapter the special properties of ComboBox controls are discussed. The ComboBox column refers to the section "ComboBox: Have Your List and Eat Your Text Too"; the ListBox column refers to the section "Making a List Box and Checking It Twice"; and the TextBox column refers to the section "TextBox: Asking for User Input (And Showing That You Care)." In the table, properties unique to combo boxes are marked as ComboBox.

Table 9-10	Where to Find Descriptions of Special ComboBox Properties		
Property	*ComboBox*	*ListBox*	*TextBox*
BoundColumn		X	
Column		X	
ColumnCount		X	
ColumnHeads		X	
ColumnWidths		X	
DropButtonStyle	X		
List		X	
ListCount			X
ListIndex		X	
ListRows	X		
ListStyle		X	
ListWidth	X		
MatchEntry		X	
MatchRequired	X		
ShowDropButtonWhen	X		
Style	X		
TextColumn		X	
TopIndex		X	
Value		X	

DropButtonStyle

```
object.DropButtonStyle [= fmDropButtonStyle]
```

Although combo boxes offer a list box component, the text box portion is all that FFOs see at first — the list box is hidden away in a drop-down list. A *drop-down list* is a list in which only the first line is shown and an FFO must press a button to see the rest of the list. After the button is pressed, the list is drawn with the first item on a line below the button and remaining items listed below the first. FFOs need a "drop button" to access the list, and the DropButtonStyle property determines what the button looks like.

The four drop button styles, shown in Figure 9-8, are listed in Table 9-11.

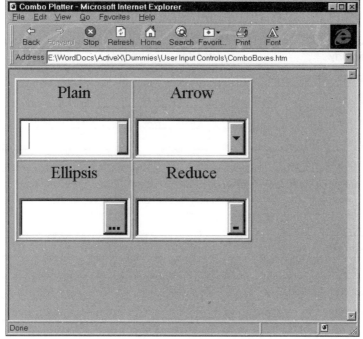

Figure 9-8:
The
ComboBox
control
offers four
button
styles for
displaying
the drop-
down list
associated
with a
combo box.

Table 9-11		Drop Button Styles
Constant	*Value*	*Description*
fmDropButtonStylePlain	0	Plain button, with no symbol
fmDropButtonStyleArrow	1	Down arrow (default)
fmDropButtonStyleEllipsis	2	Ellipsis (. . .)
fmDropButtonStyleReduce	3	Horizontal line, such as an underscore character

If all you have is a button that displays the list when clicked, use the fmDropButtonStyleArrow setting.

ListRows

```
object.ListRows [= Long]
```

The ListRows property sets the maximum number of items to display in the drop-down list before a scroll bar is shown. If you don't specify a value, the default value of 8 is used. If the number of items in the list exceeds the value of the ListRows property, a scroll bar appears at the right edge of the list box portion of the combo box.

The hidden meaning of buttons

The various styles of drop buttons weren't chosen randomly; each style has a particular meaning in the Windows interface. An ellipsis indicates that clicking it brings up a dialog box. The Font property in the Properties dialog box in Microsoft Control Pad, for example, uses an ellipsis to bring up the Font dialog box. The reduce symbol (a short underscore drawn at the bottom of the button) is used as the Minimize button in Windows 95. You should use these styles only if your design is consistent with these standards, or else you may confuse your FFOs.

If you want to use a combo box in an offbeat way (popping up a dialog box when the drop button is clicked, for example), feel free to do so. You have to write a custom procedure for the ComboBox DropButtonClick event, however, because the default action for clicking the button simply shows the drop-down list.

ListWidth

```
object.ListWidth [= Variant]
```

The ListWidth property sets the width of the drop-down list. The list is, by default, as wide as the text portion of the control, but the list and text portions can be different widths. If you set ListWidth to 0, the list is the same width as the ComboBox. If you want to display a multicolumn list, enter a value that makes the list box wide enough to fit all the columns.

Be sure to make the combo box wide enough to display your data and a vertical scroll bar.

MatchRequired

```
object.MatchRequired [= Boolean]
```

Although FFOs can enter a new value in the text box portion of a combo box, you can prevent them from doing so with the MatchRequired property. If you want to use a combo box as a fancy list box, you can force FFOs to either choose an item from the drop-down list or restrict them to entering a list item in the text portion. Although FFOs can choose whether to type an entry themselves or choose it from the list, they always have to choose one of the items you have listed. FFOs can enter nonmatching values but may not leave the control until the text that's entered matches one of the list items.

Using a combo box with MatchRequired has an advantage over a plain list box: FFOs can see what they have typed in the TextBox portion of the control. With a ListBox control, you can set the MatchEntry property to complete matching, and then the control jumps to the item whose initial characters match what the FFO has typed. The problem is that the characters that are typed aren't shown anywhere. With a combo box, the FFO always knows what has been entered because it's in the text portion. (Remember that even with MatchRequired set to TRUE, FFOs can still type partial matches but can't leave the control until there's a complete match.)

Not all ComboBox implementations support MatchRequired, so test it out before you count on it.

ShowDropButtonWhen

```
object.ShowDropButtonWhen [= fmShowDropButtonWhen]
```

Combo boxes use drop buttons to open and close the list portion of the control. As the designer, you decide when to show the drop button. You can choose from among the values of fmShowDropButtonWhen, which are listed in Table 9-12.

Table 9-12	When to Show the Drop Button	
Constant	*Value*	*When to Show the Button*
fmShowDropButtonWhenNever	0	Never
fmShowDropButtonWhenFocus	1	Only when the control has the focus
fmShowDropButtonWhenAlways	2	Always (default)

Style

```
object.Style [= fmStyle]
```

When you create a combo box, you decide whether FFOs can type an entry and choose from the list or only choose from the list. In a drop-down style combo box (the default style), FFOs can type a value in the edit region or choose from the drop-down list. In a list box style, FFOs can only choose from the list — no typing allowed. You can choose from the two styles in Table 9-13.

Table 9-13	Type and List or Just List?	
Constant	*Value*	*Description*
fmStyleDropDownCombo	0	Drop-down combo box
fmStyleDropDownList	2	List box style

Events

Although most of the Style events are discussed in Chapter 11, here's a list of the events triggered by a ComboBox:

AfterUpdate	DblClick	KeyPress
BeforeDragOver	**DropButtonClick**	KeyUp
BeforeDropOrPaste	Enter	MouseDown
BeforeUpdate	Error	MouseMove
Change	Exit	MouseUp
Click	KeyDown	

DropButtonClick

```
Sub object_DropButtonClick( )
```

The DropButtonClick event fires either because the event was triggered in a script or because of an FFO's actions. In a script, calling the DropDown( ) method initiates the DropButtonClick event. FFOs can trigger a DropButtonClick event in one of two ways: by clicking the drop-down button on the control or by pressing the F4 key. The DropDown( ) method, drop button, and F4 key all have the same effect: They make the drop-down list appear if it's not displayed or hide the list if it's already displayed. Whether the list is going up or down, a DropButtonClick event fires.

Methods

Of all the ComboBox methods, only one — DropDown( ) — is unique to the ComboBox control; all other methods are discussed earlier in this chapter, in the section "Common Methods of Form Controls":

AddItem( )	Cut( )	RemoveItem( )
Clear( )	**DropDown**	SetFocus( )
Copy( )	Paste( )	ZOrder( )

DropDown

```
object.DropDown
```

DropDown displays the list portion of a combo box or dismisses the list if it is currently displayed.

Making a List Box and Checking It Twice

Choices, choices, choices. Although the world is full of choices, there aren't many good ways to present all those choices. Enter the list box: If you want to present a list of choices, the list box may be just the ticket. A ListBox object can present a list of choices in any of three formats, as shown in Figure 9-9. Although only two different list styles are available (plain list and option button), three different appearances are possible. The meeting-scheduler application shown in the figure uses list boxes in each of the three styles:

- ✔ Plain
- ✔ Option button without MultiSelect
- ✔ Option button with MultiSelect

Using the ListStyle property, you decide whether a list box is displayed as a plain list or as a group of option buttons (for more information about option buttons, see the section "Knowing Your Option Buttons," later in this chapter). You also decide whether FFOs can choose only one or more than one item by setting the MultiSelect property. (List boxes in the OptionButton style are displayed differently if more than one item can be chosen, as discussed later in this chapter.)

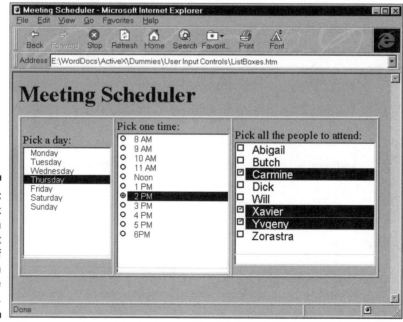

Figure 9-9:
A ListBox object can present a list of choices in these three formats.

Properties

The ListBox control can be used for more than just listing items, a capability that's reflected in its many properties:

BackColor	Height	**MultiSelect**
BorderColor	ID	**Selected**
BorderStyle	IMEMode	SpecialEffect
BoundColumn	IntegralHeight	TabIndex
CodeBase	Left	TabStop
Column	**List**	**Text**
ColumnCount	**ListIndex**	**TextColumn**
ColumnHeads	**ListStyle**	Top
ColumnWidths	Locked	**TopIndex**
Enabled	**MatchEntry**	Value
Font	MouseIcon	Visible
ForeColor	MousePointer	Width

BoundColumn

```
object.BoundColumn [= Variant]
```

Although a ListBox control can have only one value (which is stored in the Value property), it can display several columns. After an FFO has selected a row, how does the control know which value from within the row to use? That's the job of the BoundColumn property: The FFO selects a row, and the BoundColumn property picks the column that uniquely identifies one value for the control.

You can use the BoundColumn property in conjunction with the TextColumn property to display one set of values (which the FFO sees) and use another set as the "behind the scenes" values. In a calendar application, for example, you may want to use numbers for the days of the week and allow FFOs to use the familiar names to select a particular day. To create a multicolumn list box that has columns for both the days of the week and numbers, you can enter the following:

```
<OBJECT ID="ListBoxDays" WIDTH=160 HEIGHT=210
        CLASSID="CLSID:8BD21D20-EC42-11CE-9E0D-00AA006002F3">
        <PARAM NAME="ScrollBars" VALUE="3">
        <PARAM NAME="DisplayStyle" VALUE="2">
```

(continued)

(continued)

```
            <PARAM NAME="Size" VALUE="3387;4445">
            <PARAM NAME="TextColumn" VALUE="1">
            <PARAM NAME="BoundColumn" VALUE="2">
            <PARAM NAME="ColumnCount" VALUE="1">
            <PARAM NAME="MatchEntry" VALUE="0">
            <PARAM NAME="FontName" VALUE="Arial">
            <PARAM NAME="FontHeight" VALUE="200">
            <PARAM NAME="FontCharSet" VALUE="0">
            <PARAM NAME="FontPitchAndFamily" VALUE="2">
            <PARAM NAME="FontWeight" VALUE="0">
</OBJECT>
```

Because the ColumnCount is the number of columns to display, not the number of columns stored in the object, it's set to 1 rather than 2. By setting the TextColumn property to the first column and the BoundColumn to the second column, FFOs see the day names; the value of the control is the numbers corresponding to the days.

In the following code, I have created the array of days and numbers (called Days) that will be used with a ListBox object for choosing a day:

```
' Add days of the week to ListBoxDays
Dim Days(6, 1)

Days(0, 0)= "Monday"
Days(1, 0)= "Tuesday"
Days(2, 0)= "Wednesday"
Days(3, 0)= "Thursday"
Days(4, 0)= "Friday"
Days(5, 0)= "Saturday"
Days(6, 0)= "Sunday"

'Assign the numbers to days of the week
for ii = 0 to 6
   Days(ii, 1) = ii
next

'Stuff the Days array into the ListBox object
'(Assign Days to the List property instead
'   of the Column property, which transposes the
'   array values.)
ListBoxDays.List = Days
```

The text days of the week are stored in the first column, and the numbers are stored in the second. Because the ListBox object has TextColumn set to 1 and BoundColumn set to 2, the text days of the week are displayed, but the object's Value property is set to a number. If an FFO chooses Wednesday, for example, ListBoxDays.Value is 2 (Wednesday's number).

If you have trouble using TextColumn to display a column, try putting the text to display in the first column and setting TextColumn to –1. Then set the BoundColumn property to whichever column after the first you want to use as the value for the ListBox.

Don't be confused by the wacky numbering system used for different properties (even within the same controls). When you're setting the BoundColumn and TextColumn properties, you begin with column 1 as the first column and column 2 as the second column. It seems reasonable, but other properties (such as Column, List and ListIndex) use zero-based numbering, which means that the third column is column 2. Because this is simply one of life's little inconsistencies, unfortunately, you just have to be on your toes.

If you set the BoundColumn property to 0, the value of the item pointed to by ListIndex is assigned to the control.

Column

```
object.Column( column [, row] ) [= Variant]
```

In a multicolumn list box, you need some way to pluck a value from the crowd by specifying the row and column. If you specify only the value for a column, you get a whole column. You could assign a column's worth of values in this way. If you want to be specific, though, you can specify both the column and row to narrow it to one item. You can use the Column property to load an entire two-dimensional array in one shot, by specifying:

```
ListBox1.Column = MyArray
```

Arrays are usually assigned by the row first and then the column, as in (row, column), rather than the column first and then the row (column, row) format used in the Column property. That means that the array you assign is loaded into the list box *transposed* — what was in the second row, third column (2, 3) is now in the third row, second column (3, 2).

For example, your array would change as follows:

```
              1    2    3                    1    4    7
MyArray  =    4    5    6      Column  =     2    5    8
              7    8    9                    3    6    9
```

If you want to copy an array but don't want it transposed, you can assign it to the List property rather than use the Column property.

ColumnCount

```
object.ColumnCount [= Long]
```

If you're using a multicolumn list box, you can set the number of visible columns through the ColumnCount property. On a product order form, for example, you could use three columns to show the item number, item name, and price, with one item in each row. If you set ColumnCount to 0, zero columns are displayed. If you set ColumnCount to –1, the list box displays all columns that fit within the width of the list box.

ColumnHeads

```
object.ColumnHeads [= Boolean]
```

In a multicolumn list box, you can use the first row of each column as the heading for that column. To do so, set the ColumnHeads property to TRUE; the default value is FALSE. If you use the first item in each column as the heading, that item cannot be selected.

ColumnWidths

```
object.ColumnWidths [= String]
```

The ColumnWidths property gives you control over the width of each column. You can set the width of every column with a single statement by separating the width with semicolons (;). If you a specify a number without any units as a width, it's measured in points ($1/72$ of an inch). You can use another unit of measure by including the units as well. You could set the widths of three columns, for example, by using the following:

```
ListBox3.ColumnWidths = "90;3.2in;6cm"
```

If you specify a width of 0 for a column, the column is hidden. A blank value, or a width of –1 (which is replaced by a blank value), tells the control to space columns evenly. If you specify the width for several columns and leave several widths blank (or set to –1), the control allocates space evenly among the controls with blank widths. For columns whose width is calculated, the minimum width is 72 points (1 inch). If you want columns smaller than that, you have to specify it yourself.

List

```
object.List( row, column ) [= Variant]
object.List = Array
```

The values for a list box are stored in the List property, which you can use to both retrieve and set values. You can specify the entire array displayed in a multicolumn list box by assigning an array variable directly to the List property. Be careful, though, because this replaces any previous items in the ListBox array.

If you assign an array to a ListBox's Column property, the array is transposed. Assigning the array to the List property avoids the transposition. (For more information about transposing arrays, see the "Column" section, a few pages back.)

ListIndex

```
object.ListIndex [= Variant]
```

The ListIndex is the index of the currently selected item in the control. You can set this property through code to change the selected item. If no item is selected, the ListIndex is set to –1. Because ListIndex makes sense only if just one item can be "the currently selected item," it doesn't work if you have the MultiSelect property set to TRUE. (Instead, the Selected property holds the currently selected items.)

If you set the BoundColumn property to TRUE, the value of ListIndex is assigned as the object's value. If Thanksgiving is the sixth holiday listed in a list box displaying holidays and the FFO chooses Thanksgiving, for example, ListIndex is set to 6. If the BoundColumn property is 0, the list box's Value property is set to the value of ListIndex, which is now 6. (If BoundColumn were instead set to 1, the list box's Value would be the string "Thanksgiving.")

ListStyle

```
object.ListStyle [= fmListStyle]
```

The ListBox control can display lists in two different styles: plain and option button. The appearance of a list box depends on the style and whether FFOs can choose more than one item (determined by the MultiSelect property, as described in the upcoming section "MultiSelect"). The ListBox styles are summarized in Table 9-14 (the last column tells you which of the three list boxes shown in Figure 9-9 matches a particular style).

Table 9-14	A List of ListStyles		
ListStyle	*MultiSelect*	*Looks Like*	*Position in Figure 9-9*
fmListStylePlain (0)	Yes	Plain list	Left
fmListStylePlain (0)	No	Plain list	Left
fmListStyleOption (1)	Yes	List with check boxes	Right
fmListStyleOption (1)	No	List with radio buttons	Middle

The default value of ListStyle is 0 for controls with MultiSelect set to fmMultiSelectSingle and 1 (with check boxes) otherwise.

ListStyle can be somewhat confusing because it has two styles and because list boxes can be displayed in three formats. If you choose the option button style, the ListBox object's appearance depends on the value of the MultiSelect pro-perty. If you limit FFOs to selecting one of the choices, the list box is drawn as a stack of radio buttons, as shown in the middle list box in Figure 9-9. (A *radio button* is one of a group of buttons of which only one at a time can be selected — selecting one button deselects the previous button. For more information about radio buttons, see the description of the OptionButton control.) If you enable FFOs to choose more than one item from a list in the option style, they see instead a list with check boxes next to each item, as shown in the last of the three ListBox objects in Figure 9-9. If you choose the plain style, FFOs see an ordinary list of items, as shown in the first ListBox object in Figure 9-9, which looks the same regardless of whether MultiSelect is enabled.

Try to use the option button style rather than the plain style. The plain style makes it difficult to tell whether you (as the designer) intended for FFOs to choose exactly one or more than one item. Although FFOs can experiment with choosing more than one item, radio buttons and check boxes are common elements across many platforms; most FFOs know simply by looking at the ListBox object, therefore, whether more than one item can be selected. As a bonus, you know instantly, just by glancing at your handiwork, whether you have accidentally set the MultiSelect property incorrectly.

MatchEntry

```
object.MatchEntry [= fmMatchEntry]
```

The ListBox control features built-in search capabilities, which make it easier for FFOs to select a single choice from many choices. You determine the search behavior by setting the MatchEntry property. The possible values for MatchEntry are listed in Table 9-15 (in this case, "matching" means matching characters typed by FFOs to characters in the items of the list box).

Table 9-15	The Many Ways to Match Entries	
Constant	*Value*	*What It Does*
fmMatchEntryFirstLetter	0	Jumps to the next entry that begins with the character that's entered
fmMatchEntryComplete	1	Searches for an entry matching all the characters entered so far (default search)
fmMatchEntryNone	2	Performs no matching

You can choose between matching and no matching. If you choose matching, you can use either of two methods:

✔ **First-letter method:** An FFO types a letter, and the ListBox object jumps to the next item that begins with that letter. Suppose that a list box offers an array of fruit: apple, banana, cantaloupe, fig, grape, lemon, and lime. When an FFO presses l , the list box jumps to lemon. If l is pressed again, the list box jumps to lime. If the l key is pressed a third time, the list box jumps back to lemon. If b is pressed, however, the list box jumps to banana.

✔ **Complete-entry method:** The list box tries to find the item that matches all the characters typed so far. Imagine a ListBox object that lists these items: a, aardvark, . . ., far, foment, fond, fondle, fondue, forest, garage, garbage, . . ., zoo, zoology. With so many items beginning with the same letter, the first letter method would be annoying. Pressing f would jump to the first word beginning with *f*. If an FFO wants to choose forest, that's a large number of f keys. As the designer, though, you can help by setting the list box to use complete matching. Then, when an FFO types f, the list box jumps to far, jumps to foment when the FFO enters o, and then jumps to forest when the FFO enters **r**.

If you have only a few items beginning with each letter, use the first-letter method (fmMatchEntryFirstLetter). A list of states in an address form, for example, could use first-letter matching. If several items begin with the same letter, you should use complete-entry matching (fmMatchEntryComplete).

MultiSelect

```
object.MultiSelect [= fmMultiSelect]
```

Sometimes it's difficult to narrow many choices to just one. You can spare FFOs that pain by allowing multiple selections. A list box can be used to allow FFOs to choose several items from a list simultaneously. You can decide not only whether to allow only one selection or multiple selections but also how multiple selections can be made (simple or extended). The possibilities for multiple selections are shown in Table 9-16.

Table 9-16   Multiple Ways to Select Multiple Items

Constant	Value	Description
fmMultiSelectSingle	0	One item at a time (default)
fmMultiSelectSimple	1	Pressing spacebar or clicking an item selects or deselects it
fmMultiSelectExtended	2	Ctrl/Shift selections

If you choose simple selection (fmMultiSelectSimple), FFOs can select an item by pressing the spacebar while the item is highlighted or by clicking the item. (Clicking an item highlights and selects it in one step.) FFOs can deselect an item in the same way — by pressing the spacebar while the item is highlighted or by clicking the item.

If you like to complicate things, you can use extended selections by setting MultiSelect to fmMultiSelectExtended. In the world of extended selections, pressing the spacebar does nothing, and clicking an item selects the clicked item and deselects everything else. If FFOs want to select more than one item, they can do so in two ways:

✔ **Select all the items between (and including) two items:** FFOs click the mouse button and then click the second item while holding down the Shift key. (They can also press the arrow keys to extend a selection.)

✔ **Hold down the Ctrl key while clicking an item:** This method selects that item (or deselects the item if it's already selected). FFOs can select several items, none of which is adjacent to one another, by Ctrl+clicking each item.

The problem with multiple selections is that FFOs can't tell by looking at a list box how to select multiple items. Although it's possible to experiment, the Ctrl/Shift+click technique is Windows-centric and may never occur to non-Windows users. To avoid frustrating them more than necessary, make sure that they know (or can find out) how to select multiple items.

The appearance of a ListBox object depends partly on the MutliSelect property. For more information about how MultiSelect affects the appearance of a list box, flip back a couple of pages to Table 9-14.

The default value of ListStyle is 0 for controls with MultiSelect set to fmMultiSelectSingle, and is 1 (with check boxes) otherwise.

Selected

```
object.Selected(index) [= Boolean]
```

After a selection (or selections) is made from the list box, you have to know which items were chosen. Although the ListIndex property contains the number of the chosen item for single-select lists, that property can indicate only a single list item. For multiple selection lists, more than one item can be chosen; you need an array, therefore, to mark the selected items. That's where the Selected property steps in.

For multiple selection lists, the Select property is an array the same size as the array of items. Rather than hold the items in a list, though, the elements of the Selected array are either TRUE (if the corresponding item is selected) or FALSE (if the corresponding item is not selected).

Suppose that a list box offers several kinds of fruit and that the List property holds these items:

```
Index          0        1        2           3       4
FruitList.List   Apples   Banana   Cantaloupe   Figs   Grapes
```

If an intrepid Web shopper chooses bananas, figs, and grapes, the Selected property contains an array with these values:

```
Index          0        1        2        3        4
FruitList.Selected   FALSE    TRUE     FALSE    TRUE     TRUE
```

If you use an index value for the Selected array that's out of range to get a value, you receive an error message complaining about an "invalid argument." If you write the following line of code based on the preceding example:

```
MsgBox("The sixth item's selection value is: " &_
    FruitList.Selected(6))
```

VBScript complains that 6 is an invalid argument because the last item in the Selected array has index 4.

You can use the Selected property for more than just finding out what an FFO has selected — you can select (and deselect) items yourself. If you want to create a list box that starts with some items already selected, you can set the appropriate indices of the Selected property array to TRUE. If you want to display a list of people with several people selected in advance, for example, you include the following script fragment:

```
'Add people to third ListBox
People(0) = "Abigail"
People(1) = "Butch"
People(2) = "Yvgeny"
People(3) = "Zorastra"

for ii = 0 to 3
   ListBoxPeople.AddItem(People(ii))
next

ListBoxPeople.Selected(1) = TRUE
ListBoxPeople.Selected(2) = TRUE
```

Now when the ListBoxPeople object is displayed, Butch and Yvgeny are already selected.

If you try to set a value in the Selected array using an index that's out of range, you don't receive an error message, and no value is set.

Suppose that you write this piece of script:

```
If LikeBananas = TRUE then FruitList.Selected(-1) = TRUE
```

Because no item in the Selected property array has an index set to –1, nothing happens — no error and nothing is set. (Although you may think that errors are bad and that having no errors is a good thing, that's not the case. Errors such as "array index is invalid" are helpful because they help you track down mistakes more easily.)

Text

```
object.Text [= String]
```

For a list box, the Text property sets the selected row and resets the Value property.

TextColumn

```
object.TextColumn [= Variant]
```

The TextColumn property sets the column that's displayed in the list box. You can use the BoundColumn property in conjunction with the TextColumn property to display one set of values (which FFOs see) and use another set as the "behind the scenes" values. In a calendar application, for example, you may want to use numbers for the days of the week but allow FFOs to use the familiar names to select a particular day. (For more information, see the section "BoundColumn," a little earlier in this chapter.)

If you have trouble using TextColumn to display a column, try putting the text to display in the first column and setting TextColumn to –1. Then set the BoundColumn property to whichever column after the first one you want to use as the value for the list box.

TopIndex

```
object.TopIndex [= Variant]
```

Just because an item appears first in the List array of a list box doesn't mean that it must be shown first when the list is displayed. TopIndex determines which item is shown first in the list box. If TopIndex is 0 or –1, the first item in the list is displayed.

Events

Events for the ListBox control are the same as for most other form controls (each event is discussed in detail in Chapter 11):

AfterUpdate	DblClick	KeyPress
BeforeDragOver	Enter	KeyUp
BeforeDropOrPaste	Error	MouseDown
BeforeUpdate	Exit	MouseMove
Change	KeyDown	MouseUp
Click		

Methods

All the methods for the ListBox control are discussed at the beginning of this chapter, in the section "Common Methods of Form Controls":

AddItem( )   SetFocus( )

Clear( )   ZOrder( )

RemoveItem( )

Knowing Your Option Buttons

The OptionButton control is a team player that works best in a group with other option buttons. A group of option buttons can be used as radio buttons. A *group* of option buttons is the collection of all option buttons within the same container, all of which have the same value for the GroupName property. Figure 9-10 shows part of a voting application that uses radio buttons to ensure that only one candidate is chosen.

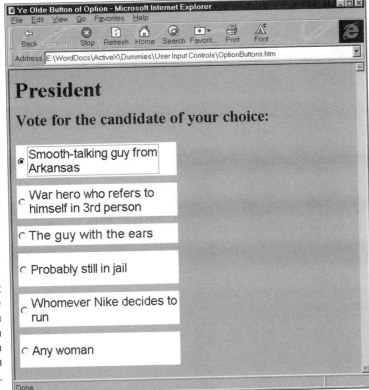

Figure 9-10:
Option buttons can be grouped together as radio buttons to ensure that only one option button within a group can be chosen.

Properties

OptionButton controls share most of their properties with other form controls (discussed in Chapter 7), except for the GroupName property (listed here in **boldface** because it's discussed in this section):

Accelerator	**GroupName**	SpecialEffect
Alignment	Height	TabIndex
AutoSize	ID	TabStop
BackColor	Left	Top
BackStyle	Locked	TripleState
Caption	MouseIcon	Value
CodeBase	MousePointer	Visible
Enabled	Picture	Width
Font	PicturePosition	WordWrap
ForeColor		

GroupName

```
object.GroupName [= String]
```

You can group related option buttons together to create a set of radio buttons. All the option buttons in the same container with the same group name are mutually exclusive: Clicking one button in a group sets all the other buttons in the same group to FALSE. Although you can use the same group name in two containers, doing so creates two groups (one in each container) rather than one group that includes both containers.

To create a set of radio buttons from several OptionButton controls, follow these steps:

1. **Create the OptionButton controls you want.**

2. **Set the ID property of each control.**

3. **For each button in a group, set the GroupName property to the common group name.**

To improve the visual appearance of your HTML Layout, you can create buttons that have a transparent background.

Events

The events for the OptionButton control are the same as for most other form controls (each event is discussed in detail in Chapter 11):

AfterUpdate	Click	KeyPress
BeforeDragOver	DblClick	KeyUp
BeforeDropOrPaste	Enter	MouseDown
BeforeUpdate	Error	MouseMove
Change KeyDown	Exit	MouseUp

Methods

Both the methods for the OptionButton control, SetFocus( ) and ZOrder( ), are discussed at the beginning of this chapter, in the section "Common Methods of Form Controls."

Popup Goes the Menu!

A pop-up menu is a menu of choices that isn't always visible on-screen; the menu pops up only when necessary. Pop-up menus are useful because you can offer FFOs many choices without using up much screen space. Figure 9-11 shows the pop-up menu from a cybercafé. The menu is displayed only after the Today's Specials button is clicked; the pop-up menu vanishes after an item is chosen.

 Popup controls include only the pop-up menu itself and not the associated button. Usually you use a Popup control by creating a button and then displaying the pop-up menu when an FFO clicks the button. To the FFO, it looks as though the button and the pop-up menu are connected. You know the truth, though: The button and menu are linked only by a call in the button's procedure for handling the Click event.

Figure 9-11:
This
cybercafe's
specials are
hidden on a
pop-up
menu and
displayed
only after
someone
has clicked
the Today's
Specials
button.
After an
item is
clicked,
the menu
disappears.

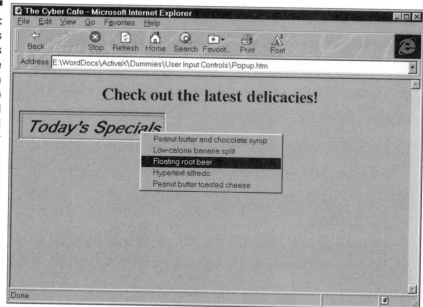

Reading the menu at the cybercafé

To set up a pop-up menu, you need two things: an instance of the Popup control and another item that triggers the pop-up menu. The following HTML code produced the menu shown in Figure 9-10 and is typical for a page with a pop-up menu:

```
<HTML>
<HEAD>
<TITLE>The Cyber Cafe</TITLE>
</HEAD>
<BODY>

<CENTER>
<P>
<FONT SIZE=5>
<B>Check out the latest delicacies!</B>
</FONT>
</CENTER>

<!-- Create the Popup Menu control, the menu
     is displayed when the ShowMenu button
     is pressed -->
<OBJECT
   ID = Iepop
   CODEBASE = "http://www.microsoft.com/ie/download/_
activex/iemenu.ocx#Version=4,70,0,1086"
```

```
    CLASSID="clsid:7823A620-9DD9-11CF-A662-00AA00C066D2"
    WIDTH=1
    HEIGHT=1>

    <PARAM NAME="Menuitem[0]"
        VALUE="Peanut butter and chocolate syrup">
    <PARAM NAME="Menuitem[1]"
        VALUE="Low-calorie banana split">
    <PARAM NAME="Menuitem[2]"
        VALUE="Floating root beer">
    <PARAM NAME="Menuitem[3]"
        VALUE="Hypertext alfredo">
    <PARAM NAME="Menuitem[4]"
        VALUE="Peanut butter toasted cheese">

</OBJECT>

<!-- Create the CommandButton (ShowMenu)
     which triggers the PopUp() menu (Iepop) -->
<OBJECT ID="ShowMenu" WIDTH=265 HEIGHT=52
 CLASSID="CLSID:D7053240-CE69-11CD-A777-00DD01143C57">
    <PARAM NAME="VariousPropertyBits" VALUE="268435483">
    <PARAM NAME="Caption" VALUE="Today's Specials">
    <PARAM NAME="Size" VALUE="5609;1100">
    <PARAM NAME="FontEffects" VALUE="1073741827">
    <PARAM NAME="FontHeight" VALUE="360">
    <PARAM NAME="FontCharSet" VALUE="0">
    <PARAM NAME="FontPitchAndFamily" VALUE="2">
    <PARAM NAME="ParagraphAlign" VALUE="3">
    <PARAM NAME="FontWeight" VALUE="700">
</OBJECT>

<SCRIPT Language="VBScript">

' When the button is clicked, the menu pops up
Sub ShowMenu_Click()
   call Iepop.PopUp()
End Sub

</SCRIPT>

</BODY>
</HTML>
```

The menu items are entered as <PARAM> elements of the menu object beginning with

```
<PARAM NAME="MenuItem[0]" VALUE="Peanut butter and chocolate
            syrup">
```

Although this line may look a little odd, it's one way to enter an array of values — one item at a time.

After the menu itself is created, a button is added, which is used to pop up the menu. Although scripting is covered in detail in Part III, you can see that when an FFO clicks on the menu (the subroutine ShowMenu_Click), the pop-up menu is displayed by calling the PopUp( ) method of the Popup object (named lepop).

Properties

Because the Popup Menu control is used only to support a menu, it has only a few properties:

CodeBase	Left	Top
Height	**MenuItem**	Visible
ID	TabIndex	Width
ItemCount	TabStop	

ItemCount

```
object.ItemCount
```

The ItemCount property stores the number of menu items in a pop-up menu. Although you can read the value of the ItemCount property, you can't set its value.

MenuItem

```
object.MenuItem(Integer) [= String]
```

You have to tell the Popup control which menu choices you want to display, and MenuItem is the way to do it. The choices are specified as an array, which begins with the zero element. (For an example of how to create this array, see the sample HTML code in the section "Reading the menu at the cybercafé," earlier in this chapter.)

The first item is index 0 because the MenuItem array begins at 0, not at 1.

Events

Because FFOs can't do much with a pop-up menu, there's only one event: Click.

Click

```
Click(Integer)
```

When you're using a Popup control, you have to know when FFOs make a choice and which item is chosen. The Click event is generated after an FFO clicks a menu choice (which also closes the menu). In addition, the Click event includes the index of the chosen item. (Don't forget that the first item is 0 because the MenuItem array begins at 0, not at 1.)

Methods

Although the Popup Menu control's methods have familiar names, they're a little different from other methods with the same names because they apply to menus. All the methods of Popup Menu controls are discussed in this section:

AddItem()	**PopUp()**
Clear()	**RemoveItem()**

AddItem ( )

```
object.AddItem(String, index)
```

Add individual menu items with the AddItem() method by passing a String value with the text of the menu item and the index at which to insert the item. If you don't pass a value for the index, the item is added to the end of the menu's list.

Clear ( )

```
object.Clear()
```

The Clear() method removes all menu items from the control. Use Clear() if you want to change the menu on the fly and start from a clean slate.

PopUp ( )

```
object.PopUp(x, y)
```

The PopUp() method pops up the menu on the screen and is usually called by another procedure (a CommandButton's Click event, for example). The *x* and *y* parameters are the coordinates indicating where the menu will pop up; both *x* and *y* are optional. PopUp() uses the current mouse position if either or both coordinates are unspecified.

RemoveItem ( )

```
object.RemoveItem(index)
```

If you don't want to throw it all away with the Clear( ) method, you can remove individual items with the RemoveItem( ) method.

Putting a New Spin on Buttons

SpinButton controls look like adjacent arrows. You use them to step through a series of values. Figure 9-12 shows three spin button controls, each next to a TextBox control. Clicking one of the arrows within a SpinButton moves the value in the corresponding text box up or down.

Spinning your values

Because spin buttons can't display anything on their own, they're really only helper controls: You never use a spin button alone. When a spin button is clicked, its internal value changes, and that's the end of the story. If you want FFOs to know which value they have chosen, you have to add another control to show the spin button's value. In Figure 9-12, for example, each spin button is linked to a text box. As an FFO clicks a spin button, the corresponding text box is updated with the new value. (The text box is still a text box, and FFOs can type a value in the text box without the spin button's help.)

Figure 9-12: SpinButton controls must be linked to another control to display a value because they have no display of their own.

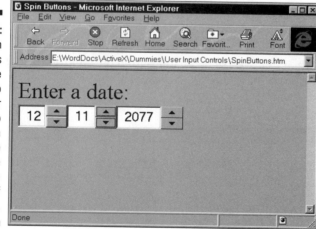

The following three procedures update the text boxes as the spin button is clicked (if these procedures look like gibberish, take a look at Chapter 11 for more details about how they work):

```
Sub SpinButtonDay_Change()
    TextBoxDay.Text = SpinButtonDay.Value
end sub

Sub SpinButtonMonth_Change()
    TextBoxMonth.Text = SpinButtonMonth.Value
end sub

Sub SpinButtonYear_Change()
    TextBoxYear.Text = SpinButtonYear.Value
end sub
```

Whenever a spin button is clicked, the SpinButton control changes its value and generates a Change event. Each SpinButton object has its own procedure for handling a Change event; the procedure simply assigns the spin button's new value to the associated text box. The TextBox object is smart enough to recognize that its value has changed and automatically displays the new value.

Properties

Like Popup Menu controls, SpinButtons are really helper controls that work with other controls. Although they have several properties, only a few are unique to spin buttons. All the properties are listed here (only properties in **boldface** are discussed in this section — the rest are in Chapter 7):

BackColor	Left	TabIndex
CodeBase	**Max**	TabStop
Delay	**Min**	Top
Enabled	MouseIcon	Value
ForeColor	MousePointer	Visible
Height	**Orientation**	Width
ID	**SmallChange**	

Delay

```
object.Delay [= Long]
```

When an FFO clicks on a SpinButton control, the control begins to either increase or decrease (depending on whether the up or down button was pressed). The Delay property lets you (the designer) decide how frequently the spin button's value is changed by setting the lag between updates.

Here's the sequence of events for updating a spin button:

1. FFO clicks and an event is generated immediately.

2. If an FFO holds down the spin button (either the up or down button), a delay occurs between the first (immediate) event and the second event. The delay is equal to five times the value of the Delay property, in milliseconds. (One *millisecond* is $1/1000$ of a second.)

3. Third and following events: If an FFO continues to hold down the mouse button after the second event is generated, successive events are generated every Delay milliseconds, where Delay is the value of the spin button's Delay property.

Because the default value of Delay is 50 milliseconds, the second event occurs 250 milliseconds (five times the specified value) after the first event. Each subsequent event occurs every 50 milliseconds.

Max, Min

```
object.Max [= Long]
object.Min [= Long]
```

The Max and Min properties set the maximum or minimum value for the spin button's Value property setting. If an FFO tries to increase the spin button's value past Max (or decrease it below Min), the spin button's value remains unchanged. The default value is 1.

Orientation

```
object.Orientation [= fmOrientation]
```

Do you prefer your spin buttons to stand up straight (up arrow on top of down arrow) or lie sideways (left arrow to the left of the right arrow)? The Orientation property has an extra twist: The spin button can automatically choose the orientation depending on its relative height and width. Table 9-17 lists the possible SpinButton orientations.

Table 9-17	Orienting a Spin Button	
Constant	*Value*	*Description*
fmOrientationAuto	−1	Automatic orientation (default)
fmOrientationVertical	0	Vertical
fmOrientationHorizontal	1	Horizontal

If you specify automatic orientation (fmOrientationAuto), the relative height and width of the control determine whether the orientation is vertical or horizontal. If a control is wider than it is tall, the spin button is displayed horizontally; if the control is taller than it is wide, the spin button is oriented vertically.

SmallChange

```
object.SmallChange [= Long]
```

Each click of a spin button changes the control's Value property by an amount equal to SmallChange; the default for SmallChange is 1. Although there is a LargeChange property, it applies only to ScrollBar controls, not to SpinButtons.

Events

Although most of the SpinButton's events are discussed in Chapter 11, the two that are unique to the SpinButton control (shown in **boldface**) are discussed in this section:

AfterUpdate	Enter	KeyPress
BeforeDragOver	Error	KeyUp
BeforeDropOrPaste	Exit	**SpinDown**
BeforeUpdate	KeyDown	**SpinUp**
Change		

SpinDown, SpinUp

```
Sub object_SpinDown( )
Sub object_SpinUp( )
```

SpinDown occurs when an FFO clicks the lower or left SpinButton arrow; SpinUp fires when the upper or right arrow is clicked. SpinDown decreases the Value property; SpinUp increases the Value property.

Methods

Both methods for the SpinButton control, SetFocus( ) and ZOrder( ), are discussed at the beginning of this chapter, in the section "Common Methods of Form Controls."

TextBox: Asking for User Input (And Showing That You Care)

When you ask for an FFO's thoughts, you often can't anticipate all possible responses, so you have to be ready for free-form responses. When you're looking for text input, the TextBox control is just what you need. FFOs can enter and edit text by using common Windows conventions, and you get input from every aspiring Hemingway to hit your site. The TextBox includes editing tools on a par with Notepad: You can select text (including auto-word select), jump from word to word, and have text automatically wrap within the control. You can't search the text, however, or have any file commands (Save or Open, for example) available.

Although text boxes are fine for short chunks of text, they lack advanced editing capabilities. If you're asking an essay question, you should either use a more advanced editing control or let FFOs edit a file on their own and then submit it.

Because TextBox controls are flexible, you can adjust lots of properties. Most properties have sane default values, so you don't have to set them yourself. A few interactions among properties, however, can lead to unintended effects. (You may think, for example, that setting the WordWrap property to TRUE would give you word wrapping. Guess again.)

Properties

Text boxes have all the usual form control properties in addition to a raft of properties for editing text. The TextBox control's special properties, shown in **boldface,** are discussed in this section:

AutoSize	Height	SelLength
AutoTab	HideSelection	SelStart
AutoWordSelect	ID	SelText
BackColor	IMEMode	SpecialEffect
BackStyle	IntegralHeight	TabIndex
BorderColor	Left	TabKeyBehavior
BorderStyle	**LineCount**	TabStop
CodeBase	Locked	Text
CurLine	MaxLength	TextAlign
DragBehavior	MouseIcon	Top
Enabled	MousePointer	Value

EnterFieldBehavior	**MultiLine**	Visible
EnterKeyBehavior	**PasswordChar**	Width
Font	**ScrollBars**	**WordWrap**
ForeColor	SelectionMargin	

CurLine

```
object.CurLine [= Long]
```

The CurLine property stores the line that the insertion point is on, counting the first line as 0 (if the TextBox control doesn't have the focus, this property is meaningless).

If you want to set the CurLine property (perhaps to start the FFO at the end of a block of text), check to ensure that the control has the focus; if it doesn't, use the SetFocus() method.

LineCount

```
object.LineCount [ =Long]
```

The LineCount property indicates the number of lines in a TextBox object. It is read-only. The returned value is from 0 to 1 less than the value of LineCount.

MultiLine

```
object.MultiLine [= Boolean]
```

If MultiLine is set to TRUE, a text box can display text across multiple lines; if MultLine is FALSE, all the text goes on one line. A multiline control can have vertical scroll bars, but a single-line text box can't have vertical scroll bars.

Because single-line controls ignore the value of the WordWrap property, don't bother to set the WordWrap property to TRUE unless MultiLine is TRUE.

If you change MultiLine from TRUE to FALSE in a text box, all the characters are combined into one line.

PasswordChar

```
object.PasswordChar [= String]
```

If you ask FFOs to enter sensitive information into a text box, you can protect their privacy by using the PasswordChar property. At design time, you set the property to a single character that appears in the text box no matter what an FFO types. (If you don't specify a character, the control displays the characters that are typed.)

You can use the PasswordChar property to protect sensitive information, such as passwords or security codes.

ScrollBars

```
object.ScrollBars [= fmScrollBars]
```

TextBox controls can display scroll bars in case there isn't enough room to show all the text in the control. You can set the ScrollBars property to any of the values of fmScrollBars (refer to Table 9-6). Whether scroll bars are actually displayed when they're enabled depends on the ScrollBars, WordWrap, and AutoSize properties.

Scroll bars are hidden or displayed according to the following rules:

- ✔ When ScrollBars is set to fmScrollBarsNone, no scroll bar is displayed.

- ✔ When ScrollBars is set to fmScrollBarsVertical or fmScrollBarsBoth, the control displays a vertical scroll bar if the text is longer than the edit region and if the control has enough room to draw the scroll bar itself.

- ✔ When WordWrap is TRUE, a multiline TextBox control does not display a horizontal scroll bar.

WordWrap

```
object.WordWrap [= Boolean]
```

If the MultiLine property of the text box is FALSE, WordWrap is ignored. Text wraps within a text box if WordWrap is TRUE.

Events

Events for the TextBox control are the same as for most other form controls (see Chapter 11):

AfterUpdate	DblClick	KeyPress
BeforeDragOver	Enter	KeyUp
BeforeDropOrPaste	Error	MouseDown
BeforeUpdate	Exit	MouseMove
Change	KeyDown	MouseUp

Methods

All the methods for the TextBox control are discussed at the beginning of this chapter, in the "Common Methods of Form Controls" section:

Copy( )	SetFocus( )
Cut( )	ZOrder( )
Paste( )	

Toggle This!

The ToggleButton control is one of the many ways to answer those pesky yes–no, true–false questions. A ToggleButton object looks like a push-down button, which is pressed down for TRUE and popped up for FALSE. ToggleButton objects switch between true and false (and null, if TripleState is TRUE).

 Although you can't group toggle buttons with a GroupName property, you can group them visually on a page. If you really want only one toggle button selected at a time, you can write a script which ensures that only one of a visual group of toggle buttons is true.

Properties

All the ToggleButton control's properties are described earlier in this chapter, in the section "Common Properties and Their Picky Little Details":

Accelerator	ForeColor	SpecialEffect
Alignment	Height	TabIndex
AutoSize	ID	TabStop
BackColor	Left	Top
BackStyle	Locked	TripleState
Caption	MouseIcon	Value
CodeBase	MousePointer	Visible
Enabled	Picture	Width
Font	PicturePosition	WordWrap

Events

The events for the ToggleButton control are the same as for most other form controls (see Chapter 10):

AfterUpdate	DblClick	KeyPress
BeforeDragOver	Enter	KeyUp
BeforeDropOrPaste	Error	MouseDown
BeforeUpdate	Exit	MouseMove
Change	KeyDown	MouseUp
Click		

Methods

The ToggleButton controls, SetFocus( ) and ZOrder( ), don't know how to do much, and what they do know isn't all that special.

Testing your newfound knowledge

1. A TextBox control is useful for:

A. Letting FFOs edit text.

B. Gift wrapping text as a present.

C. Storing text when it's not in use.

D. Restraining ferocious text that may otherwise escape.

2. Pop-up menus are a good choice:

A. With soda and candy at a movie.

B. When there isn't enough room on-screen to permanently display a menu.

C. When you want to simulate a virtual jack-in-the-box.

D. With a fruity chardonnay that's not dry.

Part III
Scripting
for ActiveX

The 5th Wave **By Rich Tennant**

" RIGHT NOW I'M KEEPING A LOW PROFILE. LAST NIGHT I
CRANKED IT ALL UP AND BLEW OUT THREE BLOCKS OF
STREETLIGHTS."

In this part . . .

ActiveX controls without scripts would be like Laurel without Hardy or Thelma without Louise. Microsoft has thoughtfully developed a stripped-down version of Visual Basic, called VBScript, which is just the right size for writing scripts for ActiveX controls. ActiveX controls are more than just another pretty face — with VBScript, you can put them to work.

Chapter 10

We Don't Need No Stinkin' Scripts

. . . .

In This Chapter

▶ Understanding why you should write a script

▶ Activating ActiveX with scripts

▶ Choosing a scripting language

▶ Understanding what can you do with scripts

. . . .

M ost people would follow a bunch of lemmings over a cliff before they would write a computer program. The process of writing a script looks much like computer programming. Part III of this book is all about writing scripts. Before you head off in search of several despondent lemmings, you should think about how scripting can change your life. You can create a sharp-looking page with ActiveX controls without doing any programming. The big attraction to ActiveX is that you don't have to know computer programming: Just drop in a control, and you look cool.

Without scripting, though, you're missing half the story. A *script* is a short piece of computer programming, written in a scripting language. *Scripting languages* are usually simpler and easier to use than traditional programming languages. Because simplicity comes at the price of power, scripting languages are less capable than their bigger siblings. That's okay, though, because scripting languages are often narrower in scope — they are usually designed for a particular task. Although you can create many special effects with scripting languages, programs you write will be very short and therefore easier to manage.

Why Write a Script?

Avoiding scripting is similar to never learning to cook because you can live on TV dinners: You save the time and effort of cooking a meal yourself, but your menu selections are limited. Scripts do two things for you: squeeze the most from each control and tie together different controls. You can get the most from a control by "adjusting" it with scripts. With scripting, for example, you can control the background displayed in the browser window. Scripts can create teams of controls by responding to some controls to change others. Different menu choices (from a pop-up menu control) can even trigger different movies to be played in an ActiveMovie control.

Although you probably can find better things to do on your vacation, you might consider scripting — it's fun and easy. If you're using the Microsoft Control Pad to build pages with ActiveX controls, you can use the Script Wizard to write scripts for you. If you don't like what the Script Wizard has conjured up, you can easily make a little magic of your own. Scripting languages are designed to be easy to use so that you don't have to be a professional programmer.

Writing Scripts to Activate ActiveX

Users who visit your sites won't be dazzled by your scripts because they won't see them. Scripting an ActiveX site is a little like directing a movie. As a designer, your job is to cast the stars by choosing the right controls to catch the eye and then direct the action. As the site's director, you have to make sure that your stars do the right thing at the right time and that they do it well. That's where scripts come in. By tying together controls through actions, you can create special effects. Just like a director, you and your scripts work behind the scenes, of course, far from the glare of the ActiveX stage. Don't worry, though — people eventually will recognize your creative genius.

What does it mean to "activate your site"? Through scripting, your pages can interact with visitors who flock to your site. You can engage them by giving them more control and keep them coming back. As an example, I created — in just a few minutes — a script that displays a color label on a page and changes the label's colors as a user moves the mouse over the label. The same script also prints the X and Y mouse coordinates in two text boxes. Although the following script is short, I wrote an even smaller part of it (just seven lines); the Script Wizard filled in the rest:

```
<SCRIPT LANGUAGE="VBScript">
<!--
dim XScale
dim YScale
dim MaxColor
MaxColor = 65535

Sub ChangingLabel_MouseMove(Button, Shift, X, Y)
    ChangingLabel.BackColor = INT(X * XScale)
    ChangingLabel.ForeColor = INT(Y * YScale)
    XVal.Text = X
    YVal.Text = Y
end sub
```

```
Sub Layout_OnLoad()
    XScale = INT(MaxColor/ChangingLabel.Width)
    YScale = INT(MaxColor/ChangingLabel.Height)
end sub
-->
</SCRIPT>
```

If you have already done some programming, you can probably figure out with just a quick glance how the script works. (If you have done any Windows programming in C, you know that you can't even say "Hello" in just a few lines of code.) If you haven't ever programmed, you will be dashing off scripts in no time. Friends and family members who knew you before you began programming will stop and stare as you rattle off the perfect script for any occasion.

Figure 10-1 shows the script in action. Although a color-changing label won't cause people to beat down the virtual door to your Web site, with a little more time (maybe another ten minutes), you can create even more dramatic effects.

Figure 10-1:
As a user moves the mouse pointer within the label, the colors change depending on the position of the mouse pointer.

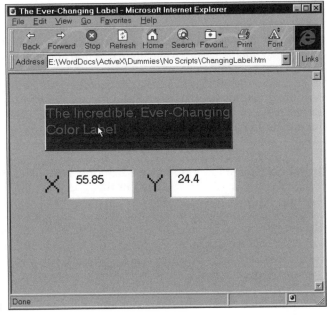

Choosing a Scripting Language (Speaking in Tongues)

Because the ActiveX framework is relatively flexible when it comes to scripting, you can choose from many different scripting languages. It even has a standard for writing your own scripting language from scratch. Personally, I try to avoid doing anything from scratch — I even make brownies from a mix. You can make your life easier by using an existing scripting language. Microsoft Internet Explorer has built-in support for two languages: VB Script and JScript. VBScript is a scaled-down version of Visual Basic, which is a Microsoft tool for writing programs quickly. If you're familiar with JavaScript (from Netscape), you might prefer to use JScript, which is a Microsoft clone of JavaScript.

Although Java and JavaScript sound like they're related, they're not. Java is a full-blown programming language that's similar to the C++ programming language. Writing programs in Java is also more difficult than writing scripts in JavaScript because the code you write with Java must be transformed into a form that Java-enabled applications can understand. With JavaScript, JScript, and VBScript, the computer sees the same code you see. Before a browser (or any other application) can run the commands in a script, the script must be interpreted. *Interpreted* languages are translated, one line at a time, from the scripting code into machine code every time you run a program. Even if the same line of code is run repeatedly (in a loop, for example), the interpreter converts the scripting commands into machine code again every time. Although that makes scripting languages easier to work with (because you don't have to do any translation in advance, as you do with Java), it also makes them run more slowly.

Because Microsoft developed ActiveX, Internet Explorer, and VBScript, VBScript has a synergy with ActiveX and Internet Explorer that you don't find with JavaScript. Unless you have a special affinity for JavaScript and you know that you will be working with Internet Explorer, you probably should write your scripts in VBScript. Until recently, JavaScript offered better coverage because scripts ran with both Internet Explorer and Netscape Navigator; VBScript worked only with Internet Explorer. NCompass Labs has developed an ActiveX plug-in for Navigator, however, that runs VBScript with Navigator.

Figure 10-2 shows the relationship among the various flavors of Visual Basic. Visual Basic, a sophisticated environment for developing applications, is often used for *prototyping* new applications. (When a new application is being developed, a prototype is often developed first. The prototype usually looks and feels like the eventual application but is usually missing the "guts" of the final application.) Visual Basic for Applications (VBA) is a scaled-down version of Visual Basic that Microsoft uses as a macro language for several desktop applications, such as Excel and Word. A *macro language* is a simplified programming language designed to automate repetitive tasks.

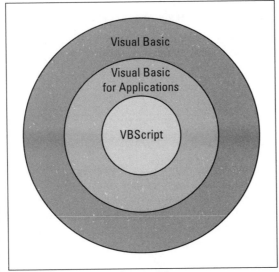

Figure 10-2:
Deeper and deeper: You can view the relationship among Visual Basic, Visual Basic for Applications, and VBScript as a series of concentric circles.

In Figure 10-2, the innermost circle is VBScript, which is a subset of VBA. VBScript is designed specifically for network applications, although developers are free to incorporate VBScript as the scripting language. Visual Basic is either available or being developed for Windows 95 and Windows NT (including native versions for Alpha, MIPS, and PowerPC architectures), 16-bit Windows, and Power Macintosh, and VBScript is being *ported* to other operating systems. (Applications and languages are usually developed on one operating system, and then the original is later changed to run on other operating systems.) Microsoft is working with other companies to provide UNIX versions for Digital, Sun, Hewlett-Packard, and IBM platforms.

What Can You Do With a Script?

Asking what you can do with VBScript is similar to asking, "What kind of things can you write in English?" You can cover a great deal of ground with VBScript, and this section suggests a few concrete ways to apply scripts to common situations. You can do many things without scripts, but your pages must be "preprogrammed": You can't design pages that react to users — you can only lead them down a well-worn path. Lots of well-worn paths are worth traveling, of course, but there's more to life.

With ActiveX controls, scripting, and servers, you can build sites by using any of the following ideas; each is described in more detail in this section.

  ✔ **Action and reaction:** React to user actions by changing colors, playing sounds, showing a movie, or changing the background.

✔ **Interactive forms:** Create forms that users can fill out and submit to place orders, request information, or register for services.

✔ **Play a game:** Build a game that users can play to keep them coming back for more (you can even award prizes to winning players).

✔ **Broadcast news:** Broadcast your own news, including up-to-the-minute animations and live audio.

Acting and reacting

Virtually every ActiveX control can sense many happenings in the world: mouse movements, mouse clicks, and even key presses. You can tie any of these happenings to other actions. Scripting lets you tell the browser what to do for each happening for every object; the actions for each event are independent of one another. Clicking one button might change a color scheme; clicking a second button might fast-forward a video.

When you design a new kitchen, for example, you have to select cabinets, countertops, sinks, appliances, and furniture and then choose colors to coordinate everything. With ActiveX, you can create color-selection objects that change color as a user glides the mouse pointer over objects; after a user clicks the mouse, the color is set and can be applied to any item: countertops, floor, or sink, for example.

Add animations to spice up your new kitchen. A user might click a dial on a gas stove and watch a flame pop up. (To add a touch of realism, you can force users to fiddle with the pilot light before the burner will light.) If you really need to sell more of the polka-dot-striped countertop but customers keep choosing solid colors, no problem — just add video testimonials from satisfied polka dot purchasers who rave about their stylish new kitchen.

After a visitor has assembled the dream kitchen, you can offer a walk-through. Using the Virtual Reality Modeling Language (VRML), you can create a three-dimensional world in which users can pick up objects and view their world from different perspectives. With ActiveX and scripting, you can bring VRML objects to life so that users can flip on a light switch to light a room or flip a fan switch to hear the roar of an exhaust fan.

Designing forms that talk back (interactive forms)

Despite the heart-pounding excitement, Web surfing has been a passive activity. As a surfer roams from site to site, information is sent to the computer, but nothing is coming back to the Web site from the user. ActiveX includes a raft of controls for designing forms that users can then fill out and send in, some of which are shown in Figure 10-3. You can create forms for purchases, requests for information, and sweepstakes entry forms.

Scripting offers you two advantages for creating forms: changing forms and form check-ups. Using scripting, you can build a form that changes as a user fills it out. An order form might keep a running total of a customer's bill and then delete the shipping fields when the customer chooses pickup rather than delivery. You can also double-check the data in a form before sending it off. A script included in a page with a form can check each field in a form to be sure that the information that's entered is reasonable. For example, an address checker might verify that a zip code doesn't contain any letters. You probably can't guarantee that everything a user has entered makes sense, but you can at least catch the most common errors.

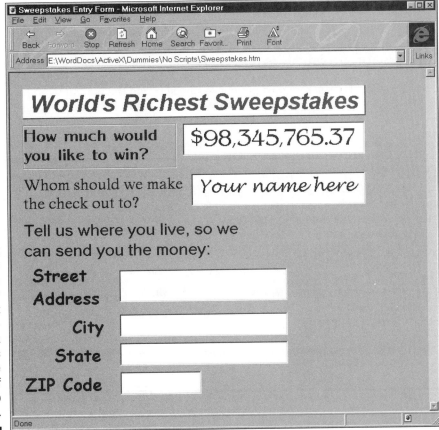

Figure 10-3: Scripting for dollars: You can create forms for users to fill out that change as information is entered or forms that double-check themselves before rushing off to your Web server.

Sharing your view of the world with broadcast news

Start your own news program! If you want to let the world know what you or your company are up to, create a news page. Companies can include stock tickers that show the latest prices, billboards updated with the latest prices and products, and video interviews with the employee of the month. With scripts, you can add boilerplate video to recent sound bites. Imagine your company's news anchorperson declaring, "This just in: Mary in the Do Nothing division of our Big City office has just been promoted to Chief Sales Overseer of All the People Who Sell Those Little Green Things to the Suckers at Those Other Companies."

Playing a game

ActiveX gives you everything you need to create Web-based games for users to play. Well-done games can be a powerful draw for a site and distinguish your site from many others. A medical-supply company might build an emergency room game that lets users operate on patients. A visitor could wield a virtual scalpel to operate on a patient — one slip, and the patient would howl! If a user does poorly, the game can end with that person being served papers announcing that he or she is being sued for medical malpractice.

Testing your newfound knowledge

1. If you add script writing to your ActiveX repertoire, you can:

A. Communicate with animals, just like Dr. Doolittle.

B. Activate ActiveX controls by linking them together.

C. Impress your friends and relatives.

D. Write computer viruses that will bring nations to their knees.

2. VBScript is a good choice for a scripting language because:

A. Hollywood prefers scripts written in VBScript.

B. What's a scripting language?

C. The Script Wizard says so.

D. Microsoft designed VBScript, Internet Explorer, and ActiveX to work together.

Chapter 11

The Basics of Scripting

. . . .

In This Chapter

▶ Writing your first script

▶ Understanding the fundamentals of VBScript

▶ Practicing good scripting habits

▶ Creating variables in scripts

▶ Working with characters and text by using strings

▶ Repeating actions repeatedly within a script

▶ Handling an uncertain world with alternatives

▶ Building complex expressions with operators

▶ Understanding procedures inside and out

▶ Commenting on code you write

. . . .

*A*lthough you can insert ActiveX controls into your pages without scripting a single line, writing programs of your own opens new doors. Microsoft has designed VBScript to work with Internet Explorer and ActiveX controls and to be easy to use. If you have done any programming, you should recognize much of what's in VBScript and learn it quickly. Even if you have never written a program, you can learn to use VBScript. This chapter introduces VBScript, but it doesn't talk much about ActiveX controls. Chapters 12 and 13 describe some techniques for integrating VBScript and ActiveX controls.

What's a Script?

A popular misconception is that computers are smart. The truth is that a computer is as dumb as a rock. Because computers aren't very bright, you can't trust them to do the right thing unless you give them explicit, step-by-step instructions. That's what scripts are for: so that you (and *you* know how to do something) can explain how to do it in terms that are simple enough for a computer to understand. A *script* is a short set of instructions that tell a computer how to do a small job.

Why Write a Script?

Scripts are written to save time. Because computers don't understand much, explaining anything to them involves a great deal of work. To avoid having to give the same set of instructions repeatedly, all the instructions for a task are rounded up in one script. The next time you (or someone else) want the computer to do the same thing, you just tell it to follow the script.

Writing Your First Script

Although it's not widely known, everyone has the muscles that are necessary to wiggle their ears. If you don't practice much, though, your ear-wiggling muscles are probably pretty weak. If you start with regular workouts for your ears, you can build up those muscles and become a full-blown wiggler. (I hear that you can even fan yourself on hot days — if you're really good.) Scripting is much like ear-wiggling because everyone is bad at it to start with, but you can become much better with practice. Remember that the longest journey begins with a single step.

Although you can use many scripting languages for your script writing, I stick with VBScript in this book. VBScript is a free scripting language, created by Microsoft, that is compatible with ActiveX standards for a scripting language.

Introducing "Hello, world!"

Ever since two guys wrote a book about programming in the C language, the traditional first program has been one that prints "Hello, world!" Whenever you agree to write a book that talks about computer programming, you have to swear that you too will use "Hello, World!" as your first example. Here's a short script that follows in the (very deep) footsteps of tradition.

```
<HTML>
<HEAD>
<TITLE>Hello, world!</TITLE>
</HEAD>
<BODY>

<SCRIPT LANGUAGE = "VBScript">
    MsgBox "Hello, world!"
</SCRIPT>

</BODY>
</HTML>
```

If you type this text and then load the page into Internet Explorer, you should see a box just like the one shown in Figure 11-1.

Figure 11-1:
"Hello,
world!"

Understanding how "Hello, world!" works

Because Internet Explorer is, for now, the only program that understands
VBScript, you have to load the script into Explorer. (Because VBScript is an
interpreted language, VBScript programs can't stand on their own. For more
information about interpreted languages, see the nearby sidebar "If you don't
understand VBScript, you need an interpreter.") Internet Explorer understands
only HTML files, so you have to stick the script in the middle of an HTML file.
Most of the text in the preceding example is necessary for the HTML file.

All the lines in the script are contained between the <SCRIPT> tags:

```
<SCRIPT LANGUAGE = "VBScript">
   MsgBox "Hello, world!"
</SCRIPT>
```

The <SCRIPT> tag is a signal that says to the browser, "Hey, don't expect to see
any more HTML code until you come to the next </SCRIPT> tag — it's all code in
a scripting language." Because no law says that a browser can support only one
scripting language, you also have to tell the browser which language you're
using. (If you forget the Language attribute, Internet Explorer assumes that
you're using VBScript, but it's a good idea to include the attribute anyway.)

The entire script is in one line:

```
MsgBox "Hello, world!"
```

This line consists of two parts: a call to the VBScript procedure MsgBox() and a
single argument to the procedure (the string "Hello, world!"). The procedure
MsgBox() is a small script that the VBScript designers have written to display a
message to users. One way to call a procedure in VBScript is to write the
procedure name followed by a space and the procedure's first argument. (An
argument is a value a procedure uses internally; some arguments are required,
and others are not.) When you call a procedure to display a message, you gotta
give it a message to display. In the example, the message is "Hello, world!"; the
message is enclosed in quotation marks so that Internet Explorer knows that
you mean literally the sequence of characters in "Hello, world!" — beginning
with H-e-l-l-o.

If you don't understand VBScript, you need an interpreter

Because computers aren't smart enough to understand even the simplest computer languages that people use, the languages must be translated into an even simpler form that computers can understand. The process begins with your writing some instructions in the language of your choice — VBScript, for example. The scripts you write are called *source code* because those scripts are the source of the computer's instructions. (The term *source code* is used for the instructions people type in any programming language, not just in VBScript.) Although people find source code convenient, computers don't understand a word of it, so it must be translated into an even simpler language.

Computer programming languages come in two flavors, depending on how the source code is translated: compiled and interpreted. In a *compiled* programming language, a translator (called a *compiler*) reads the source code you have written and converts it into *machine code,* which is the only language simple enough for computers to understand. After the program is compiled, the computer can understand it, and you can run it by just typing the name of the program. Compiling a program is similar to translating a book from one language to another: Although it involves a great deal of work, after the work is done, the new book can be taken anywhere and you don't need the original.

Interpreted languages work a little differently. In an *interpreted language,* the source code isn't translated into machine code until the program is actually run. If you're using an interpreted language, you can't do anything without an interpreter. The interpreter reads a line of the source code, translates it into machine code, and then runs the freshly translated line of machine code, which is then run by the computer. Whereas compiling is similar to a translating a book into a new book all at one time, interpreting is similar to reading aloud from a book and translating it as you read each line.

Because VBScript is an interpreted language, you need an interpreter to translate any programs you write. That's where Internet Explorer comes in: Explorer has a VBScript interpreter built into it. When you want to run a VBScript program, you need an interpreter. Although you don't have to use Internet Explorer as your interpreter, all the examples in this book do.

If you have understood this example, you're well on your way to writing your own scripts. Scripting primarily involves calling the right procedure at the right time. Sure, you have to write many of your own procedures, but they too consist of calling other procedures. The hardest part of writing a program is learning to think like a computer — a really dumb computer.

It's not a script — it's a comment

To be properly recognized in HTML, all your VBScript code must be bracketed by <SCRIPT LANGUAGE="VBScript"> and </SCRIPT> tags. You can have as many sets of <SCRIPT> and </SCRIPT> tags as you want, but all your code must be inside one of those sets. You add scripts by using this template:

```
<SCRIPT LANGUAGE="VBScript">
<!--
your code here
-->
</SCRIPT>
```

Although I haven't included the HTML comment tag in my examples, you should use the comment tags (<!-- and -->) inside your <SCRIPT> tags. *Comment tags* mark a section of HTML as a comment the browser should ignore. They prevent browsers that don't understand scripting languages from displaying your script code in the browser window. By adding the comment tags, you guarantee that a browser that doesn't understand the <SCRIPT> tags doesn't display your script as part of the page. Browsers that do understand the <SCRIPT> tags ignore the inner, HTML comment tags and process your script.

Working with Variables

Life is full of uncertainties, and scripts are no exception to the rule. In life (and in scripts), you often know *what;* you just don't know *how much* — and that's where variables come in. On my morning commute, for example, I know that I will encounter traffic delays along the highway, but I don't know how long those delays will last. Or you might know that every employee has a Social Security number, but because you don't know which employee will use your script next, you don't know the Social Security number to use. A *variable* is a name for something whose value is unknown when you write a script. In the two examples just mentioned, I might create variables called TrafficDelay or SocialSecNum to stand in for the unknown values. When you write a script, you create a variable and then use it wherever you need that variable's value in your program. Later, when your script runs, the variable's value is filled in, and everything works out right.

Naming variables

You can't name a variable just any old thing — you have to follow some rules. Although the rules for variable naming are somewhat lax, to be valid, a variable name must

- Begin with a letter
- Be shorter than 256 characters
- Not contain a period
- Not be a *reserved word* — one that's already part of Visual Basic (Sub or Dim, for example)

Here are some variables that pass muster:

- ✓ TrafficDelay
- ✓ Address23
- ✓ DinnerEntree67Tuesday

These variable names are no good:

- ✓ 123Start
- ✓ Today.Year
- ✓ 45Skedoo

The second bad example (Today.Year) might look familiar, but it's not a valid variable name. VBScript has objects, such as embedded ActiveX controls, as well as variables, and objects can have properties (called *members* in other languages).

Here's the syntax for accessing an object member's value:

```
object-name.property-name
```

If an object called Today had a Year property, Today.Year would be the correct way to access the property's value. If VBScript allowed variable names to include a period, VBScript couldn't tell objects' properties from variables whose names include a period. To avoid confusing VBScript (or you), the period (.) is excluded from variable names.

Declaring the independence of variables

After you have settled on a good name, you have to tell VBScript. The process of telling it about your variables is called *declaring* a variable. You declare a variable by using the Dim statement:

```
Dim varname1
```

You can also declare more than one variable at a time by writing a list of variable names after Dim:

```
Dim varname1, varname2, varname3, ...
```

Because it's common practice to declare all your variables up front, the Dim statement should be in either the first few lines of the opening <SCRIPT> tag or the first few lines of a procedure.

In VBScript (and in most versions of Basic), you don't have to use a Dim statement to declare a variable; you can just begin using a variable's name. This idea is a bad one: You can accidentally declare a new variable just by misspelling the name of an old one. If you lack self-discipline, you can ask VBScript to force you to declare all your variables using the Dim statement. The Option Explicit statement tells VBScript, "Don't let me use a variable without declaring it!" If you do try to use an undeclared variable, VBScript signals an error.

To make sure that you walk the straight and narrow, include the Option Explicit statement in your script, before you define any procedures. Your scripts then look like this:

```
<SCRIPT LANGUAGE="VBScript">
Option Explicit
      :
SUB FirstProcedure(...)
      :
SUB LastProcedure(...)
      :
</SCRIPT>
```

Scopin' out variables

Highways all over the United States are named Route 66, and one big highway that runs over most of the United States is also called Route 66. Now *there's* an opportunity for confusion; lots of people drive down a Route 66 every day, however, without getting confused. Suppose that you live in a small county in which the main thoroughfare is Route 66. If you tell me that I should drive down Route 66 and then take the third right, I wouldn't have to ask, "Do you mean the big Route 66 or the one right here in town?" I wouldn't think that you were talking about the Route 66 in another county 200 miles away, either. On the other hand, if neither of us lives anywhere near a Route 66 and you ask whether I have driven down Route 66, I would think that you were talking about the big Route 66. If all this makes sense to you, you already understand variable scoping.

If you declare a variable in a procedure, that variable's scope is limited to the procedure in which it's defined. A variable with procedure-level scope (also called *local scope*) is similar to a county road named Route 66: In that county, Route 66 refers to the county road; after you leave the county, however, Route 66 means something else. Because variables declared in a procedure have only procedure-level scope, you can use the same variable name in every procedure and never worry about confusing VBScript. Sometimes, though, you do want to use the same variable in more than one procedure. *Global variables* apply in every procedure and are said to have script-level scope (because they're visible everywhere inside a script). When people talk about the "big" Route 66, they're using a global variable.

The following script example shows the difference between global and local variable declarations:

```
<SCRIPT LANGUAGE = "VBScript">
Dim ThisIsGlobal    'Global variable

Sub SomeProcedure(...)
   Dim ThisIsLocal    'Local variable
         :
end sub

</SCRIPT>
```

What happens when you create a global variable at the script level and then use the same name for a variable you declare within a procedure? This situation is the same as in counties that have their own Route 66 — there's a global Route 66 (the big one) and a local Route 66 (the county one). In those counties, when somebody says Route 66, they're talking about the local Route 66. It's the same for procedure-level variables — if you use the name of a global variable, the procedure-level variable (the county Route 66) takes precedence.

The following script demonstrates what happens when a procedure-level and a script-level variable have the same name:

```
<SCRIPT LANGUAGE = "VBScript">
Dim LocalRoad 'Global variable (script-level)
LocalRoad = "Big Route 66"

Navigate

Sub Navigate()
   Dim LocalRoad 'Local variable (procedure-level)
   LocalRoad = "County Route 66"
   MsgBox "Local road is: " & LocalRoad
end sub

MsgBox "Local road is: " & LocalRoad
</SCRIPT>
```

If you run the script, a message box pops up saying that LocalRoad is "County Route 66" because it uses the local value. The second message box uses the global value ("Big Route 66"), which is unchanged by the procedure Navigate( ).

Keeping things constant with constants

Few things in life are certain, and for those things VBScript has constants. A *constant* is a variable whose value doesn't change. (Not very variable, is it?) Although death and taxes might be the only certainties in life, a computer's world is a little more stable. Constants commonly used in programming include the ratio of Celsius to Fahrenheit degrees, pi (the ratio of a circle's circumference to its diameter), and TRUE and FALSE.

Although VBScript doesn't allow you to declare your own constants, VBScript does include several predefined constants, as listed in Table 11-1.

Table 11-1	Defined Constants in VBScript
Constant	*What It's Used For*
Empty	Value of uninitialized variables; not the same as Null
False	0
Nothing	Used to break reference links
Null	No valid data; not the same as Empty
True	−1

The constant True has the value −1 for good reason. Digital computers store numbers as a series of bits, which are either on (=1) or off (=0). Because of the way computers store negative numbers, the number whose bits are all on (all equal to 1) is actually −1.

Just because VBScript doesn't give you a way to declare a variable as a constant doesn't mean that you can't pretend that a variable is a constant. If you frequently use a value that doesn't change, use a variable name that is all uppercase to mark the value as a constant and pledge not to change its value. Constants are an important part of your scripts because they make scripts more readable and easier to change.

Suppose that you have a procedure that calculates the circumference of a circle. The following formula

```
Circumference = 2 * PI * radius
```

is more readable than the same formula without constants:

```
Circumference = 2 * 3.141592654 * radius
```

Realizing that all variables are created equal (sort of)

Variables are often created to hold a specific kind of information: Social Security numbers, addresses, or names, for example. In programming, the kind of information a variable is supposed to hold is the variable's *type*. VBScript could treat variables with different kinds of information as different types, but that would involve more work for you. Instead, VBScript uses a compromise — all variables are of the same type: variant.

One of the most common variable types is the string type. A *string* is just a literal sequence of characters, usually enclosed in quotation marks. The "Hello, world!" example used the string "Hello, world!" as the message to display. Because numbers are also important to computers, most programming languages have several different types of numbers. Because TRUE–FALSE values are fairly common, some programming languages include a Boolean type; Boolean values can be only TRUE or FALSE. (*Boolean* is from George Boole, who developed a system of logic using true and false values.)

With VBScript, you don't have to worry about variable types because when you create a variable, it's ready to hold any type of data: numbers, strings, or Boolean (TRUE–FALSE), for example. VBScript is smart enough to recognize some values as being of one type or another. If you assign the variable StepNum the value 2, VBScript realizes that you want StepNum to be a number. If you then want to display StepNum's value using the MsgBox() procedure (from the "Hello, world!" example), you can just write

```
MsgBox StepNum
```

Because MsgBox() expects a string and not a number, VBScript converts the number 2 into the string "2" and hands it off to MsgBox().

Because there are some advantages to dividing variables into different types, VBScript includes subtypes of the one variant type; a *subtype* is a further division of types. Subtypes are really for the benefit of VBScript — you don't have to worry about them because everything is still a variant type. Table 11-2 lists the subtypes in VBScript.

Table 11-2	Subtypes of the VBScript Type Variant	
Subtype	**VarType( ) #**	**Description**
Empty	0	Uninitialized; either 0 for numeric variables or a zero-length string ("") for string variables
Null	1	No valid data
Integer	2	Integers bigger than a byte
Long	3	Big integers
Single	4	Floating-point numbers
Double	5	Really big floating-point numbers
Date	7	Dates between January 1, 100, and December 31, 9999

Subtype	VarType() #	Description
String	8	Variable-length string (no more than about 2 billion characters)
Object	9	OLE Automation object
Error	10	Error number
Boolean	11	Either TRUE or FALSE
Byte	17	Small integer

If you want to know which type of data is stored in a variable, you can use the VarType() function to find out. For each subtype, VarType() returns a different number.

For array variables, VarType() returns a number equal to 8,192 plus a number for the type of array elements. An array of dates VarType(), for example, returns 8,192 (for the array) plus 7 (because of the date elements), for a total of 8,199. The following section has more information about arrays.

Declaring arrays

Although variables are a necessity for programming, sometimes one just isn't enough. An *array* is a single variable that contains other variables in a numbered list. The List property of a ListBox control is an example of an array. A typical ListBox that displays a list of names would use an array of strings:

```
'Add people to third ListBox
People(0) = "Abigail"
People(1) = "Butch"
People(2) = "Carmine"
```

The single variable People is an array that has three elements. (An *element* is a single item in an array.)

To declare an array, you use the VBScript statement Dim:

```
Dim varname(lastIndex)
```

To declare an array of three people, for example, you write

```
Dim People(2)
```

The number you include in parentheses tells VBScript the index of the last item in the array.

The first element of an array is stored at index 0, so the number you include in the Dim statement is one less than the array's total size. In the preceding People example, the number is 2, but the array's size is one more (3).

Arrays aren't limited to being one-dimensional lists; they can be two, three, or even eight dimensional. To add extra dimensions to an array, you still use the Dim statement, but you also include a list of numbers that give the size of the array along each dimension:

```
Dim MultiPeople(3, 4, 5)
```

This statement creates a three-dimensional array that has 120 (4 x 5 x 6) elements in a cube that's four units high by five units wide by six units high.

Creating reference material

With most VBScript variables, when you assign one variable to another, the value of one is copied into another. The following script, for example, assigns one variable's value to another:

```
<SCRIPT LANGUAGE = "VBScript">
    Dim OldVariable, NewVariable

    OldVariable = 32
    NewVariable = OldVariable
        :
    NewVariable = 37        'OldVariable still equals 32
        :
</SCRIPT>
```

In this example, the last line copies OldVariable's value into NewVariable. In later lines of the same script, changing either OldVariable or NewVariable has no effect on the other.

VBScript does have a different type of variable, though, called a reference. A *reference* is a new name for an old variable. When you create a reference, you're saying to VBScript, "I want to use a different name to refer to the same object." References are created by the Set statement, whose syntax is

```
Set objectvar = {objectexpression | Nothing}
```

If you need to break the link between a reference and its value, you assign the reference variable to the VBScript constant Nothing.

Because a reference is really just another name for the same object, changing the value of a reference variable changes the value for all references to the same variable. If you buy a book written by me, for example, you also buy a book written by my wife's husband. The following script illustrates how references work:

```
<SCRIPT LANGUAGE = "VBScript">
   Dim OldVariable, NewVariable

   OldVariable = 32
   Set NewVariable = OldVariable    'New Variable is a
            reference to OldVariable
     :
   NewVariable = 37     'Now OldVariable equals 37 too
     :
</SCRIPT>
```

Stringing Your Data Along

Strings are everywhere because strings are the variables used to store text. Strings are versatile because they're so simple: A *string* is a literal sequence of characters. The message displayed in the "Hello, world!" script was a string. If you need a variable to store an address or record a name, you need a string variable. You can always tell a string when you see it because strings are always enclosed in quotes. The spaces, commas, and other characters would just confuse VBScript, so everything is wrapped up in one set of quotation marks. You can generally put anything you want between the quotes because nobody ever looks inside them.

Because strings are so important, VBScript includes lots of tools for working with strings. The most important string tool is the concatenation operator, whose symbol is the ampersand (&). The concatenation operator combines two strings into one. Here's the syntax for the concatenation operator:

```
result = expression1 & expression2
```

You could have created the string "Hello, world!," for example, by combining two others:

```
HelloWorld = "Hello, " & "world!"
```

In this line, the two separate strings are combined into one, and the result is stored in a variable called HelloWorld. Notice that the left side isn't a string because it's not in quotes — it's just a variable called HelloWorld.

VBScript has many more tools for working with strings to perform the following tasks:

- ✔ Trim extra spaces from the beginning and end of strings
- ✔ Compare two strings
- ✔ Change from uppercase to lowercase and vice versa
- ✔ Select portions from the beginning, middle, or end of strings
- ✔ Create special control characters that can't be typed

Descriptions of each of the string tools are in the Microsoft documentation for VBScript, which is available from the Microsoft Web site. Look for it at `http://www.microsoft.com/vbscript/`.

Going with the Flow of Control

Although it's possible to write a script that moves from one line to the next and never looks back, it's rare. Sometimes you will want to check a variable and do something different depending on its value; at other times, you may want to do the same thing over and over. The *flow of control* is the order in which statements in a script are executed, which could be much different from the order in which they appear in the file. VBScript includes many ways to decide what you want to do next.

Playing what-if?

If you drive to work, you probably know more than one way to get there. If you encounter a problem on one route, you take another. You can't plan in advance, though, because you don't know what's going to happen on any given day. Scripts can be the same way: You have more than one way to go, but you can't decide in advance. VBScript uses the If...Then...Else statement to let you choose between two courses of action.

When it comes to the If statement, you can go it high or you can go it low. Here's the bare-bones syntax:

```
If condition Then statements [Else elsestatements]
```

If you really want to go for the gusto, try this:

```
If condition Then
    [statements]
[ElseIf condition-n Then
    [elseifstatements]] . . .
```

```
[Else
    [elsestatements]]
End If
```

Notice that this definition has lots of square brackets, which means that most of it is optional. The bare-bones version of the syntax in the preceding paragraph just tests a variable's value and does something if it's true:

```
If StoppingByOnASnowyEvening Then Follow RoadLessTraveled
```

If the variable StoppingByOnASnowyEvening is TRUE, you take the road less traveled. You're not limited to testing just one condition, though, because you can use the ElseIf clause:

```
If Personality = "PartyAnimal" Then
    Dress(GorillaSuit)
ElseIf Personality = "WallFlower" Then
    Dress(Ghost)
ElseIf Personality = "Teenager" Then
    Dress(Badly)
End If
```

If you're using an If statement, you have to test a condition and choose what to do based on the value of the condition. A condition is acceptable for an If statement if it's a numeric or string expression that evaluates to TRUE or FALSE. If the condition is Null, it's the same as FALSE.

Looping

Because programming involves as much monotony as anything else, you have to be prepared to do the same thing over and over and over. . . .

VBScript has two kinds of loops:

- ✔ Loops that run a fixed number of times
- ✔ Loops that repeat until a condition becomes TRUE (or FALSE)

"For he's a jolly good Next"

The For...Next loop is one of the most common in programming. Here's the syntax:

```
For counter = start To end [Step step]
    [statements]
    [Exit For]
    [statements]
Next
```

A For...Next loop works by comparing the *counter* variable to the *end* value. If they're equal, nothing happens; if they're not equal, the statements inside the For...Next loop are executed one after another. After all the statements have been run, the value of Step is added to the counter, and the value of *counter* is compared to *end,* and then the process starts over again.

Suppose that an array lists times throughout the day and that you want to add each item to a ListBox control, using the AddItem() method:

```
' Add times to second ListBox
Times(0) = "8 AM"
Times(1) = "9 AM"
'        :              You can do this in VBScript.
'        :              You're just saving some space.
Times(10) = "6PM"

for ii = 0 to 10
   ListBoxTimes.AddItem(Times(ii))
next
```

The For...Next loop starts with a counter equal to 0 (because that's the first item in the array) and adds each item in the array, one at a time. There's no line where the value of the counter ii is increased because the For...Next loop does it automatically. The counter ii eventually reaches 10, the last item is added, and the loop stops. When the loop is finished, VBScript starts with the first statement following the loop.

It's considered poor taste to change the value of the loop's counter within the loop. You can use the value of the counter in the loop, but don't assign a new value to it. The following code, for example, would be frowned on by most programmers:

```
for ii = 0 to 7
   MsgBox "The current counter is " & ii
   if Today = "Tuesday" then ii = 3
next
```

In the second line of the For...Next loop, the loop counter (ii) is assigned to 3.

Adding a little spice to your For...Next loop

The For...Next loop syntax has two extras: Step and Exit For. The Step parameter lets you change the value that's added to the counter after each pass through the loop. By setting Step to 3, you can count up three at a time. The loop still runs only once for each change, but the counter variable is increased by the size of Step.

You can use a For...Next loop to count down by setting Step to a negative number. After each pass through the loop, Step is added to the counter variable; if Step is negative, the counter goes down after each pass.

Sometimes in the middle of a loop, you realize that you want to stop without continuing the loop. If VBScript encounters an Exit For statement in your loop, it jumps out of the loop and begins executing the statement following the loop (just as though it had finished with the loop on its own). The Exit For statement is usually executed as part of an If statement:

```
for ii = 0 to 7
   MsgBox "The current counter is " & ii
   if Today = "Tuesday" then Exit For
next
```

Doing the loop thing

Although the For...Next loop is handy, it has a drawback: You have to know how many times the loop should run before starting the loop for the first time. (Remember that you have to set a start and end value for the loop, which must be done before the loop's first cycle.) Other VBScript loops let you keep looping until something happens (until a condition becomes TRUE or FALSE). The Do loop is the most flexible loop in VBScript, which also means that it's the most complicated. The syntax for Do is

```
Do [{While | Until} condition]
   [statements]
   [Exit Do]
   [statements]
Loop
```

While you're waiting

If you use the While form of a Do loop, the loop keeps going over and over as long as the condition you have specified is TRUE. If you were writing a political campaign simulation game, for example, you might use a Do loop:

```
Do While CampaignSeason
   MakeSpeech HotTopic, Constituents
   AcceptContributions InterestGroup
   KissBabies
      :
   CampaignSeason = CheckCalendar Today, ElectionDay
Loop
```

In this Do loop, VBScript keeps going (making speeches, kissing babies, and other things) until the campaign season is over. At the end of each cycle, the script checks the calendar to see whether ElectionDay has arrived. If there's still another day, then CampaignSeason is still TRUE and the loop runs again. Eventually, ElectionDay comes and CampaignSeason's value becomes FALSE; then the loop stops running.

In a For...Next loop, you're not supposed to change the value of the loop counter. With a Do loop, however, you must change the value being tested. Suppose in the preceding example that the last line were left out (so that the value of Campaign Season never changed). The loop's condition would always be TRUE (assuming that it started out that way), and the loop would run forever (called an *infinite loop*).

Until we meet again

With the Do loop, you don't have to wait for a TRUE condition to become FALSE. You can also turn it around by looping as long as a condition is FALSE and then stopping when it becomes TRUE. A Do loop of the following form starts if the condition is FALSE and keeps looping until it becomes TRUE:

```
Do Until condition
    [statements]
Loop
```

Turning things upside down

In all the loops I have discussed in this section, the condition is tested before the statements in the loop are executed. If the loop fails the test, the statements in the loop are never executed and VBScript jumps to the line following the end of the loop. With a Do loop, though, you can guarantee that the loop executes at least once by moving the loop test to the end of the loop. The following syntax for the Do loop works just like the other Do loop syntax except that the loop runs once before the test is done, so you get at least one cycle from it:

```
Do
    [statements]
    [Exit Do]
    [statements]
Loop [{While | Until} condition]
```

Please head for the nearest Exit

As with the For...Next loop, you can jump out of a Do loop if things aren't going your way. If VBScript stumbles across an Exit Do statement in a Do loop, VBScript jumps out of the loop and starts with the first statement following the end of the loop.

The Exit Do usually happens as the result of some test, as with an If statement. You could modify the political game in the preceding example as follows:

```
Do While CampaignSeason
    MakeSpeech HotTopic, Constituents
    AcceptContributions InterestGroup
    If BribeScandal Then Exit Do
    KissBabies
       :
```

```
      CampaignSeason = CheckCalendar Today, ElectionDay
Loop
```

The third statement in the Do loop now tests for a bribery scandal (following campaign contributions); if a scandal has occurred, the loop exits because the campaign is over.

Pick a case — any case

The VBScript If statement works well if you're testing a single condition and you care only whether it's TRUE or FALSE. If you have lots of tests, each with its own actions, the If statement can be cumbersome. VBScript includes a special statement for cases in which you're testing just one expression that could have many values (not just TRUE or FALSE) and you want do something different for each value. The Select Case statement has the following syntax:

```
Select Case testexpression
   [Case expressionlist-1
      [statements-1]]
          :
   [Case expressionlist-n
      [statements-n]]
   [Case Else
      [elsestatements-n]]
End Select
```

The Select Case statement checks a *testexpression* and then looks for a Case clause that has a matching value. If a matching Case clause is found, VBScript begins executing statements until it reaches the next Case clause and then jumps to the statement following the Select Case...End Select statement.

If your *testexpression* matches more than one case, only the block of statements from the first Case clause is executed; later, matching Case clauses are ignored.

An example: Which was it?

The MouseMove event (described in Chapter 11) includes an argument to tell the script which (if any) of the modifier keys (SHIFT, CTRL and ALT) were pressed when the MouseMove event was generated. Testing the Shift argument of the MouseMove event is a great application of the Select...Case statement, as shown here:

```
Select Case Shift
   Case fmShiftMask
      MsgBox "SHIFT"
```

(continued)

(continued)

```
    Case fmCtrlMask
      MsgBox "CTRL"
    Case fmShiftMask + fmCtrlMask
      MsgBox "SHIFT and CTRL"
    Case fmAltMask
      MsgBox "ALT"
    Case fmShiftMask + fmAltMask
      MsgBox "ALT and SHIFT"
    Case fmAltMask + fmCtrlMask
      MsgBox "ALT and CTRL"
    Case fmAltMask + fmShiftMask + fmCtrlMask
      MsgBox "All of 'em (ALT, SHIFT, and CTRL)"
    Case Else
      MsgBox "Whoops!"
 End Select
```

Select a Case or Else!

You can include an else clause in your Select Case statement using Case Else. If none of the Case clauses listed has an expression whose value matches, the statements following the Case Else are executed. You don't have to include a Case Else, but it's a good idea. You may think that you have covered all the bases with your cases, but a surprise value is always lurking in your code. If you're confident that you should never reach the Case Else clause, you can include a statement that pops up a message saying that an error occurred.

Although some versions of the Microsoft documentation for VBScript indicate that you must include a list of expressions following the Case Else, don't do it. If you do include a list of expressions (or a single expression) following the Case Else, it's an error.

Smooth Operators

VBScript has operators to do everything from adding two numbers to combining two strings. The operators fall into three categories:

- Arithmetic
- Comparison
- Logical

Arithmetic operators handle anything having to do with numbers, including addition, exponentiation, division, and others, as listed in Table 11-3. The comparison operators compare two expressions, as listed in Table 11-4. Logical operators are used with Boolean (TRUE–FALSE) expressions; in Table 11-5, operators are listed in order of precedence from top to bottom.

Table 11-3   **Arithmetic Operators in VBScript**

Name	Symbol	What It Does
Addition	+	Adds two expressions
Subtraction	–	Subtracts
Exponentiation	^	Raises to a power
Modulus arithmetic	Mod	Calculates remainder after division
Multiplication	*	Multiplies two expressions
Division	/	Divides two expressions
Integer division	\	Divides two expressions and throws away fractional part
Negation	–	Switches between positive and negative numbers and vice versa

Table 11-4   **Comparison Operators in VBScript**

Name	Symbol	True If
Equality	=	Two expressions are equal
Inequality	< >	Two expressions are *not* equal
Less than	<	Value on left is less than value on right
Less than or equal to	<=	Value on left is less than or equal to value on right
Greater than	>	Value on left is greater than value on right
Greater than or equal to	>=	Value on left is greater than or equal to value on right
Is	Is	Test whether two variables refer to the same object

Table 11-5   **Logical Operators in VBScript**

Name	Value of Expression
Not	True if expression is false; false if expression is true
And	True if both expressions are true
Or	True if either (or both) expression is true
Xor	True if the two expressions have a different value (one true and the other false)
Eqv	True if both expressions have the same value (both true or both false)
Imp	True if the first expression implies the second

The third R: 'rithmetic

Most of the arithmetic operators probably look familiar, although you may see a few oddballs. The exponentiation operator raises an expression to a power. To find the fourth power of 7, for example, you write:

```
7^4
```

The modulus operator gives you the remainder that's left after dividing two expressions:

```
3 Mod 5 = 3
17 Mod 4 = 1
28 Mod 6 = 4
```

If you don't care about the remainder, you can use the integer division operator, which throws away the remainder:

```
6 \ 7 = 0
9 \ 4 = 2
17 \ 3 = 5
```

When an expression has several operators, it's important to know the order in which operators are applied. Three rules apply in deciding which operators are applied first:

- Expressions in parentheses are evaluated first; the innermost parentheses are evaluated before outer parenthetical expressions.
- Operators with higher precedence are applied before those with lower precedence.
- If the first two rules don't apply, expressions are evaluated from left to right within an expression.

The precedence rules for VBScript state the order of precedence as follows:

1. Arithmetic operators
2. String concatenation (&)
3. Comparison operators
4. Logical operators

Compare and contrast

All expressions are not created equal, and the VBScript comparison operators tell you which are more equal. The comparison operators are mostly the usual collection of greater than, less than, and so on. One unusual operator, though, is the Is operator. It tests two expressions and is TRUE only if the two expressions refer to the same object. (For more information about object references, check out the Microsoft documentation of the VBScript Set statement.)

Logically speaking

VBScript has several operators for creating logical expressions. Of the logical operators, the Xor, Eqv, and Imp operators aren't common in everyday life, but are useful in programming. All these operators operate on two expressions, as shown in this expression:

```
exp1 operator exp2
```

The name Xor is shortened from exclusive *or,* which means that the two values must be different in order for the entire Xor expression to be TRUE. The Eqv operator is TRUE only if two expressions are the same. It is the mirror image of the Xor operator, in other words:

```
exp1 Xor exp2 = Not (exp1 Eqv exp2)
```

The Imp operator is a little strange unless you're familiar with the rules of logic for If...Then expressions. This operator is defined so that

```
exp1 Imp exp2 IFF If exp1 Then exp2
```

where IFF means "if and only if."

Procedural Anatomy

Whenever you need to do something more than once, you have a procedure on your hands. To most people, *procedure* means a sequence of steps to complete a task — and that's what it means in scripts, with one addition: A script procedure is a named sequence of steps. VBScript has two kinds of procedures:

- ✔ Sub
- ✔ Function

"We all live in a yellow Sub procedure"

Most procedures you write are Sub procedures. VBScript is picky about the format of its Sub procedures, which must look like this:

```
Sub name ([arglist])
    [statements]
    [Exit Sub]
    [statements]
End Sub
```

A summary of syntax (like that for the preceding Sub procedure) has several conventions. Anything that appears in square brackets ([ ]) is optional. The statement Exit Sub doesn't have to be included, for example, because it's given in square brackets. Words that appear in *italics* are just placeholders. The term *name* means that's where the name of the procedure goes, but you don't actually have to put the word *name* there.

The first line of a Sub procedure has three elements:

- **Keyword Sub:** *Keywords* are words that are part of the VBScript language. They're sometimes called *reserved words* because VBScript has reserved them for its own use. You can't write a procedure named Sub, for example, because VBScript already uses the word *Sub* for something else.

- **Procedure name:** Because it's your procedure, you can name it pretty much anything you want.

- **Procedure's argument list in parentheses:** The arguments are just a list of things the procedure needs in order to work.

Knowing how to argue with VBScript

Imagine that you're writing a procedure to bake a cake, which is something you plan to do more than once. Before you begin baking, you need a few items, including ingredients, a cook, a cake pan, an oven, a cooling rack, and a taste tester. The first line of your procedure looks like this:

```
Sub BakeCake(cook, ingredients, cakePan, oven, coolRack,
        tasteTester)
```

As you write the procedure, you use each of these items while baking the cake. Whenever you need to use the oven during the procedure, for example, you just refer to the argument oven. Because some arguments are optional, they don't have to be supplied. If no tasteTester exists, for example, you can assume that the cook does the tasting or that no tasting takes place.

You don't have to have arguments to a procedure. If you don't have any arguments, you still have to include the parentheses after the procedure name:

```
Sub NoArgumentProcedure()
```

Proceeding with Function procedures

When you ask somebody to do a job for you, you usually expect some feedback. If you want a package brought to you, you expect to receive the package. If you ask someone to make a phone call, you might want that person to let you know after the call has been made. When you ask a Sub procedure to do something for you, though, you get no feedback because Sub procedures can't return values. If you want to get a value back, you must use a Function procedure.

Just because a Sub procedure can't return a value doesn't mean that it must work in isolation. A Sub procedure could change a global variable's value, and you could check the value after you have called the procedure. This process is similar to asking someone to make a phone call for you and then jotting a note on a bulletin board you check later.

A Function procedure is just like a Sub procedure, with two exceptions: The word *Function* is used to begin and end the procedure (just like the word *Sub* for Sub procedures), and every Function must contain at least one statement that assigns the function a value. The syntax for a Function procedure is

```
Function name [(arglist)]
    [statements]
    [name = expression]
    [Exit Function]
    [statements]
    [name = expression]
End Function
```

One reason that the metric system hasn't caught on in the United States is the difficulty of converting from English to metric. VBScript can help bring the United States into the twentieth century by doing the conversions for us. The following function converts from English inches to metric centimeters:

```
<SCRIPT LANGUAGE="VBScript">
<!--
Sub ConvertToMetric()
    temp = InputBox("Please enter the measurement in inches:
        ", "Inches to Centimeters")
    MsgBox temp & " inches is " & InchesToCms(temp) & "
        centimeters."
End Sub
```

(continued)

(continued)

```
Function InchesToCms(inches)
    InchesToCms = (inches * 2.54)
End Function
-->
</SCRIPT>
```

Using Sub and Function procedures in code

Writing a procedure is only half the job because you want to call the procedure later. Because calling a Sub procedure is a little different from calling a Function procedure, the two are described separately.

Calling all Subs

Sub procedures are written to be called by other procedures; you can call a Sub procedure from another procedure in two different ways:

- ✔ Just type the name of the procedure along with values for any required arguments, each separated by a comma.
- ✔ Use the Call statement and enclose any arguments in parentheses.

Although the examples in this chapter have all used the first method, there's nothing wrong with the second. The following example shows both methods, each calling a procedure named HardWork():

```
<SCRIPT LANGUAGE="VBScript">
<!--
Call HardWork(firstarg, secondarg)
HardWork firstarg, secondarg
-->
</SCRIPT>
```

The parentheses are omitted if you don't use the Call statement.

Functioning functions

You can think of a function as another name for a value. The following function call, for example, is just another name for the value 25.4:

```
InchesToCms (10)
```

You can use a function anywhere you can use a value, but nowhere else. For example, you could write

```
<SCRIPT LANGUAGE="VBScript">
<!--
 Temp = InchesToCms(inches)
-->
</SCRIPT>
```

Because it's okay to say Temp = 25.4, this example is also correct. You can also use a function call as part of an expression:

```
<SCRIPT LANGUAGE="VBScript">
<!--
   MsgBox temp & " inches is " & InchesToCms(temp) & "
          centimeters."
-->
</SCRIPT>
```

You could just as easily insert 25.4 for the expression InchesToCms(temp), so the function call is valid. You can't assign a value to InchesToCms(temp), however, any more than you can assign a new value to 25.4:

```
InchesToCms(temp) = 73
```

This line is wrong for the same reason that you can't assign 73 to 25.4:

```
25.4 = 73
```

(The preceding line could be correct in a certain context — if you were using the equal sign to compare the two values — but I'm talking about using it to assign one value to another.)

Knowing where to declare

In VBScript, you have to define procedures before they are used. Other than that, you're on your own. In the VBScript documentation, Microsoft recommends that you define your procedures in the HEAD section (between the <HEAD> and </HEAD> tags) of your HTML page. That's a fine idea, but some people prefer to put all their code at the end of the HTML file, and that's okay too. As long you don't try to call a procedure (either a Sub or a Function) before you have defined it, you can do whatever you want. You should, however, stick with your choice. Consistency is a good thing in programming — strive for it.

"No Comment" Is No Good

No computer code, including the simplest script, is well written unless it includes comments. With good comments, your code can be understood by other script writers and by you when you look back at it six months after you write it. Because I'm not above self-flagellation, I use myself here to demonstrate. Here's a procedure I wrote to change the colors of a Label control depending on the mouse pointer's position above the label:

```
Sub ChangingLabel_MouseMove(Button, Shift, X, Y)
    ChangingLabel.BackColor = INT(X * XScale)
    ChangingLabel.ForeColor = INT(Y * YScale)
    XVal.Text = X
    YVal.Text = Y
end sub
```

Notice that there's not a comment anywhere. As I look at it now, I have no idea what XScale and YScale are. To make matters worse, both variables are global variables that are defined elsewhere. I can read through the rest of the code and figure it out, but it would have been simpler to have included a comment describing both variables when I wrote the procedure.

Another part of commenting your code is the use of descriptive names for variables and procedures. Because you don't gain anything by using short, generic variable or procedure names, don't do it. The color-changing label in this example is called ChangingLabel, not the ubiquitous Label1.

Testing your newfound knowledge

1. If you have to do something different for each of many different values for the same expression, you should use:

   A. The Select...Case statement.

   B. A large menu that includes appetizers, entrées, and desserts.

   C. Write a loop that counts from 1 to 100 and back down again.

   D. Just do the same thing for every value, and it will even out in the end.

2. Why should you enclose your script code within the HTML comment tags (<!-- and -->)?

   A. If you don't use the comment tags, Internet Explorer thinks that you're just kidding.

   B. Because the code you write is a comment on society.

   C. So that browsers that are too dumb to appreciate the power of VBScript don't try to display your code as part of the page.

   D. Those are comment tags? I thought that they were arrows!

Chapter 12

World Events and
How to Handle Them

• •

In This Chapter

▶ What is an event?

▶ How events are used in scripts

▶ Common events of ActiveX controls

• •

*T*oday's programs are written to respond to a user's actions — users
expect that they can do anything at any time. In *event-driven programming*,
developed to make it easier for developers to write the programs users want,
events are generated to notify a program what's going on in the world.

As users interact with your stunning ActiveX-enabled pages, things happen.
Users may move the mouse pointer or press the Tab key, for example. They
may also get up for a cup of coffee or consult with a psychic friend. Although
these are examples of things that happen, they're not all events. An *event* is
something that happens that another programmer thought your script should
know about. For example, the Label control generates events as the control's
caption changes, the mouse moves, or objects are dragged and dropped. The
Label control generates those events and not others because the programmers
who wrote the Label control thought that those were the things you, as a script
writer, would want to know about.

Unfortunately, because programmers have fewer psychic friends than most
people, they sometimes have trouble second-guessing script writers. Occasionally something happens that you want to know about, but the control you're
using doesn't have the event you want. You either have to find another control,
write your own control, or just do without. Although writing your own control
sounds tough, the new version of Visual Basic (Version 5.0) includes tools for
creating your own controls. After you have settled on a control with the event
you need, you have to write an event handler.

If you're having trouble finding the right event, look for similar events that work a little differently. The KeyDown and KeyUp events are virtually identical, but the KeyPress event is a little different from both and might work when neither KeyDown nor KeyUp will. MouseMove, which is a little different from MouseDown and MouseUp, may be just what you're looking for.

Don't forget that most controls discussed in this book are free. Although they're pretty good, you get what you pay for — if you spend the money to buy your own controls, you can expect them to be more flexible. For examples of commercial controls, take a look at the CD-ROM in the back of this book.

Handling Events

Procedures written to respond to events are known as *event handlers.* ActiveX supplies the events, and you supply the event handlers. Events are one of the most important components of an ActiveX Web site because events are where the activation kicks in. If you want a page that interacts with users, you have to know what users are doing — and that's what events are for.

Event handlers are written in a standard way in VBScript. They're usually written as Sub procedures (see Chapter 11). An event handler for an object called ObjectName looks like this:

```
Sub ObjectName_EventName(EventArg1, EventArg2, ...)
   Stuff to do when the event occurs
end sub
```

Event handlers use a standard form so that VBScript can call them when the time is right. Suppose that you have created a Label called Banner and you want to know when a user moves the mouse while the mouse pointer is positioned over the label. You would write an event handler like this:

```
Sub Banner_MouseMove(Button, Shift, X, Y)
   MsgBox "The mouse moved while over the Banner label!"
end sub
```

As a user interacts with your program, the mouse eventually moves over your Banner label. VBScript keeps a watchful eye on the user: When the mouse moves, the Label control fires off a MouseMove event. VBScript checks and, sure enough, a procedure has been written to handle mouse movement over the Banner label. VBScript runs the procedure, and the message you have written pops up.

Living within the limitations of VBScript

Be careful about your event handlers' procedure prototypes. A *prototype* specifies whether the procedure is a Sub or Function procedure, indicates the procedure's name, and provides information about a procedure's arguments. A procedure's prototype is similar to a signature because it uniquely identifies the procedure. Many prototypes you see, including some of those mentioned in the Microsoft Control Pad online Help feature, were written for more advanced versions of Visual Basic. If you look up the MouseMove event in the Control Pad online Help system, for example, you see

```
Private Sub object_MouseMove(ByVal Button As fmButton, ByVal
          Shift As fmShiftState, ByVal X As Single, ByVal Y
          As Single)
```

Because VBScript doesn't include most features used in this prototype, trying to use it in a VBScript program would be an error. If you use the Control Pad Script Wizard (described in Chapter 5) to write the MouseMove event handler, it inserts the following (much simpler) prototype:

```
Sub object_MouseMove(Button, Shift, X, Y)
```

Here are two common problems to watch out for:

- ✔ The Private keyword, often written immediately before the Sub keyword
- ✔ The As keyword (Button As fmButton, for example)

The ByVal keyword also appears often in event handlers, but it's okay because VBScript includes the ByVal keyword. You usually don't need ByVal, though, and the Script Wizard doesn't bother to insert it.

If you have any doubt about what to include and what to leave out when you're writing an event handler, use the Script Wizard to insert your event handlers. If you switch to code view after you have selected an object and an event, Script Wizard inserts the procedure prototype for you and all you have to do is type the event handler. (You can certainly use Script Wizard list view as well, but it's less flexible than code view.)

The Private keyword is an access modifier that determines which procedures can call the Private procedure. All procedures in VBScript are Public, and there's no way to change that. The As keyword is used to set an argument's type, but VBScript has only one type: variant. The ByVal keyword tells VBScript to make a copy of the variable being passed as an argument and use the copy as the procedure's argument. Although this process seems inefficient, it ensures that the procedure can't change the value of the original variable (because it's working with a copy). In computer science, this method is called *pass by value,* and so the keyword ByVal (short for *by val*ue) is used.

Writing an event handler

After you have found a control with the events you need, writing an event handler is just like writing any other procedure. It can even be a little easier because you already know the name of and all the arguments for the procedure. Usually, as you're designing a page, you think, "Wow, it would be neat if I could draw a picture, and whenever the mouse pointer were positioned over the picture, a song would play. Better yet, if I could play a different song depending on where the mouse pointer was located within the picture, people would flock to my Web site." Event handers are the scripting glue that tie together events (such as "whenever the mouse pointer is positioned over the picture") and actions (for example, "a song plays").

As you write your event handlers, you can refer to this chapter and the sample code on the CD-ROM in the back of this book to help you along. As with any script writing, you get better with practice, which can include figuring out how other event handlers work. If you notice something cool at another Web site, use your browser's View Source command to look at the underlying HTML and scripts. (Most people don't mind if you use a technique you find there, but don't copy someone else's scripts without permission.)

The following section discusses the most common events for ActiveX controls and provides details about the event procedure's arguments.

Common Events of ActiveX Controls

Most ActiveX controls have a heaping helping of events. The most common events fall into one of several categories:

- **Change:** Generated by controls whenever the control's value changes
- **Drag and drop:** Fired as objects are dragged or dropped
- **Keyboard:** Generated as users press keys
- **Mouse:** Generated by clicks, double-clicks, and mouse movements

Change events

Change events are generated by controls whenever the control's value changes. If you delete a character from a TextBox object, for example, the TextBox fires off a Change event. The most common Change events are listed in Table 12-1.

Table 12-1	Change Events of ActiveX Controls
Event	**When It Fires**
AfterUpdate	After user has changed data in a control
BeforeUpdate	Before data in a control is changed
Change	Whenever Value property of a control changes
Enter	Before a control receives the focus from another control on the same HTML Layout
Exit	Immediately before a control loses the focus to another control on the same HTML Layout

Here's the ordering of Change events:

1. BeforeUpdate event

2. AfterUpdate event

3. The Exit event for the current control

4. The Enter event for the next control in the tab order

AfterUpdate

```
Sub objectName_AfterUpdate()
```

The AfterUpdate event fires after a user has changed a control's data. If you want to cancel the update (to restore the previous value of the control), you can't cancel the AfterUpdate event (because it's too late). Instead, use the BeforeUpdate event and set the event's Cancel argument to True.

BeforeUpdate

```
Sub objectName_BeforeUpdate(Cancel)
```

BeforeUpdate is an early warning event that fires before a user has changed the data in a control. Because the BeforeUpdate occurs before the data has been changed, you can cancel the update by the user and restore the control's previous value. If you want to cancel the update, you must set the event's Cancel argument to True:

```
Sub SomeObject_BeforeUpdate(Cancel)
    If SomeObject.Value <> 7 Then Cancel = True
       :
end sub
```

If you set the Cancel argument to True (canceling the update), the focus stays on the control, and neither the AfterUpdate event nor the Exit event fires.

Change

```
Sub objectName_Change( )
```

If a control's Value property changes, a Change event fires. Unlike AfterUpdate and BeforeUpdate, it doesn't matter whether the change in the Value property was scripted or made by a user.

Some actions change the Value property:

- ✔ Scrolling with a scrollbar
- ✔ Clicking an option button or toggle button
- ✔ Clicking an arrow on a spin button
- ✔ Typing text in a combo box or text box
- ✔ Switching tabs on a TabStrip

The Change event is just what you need to keep controls marching together in lock step. The SpinButton control maintains its value internally, for example, but you usually want to display the spin button's value in a text control.

Suppose that you have a series of spin buttons for setting a date (as shown in Figure 12-1). You could use a TextBox control to display part of the date (the day, for example) and a SpinButton control to update the TextBox object. The Change event for the SpinButtonDay control does exactly that:

```
Sub SpinButtonDay_Change()
    TextBoxDay.Text = SpinButtonDay.Value
end sub
```

A Change event often goes in hand in hand with a Click (which fires whenever a user clicks the mouse button). Despite this coincidence, you should use the Change event whenever you're interested in learning about changes. Using the Change event makes it easier for another script writer to look at your code and understand it.

If you have written a script for a worksheet application, you can use the Change event to link work done in a work area to results displayed somewhere else. For example, if a bank's pages include a mortgage worksheet that calculates the monthly payment for different mortgage amounts, a user begins by filling out a monthly budget, including an item called Housing Expense. After completing the budget, that person fills in the mortgage information in one area, and the bottom-line figure (the monthly payment) is then displayed on the Housing Expense line of the budget worksheet.

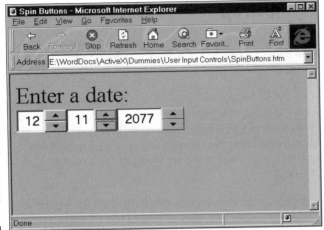

Figure 12-1:
The spin
button's
Change
event is
used to
update the
value shown
in the text
box.

Enter, Exit

```
Sub object_Enter()
Sub objectName_Exit(Cancel)
```

The Enter and Exit events fire as the focus moves from one control to another on an HTML Layout. The Enter event occurs just before a control gets the focus from a control on the same HTML Layout; Exit occurs immediately before a control loses the focus to another control.

Suppose that a user is at a text box and then clicks a check box — the check box fires an Enter event. If the user then selects another control in the same HTML Layout, the check box's Exit event fires (because the focus is moving to a different object in the same HTML Layout), and an Enter event fires for the control the user is jumping to.

Because the Enter event fires before the focus has switched to a control, your script can get a jump on users. The Enter event is your chance to tell users something about the new control before they have a chance to do any damage (because, at the time of the Enter event, the focus hasn't switched yet). On a page that includes a form, for example, you can offer suggestions for filling out a particular field.

If you don't want the control to lose the focus, you can set the Cancel argument of the Exit event to True.

The Enter and Exit events in VBScript are similar to the GotFocus and LostFocus events in Visual Basic. The events have one important difference, however: They don't occur when an HTML Layout receives or loses the focus.

Drag 'til you drop

A fad started a while ago in user interface design, and suddenly every Windows software package touted its use of the drag-and-drop feature — it's really just the old wine of cut-and-paste packaged in new bottles. In the past, if you wanted to move text from one place to another, you had to select it, cut it, move the insertion point to the new location, and then paste the text into its new home. With *drag-and-drop,* you don't have to cut or paste; to move text, you just select it, click the mouse button within your selection, and hold the mouse button down while you move the mouse pointer (or drag). After you place the insertion point where you want the text to be inserted, you release the button to drop the text into place.

Although drag-and-drop isn't much of a breakthrough for text, the operation isn't limited to just text — it can apply to any object. The most common drag-and-drop events are listed in Table 12-2. If you drag a Microsoft Word document and drop it on the icon for Word, for example, the Word program starts up and loads the document. For the near future of ActiveX page design, though, most dragging and dropping is confined to moving text around.

Table 12-2   Drag-and-Drop Events of ActiveX Controls

Event	When It Fires
BeforeDragOver	As a drag-and-drop operation is beginning
BeforeDropOrPaste	When user is about to drop (or paste) data on an object

BeforeDragOver

For TabStrip:

```
Sub ObjectName_BeforeDragOver(Index, Cancel, Data, X, Y,
          DragState, Effect, Shift)
```

For other controls:

```
Sub ObjectName_BeforeDragOver(Cancel, Data, X, Y, DragState,
          Effect, Shift)
```

The BeforeDragOver event fires when a user begins a drag-and-drop operation. It usually means that a user has selected some text and has clicked within the selection and begun to drag it. With BeforeDragOver, you can track the mouse pointer as it enters or leaves a valid target or sits directly over it. The current location of the mouse pointer determines which object receives the BeforeDragOver event.

When a user cuts (or copies) a selection, the selection is either moved (or copied) to the Windows Clipboard. (The *Clipboard* is an area of system memory used as a temporary storage area for cutting, copying, and pasting.) When a user drags and drops text, however, no change occurs in the Clipboard.

The BeforeDragOver event carries quite a bit of information along with it. Table 12-3 briefly describes each of its arguments.

Table 12-3	Arguments to BeforeDragOver Event
Argument	*Description*
Cancel	Indicates what to do with event: If False (the default), control should handle the event; True tells the object to forget about the event and allow the event's container (Internet Explorer, if you're using Explorer) to handle the event
Data	Whatever is being dragged in a drag-and-drop operation; data is packaged in a DataObject
X, Y	Horizontal and vertical coordinates of control's position measured in points; X is measured from left edge of control, and Y is measured from top of control
DragState	Transition state of data being dragged
Effect	Operations supported by drop source
Shift	Specifies state of Shift, Ctrl, and Alt keys

Most controls do not support drag-and-drop while Cancel is False, which is the default setting. The control therefore rejects attempts to drag or drop anything on it, and it does not initiate the BeforeDropOrPaste event. The TextBox and ComboBox controls are exceptions: They support drag-and-drop operations even when Cancel is False.

After trying several test scripts with different controls, I have been unable to cancel an event using the Cancel parameter.

Not all objects can receive a dropped object. A user can tell which objects are valid targets because the mouse pointer changes to a circle with a slash through it while it's positioned over an invalid drop target. With scripting, you too can determine from the mouse position whether the cursor is positioned over a valid target. The argument DragState is set to different values (listed in Table 12-4) depending on the mouse pointer's location when the BeforeDragOver event fires.

Table 12-4   Settings for DragState (fmDragState)

Constant	Value	Mouse Pointer Location
fmDragStateEnter	0	Within range of target
fmDragStateLeave	1	Outside range of target
fmDragStateOver	2	At new position but within range of same target

When a control handles the BeforeDragOver event, you can use the Effect argument to identify the drag-and-drop action to perform; the Effect argument has several possible values, which are listed in Table 12-5.

Table 12-5   Settings for Effect (fmEffect)

Constant	Value	What It Does
fmDropEffectNone	0	Nothing (does not copy or move source to target)
fmDropEffectCopy	1	Copies source to target
fmDropEffectMove	2	Moves source to target
fmDropEffectCopyOrMove	3	Copies or moves source to target

The value of fmEffect passed through the Effect argument is cumulative, as shown in Table 12-6.

Table 12-6   Effects of Different fmEffect Values

When Effect Is Set to This	Drop Source Supports This
fmDropEffectCopy	Copy and Cancel operations
fmDropEffectCopyOrMove	Copy, Move, and Cancel operations
fmDropEffectMove	Move or Cancel operation
fmDropEffectNone	Cancel operation

Users can modify a drag-and-drop operation by holding one of the modifier keys (Shift, Ctrl, or Alt) while dragging a selection. The BeforeDragOver event tells you which key, if any, was held by setting the Shift argument to one of the values listed in Table 12-7.

Table 12-7		Settings for Shift (fmShift)
Constant	**Value**	**What Happened**
	0	No modifier was pressed
fmShiftMask	1	Shift was pressed
fmCtrlMask	2	Ctrl was pressed
fmAltMask	4	Alt was pressed

The Ctrl key is usually used to indicate a Copy operation rather than a Move. Without any modifier keys, dragging and dropping text cuts and pastes the text. With the Ctrl key, the selection is copied and pasted.

BeforeDropOrPaste

For TabStrip:

```
Sub objectName_BeforeDropOrPaste(Index, Cancel, Action, Data,
          X, Y, Effect, Shift
```

For other controls:

```
Sub objectName_BeforeDropOrPaste(Cancel, Action, Data, X, Y,
          Effect, Shift)
```

The BeforeDropOrPaste event fires when a user is about to drop or paste a dragged selection (or object) on a target. The BeforeDropOrPaste event is similar to the BeforeDragOver event except for the addition of the Action argument, which distinguishes a paste from a drop. The arguments for BeforeDropOrPaste are listed in Table 12-8. For a TabStrip, VBScript fires a BeforeDropOrPaste event as it transfers a data object to the control.

Table 12-8	Arguments to BeforeDropOrPaste Event
Argument	**Description**
Cancel	Indicates what to do with event: If False (the default), control should handle event; if True, cancels the event
Action	Result of pending drag-and-drop operation
Data	Whatever is being dragged in drag-and-drop operation; data is packaged in a DataObject
X, Y	Horizontal and vertical coordinates of control's position measured in points: X is measured from left edge of control, and Y is measured from top of control

(continued)

Table 12-8 *(continued)*

Argument	Description
DragState	Transition state of data being dragged
Effect	Operations supported by drop source
Shift	Specifies state of Shift, Ctrl, and Alt keys

Because the DragState, Effect, and Shift argument values are the same for the BeforeDropOrPaste event as for BeforeDragOver, they are listed in Tables 12-4, 12-5, and 12-7, respectively.

Most controls do not support drag-and-drop while Cancel is False, which is the default setting. The control therefore rejects attempts to drag or drop anything on it, and it does not initiate the BeforeDropOrPaste event. The TextBox and ComboBox controls are exceptions: They support drag-and-drop operations even when Cancel is False.

After trying several test scripts with different controls, I have been unable to cancel an event using the Cancel parameter.

The Action argument indicates the soon-to-be result (remember that this is the *Before*DropOrPaste event) of the imminent paste or drop. The two possibilities are listed in Table 12-9.

Table 12-9 **Settings for the Action Argument**

Constant	Value	What Happened
fmActionPaste	2	Selected object was pasted into drop target
fmActionDragDrop	3	Object was dragged from its source and dropped on drop target

When a control handles the BeforeDropOrPaste event (as opposed to the system handling the event), you can update the Action argument to identify the drag-and-drop action to perform. When Effect is set to fmDropEffectCopyOrMove, you can assign Action to fmDropEffectNone, fmDropEffectCopy, or fmDropEffect Move. When Effect is set to fmDropEffectCopy or fmDropEffect Move, you can reassign Action to fmDropEffectNone. You cannot reassign Action when Effect is set to fmDropEffectNone.

The keys to the kingdom

Although most people enjoy mousing around, the keyboard is still an important input device. As a script writer, you have to know what users are doing as they bang away on their keyboards. Text controls depend on keyboard input, and so do many other controls. The keyboard events are summarized in Table 12-10.

Table 12-10	ActiveX Keyboard Events
Event	*When It Fires*
KeyDown	When user presses a key
KeyPress	When user presses an ANSI key
KeyUp	When user releases a key

The sequence of keyboard-related events is

1. KeyDown

2. KeyPress

3. KeyUp

The KeyDown event occurs when a user presses a key on a running HTML Layout while that HTML Layout or a control on it has the focus. The KeyDown and KeyPress events alternate repeatedly until the user releases the key, at which time the KeyUp event occurs. The HTML Layout or control with the focus receives all keystrokes. An HTML Layout can have the focus only if it has no controls or all its visible controls are disabled.

The KeyDown and KeyUp events apply only to HTML Layouts and controls on an HTML Layout. To interpret ANSI characters or to determine the ANSI character corresponding to the key that's pressed, use the KeyPress event.

TECHNICAL STUFF

Fancy ANSI

The American National Standards Institute (ANSI), pronounced "an-see," has created a character set based on the older ASCII character set. Microsoft Windows uses the ANSI character set, which has 256 characters. The first 128 characters (codes 0–127) are from the original ASCII character set, which contains 128 characters; the second 128 characters (codes 128–255) include special characters, such as letters with accented characters, international currency symbols, and common fractions.

KeyDown, KeyUp

```
Sub objectName_KeyDown(KeyCode, Shift)
Sub objectName_KeyUp(KeyCode, Shift)
```

The KeyDown and KeyUp events split the user's act of pressing a key into two parts: going down and going up. The KeyCode argument tells you which key was pressed, and the Shift argument specifies which modifier key was pressed, as listed in Table 12-11.

Table 12-11		Settings for Shift (fmShift)
Constant	**Value**	**Key Pressed**
	0	No modifier key was pressed
fmShiftMask	1	Shift
fmCtrlMask	2	Ctrl
fmAltMask	4	Alt

The KeyDown and KeyUp events are typically used to distinguish among these keys:

- ✔ Extended character keys, such as function keys
- ✔ Cursor-movement keys (End, Home, and PgUp, for example)
- ✔ Keys modified with the Shift, Ctrl, or Alt keys
- ✔ Number keys on the numeric keypad
- ✔ Number keys at the top of the keyboard

You can tell whether a modifier key (and which one) was pressed by examining the Shift argument to the KeyDown and KeyUp events.

The KeyDown and KeyPress events occur when you press an ANSI key. If a key is pressed while a control has the focus, the KeyUp event occurs after any event for the control, which is triggered by a key press. If a keystroke switches the focus from one control to another, the KeyDown event occurs for the first control, and the KeyPress and KeyUp events occur for the second control.

KeyPress

```
Sub objectName_KeyPress(KeyANSI)
```

When a user presses a key that displays a character from the ANSI character set, a KeyPress event fires. The event can occur either before or after the key is released. If a keystroke switches the focus from one control to another, the KeyDown event occurs for the first control, and the KeyPress and KeyUp events occur for the second control.

A KeyPress event can occur when any of the following keys is pressed:

- Any printable keyboard character
- Ctrl combined with a character from the standard alphabet
- Ctrl combined with any special character
- Backspace
- Esc

A KeyPress event does not occur under any of these conditions:

- Tab is pressed
- Enter is pressed
- An arrow key is pressed
- A keystroke causes the focus to move from one control to another

The Backspace key is an ANSI character, but the Delete key is not. If a user deletes a character by pressing the Backspace key, a KeyPress event fires; deleting a character by pressing the Delete key doesn't produce a KeyPress event.

If you want to handle keystrokes not recognized by the KeyPress event (function keys, navigation keys, and any combination of these keys with keyboard modifiers), you must use the KeyDown and KeyUp events rather than the KeyPress event.

Mousin' around

The mouse is a key part of the user interface, and VBScript has many mouse events for keeping your scripts informed (see Table 12-12). Most ActiveX controls support several mouse events, even for controls that don't seem to be "mouse controls." The Label control, for example, generates events for many different mouse actions by users. The wide-ranging support for mouse events means that you can link effects to almost any control: Label controls can change color, TextBox controls can change text, and CommandButton controls can light up — all in response to a user's playing with the mouse. Each of these types of events is discussed in this section.

Table 12-12 Common Mouse Events of ActiveX Controls

Event	When It Fires
Click	When user either chooses one value from many-valued control or clicks control with mouse
DblClick	When user points to object and then clicks mouse button twice
MouseDown	When user presses mouse button
MouseEnter	When user moves mouse pointer over control
MouseExit	When user moves mouse pointer away from control
MouseMove	When user moves mouse
MouseUp	When user releases mouse button

The following sample HTML code demonstrates some basic applications of mouse events and their use. The page has three Label controls and a CommandButton. The Caption property of the last Label (InfoLabel) is changed to show one of several different mouse events generated by the other two Label controls and the CommandButton:

```
<HTML>
<HEAD>
<TITLE>Tracking the mouse with VBScript Mouse Events</TITLE>
</HEAD>

<BODY>
<SCRIPT LANGUAGE="VBScript">
<!--
' Change the Info label when a user presses
' the mouse button while the mouse is positioned
' over the first label control, Label1.
Sub Label1_MouseDown(Button, Shift, X, Y)
   InfoLabel.Caption = "We have a MouseDown over Label One"
end sub
-->
</SCRIPT>

<OBJECT ID="Label1" WIDTH=265 HEIGHT=43
    CLASSID="CLSID:978C9E23-D4B0-11CE-BF2D-00AA003F40D0">
    <PARAM NAME="Caption" VALUE="Hi, I'm Label One">
        :
</OBJECT><BR><BR><BR>
```

```
<SCRIPT LANGUAGE="VBScript">
<!--
' Change the info label when a user releases
' the mouse button while over the second
' label control, Label2.
Sub Label2_MouseUp(Button, Shift, X, Y)
    InfoLabel.Caption = "Going up! MouseUp over Label Two"
end sub
-->
</SCRIPT>

<OBJECT ID="Label2" WIDTH=428 HEIGHT=37
    CLASSID="CLSID:978C9E23-D4B0-11CE-BF2D-00AA003F40D0">
    <PARAM NAME="Caption" VALUE="Label Two, pleased to meet
            you!">
        :
</OBJECT><BR><BR><BR>

<SCRIPT LANGUAGE="VBScript">
<!--
' Change the info label as a user moves
' the mouse pointer down while over the
' CommandButton control, CommandButton1.
Sub CommandButton1_MouseMove(Button, Shift, X, Y)
    InfoLabel.Caption = "Mouse is moving over the Command
            button"
end sub
-->
</SCRIPT>

<OBJECT ID="CommandButton1" WIDTH=330 HEIGHT=73
    CLASSID="CLSID:D7053240-CE69-11CD-A777-00DD01143C57">
    <PARAM NAME="Caption" VALUE="Command's the name, running
            things is my game!">
        :
</OBJECT><BR>

<HR>
<!-- The last label, InfoLabel, is used to display
        what's going on with the other labels and the
        button. InfoLabel's Caption property is changed
        in response to mouse events fired by other
        controls on the page.
-->
```

(continued)

(continued)

```
<H2>What's going on?</h2><BR>
<OBJECT ID="InfoLabel" WIDTH=498 HEIGHT=135
      CLASSID="CLSID:978C9E23-D4B0-11CE-BF2D-00AA003F40D0">
            :
</OBJECT><BR><BR><BR>

</BODY>
</HTML>
```

A summary of the most common mouse events is shown in Table 12-12, followed by detailed explanations of each event.

Click

```
Sub objectName_Click( )
```

The Click event fires when a user performs either of these actions:

- Selects a value for a control with more than one possible value (CommandButton, Image, Label, ScrollBar, and SpinButton controls)
- Clicks a control with the mouse (CheckBox, ComboBox, ListBox, TabStrip, TextBox, and ToggleButton controls)

A Click event occurs, for example, whenever a user clicks on an HTML Layout, clicks a Command button, or presses a control's *accelerator key* (a shortcut key that causes the focus to jump directly to a control without using the mouse).

When the Click event results from clicking a control, the sequence of events leading to the Click event is

1. MouseDown
2. MouseUp
3. Click

A Change event often goes in hand in hand with a click (which fires whenever a user clicks the mouse button). Despite this coincidence, you should use the Change event whenever you're interested in learning about changes to a control's value. Using it makes it easier for another script writer to look at your code and understand it.

DblClick

For TabStrip:

```
Sub objectName_DblClick(Index, Cancel)
```

For other controls:

```
Sub objectName_DblClick(Cancel)
```

A DblClick event occurs when a user clicks the mouse button twice in rapid succession. The Cancel event determines what handles the DblClick event. If Cancel is set to False (the default), the control should handle the event. If Cancel is set to True, your script should handle the event (possibly by ignoring it). For TabStrip controls, the Index argument gives the position of a Tab object within a Tabs collection.

If the return value of Cancel is True when a user clicks twice, the control ignores the second click. You might want to ignore a double-click if a second click would reverse the effect of the first click, such as double-clicking a toggle button. The Cancel argument enables your HTML Layout to ignore the second click so that either clicking or double-clicking the button has the same effect.

For controls that support Click, the following sequence of events leads to the DblClick event:

1. MouseDown
2. MouseUp
3. Click
4. DblClick

If a control, such as TextBox, does not support the Click event, the sequence is

1. MouseDown
2. MouseUp
3. DblClick

 A DblClick event is distinguished from two successive Click events based on the delay between the first and second clicks. To count as a double-click, the two clicks must occur within the time span specified by the system's double-click speed setting. In Windows, the delay is set by using the Control Panel's Mouse option.

MouseDown and MouseUp

For TabStrip:

```
Sub objectName_MouseDown(Index, Button, Shift, X, Y)
Sub objectName_MouseUp(Index, Button, Shift, X, Y)
```

For other controls:

```
Sub objectName_MouseDown(Button, Shift, X, Y)
Sub objectName_MouseUp(Button, Shift, X, Y)
```

The MouseDown and MouseUp events fire as the mouse button is pressed down and released, respectively.

The sequence of mouse-related events is

1. MouseDown
2. MouseUp
3. Click
4. DblClick
5. MouseUp

Arguing with the mouse

MouseDown and MouseUp events enable you to distinguish among the left, right, and middle mouse buttons (the events are listed in Table 12-13). You can also write code for mouse–keyboard combinations that use the Shift, Ctrl, and Alt keyboard modifiers.

Table 12-13	Arguments to MouseDown and MouseUp Events
Argument	**Description**
Index	Index of tab within a TabStrip (TabStrip controls only)
Button	Mouse button that caused the event
Shift	State of Shift, Ctrl, and Alt modifier keys
X, Y	Horizontal or vertical position from left or top edge of the layout, measured in points

For a TabStrip, the index argument identifies the tab where the user clicked. An index of –1 indicates that the user did not click a tab. If no tabs are in the upper right corner of the control, for example, clicking in the upper right corner sets the index to –1.

If a user presses a mouse button while the mouse pointer is positioned over an HTML Layout or a control, the object underneath the mouse pointer "captures" the mouse and receives all mouse events up to and including the last MouseUp event. Suppose that a user with more than one mouse button begins pressing the buttons one after the other. If the user never releases all the mouse buttons simultaneously (so that at least one button is always pressed), the events generated by successive mouse presses continue to fire from the original control or layout regardless of the mouse pointer's current location. Because of this behavior, the X and Y coordinates returned by a mouse event might not fall within the boundaries of the object that's firing off those events.

Which button was pressed?

The value of the Button argument can tell you which mouse button was pressed (see Table 12-14).

Table 12-14	Values for Button Argument for Mouse Events	
Constant	*Value*	*Mouse Button Pressed*
fmButtonLeft	1	Left button
fmButtonRight	2	Right button
fmButtonMiddle	4	Middle button

Shifting the mouse

If you want to do something different when a user holds down a key while pressing a mouse button, you can check the Shift argument to figure out which, if any, modifier keys were pressed. The values for each modifier key (and key combinations) are shown in Table 12-15.

Table 12-15	Values for Shift Argument for Mouse Events
Value	*Modifier Key (or Keys) Pressed*
1	Shift
2	Ctrl
3	Shift and Ctrl
4	Alt
5	Alt and Shift
6	Alt and Ctrl
7	All of 'em (Alt, Shift, and Ctrl)

If you want to identify individual key modifiers, you can use the constant values shown in Table 12-16.

Table 12-16	Settings for Shift (fmShift)	
Constant	**Value**	**Key Pressed with Mouse**
fmShiftMask	1	Shift
fmCtrlMask	2	Ctrl
fmAltMask	4	Alt

Although the values for fmShift might seem a little odd (1, 2 and 4?), they have an important advantage: If more than one key was pressed simultaneously, you can tell which set of two or three keys was pressed by checking the value of the Shift argument. If Ctrl and Alt were both pressed, for example, Shift is

fmCtrlMask + fmAltMask = 6

If you look again at the values in Table 12-16, you can see that you have no way to add the values in the first column to add up to 6, except by adding 2 (Ctrl) and 4 (Alt). Table 12-16 lists 6 as the value for Shift, therefore, when both the Ctrl and Alt keys were pressed.

MouseMove

For TabStrip:

```
Sub objectName_MouseMove(Index, Button, Shift, X, Y)
```

For other controls:

```
Sub objectName_MouseMove(Button, Shift, X, Y)
```

The MouseMove event fires when a user moves the mouse pointer over a control. As long as the mouse pointer is moved within the control's boundaries, the control continues to fire off MouseMove events. The MouseMove event's arguments are listed in Table 12-17.

Table 12-17	Arguments to the MouseMove Event
Argument	**Description**
Index	Index of tab within a TabStrip (TabStrip controls only)
Button	Mouse button (or buttons) pressed when MouseMove is fired
Shift	State of Shift, Ctrl, and Alt modifier keys
X, Y	Horizontal or vertical position from left or top edge of the layout, measured in points

Don't be fooled by the Button argument (whose values are listed in Table 12-18). The Button argument tells you which button or buttons were pressed when the MouseMove event fired, but it doesn't mean that the button was pressed over the control that fired the MouseMove event. It's possible, for example, for a user to click the mouse button on one control and then move the mouse pointer to a second control that then generates the MouseMove event. The second control dutifully reports the button that was pressed, but the button was pressed over the first control, not the second one. Unlike the MouseDown and MouseUp events, the MouseMove event can tell whether several buttons were pressed simultaneously.

Table 12-18	Mouse Buttons Users Press
Value	*Buttons Pressed*
0	None
1	Left
2	Right
3	Left and right
4	Middle
5	Left and middle
6	Middle and right
7	Left, middle, and right

You can use the Shift argument's value (listed in Table 12-19) to figure out which, if any, modifier keys were pressed at the time of the MouseMove. If both the Ctrl and Shift keys were pressed, for example, the value of Shift is 3.

Table 12-19	Values for Shift Argument for Mouse Events
Value	*Modifier Key (or Keys) Pressed*
1	Shift
2	Ctrl
3	Shift and Ctrl
4	Alt
5	Alt and Shift
6	Alt and Ctrl
7	All of 'em (Alt, Shift, and Ctrl)

If you want to identify individual key modifiers, you can use the constant values shown in Table 12-20.

Table 12-20	Settings for Shift (fmShift)	
Constant	*Value*	*Key Pressed with Mouse*
fmShiftMask	1	Shift
fmCtrlMask	2	Ctrl
fmAltMask	4	Alt

You might think that the mouse would have to move for a control to generate a MouseMove event, but that's not true for an HTML Layout control. If a user moves the mouse while the pointer is positioned over a blank area within the layout, the HTML Layout control fires off a MouseMove event. A MouseMove event is also generated, however, when the HTML Layout moves beneath the mouse pointer. (The Move() method applies to HTML Layouts and objects on a Layout.)

A miscellaneous event: Error

```
Sub objectName_Error(Number, Description, SCode, Source,
          HelpFile, HelpContext, CancelDisplay)
```

The Error event is generated by a wide array of controls, but it doesn't fall into any of the neat categories listed in this chapter. You probably won't need to use the Error event, which is intended primarily for use with more advanced Visual Basic versions. In case you do need to use it, however, it's briefly described in this section.

A control fires an Error event when an error occurs, but the control can't return the error information to the calling program. This usually means that the calling program wasn't prepared for the particular problem encountered by the control. The purpose of the Error event is to bundle into one neat and tidy package all the information necessary to debug the error. The Error event's arguments, shown in Table 12-21, have all the error information you could want. The code written for the Error event determines how the control responds to the error condition.

Table 12-21	Arguments to the Error Event
Argument	*Description*
Number	Unique value used to identify error
Description	Textual description of error
SCode	OLE status code for error
Source	String which identifies control that initiated the event
HelpFile	Fully qualified pathname for Help file that describes error
HelpContext	Context ID of Help file topic that contains description of error
CancelDisplay	Indicates whether to display error string in message box

The Error event gives you two things: enough information to track down the error (assuming that you're familiar with OLE programming) and a way to break the bad news to users. The Number and SCode arguments tell you which error occurred, and the Source argument tells you which control initiated the error (which is not necessarily the control that caused the error). All these arguments are designed to help programmers track down errors. The remaining arguments (Description, HelpFile, HelpContext, and CancelDisplay) give you information that helps users figure out what to do next.

Testing your newfound knowledge

1. What's an event handler?

A. One of those people who makes sure that politicians don't make even bigger fools of themselves.

B. Someone who promotes concerts, circuses, and other events.

C. A procedure that tells VBScript what to do when an event occurs.

D. A person just like an elephant handler, but who handles events instead.

2. The MouseMove event fires whenever:

A. A rodent packs up and heads out of town.

B. The mouse pointer is moved over a control or an HTML Layout moves underneath the mouse pointer.

C. When a cat appears and there's a mouse in the same room.

D. Every time a mouse anywhere twitches a muscle, which is why it's always going off.

Chapter 13

The High-Fashion World of Object Modeling

• •

In This Chapter

▶ Understanding the Internet Explorer Object Model

▶ Looking at the Window object

▶ Documenting the Document object

▶ Linking things together with the Link object

▶ Dealing with the Anchor object

▶ Designing forms with the Form object

▶ Handling the Navigator object

▶ Looking at the past with the History object

• •

*I*f you ask most people what the intestines of Internet Explorer look like, they usually will walk away from you at a brisk pace. You too could consider the innards of Explorer with fear and loathing (although you really should move to Las Vegas if you're into fear and loathing). If you're willing to delve into the heart of Explorer, you can amaze your friends, confound your enemies, and win the adulation of Web surfers across the globe.

With some knowledge of Explorer internals, you can change background and foreground colors, alter links on the fly, and send messages. Wait — put away your checkbook! You can also change history! That's right — if you understand the Internet Explorer Object Model for Scripting, the sky's the limit.

Because Internet Explorer has many faces, it looks different to different people. Explorer has one face for the programmers who work on Explorer, another for users who cruise with Explorer, and still another for people who write scripts to run under it. The scripting personality of Explorer is known as the Internet Explorer Object Model for Scripting. The Object Model is a description of what Explorer looks like from a script's-eye view. You can write scripts without knowing about the Object Model — you may have already written scripts for button presses or to process text — but you can't change the browser itself without the Object Model. Because the developers of Explorer anticipated that you would want to tinker with the browser, they created the Object Model.

 Although fiddling with the Object Model is the only way to change a browser's attributes, changing a control's properties can seem to change the browser — don't be fooled. If a designer has used an Image control to create a background image for a page, changing the properties of the Image control seems to change the browser window. How can you tell for sure? Take a look at the HTML source for the page that's being viewed.

In this chapter, the (capitalized) term Object Model means specifically the Internet Explorer Object Model. The closely related (all lowercase) term object model refers to any model that breaks something big into smaller pieces called objects.

Who Do Voodoo? You Do!

If you know how voodoo dolls work, you know what an object model is. To punish someone with a voodoo doll, you build a doll that represents that particular person, whom I'll call the target. If you stab the voodoo doll in the shoulder with a pin, the target suddenly feels a pang in the shoulder. You're not really stabbing the person in the shoulder — you're stabbing the doll that represents the person.

Why even bother with the doll? Because it's much easier to stab a doll than a crabby person. (If you want to antagonize someone while you're on vacation, it's much more difficult to pack a real person in a suitcase.) The bottom line is that it's easier to deal with dolls than with people — dolls are much less complicated. The Internet Explorer Object Model for Scripting is just a long name for a doll you can poke with pins written in a scripting language.

Objects for Peace, Love, and Understanding

The Object Model is more than just a doll because it gives you a window into the workings of Explorer. If you understand the Object Model, you know a great deal about how Explorer works. Although the model is not the object, it tells you how the designers of Explorer view Explorer (or at least how they want you to think they view it). The Object Model seems complicated because Explorer is a complex program; one of the advantages of object-oriented design, however, is that you can break the whole mess into bite-size chunks and find out about the parts without having to understand the whole.

If you look at a picture of the Object Model, it looks like a Christmas tree, with Window at the top. (Most computer experts call it a *hierarchy* because they don't want anyone to know that it's as simple as a tree.) The next time you're wandering in the wilderness, you can impress your friends by pointing to a large pine tree and declaring, "That's exactly what the Internet Explorer Object Model for Scripting looks like!"

Who's in Control Here?

Don't confuse the Object Model with the Internet Explorer control. The Object Model is an abstract version of the Explorer — a version that does two things: gives you a way to think about how Internet Explorer works and, through scripts, provides access to the inner workings of Internet Explorer. When you use the Object Model to tinker with Explorer, you change the browser in which your pages are viewed.

An Internet Explorer control is also available, however, which is the Internet Explorer browser packed into an ActiveX control. The Internet Explorer control looks like the Object Model because the properties and methods of the control resemble those of the Object Model. Despite their similarity, the two are different animals. You use the Object Model to abstractly understand and modify a running version of the browser. You use the Internet Explorer control as you would use any other control: To add the functionality of Internet Explorer to a page, you embed the control in the page, by using the <OBJECT> tag. You might use the Internet Explorer control to create, for example, a browser for someone who's using a Microsoft Access database application. When an Access user gets to your control, all the capabilities of Internet Explorer are added to those of Access.

The following example creates two buttons: one that changes the background for the browser and another that changes the background of an Explorer control. As you read through the example, try to separate the wheat from the chaff. Glance at the objects that are defined (with the <OBJECT> tags), and then look at the scripts and how the objects are used. When you skim through the objects, don't worry about the many properties the Control Pad has filled in — focus on which controls are being used and how they're labeled. (You can find the label for a control by looking at the ID attribute within the <OBJECT> tag. You have to know the ID for a control because that's how it is referred to in scripts.) As you look through the HTML code, notice the difference between the WebBrowser control and the Internet Explorer Object Model:

```
<HTML>
<HEAD>
<TITLE>Control versus Object</TITLE>

<SCRIPT LANGUAGE="VBScript">
<!--
Sub GoHome_Click()
```

(continued)

(continued)

```
' The Navigate method loads the page at the
' specified URL
  call WebBrowserControl.Navigate("http://www.dummies.com/
          E:\WordDocs\ActiveX\Small-page.htm")
end sub

Sub ControlButton_Click()
' A subtle trick here ensures that
' you can see the WebBrowser window.
' Because the browser control takes on the
' background color of its container, I've:
  ' 1) Changed the background color to blue
  ' 2) Forced a redraw of the browser control
  ' by changing its width
' 3) Changed the background color back again
  window.Document.bgColor = "blue"
  WebBrowserControl.Width = 350
  window.Document.bgColor = "red"
end sub

Sub BrowserButton_Click()
' Using the object model, I have changed the
' background for the browser window. (If
' you're familiar with C++, you'll recognize
' the format for referring to class members.)
' The statement below tells you that windows
' have documents and that documents have an
' attribute called background color:
  '     window
  '       |
  '     document
  '       |
  '     bgColor

  window.Document.bgColor = "red"
end sub
-->
</SCRIPT>

</HEAD>

<BODY>

<!-- The following three objects create the buttons and the
          buttons that are scripted to give the effects you
          see. -->

  <OBJECT ID="BrowserButton" WIDTH=397 HEIGHT=45
    CLASSID="CLSID:D7053240-CE69-11CD-A777-00DD01143C57">
```

```
                    <PARAM NAME="VariousPropertyBits" VALUE="268435483">
                    <PARAM NAME="Caption" VALUE="Change Browser
                        Background Color">
                    <PARAM NAME="Size" VALUE="8396;953">
                    <PARAM NAME="FontHeight" VALUE="280">
                    <PARAM NAME="FontCharSet" VALUE="0">
                    <PARAM NAME="FontPitchAndFamily" VALUE="2">
                    <PARAM NAME="ParagraphAlign" VALUE="3">
                    <PARAM NAME="FontWeight" VALUE="0">
            </OBJECT>

<BR>
<BR>

<OBJECT ID="ControlButton" WIDTH=262 HEIGHT=45
 CLASSID="CLSID:D7053240-CE69-11CD-A777-00DD01143C57">
    <PARAM NAME="VariousPropertyBits" VALUE="268435483">
    <PARAM NAME="Caption" VALUE="Change Control Width">
    <PARAM NAME="Size" VALUE="5539;953">
    <PARAM NAME="FontHeight" VALUE="280">
    <PARAM NAME="FontCharSet" VALUE="0">
    <PARAM NAME="FontPitchAndFamily" VALUE="2">
    <PARAM NAME="ParagraphAlign" VALUE="3">
    <PARAM NAME="FontWeight" VALUE="0">
</OBJECT>
<BR>
<BR>

<OBJECT ID="GoHome" WIDTH=127 HEIGHT=45
 CLASSID="CLSID:D7053240-CE69-11CD-A777-00DD01143C57">
    <PARAM NAME="VariousPropertyBits" VALUE="268435483">
    <PARAM NAME="Caption" VALUE="Go Home!">
    <PARAM NAME="Size" VALUE="2668;952">
    <PARAM NAME="FontHeight" VALUE="280">
    <PARAM NAME="FontCharSet" VALUE="0">
    <PARAM NAME="FontPitchAndFamily" VALUE="2">
    <PARAM NAME="ParagraphAlign" VALUE="3">
    <PARAM NAME="FontWeight" VALUE="0">
</OBJECT>

<H1>Web Browser Control</h1><BR>

<!-- The nice thing about ActiveX controls is how easy it is
        to add sophisticated touches to your pages. If
        you had to write a Web browser from scratch, you
        probably wouldn't bother. With Control Pad, you
        just insert an already-written Web browser. -->
```

(continued)

(continued)

```
     <OBJECT ID="WebBrowserControl"
  CLASSID="CLSID:EAB22AC3-30C1-11CF-A7EB-0000C05BAE0B">
     <PARAM NAME="Height" VALUE="250">
     <PARAM NAME="Width" VALUE="200">
     <PARAM NAME="AutoSize" VALUE="0">
     <PARAM NAME="ViewMode" VALUE="1">
     <PARAM NAME="AutoSizePercentage" VALUE="0">
     <PARAM NAME="AutoArrange" VALUE="1">
     <PARAM NAME="NoClientEdge" VALUE="1">
     <PARAM NAME="AlignLeft" VALUE="0">
</OBJECT>

</BODY>
</HTML>
```

The Object Model has a logical organization, shown in Figure 13-1. Because Window is at the top, it's a good place to begin.

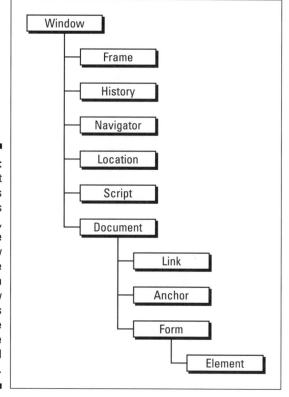

Figure 13-1:
The Object Model is organized as a hierarchy, with the Window object at the top. Each Window object has exactly one of the shaded objects.

The Door to the Object Model: The Window Object

The Window object represents the browser itself; each running instance of Internet Explorer has one Window object. (Remember that a user can start more than one instance of Explorer by choosing File⇨New Window — doing so also creates a new Window object. The object above all other objects is a window, and it's the top-level *container* (an object that can hold other objects). Windows contain exactly one of each of the following objects: History, Navigator, Location, and Document. In addition, every Window object contains one Frame object; the Frame object is an array that holds one or more frames. (For more information about arrays, see Chapter 11.) A Window object can contain any number of Script objects, including none. A Window object is more than just another pretty container, though — the Window object has properties, events, and methods of its own.

Properties

Every object underneath the Window object in the hierarchy is also a property of the Window object. For example, the Document object (shown underneath the Window object in Figure 13-1) is a property of the Window object. You access the properties of the Window object, listed in Table 13-1, just as you access any other object's properties:

```
Window.property
```

With the Window object (and only with the Window object), you can omit the Window object label and simply use this syntax:

```
property
```

You can refer to the current window's parent, for example, as follows:

```
<SCRIPT LANGUAGE="VBScript">
    '...
    pName = Parent.Name 'get the name of parent window
    '...
</ SCRIPT>
```

Table 13-1	Properties of the Window Object
Property	*Description*
DefaultStatus	Default text written on the status bar
Document	Document in the current window
Frame	Array of frame windows contained by a parent window
History	Used to access the history list from the browser
Location	Information about the location of the window's URL
Name	Name of the window
Navigator	Contains information about the browser application
Opener	Window that opened the current window
Parent	Parent of the current window
Self	Current window
Status	Text displayed on the status bar (lower left corner of browser window)
Top	Topmost window

DefaultStatus

```
[window.]DefaultStatus[=string]
```

Every Internet Explorer window has a status bar along the bottom. The status appears on the left side of the status bar. The status bar is usually used to update Internet Explorer users about the progress of the current operation. When a user follows a link, for example, Internet Explorer displays this message on the status bar:

```
Opening page http://somewhere.com/next-page.html
```

You can write your own message by assigning a string value to the DefaultStatus property:

```
DefaultStatus = "Your message here"
```

If you want to insert your own status text, offer users additional information. If a user follows a link to a subscription form, for example, you might change the status text to "Loading subscription form."

If you want the status text to be displayed as soon as a user loads a new page, use the Window_onLoad event to assign the new status text. Part of your script looks like this:

```
Sub Window_onLoad()
   window.dDefaultStatus = "New and improved status text!"
end sub
```

Name

```
[Window.]Name
```

Every window must have a name, and the name property is where it's at. Although you can read the value of the Name property, you can't change it. You can, however, create a new window and name it when it's created. You can create a window and name it in one of three ways:

- ✔ Use the Window.Open() method.
- ✔ Name the window by using the <FRAMESET> element's NAME attribute.
- ✔ Create a link to a new window named by the link's TARGET attribute.

The Open() method of the Window object opens a new instance of Internet Explorer, and you can pass the page to load and the window name as arguments to the Open() method:

```
<SCRIPT Language="VBScript">
   window.open("next-page.html", "Crazy Name");
</SCRIPT>
```

You can also split the Internet Explorer window into frames by creating a frameset that in turn contains frames you have named. (For more information about frames, see Chapter 3.) The following HTML code creates a frameset with two frames: one called "Crazy Name" and a second named "Really Crazy Name":

```
<FRAMESET
   COLS = "200, *"
   FRAMEBORDER = 0>
   <FRAME
      name = "Crazy Name"
      src = "next-page.html">
   <FRAME
      name = "Really Crazy Name"
      src = "page-after-that.html">
</FRAMESET>
```

The third way to name a window is to include an anchor that uses the TARGET attribute of the <A> tag:

```
<A HREF="next-page.html" TARGET = "Crazy Name">Next page
         (displayed in window called "Crazy Name").</A>
```

Opener

```
[Window.]Opener
```

Although the Opener property is documented as a property of the Window object, it's not available by using the Script Wizard or hand-written scripts. Although the property may be accessible in later versions, you should check any script that uses this property.

Parent

```
[Window.]Parent
```

Just as every window has a name, every window has a parent. For a window, the parent is the frame that contains the window. If no frame is holding the window, then the window is its own parent. Weird.

The expression `window.parent` evaluates to a window, and you can access that window's properties just as you can access any other. To display the name of the window's parent in a variable, for example, you could write:

```
parentName = window.parent.name    'Get name
MsgBox(parentName)    'Display name
```

Self

```
[Window.]Self
```

Everyone should have a sense of self, and Internet Explorer is no exception. If you want to refer to the current window, you can do so by using the Self property. The Self property evaluates to the window object of the current window. Although it may be fun to try, you can't change the value of this property: It's read-only.

Status

```
[Window.]Status[=string]
```

Like DefaultStatus, the Status property sets the text that appears on the left side of the status bar. The *status bar* is an unobtrusive way (compared to popping up a message box) to inform users about what's going on. Many people don't notice status text, though, so don't depend on it to convey critical information.

You can write your own message by assigning a string value to the Status property:

```
Status = "Your message here"
```

If you want to insert your own status text, offer users additional information. If a user follows a link to a subscription form, for example, you might change the status text to "Loading subscription form."

Top

```
[Window.]Top
```

Top is a read-only property whose value is the *topmost window* (the containing window of all frames in the current browser instance).

Events

The Window object supports two events: one for loading pages and another for unloading them. The onLoad event fires after the browser has processed all the HTML. The onUnload event fires when the page's contents are unloaded. A page is unloaded either just before a new page is loaded or just before the browser quits.

If you want to run a procedure when a Window event fires, you can do so in one of two ways:

- ✔ **Simply include your code in a procedure called Window_onLoad().** Whenever the Window object generates an onLoad event, your code runs.

- ✔ **Use an extension of the <BODY> tag in an HTML page.** Most HTML documents begin with the <HTML> tag and include both a head section (inside the <HEAD>...</HEAD>) and a body section (within the <BODY>...</BODY> tags). The exception is HTML files that use the <FRAMESET> tag; these files have a <HEAD> section but no <BODY>. (Perhaps they should be called Ichabod Crane files?)

If you want your procedure named DoThis() to run when the window's contents are loaded, you create a page similar to this one:

```
<HTML>
...
<BODY Language = "VBScript" onLoad = "DoThis">
...
<SCRIPT language = "VBScript">
...
Sub DoThis
  MsgBox "Hi, I'm the onLoad procedure!!"
End Sub
...
</SCRIPT>
....
</BODY>
</HTML>
```

You can also use the <BODY> tag to trigger the onUnload procedure:

```
<BODY Language = "VBScript" onUnload = "DoThat">
```

onLoad

```
onLoad = function-name
```

The onLoad event fires after all HTML has been parsed. *Parsing* is the action of reading the HTML code and interpreting it to display the page's content. The function-name must be a string that names an existing scripting function.

Because the onLoad event doesn't fire until *after* the HTML code has been parsed, you can't write a procedure that changes the HTML code for the document that was just loaded. (If you want to create new HTML documents on the fly, see the description of the Document.Write() method later in this chapter, in the "Write" section.)

To call the VBScript function DoWhenLoaded() when the page is loaded, use this line:

```
<BODY LANGUAGE = "VBScript" onLoad = "DoWhenLoaded">
```

onUnload

```
onUnload=function-name
```

The onUnload event fires whenever a page is unloaded. A page is unloaded when a user either jumps to a new page from the current page or quits the browser.

The onUnload event is your chance to clean up the mess you have made. If you have changed the browser's attributes, such as foreground or background color, you should change everything back before the user leaves. How do you know what the original values were? You make a copy of any values you will change in a procedure that fires the onLoad event. When a user arrives at your page, the page's scripts record the user's preferences. While a user is interacting with your page, you can make any changes you want to the browser and then restore the changes when the page is unloaded.

Methods

The methods of the Window object are listed in Table 13-2.

Table 13-2   What Can the Window Object Do for Me?

Method	What It Does
Alert	Displays a message in a pop-up window
ClearTimeout	Forgets all about a timer set with setTimer
Close	Closes the specified window
Confirm	Asks for user input
Navigate	Jumps to a new location
Open	Opens a new window from a script
Prompt	Asks the user for input
SetTimeout	Sets a timer and then performs an action when the timer goes off

Alert

```
Alert string
```

If you have to get a message across, the Alert() method can do the job. Calling Alert() and passing your message as a string argument pops up a window that displays your message. A simple click of the OK button, and the message vanishes as quickly as it appeared.

ClearTimeout

```
[Window.]ClearTimeout ID
```

If you started a countdown that you later decide to stop, you can use ClearTimeout(). You specify the timer by using the ID, which was returned by SetTimeout() when you first created the timer. Why set a timer only to get rid of it? You might start a timer, test for some condition, and then kill the timer depending on the condition. You can create a tutorial by using a series of Web pages, for example, and automatically flip from one page to the next unless the user clicks the Next Page button. To do so, you set a timer with SetTimer() and then cancel the timer if the user clicks the Next Page button.

Close

```
Window.Close
```

What do you do if Internet Explorer starts to get drafty? You close a window, of course! To close a window, call the Close() method. Calling Close() closes only the single Window object that invoked Close(). If more than one instance of Internet Explorer is running when you call Close(), other instances still run after Close() fires.

The Window object reference must be included for the Close() method to work. The following line of script closes the current browser instance:

```
Window.Close
```

Internet Explorer signals an error if you call the Close () method without the Window reference.

Confirm

```
[Boolean =] Confirm (string)
```

The Confirm() method is a handy way to double-check what a user wants. Calling Confirm() displays a dialog box with two buttons: OK and Cancel. A user clicks one of the two buttons to dismiss the dialog box, and the Confirm() method then stores either TRUE (for OK) or FALSE (for Cancel) in a Boolean variable.

It's always a good idea to ask users before embarking on any long or irrevocable actions. You can use Confirm, for example, to get user approval before erasing a hard disk:

```
eraseDrive = Confirm("Erase hard disk?")
if eraseDrive then
  ' User confirmed hard disk wipeout
  ...
else
  ' User decided not to erase
end if
```

Navigate

```
[Window.]Navigate URL
```

If you know where you're going, the Navigate method can get you there. Calling Navigate with a URL is similar to choosing File⇨Open and entering a new URL, except that you can do it within a script. Pick a URL, call Navigate, and away you go.

Open

```
[NewWindow = ]Window.Open URL, Target, ["[Toolbar=Boolean] [,
            Location = Boolean][, Directories=Boolean][,
            Status=Boolean][, Menubar=Boolean][,
            Scrollbars=Boolean][, Resizeable=Boolean][,
            Width=Pixels][, Height=Pixels]"
```

The Open() method looks complicated, but it's not bad if you take it one piece at a time. Microsoft designed the Object Model to be compatible with the existing object model for Netscape Navigator, which includes an Open() method. By including the Open() method in the Object Model, Microsoft has said, in effect, "Although it doesn't work today, we'll probably add it later."

Although some of the Microsoft documentation claims that the Open() method doesn't work, it does. You must, however, include the Window object reference. You could write the following line, for example:

```
Window.Open "http://www.dummies.com", "myWindow",
             "toolbar=no"
```

You cannot, however, use the short form (without the Window object):

```
Open "http://www.dummies.com", "myWindow", "toolbar=no"
```

What do all those parameters mean? The bottom line is that you have lots of control over the window being opened. You can specify the window whose Open() method is called by specifying a window parameter, but you can skip it if you just want to open a window from the current window. The rest of the parameters refer to the window being opened.

Just because you can't use the Open() method to open a new browser window doesn't mean that it can't be done. You can open a new browser window by specifying the TARGET attribute in a link as blank. (The TARGET attribute is used to specify a frame, and the blank target is a special target that tells the browser to open a new window. You can read about the details of frames in Chapter 3.) If a user clicks the following link, for example, a new browser window opens and the page is loaded into the new window:

```
<A HREF="new-window.html" TARGET="_blank">Open a new window</A>
```

The ActiveX Resource Guide on the CD-ROM in the back of this book uses this trick: If you click the link for the SoftQuad HoTMetaL Pro editor, a new window opens up and displays the home page for HoTMetaL Pro.

URL

If you want to open a new browser window for a user, you probably have a destination in mind. The URL parameter tells the new window where to begin browsing, and the parameters aren't optional because ya gotta start somewhere. If you're the indecisive type who just can't select the right URL from the millions available, just use the current URL. (Don't know how to figure out the current URL? No problem — it's part of the Object Model! (Check out the description of the Location object later in this chapter, in the "Location" section.)

Target

You have to tell Explorer where to go with your new browser window. Because every window has to have a name, you can, fortunately, tell them apart; the Target parameter picks the window. If you're environmentally conscious, you can recycle an existing window by giving its name as the target. If you're more of a conspicuous consumer, you can have a new window created for you by specifying a new name as the target. (Although the term *target* may sound somewhat aggressive, the parameter works the same as the TARGET attribute of an HREF in HTML.)

Toolbar, Location, Directories, Status, Menubar, Scrollbars, Resizeable

Together, these parameters control the appearance of the opened window. You choose each attribute for the window by setting the relevant parameters to either Yes or No. In a sense, these parameters (and Height and Width) are all one parameter because you pass the entire mess as a single string to the Open( ) method with commas separating each of the properties.

Width, Height

No surprises here: You set the size of the window (in pixels) by setting the Height and Width properties to the desired number of pixels. (Remember that the width and height are passed with the other appearance parameters as one big string.)

Suppose that you want to create a new window. You can create a resizable window (starting at 300 pixels high x 400 pixels wide) with a toolbar and scrollbars by including this command:

```
BrandNewWindow = open "http://www.microsoft.com", "myWindow",
        "Toolbar=Yes, Resizeable=Yes, Scrollbars=Yes,
        Height=300, Width=400"
```

As mentioned, you pass all the appearance parameters as one long string, with commas separating each item.

Prompt

```
[string =]Prompt [prompt] [, default]
```

Sometimes you want more information from users than the simple yes–no answer you can get from the Confirm( ) method (described earlier in this chapter, in the "Confirm" section). If you want users to enter a value, use the Prompt( ) method. Using Prompt( ), you can provide a message to be displayed (for example, "What's your lucky number?") and even offer a default value (for me, "7"). When the Prompt( ) method returns, you have your value. The following script fragment asks which lottery number the user wants:

```
LotteryNum = Prompt "Please enter a lottery number: ", "123-456"
```

The Prompt( ) method pops up a dialog box with the question and then lets users enter a number. After a user presses the OK button, the value that's entered is assigned to the variable LotteryNum. (If the user didn't enter a value and simply clicked OK, the default value of $123\text{-}456$ is used.)

SetTimeout

```
ID = [Window.]SetTimeout expression, msec
```

The SetTimeout( ) method sets a timer and then performs an action when the timer goes off.

If you have done any cat skinning, you won't be surprised to realize that there's more than one way to set a timer. You could use a Timer control, but who needs them? Every Explorer window comes with its own built-in timer, which you can use also. Every window comes with an unlimited number of timers, in fact, which all can count down simultaneously.

To set a timer, you have to tell Explorer two things: how long the timer should run and what to do when it goes off. You set the timer duration in milliseconds (1000 milliseconds = 1 second) by passing a number as the second parameter. To tell Explorer what to do, you give it an expression that evaluates to a procedure. To simulate a double-click on the button ClickTwice, for example, you write a procedure to handle the double-click (call it ClickTwice_DblClick) and then pass the name of the procedure to the timer:

```
SUB ClickTwice_DblClick()
  :
END SUB

ClickTimer = SetTimeout() ClickTwice_DblClick, 500
```

After the timer counts down for half a second, it calls your procedure, just as though someone had double-clicked the button.

The SetTimeout( ) method doesn't just ask without giving, though. In return for calling the method, you get back an ID. You need the ID to refer to the timer because several timers may be counting down simultaneously. Why refer to timers at all? If you change your mind, you can get rid of a timer with the ClearTimeout( ) method, which was described earlier in this chapter, in the "ClearTimeout" section.

When you use a timer, you probably set it, do something else, and then return to the timer when it goes off. Timers you create with SetTimeout( ) also work this way: You set the timer and do something else, and then the timer goes off. Computers like to finish one task before starting another, however — they prefer to start a timer, wait for it to count down, and then move on to another task. If timers created with SetTimeout( ) worked that way, they wouldn't be very useful because the line in your script following the call to SetTimeout( ) wouldn't be run until the timer was done. Usually you want timers to work just as you do: Set the timer, go on with the script, and then return to the timer when it goes off. When computers start on one task, move on to another task, and then return to the first task when notified, they are said to operate *asynchronously*. Timers created with SetTimeout( ) are asynchronous: The timer is set up, Explorer moves on to process the next script line and keeps processing your script until the timer goes off. After the timer goes off, Explorer evaluates the expression you gave when you created the timer.

Documenting the Document Object

The Document object reflects the HTML document currently in the browser and objects on the page — links, forms, buttons, and ActiveX objects. Methods and properties of the Document object must be called in a script by placing the document first in the statement. If you want to set the background color on the page, therefore, the script looks like this:

```
<SCRIPT LANGUAGE = "VBScript">
    Document.bgColor = "Blue"
</SCRIPT>
```

All properties and methods that modify the HTML contents must be called during HTML parse time. *Parsing* is the action of reading the HTML code and interpreting it to display the page's content. The Window object's onLoad event doesn't work because it doesn't fire until the parsing is complete. Instead, any script code that modifies HTML must be written in a script block that runs inline during the loading of the HTML document. (Running *inline* means that the code is executed as soon as the browser encounters the text of the script.) In the ActiveX scripting model, this process is known as *immediate execution*.

To change a link color, you insert into your document a script like the following:

```
<SCRIPT LANGUAGE="VBScript">
    Document.linkColor = "green"
</SCRIPT>
```

Notice that the script isn't attached to any event handler — it's just a chunk of VBScript dropped directly into the page.

Properties

The Document object has its own properties apart from the properties of the Window object that contains the document. The properties of Document objects are listed in Table 13-3.

Table 13-3   Documenting the Properties of the Document Object

Property	Description
aLinkColor	Current color of active links (disabled in Internet Explorer)
Anchors	Array of anchors on a given document
bgColor	Current color of background in a document
Cookie	Cookie for current document
fgColor	Foreground color of a document
Forms	Array of FORMs on a given document
LastModified	Last modified date of current page
LinkColor	Color value of current link color
Links	Array of hyperlinks in a given document
Location	Read-only representation of location object
Referrer	String containing URL of referring document
Title	Document's title (read-only)
vLinkColor	Current color of visited links in a document

The properties listed in Table 13-3 are properties of the current document, not the browser window. Because the status text displayed on the status bar is part of the browser window, it's included as a property of the Window object. Because the background color of a page is an attribute of that page, however, background color is a property of the Document object.

To make things a little more confusing, the Document object also contains objects, some of which are accessed through the Document object's properties. The Object Model says, for example, that a Document object contains a Link object. The Link object represents an array that holds all the links in an object. Like most objects, each Link object has its own properties and events, which are accessed by using the Link object. The trick is that you access the Link *object* through the Links *property* of a Document object.

To refer to the HREF property of the Link object's third link (remember that the Link object is a zero-based array), you write:

```
Document.links(2).href
```

The Form object and Anchor object work just like the Link object does. Each is a separate object, contained within a Document object, and is accessed through a property of the Document object. The Form object is accessed through the Forms property; the Anchor object, through the Anchors property.

aLinkColor

```
Document.aLinkColor [=rgb-value|string]
```

The aLinkColor property stores the color of active links. (A link is *active* while the mouse pointer is positioned over the link and the mouse button is pressed but not yet released. Because Internet Explorer doesn't support active links, this property isn't useful. The property is included for two reasons: to maintain compatibility with the Netscape object model for the Navigator browser and in case active links are added later.

As with other link colors, this property can be set only at parse time, so you have to assign the value in a script that executes before the browser is finished parsing the HTML:

```
<SCRIPT LANGUAGE="VBScript">
    Document.alinkColor = "green"
</SCRIPT>
```

Anchors

```
Document.Anchors[integer]
```

The Anchors property is the back door into the Anchor object, which is contained in the Document object. The Anchor object contains the anchors embedded within a document, and each anchor is stored as an element of the Anchors property array. (You can find more details about the Anchor object in the section "Anchor Objects Aweigh!" later in this chapter.)

The Anchors array is zero-based, so to access the first anchor in the document, you write:

```
Document.Anchors[0]
```

bgColor

```
Document.bgColor [=rgb-value|string]
```

The background color of the document is kept in the bgColor property. You can set the background color by using either an RGB color value or a predefined color name. (An *RGB color value* is a hexadecimal number that tells the computer the relative amounts of red, green, and blue to mix for a particular color. #FF0000 is red, for example, because it uses the maximum amount of red but no green or blue.) Internet Explorer has many predefined color names:

Aqua	Gray	Navy	Silver
Black	Green	Olive	Teal
Blue	Lime	Purple	White
Fuchsia	Maroon	Red	Yellow

If you use the bgColor property to find out the current background color, you get back the RGB value, not the color name.

Cookie

```
Document.Cookie [= string]
```

A *cookie* is a string expression that's stored on a user's computer and associated with the a particular page. Cookies are generally used to store information between a user's visits to a page. For example, login names, records of past purchases, and personal preferences are often stored in cookies. When a user returns to a page, the cookie for that page is sent and can be read by a script you have written. The nearby sidebar "Oatmeal raisin or chocolate chip?" provides more details about cookies, including why they're necessary.

If you set a cookie, you overwrite the current cookie information (for the current document). If you want to add incremental information to a page (for example, a new purchase by a user at an online store), you must create a new string that includes both the old and new information and then set it equal to the document's Cookie property.

As a designer, you have to include all the information for a document in a single string because there's only one string per cookie and only one cookie per document. You can create one long string, however, that includes all the information you need and then use string-manipulation procedures to pick out the relevant information. You might use the first eight characters to store a user's login name, for example, and then use the next four characters for the number of previous visits by a user. Both VBScript and JavaScript have operations for manipulating strings.

The following example code lets users create a new cookie and assign it a value. The new name and value are assigned to the Document object's Cookie property. To run the following code, create a blank HTML page and a CommandButton named cookieButton, and then insert the code. If you run this code with the "cookie warning" turned on (see the nearby sidebar, "Oatmeal raisin or chocolate chip?"), you immediately see the results of running this script:

```
Sub CreateCookie(cookieName, cookieValue)
    ' Assign the Document object's Cookie
    ' property to one long string which looks
    ' like an assignment of the cookieValue
```

(continued)

(continued)

```
        ' to the variable cookieName
        Document.Cookie = cookieName & "=" & cookieValue
End Sub
Sub cookieButton_onClick
    Dim cookieName
    Dim cookieValue

    cookieName = InputBox("Enter a name for the cookie ")
    cookieValue = InputBox("Enter value for '" & cookieName &
            "'")

    CreateCookie cookieName, cookieValue
End Sub
```

Oatmeal raisin or chocolate chip?

One of the problems Web developers have had is that *HTTP* (the protocol for communication on the Web) is a stateless protocol. Under HTTP, a connection is made from a user's browser (the client) to the Web server, information is exchanged, and then the connection is broken. A user typically clicks a link in a document, which points to a page located on a remote server. The client contacts the server and establishes a connection. Then the client tells the server which page it wants (based on the link the user clicked). As soon as the page is sent from the browser, the link between the client and the server is broken.

The problem is that the server has no way to track the client. Several proposals have been made to enable the server to maintain some information about the client; the most popular approach uses a *cookie,* which is a chunk of information the server sends, along with the page contents, to the client. The cookie is then tossed in with the rest of the client's cookies and stored on the user's hard disk. The next time the client connects to a server, the corresponding cookie is sent to the server.

Cookies offer many new possibilities for Web design. A shopping service can use cookies to track which items a user has tossed into a virtual cart. Many login-based services on the Web use cookies to save users the trouble of entering a login name and password by storing both in a cookie. Cookies are a good way to store all sorts of user preferences so that every time a user visits your page, you can remember what you found out during the last visit. If you want to know just how widely used cookies are, you can ask Internet Explorer to notify you every time you receive a cookie: Choose View⇨Options and then click the Advanced tab. Check the box next to the line "Warn before accepting 'cookies.'" As you cruise around the Web, Internet Explorer asks for permission to accept a cookie every time one is sent. Netscape Navigator also notifies you about incoming cookies if you do the following: Choose Options⇨Network Preferences from the menu bar, click the Protocols tab, and then check the "Accepting a Cookie" box.

fgColor

```
Document.fgColor[= rgb-value | string]
```

The foreground color of the document is kept in the fgColor property. You can set the foreground color by using either an RGB color value or a predefined color name. An *RGB color value* is a hexadecimal number that tells the computer the relative amounts of red, green, and blue to mix for a particular color. #FF0000 is red, for example, because it uses the maximum amount of red but no green or blue. Internet Explorer has many predefined color names:

Aqua	Gray	Navy	Silver
Black	Green	Olive	Teal
Blue	Lime	Purple	White
Fuchsia	Maroon	Red	Yellow

If you use the fgColor property to find out the current foreground color, you get back the RGB value, not the color name.

Forms

```
Document.Forms [integer]
```

The Forms property is the back door into the Form object, which is part of the Document object. (You can get more details about the Form object in the section "The Object of My Form Desire," later in this chapter.)

The Form object contains the forms embedded within a document, stored as a zero-based array. If you want the first form in the document, you write:

```
Document.Forms[0]
```

LastModified

```
Document.LastModified
```

The LastModified property stores the date on which the page was last updated. You can't set this property to a new value, but you can use it to find out how recently the page was changed. To set a variable to the date value, include a line like this one:

```
ModifiedDate = Document.LastModified
```

LinkColor

```
Document.LinkColor [=rgb-value | string]
```

The LinkColor property stores the color of links in a document. Redoing all the links after the page has been displayed would be time-consuming, so you have to set the value of LinkColor before the page is painted.

The following script sets the link color:

```
<SCRIPT LANGUAGE="VBScript">
  Document.LinkColor = "green"
</SCRIPT>
```

Links

```
Document.Links [integer]
```

The Links property is the back door into the Link object, which is contained in the Document object. The Link object is a zero-based array of the links embedded in a document; each link is an element of the array. You can find more details about the Link object in the section "Tying Things Together with a Link Object," later in this chapter.

Location

```
Document.location
```

The Location property gives you the location of the current document in cyberspace. You can't set this property to a new value, but you can check its value. To jump to a new location, use the Document object's Navigate() method. To assign the document's location to a variable, use this line:

```
whereAmI = Document.location.href
```

Referrer

```
Document.referrer
```

If you move to a new town, you may find a doctor but still be looking for a new dentist. Your doctor, Dr. Quack, may suggest that you see Dr. Tooth as your dentist. After you're nestled safely in the dental chair but only after the longest instrument in the office is halfway down your throat, Dr. Tooth may ask, "Who referred you?" If you were a Document object, Dr. Tooth wouldn't have to ask — a quick glance at your Referrer property, and the question would be answered.

In the Web world, the Referrer property is defined only when you reach Page B by clicking a link from Page A. (In this case, Page A is the referrer for Page B.) If a user types an address directly in the Internet Explorer Address box, Referrer is NULL.

Title

```
Document.title
```

Documents in HTML are assigned a title by the required tag <TITLE>. The page title is stored in the Title property for your use. Because Title is read-only, don't even think about changing a page title with this property.

vLinkColor

```
Document.vLinkColor [=rgb-value | string]
```

The vLinkColor property stores the color of visited links in a document. A *visited link* is one that points to a page the user has recently seen. You have to set the value of LinkColor before the page is painted on-screen, because it's too costly to bother repainting the page just to change the link color.

The following script sets the color of visited links:

```
<SCRIPT LANGUAGE="VBScript">
 Document.vLinkColor = "gray"
</SCRIPT>
```

Events

The document object currently has no events, although some may be added later.

Methods

The methods of the Document object (listed in Table 13-4) all treat the document as a *stream,* which is an abstract structure for input and output. You usually can write to a stream, which adds characters to the end of a stream, and read from it, which removes characters. You probably won't use these methods unless you want to create HTML pages on the fly, which you can do with the Write() method.

Table 13-4	Methods for the Document Object
Method	*What It Does*
Clear	Updates screen to display all the strings written after the last Open() method call
Close	Closes document output stream and writes data to the screen
Open	Opens document stream so that it can be written to
Write	Inserts string into current document
WriteLn	Inserts into current document a string followed by a newline character

Clear

```
Document.Clear
```

The Clear() method flushes out the document stream and in the process writes all the data in the stream to the screen. If you want to display what you have written to an open stream but aren't ready to close it yet, use Clear().

Close

```
Document.Close
```

The purpose of the Close() method isn't surprising: It closes the open document stream and displays the output on the stream. If you want to display what has been written to the stream and continue writing to the stream, use the Clear() method.

Open

```
Document.Open
```

The Open() method opens a stream, which then can be written to by the Write and WriteLn() methods. After you're done writing, the Document.Close() method closes down the stream. If the referenced document already exists, any information contained in the document is cleared. To write "Howdy folks!" to the document, use:

```
Document.Open
Document.WriteLn "Howdy folks!"
Document.Close
```

This example is identical to the following:

```
Document.WriteLn "Howdy folks!"
```

with two exceptions. When you write to an open document stream, nothing is displayed until the stream is closed. In the second example, however, calling the WriteLn() method without first opening a stream displays the string immediately on-screen. The second exception involves clearing the document: In the first example, Document.Open clears the document; in the second, "Howdy folks!" is appended to the end of the current document.

Write

```
Document.Write string
```

The Write() method writes a string to the document stream.

The document being written to by the Write() method is usually the same document in which the Write() method appears. Loading the following HTML code into a browser prints a question followed by a statement:

```
<HTML>
<BODY>
<SCRIPT LANGUAGE="VBScript">
 Document.Write ("Is this a document?")
</SCRIPT>
This is a Document.
</BODY>
</HTML>
```

This HTML code produces the following text:

```
Is this a document? This is a Document.
```

Because the Write() method simply appends text if a stream hasn't been opened, it matters where you put the call to the Write() method within your code:

```
<HTML>
<BODY>
This is a Document.

<SCRIPT LANGUAGE="VBScript">
   Document.write ("This doesn't look like a document to me!")
</SCRIPT>

</BODY>
</HTML>
```

This code now produces the inline text ("This is a Document.") followed by the result of the Write() method:

```
This is a document. This doesn't look like a document to me!
```

WriteLn

```
Document.WriteLn string
```

The WriteLn() method is similar to the Write() method, except that WriteLn() tacks on a newline character to the end of its string argument. The addition of a newline is more complicated than it seems at first because the browser ignores newlines in the HTML code. If you want to display the newline appended by WriteLn(), you must wrap the WriteLn() statement in a preformatted tag (<PRE>).

If you use the WriteLn() method but without the enclosing <PRE> tags, you may as well have used Write(). The following code fragment lacks the <PRE> tags:

```
<SCRIPT LANGUAGE="VBScript">
Document.WriteLn ("Howdy folks!")
   Document.Write ("Howdy folks!")
</SCRIPT>
```

Here's the result without the <PRE> tags:

```
Howdy folks! Howdy folks!
```

If you want to preserve the newline added by WriteLn(), you must change the preceding script to

```
<PRE>
   <SCRIPT LANGUAGE="VBScript">
Document.WriteLn ("Howdy folks!")
      Document.Write ("Howdy folks!")
   </SCRIPT>
</PRE>
```

Now the result of the script fragment displays the text with the included newline:

```
Howdy folks!
Howdy folks!
```

Tying Things Together with a Link Object

The Link object is a zero-based, read-only array. As the browser reads a document, each link it encounters is given its own Link object. A *link* is defined in scripting as any anchor tag (<A>) that contains an HREF attribute, as shown in this example:

```
<A HREF="http://www.microsoft.com">
```

The properties of the Link object, which are the same as the Location object's properties, are accessible only through the indexed array of links.

The lines in the following script example set LinkText to the location pointed to by the third link on the page (if it exists):

```
<SCRIPT language="VBScript">
   [Preceding VBScript code]
   LinkText = Document.links(2).href
```

```
[Following VBScript code]
</SCRIPT>
```

Properties

Each Link object represents a URL. As discussed in Chapter 3, a URL has several components, and the Link object has properties (listed in Table 13-5) for each of these components. Because you often want just part of a link's URL, the Link object has the component parts split out into separate properties so that you get only what you need by picking and choosing among the properties.

Table 13-5	Properties of the Link Object
Property	*Portion of URL Represented*
Hash	Hash portion, if specified
Host	Host and port portions (hostname:port)
Hostname	Host portion (either a name or an IP address)
Href	Compete URL for the link
Pathname	Pathname
Port	Port number
Protocol	Protocol portion
Search	Search portion (if specified)
Target	Link TARGET (if specified)

All the Link object's properties are read-only: Look — but don't touch.

Hash

```
Link.Hash
```

If you want to send a user to a particular location on a page, you can do so by inserting a <NAME> tag in the HTML and including a link to the page that specifies the name. You specify a particular <NAME> tag by including the name after the hash mark (#) in the URL that points to the page. The hash portion of the following URL, for example, is #user:

```
http://www.microsoft.com/intdev#user
```

If no hash is specified in the link object, the Hash property is set to NULL.

Host

```
Link.Host
```

The Host property of a Link object includes the host and port portions of the URL. In the `http://www.microsoft.com` example, the Host property is set to `www.microsoft.com:80`. (The port number of 80 was not included in the original URL; because it's the default port for HTTP service, however, it's the port that's used.)

Hostname

```
Link.Hostname
```

The hostname portion of the URL is stored in the Hostname property. In the following URL, the hostname is `www.microsoft.com`:

```
http://www.microsoft.com
```

Href

```
Link.Href
```

If you want the full URL for a link, you don't have to put all the pieces of a link object back together: Just use the Href property.

Pathname

```
Link.Pathname
```

Although the host portion of a URL tells the browser which server to connect to, the server has to know which directory the client wants. The pathname tells the server where to look in the directory structure for the linked-to page. If the full URL is

```
http://www.some-server.com/one/two/three
```

the pathname is `/one/two/three`.

Port

```
Link.Port
```

Network servers often must wear many hats: file server, Web server, mail server, and so on. Because one computer may have to play all these roles, it has to have a way to tell the different roles apart. The solution is to designate different ports for different services. Although Web service is offered at port 80 by default, Web servers can provide service from another port. If the Web port is a port other than port 80, the port number must be included in all URLs that point to pages on that Web server. The port is included in the URL after the hostname, following a colon (:). The following URL, for example, hides a port number of 123:

```
http://www.some-server.com:123/one/two/three
```

Protocol

```
Link.Protocol
```

Although the protocol of choice on the Web is HTTP, browsers often support other protocols too. A *protocol* is a set of conventions for communicating between computers. The most common protocols on the Internet are Telnet and FTP, but others exist. Every URL first specifies the protocol, before a colon (:). A link to an FTP server may point to `ftp://ftp.file.com/`, whose protocol is `ftp`. The Protocol property includes the colon in the protocol name.

Search

```
Link.Search
```

Most Web sites include search engines that enable users to search for text throughout the Web site. The search engine knows which terms to look for on the site because the search terms are specified in the query portion of a URL. The following URL includes the term *user* in the search portion:

```
http://www.microsoft.com/intdev?user
```

Target

```
Link.Target
```

When you create a link to a page, you can designate the window in which the new page is displayed. The new window's name is specified by the TARGET attribute of the anchor tag, <A>. (You can read more about targets in Chapter 3.) A typical URL with a target resembles this example:

```
<A HREF="next-page.html" TARGET = "Crazy Name">Next page
          (displayed in window called "Crazy Name").</A>
```

The Target property for this link is "Crazy Name."

Events

Although living the life of a link is boring, it does have three noteworthy events, as listed in Table 13-6.

Table 13-6	Events in the Life of a Link
Event	**When It Fires**
onClick	When user clicks a link
onMouseMove	When user moves mouse while it's over the link
onMouseOver	When user first moves mouse over the link

Each of the three events can be used in either of two ways. In one method, you can name a procedure to be called when the event fires:

```
<SCRIPT LANGUAGE=VBScript
    FOR = link-name EVENT = "onMouseOver">
```

Another method lets you include script commands directly in the link:

```
<A HREF="http://www.microsoft.com"
    onClick="alert ('Clicked here')">
To Microsoft</a>
```

onClick

```
link.onClick
```

The onClick event fires whenever a user clicks a link.

onMouseOver

```
link.onMouseOver
```

Like the onMouseMove event, the onMouseOver event fires whenever a user moves the mouse pointer over a link. Unlike that other mouse movement event, though, the onMouseOver doesn't include any additional information. If you want to know where the mouse was clicked, you should use the onMouseMove event instead.

onMouseMove

```
Link.onMouseMove Shift, Button, X, Y
```

The onMouseMove event fires whenever a user moves the mouse pointer over a link. The event includes some useful information, such as the state of the Shift key and which mouse button was pressed. The x and y parameters give the coordinates of the mouse click in pixels.

Although the shift and button parameters are included in the description of the onMouseMove event, the current version of the Object Model sets both to zero.

Methods

The Link object doesn't currently support any methods.

Anchor Objects Aweigh!

An Anchor object is built for each anchor tag (<A>) in a document. Each Anchor object is simple: no events, no methods, and only one property. You can read or change the name of an Anchor object by using the Name property. Here's the syntax:

```
Document.Anchors(i).Name
```

Each Document object has an array of Anchor objects (called anchors), and each Anchor object in the array has the sole property Name.

Because every anchor is a link (although not every link is an anchor), if you want detailed information about a link, you can find it in the Link object created for that particular link (which is accessed through the Links array property of the Document object).

The Object of My Form Desire

Although you can design some dandy forms with ActiveX controls, forms have been around longer than ActiveX. A *form* is a collection of elements designed for user input. A user fills out an online form and then sends off the responses by clicking a Submit button. Every HTML form is enclosed in a pair of <FORM>...</FORM > tags. For each form a browser encounters, a Form object is created. Because more than one form can be on a page, the Document object contains an array of Form objects, which are stored in the Forms property of the Document object.

Form objects are stored (within the Forms property) by name and by index, and you can access a form in either of two ways:

- ✔ **By index:** The Document object's Forms array
- ✔ **By name:** Given in the NAME="form-name" attribute of the HTML <FORM> tag

In the following example, the Sub procedure PressedByName() uses the form's name, and PressedByIndex() uses the index value:

```
<SCRIPT LANGUAGE = "VBScript">
' ...first way, by name ...

SUB PressedByName()
    ' access the form by name
 Document.ButtonForm.Easy.Value = "Hey, take it easy"
END SUB


' ... second way, by index...

' Note that indexes start at 0, not 1!

SUB PressedByIndex()
    ' access the form by index
Document.Forms(0).Hard.Value="Not so hard"
END SUB
</SCRIPT>

<FORM NAME = "ButtonForm">
    <INPUT TYPE = "button"
        NAME = "Easy"
        VALUE="Hi, I'm Button1"
        onClick="PressedByName"
        LANGUAGE="VBScript">
    <INPUT TYPE="button"
        NAME="Hard"
        VALUE="Hi, I'm Button2"
        onClick="PressedByIndex"
        LANGUAGE="VBScript">
</FORM>
```

Properties

The properties of the Form object, listed in Table 13-7, duplicate many of the settings included in the <FORM> tag. As a reminder, the <FORM> tag in HTML looks like this:

```
<FORM
    ACTION=url
    METHOD=get-post
    TARGET=window>
...
</FORM>
```

Table 13-7	Properties of the Form Object
Property	*Description*
Action	Address used to carry out the action of the form
Elements	Array of elements on the form
Encoding	Encoding for the form
Method	How form data should be sent to the server
Target	Target window in which to display form results

Action

```
Form.Action [= string]
```

If no URL is specified, the base URL of the document is used. Changing the Action property of a Form object is the same as changing the ACTION attribute of the <FORM> tag. The following script, therefore:

```
Document.Form[0].Action = "http:// www.sample.com/bin/search"
```

is identical to this one:

```
<FORM
    ACTION="http:// www.sample.com/bin/search">
</FORM>
```

Elements

```
Form.Elements [= string]
```

Forms wouldn't be useful for user input unless they contained user input doo-hickeys, such as buttons and check boxes. Thanks to the democracy of the standards-setting process, however, doohickey lost out as the official name. Instead, each of the little buggers is known as an *intrinsic element*. In addition to intrinsic elements, forms can include embedded objects (such as ActiveX controls).

The following HTML fragment has several elements of both kinds:

```
<FORM ACTION="http://www.somewhere.com/search"
   METHOD=GET>
   <OBJECT NAME="anObject"
     DATA=...>
   </object>
   <INPUT NAME="aCheckBox"
     TYPE ... >
```

(continued)

(continued)

```
    <INPUT NAME="aButton"
        TYPE ... >
    <INPUT NAME="aRadio" TYPE ... >
</FORM>
```

This HTML code example creates an Elements array within the Form object. The array is four elements long (specified by `form.elements.length`). The name of the first element is "aCheckbox," which is specified by `form.elements[1].name`.

Grab the secret Encoding ring!

```
Form.Encoding [= string]
```

Data is often *encoded,* or transformed from one format into another, before it is sent across a network. The encoding process ensures that no matter how strange the data format, the content travels across the network unscathed. The Internet standard for specifying encodings is *MIME,* which is the acronym for Multipurpose Internet Mail Extensions. MIME types are of the form `type/subtype`; a common Web encoding is `text/html`. If no MIME type is specified, the encoding `text/html` is assumed.

Changing the encoding of a form by setting the Encoding property is similar to setting the ENCTYPE attribute of the <FORM> tag. The following script fragment uses the Encoding property:

```
Document.Form[0].Action = "http://www.somewhere.com/search"
Document.Form[0].Encoding = "text/html"
```

This script has the same effect as setting the ENCTYPE attribute:

```
<FORM ACTION=" http://www.somewhere.com/search "
    ENCTYPE="text/html">
</FORM>
```

Method

```
Form.Method[GetOrPostString]
```

After a user fills out a form, it's time to send off the results. Form results can be sent to a server in two ways:

✔ **GET:** Appends the arguments to the action URL and opens it as though it were an anchor

✔ **POST:** Sends the data by way of HTTP post

As with the other properties, the FORM tag has an attribute analogous to the Method property of the Form object. Changing the METHOD attribute by using the Form object works as follows:

```
Document.Form[0].Action = "http://www.somehwere.com/search"
Document.Form[0].Method = "GET"
```

This HTML fragment is identical to setting the METHOD attribute of the FORM tag:

```
<FORM ACTION="http://www.somehwere.com/search"
    METHOD=GET>
</FORM>
```

Target your results

```
form.target [=string]
```

When you design a form, you can specify the window in which you want the form results displayed; the TARGET attribute designates the window. For each form created by a pair of <FORM>...</FORM> tags, a Form object is created and the form's target is placed in the Target property of the object. Setting the TARGET attribute of a <FORM> tag and changing the value of the Target property produce the same result.

Events

If you're going to ask users for input, they're going to give you mistakes. Although users submit primarily flawless forms, they occasionally enter state abbreviations where zip codes should be and type telephone numbers in place of addresses. By using the Form object's lone event, onSubmit, you can head off mistakes before the invalid forms are sent to your server.

The Form object supports one event: onSubmit. The onSubmit event fires when the form is submitted. A form is usually submitted when a user clicks a button labeled Submit. The Submit button is usually an intrinsic button control whose TYPE attribute is "submit." With the onSubmit event, you can check the data on a form and then either send it to the server or cancel the submission.

Here's the syntax for onSubmit:

```
Form.onSubmit = action
```

If you just want to run a form through another procedure before it's submitted, you can use this syntax:

```
Form.onSubmit = "PostProcessForm()"
```

The preceding script code calls PostProcessForm() and submits the form regardless of the return value of PostProcessForm(). If you have to encode some of the form data or transform it before the data is sent to the server, using the following syntax is the easiest way:

```
Form.onSubmit = action
```

You can also make the form's submission depend on the value of the *action* function. Suppose that you create a form for users to register at your Web site and you want to be sure that they have entered an e-mail address before they continue. You could write a script called CheckEmail() and use the script to verify the form data:

```
Form.onSubmit = "return CheckEmail()"
```

The addition of the word *return* tells the onSubmit routine, "If the CheckEmail() procedure returns TRUE, go ahead and submit the form; if CheckEmail() returns FALSE, cancel the form submission."

Methods

The Form object has only one method: Submit(). The Submit() method takes no arguments and does nothing other than send the form on its merry way. Here's the syntax for Submit:

```
Form.Submit
```

If you have ever used the <FORM> tag to create user-input forms, you should know that calling the Submit() method is the same as a user clicking a form input whose TYPE is SUBMIT. (The <FORM> tag isn't discussed in this book because ActiveX has alternatives for building forms — see Chapter 9.)

Sailing Away with the Navigator Object

The Navigator object is a treasure trove of information about the browser application. Whether you want to know the name of the browser application that's running or the browser's version number, the Navigator object knows it all. (If Navigator seems like an odd choice for part of the *Microsoft* Internet Explorer Object Model, check out the nearby sidebar "How did an Explorer turn into a Navigator?")

How did an Explorer turn into a Navigator?

You may think that the Microsoft marketing department must have let this one slip by: naming a major part of the Object Model after Explorer's biggest competitor. This time, the company was stuck: It had to ensure compatibility between the Netscape object model for Navigator and the Microsoft object model for Internet Explorer. Netscape chose to name the object that stored application information after the Netscape browser, Navigator.

If Microsoft had chosen instead to create an object model that referred to the application as an object named Explorer, there would have been trouble: All the scripts that had been as-

sumed to be the Netscape object model (which has a Navigator object) would break when run by Internet Explorer.

If you had written a script that read the application name using the Navigator object, for example, you would use a line like this:

```
ApplicationName =
    Navigator.appName
```

If Microsoft had renamed the Navigator object to Explorer, however, your script would no longer work. Because Netscape got there first, Microsoft decided to go with the name Navigator.

Properties

Although the Navigator object doesn't do anything, it does have some useful properties, listed in Table 13-8.

Table 13-8	Properties of the Navigator Object
Property	*Description*
AppCodeName	Code name of application
AppName	Name of application
AppVersion	Application version number
UserAgent	User agent of application

Because different browsers have different capabilities, you can often design more stunning Web sites if you're certain which browser a Web surfer will use to access your site. You can either limit enjoyment of your site to users with particular browsers or design your site to accommodate the lowest common denominator. A more elegant solution is to design versions of your sites for specific browsers and then send users to the pages for their browser. (This solution is elegant, but it also requires more work because you have to design multiple copies of each page.)

You can send users to the appropriate pages in two ways:

- ✔ Ask which browser they're using.
- ✔ Use the Navigator object to find out for yourself.

To use the second method, you can write a script that checks the browser's UserAgent property (refer to Table 13-8) and then jumps to a browser-specific page based on the results.

AppCodeName, AppName, AppVersion, UserAgent

```
Navigator.appCodeName
Navigator.appName
Navigator.appVersion
Navigator.UserAgent
```

All the properties of the Navigator object are similar, in both syntax and results. Each property provides slightly different information. The values of each property version for Version 3.01 of Internet Explorer are listed in Table 13-9. As new versions of Internet Explorer (or Netscape Navigator) are released, some of this information will change, so double-check the values before relying on them.

Table 13-9	Navigator Properties for Internet Explorer Version 3.01
Property	**Value**
AppCodeName	Mozilla
AppName	Microsoft Internet Explorer
AppVersion	2.0 (compatible; MSIE 3.0A; Windows 95)
UserAgent	Mozilla/2.0 (compatible; MSIE 3.0A; Windows 95)

The values in Table 13-9 apply to Internet Explorer Version 3.0 (4.70.1215); these values can (and probably will) change. (If you want to know which version you have, choose Help⇨About Internet Explorer.) The values for Netscape Navigator 3.0 are similar, but don't include any references to Internet Explorer or MSIE, of course. The values are listed here to give you an idea of what's stored in each property.

Because *Mozilla* was the original name for the Netscape browser, it is used in the Netscape object model. (Mozilla appears twice in Table 13-9.) Because Microsoft wanted to maintain compatibility with the Netscape model, Mozilla is also used for Internet Explorer.

Setting sail with a script

Figure 13-2 shows a message box that displays each of the Navigator properties (for a version of Internet Explorer, not Navigator). The script that produced the message box demonstrates the use of the Navigator object in action:

```
<SCRIPT LANGUAGE="VBScript">
<!--
Sub Window_onLoad()
    ' Create a newLine variable to space output
    ' in dialog box.
    newLine = chr(10) & chr(13)

    ' Each of the Navigator object properties
    ' is assigned to a variable, which is then
    ' displayed by the MsgBox routine
    ApplicationName = "Application: " & Navigator.appName
    Version = "Version: " & Navigator.appVersion
    CodeName = "Code name: " & Navigator.appCodeName
    SecretAgent = "User agent: " & Navigator.userAgent

    MsgBox(ApplicationName & newLine & Version & newLine &
              CodeName  & newLine & SecretAgent)


end sub
-->
</SCRIPT>
```

Events

The Navigator object is all properties and no events. In the future, however, events may be added, so keep your eyes peeled.

Methods

The Navigator object has no methods yet, but you never know.

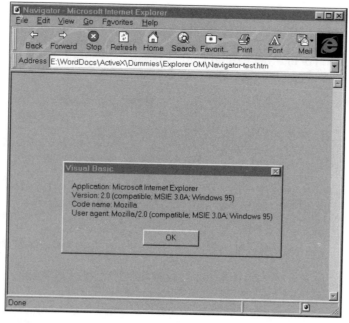

Figure 13-2:
Displaying
the
properties
of the
Navigator
object.

Knowing Your History Object

The History object (which sits under the Window object in the Object Model) lets a script writer access the browser's *history list,* which is a list of the addresses a browser has visited. Browsers often maintain several different lists of recently visited places. Both Internet Explorer and Netscape Navigator, for example, keep a short list on the Go menu, which is much like the list of recently opened files that many applications offer on their File menu. A history list, however, displays more detail about each page than is on the Go menu. A typical history list often includes dozens of pages rather than the few that are listed on a Go menu list. You can check out the Internet Explorer history list by choosing Go⇨Open History Folder; in Navigator, choose Window⇨History.

Microsoft uses the term *history list* to refer to the list shown on the Go menu; it uses *History folder* for the list of all sites visited since Internet Explorer was started. Because history list, more commonly means the full list, however (not the shorter list shown on a menu), I stick with that term in this chapter.

You can use the History list to see where a user has been on the Web. You get no guarantees of coverage, though — the history list doesn't necessarily list the last 100 pages or cover the past 10 days. If you want to know whether a user has visited other pages at your site recently, you can probably find out from the history list, through the History object.

Properties

The History object has just one lone property: Length. It tells you how many items are currently on the history list. Here's the syntax:

```
History.Length
```

The Length property always returns 0, but that could change — don't give up on Length yet.

Events

Here's another boring object — History doesn't generate any events.

Methods

The History object supports the methods listed in Table 13-10, which enable you to step back and forth through the history list and send a user's browser to pages in the history list.

Table 13-10	Methods for the History Object
Method	**What It Does**
Back	Goes back, just like the browser's Back button
Forward	Moves forward one page, just like the browser's Forward button
Go	Jumps to an item within the history list

Back, Forward

```
History.Back n
History.Forward n
```

The Back() and Forward() methods send users backward and forward, respectively, through the history list; the argument *n* sets the number of steps to jump backward or forward. If you invoke the Back() method in a script and pass it a parameter (*n*), it's the same as a user's clicking the Back button on the browser *n* times; the same is true of the Forward method.

Go

```
History.Go n
```

The Go() method send the browser to the *n*th item in the history list. The following call, for example, sends a user's browser to the third item in the list:

```
History.Go 3
```

Good programming practice suggests that you check the length of the list before calling Go() to ensure that you don't send the user to a non-existent item (the tenth item on a list of four items, for example). In Internet Explorer Version 3.01, the History object's Length property is, unfortunately, broken and always returns 0. Be prepared for things to go slightly awry.

Testing your newfound knowledge

1. **Within the Internet Explorer Object Model, the Window object is:**

A. The object that represents the browser application's window.

B. A magnifying glass that makes the rest of the Object Model look very big.

C. The part of the Object Model that is most easily broken.

D. I don't know what the Window object is, but it sure gets dirty fast.

2. **If you want to know which browser a user has, you can find out by:**

A. Who cares which browser a user has?

B. A user's browser is the user's business, and I'm not going to pry.

C. Checking the properties of the Navigator object.

D. Wait for the user to mention it in casual conversation.

Part IV
The Part of Tens

"OH, IT'S NICE HAVING A COMPLETELY COMPUTERIZED HOUSE. EXCEPT ONCE IN A WHILE IT LOSES ALL OF THE FURNITURE AND REFUSES TO LET ME IN THE FRONT DOOR, CALLING ME AN 'INVALID FILE.'"

In this part . . .

This part of the book is the ...*For Dummies* answer to David Letterman's lists. Ten cool controls that aren't covered elsewhere in the book await your perusal. You can also find handy VBScript tips, including where to get more information and a few programming tricks.

Chapter 14
Ten Cool ActiveX Controls

In This Chapter

▶ A gallery of cool controls (some free and some not)

. . . .

Adobe Acrobat Reader

http://www.adobe.com/

Despite the Web's fondness for text, it's difficult to produce documents requiring advanced layout features. Adobe, which has been in the desktop publishing game for a while, has developed the Acrobat system for displaying fancy text.

As a designer, you create documents in the Adobe Portable Document Format (PDF) and include links to those documents on your pages. People who surf by your site can then use the Acrobat Reader to view — but not edit — documents in PDF format.

With the Acrobat Reader ActiveX control, users can read documents directly in the browser window, as shown in Figure 14-1. The Acrobat Reader lets users jump to bookmarked locations within a document and print copies.

The Acrobat Reader is free, but the tools for creating PDF documents are not. If you choose to serve PDF documents, users will have no trouble getting the reader, but you have to buy the tools to create your own PDF documents.

HotSpot in Town

The HotSpot invisible control lets you add mouse events to any location. Even better, it comes free with the Microsoft Control Pad. With the HotSpot control, you can do the following:

✔ **Turn any image into a image map:** Just cover the image with multiple HotSpot objects, and link each control's Click event to a different destination.

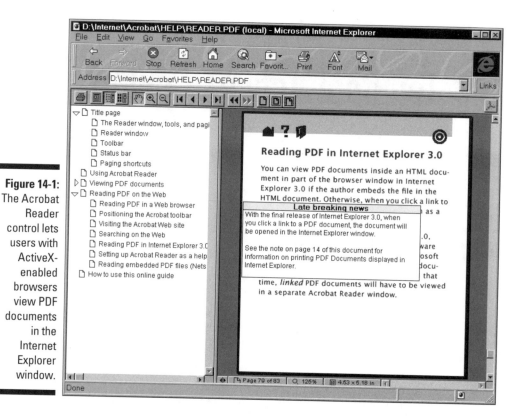

Figure 14-1:
The Acrobat
Reader
control lets
users with
ActiveX-
enabled
browsers
view PDF
documents
in the
Internet
Explorer
window.

✔ **Build a jukebox that plays different songs depending on the mouse pointer's location:** Lay down a HotSpot over a jukebox image and use the HotSpot MouseMove event to track the mouse location.

MicroHelp Calendar (Mh3DCalendar)

http://www.microhelp.com/devtools/samples/mhcal32.html

If you need to find a date, the MicroHelp Calendar control is here to help. When the Calendar control pops up on-screen, as shown in Figure 14-2, users can choose the day, month, and year from a calendar. You can also add your own bitmap and even use a fold-out calendar style.

Figure 14-2:
The MicroHelp Calendar control displays a calendar — a snazzy way to have users choose a date.

MicroHelp Clock (MhClock)

```
http://www.microhelp.com/devtools/samples/mhclck32.html
```

Adding a digital clock to your page is no problem, but how about analog? With the MicroHelp Clock control, you can create analog clocks with custom bitmaps. You can even set an alarm that triggers an Alarm event at a set time. Figure 14-3 shows a typical analog clock, side by side with a digital version.

Find an image that says "clock" to you, and you can use it as your clock's background. You can even set the alarm time and let the Clock control generate an Alarm event when the time comes.

MicroHelp Fax Plus

```
http://www.microhelp.com/devtools/pressrel/
              faxplusshippress.html
```

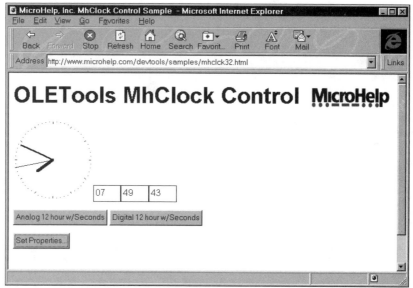

Figure 14-3:
The Clock
control can
be displayed
in both
analog and
digital
versions.
You can
create your
own clock
images for
both analog
and digital.

MicroHelp has created in the Fax Plus package a set of controls that let you print, send, and receive faxes from applications you design. Shoot, Fax Plus even supports Caller ID with modems that support that feature.

MicroHelp Wave (MhWave)

    http://www.microhelp.com/devtools/

The Wave control (included in the MicroHelp OLETools 5.0 collection) stores and plays Windows wave (.WAV) files. You can either store the wave files in the control or load them at run time. In addition, the control includes prerecorded sounds for dates and numbers; by setting the Date or Number properties of the control, you can sound out specified dates and numbers.

Microsoft Internet Control Pack

    http://www.microsoft.com/icp/icpcategories.htm

With the Microsoft Internet Control Pack, you can add Internet services to any application. Each ActiveX control in the pack focuses on a different Internet service; together, they cover the most common services: e-mail, Web, network news, and FTP. If those services aren't what you want, you can get your hands dirty with the Winsock control, which lets you send and receive Internet packets (both TCP and UDP) yourself.

The Internet Control Pack includes these controls:

- **FTP:** A system for sending and receiving files
- **HTML:** A Web browser
- **HTTP:** A simple Web server
- **NNTP:** A news reader
- **SMTP/POP3:** Internet e-mail
- **Winsock:** Interface to the Winsock Application Programming Interface

EarthTime (Starfish Software)

```
http://www.starfishsoftware.com/products/et/activex/
activeet.html
```

EarthTime, from Starfish Software, isn't the type of thing you would use to decorate pages you design for public consumption — you keep this one for yourself. The EarthTime ActiveX control displays the cool map of the world shown in Figure 14-4 in addition to clocks from as many as eight cities. You can even synchronize your computer's clock with an Internet time server.

Envoy Viewer (Tumbleweed)

```
http://www.tumbleweed.com/eax.htm
```

Envoy Viewer, from Tumbleweed, is similar to the Adobe Acrobat Reader; the Envoy format is different, however, from the Portable Document Format Adobe uses. The Envoy document format handles graphics and fonts in a document much smaller than the original. To create an Envoy document, you print from the application using the Envoy driver as your printer.

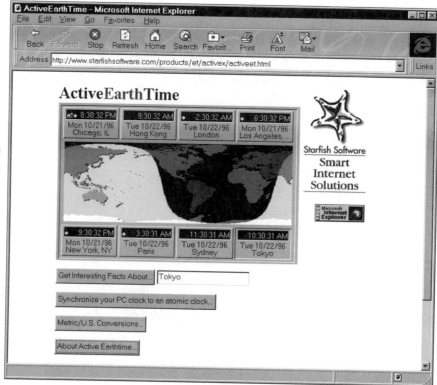

Figure 14-4:
Now, that's
a clock!
EarthTime
displays the
time in eight
different
locations
around the
world and
shows you
who's in the
dark at the
moment.

The VREAM WIRL (VRML)

```
http://www.vream.com/3d11.html
```

The Virtual Reality Modeling Language (VRML) adds limited virtual reality to
Web pages. With VRML, you design worlds; users with VRML-enabled browsers
then can move through three-dimensional space.

Thanks to the VREAM WIRL ActiveX control, every ActiveX browser can be
VRML enabled. (WIRL is included in the Microsoft Internet Explorer Starter Kit.)

WIRL supports VRML 1.0 and adds extensions of its own; VREAM expects to
support VRML 2.0 soon.

Chapter 15

Top Ten VBScript Tips

In This Chapter

▶ How to dig up even more information about VBScript

▶ Style tips for writing scripts

▶ VBScript tricks for the Web

Get a Copy of the Documentation

If you're going to write scripts with VBScript, you will want all the gory details about VBScript. You can always find the latest reference information at the Microsoft Web site, but why not install your own personal copy? You can find the reference documentation and a guide to using VBScript bundled together at: `http://www.microsoft.com/vbscript/us/vbsdown/vbsdown.htm#DOC`.

After you have downloaded your copy, run the VBSDOC.exe program, which decompresses the documents "Language and run-time reference" and "Using VBScript in HTML." Then you will always have the documentation as close as your nearest copy of Internet Explorer.

Check Out Samples at the Microsoft Web Site

One of the best ways to find out about any programming language is to read well-written programs other people have written. The Microsoft Web site has links to many different VBScript samples: `http://www.microsoft.com/vbscript/us/vbssamp/vbssamp.htm`.

The examples are targeted toward specific problems. A flower-ordering sample, for example, shows you how to check out a user's form for mistakes. You can also find some great games you can play, including Web versions of Hangman, Yahtzee, and Connect Four. The best part is that you can claim that you're not just playing games — you're becoming a better VBScript programmer.

Another good source of samples is the VBScript and ActiveX demo site, maintained by John Walkenbach, the author of *VBScript For Dummies* (published by IDG Books Worldwide, Inc.): `http://www.j-walk.com/vbscript/`.

Join the Mailing List

Microsoft maintains a mailing list of people who share tips and tricks for working with VBScript. You won't find any official support on the mailing list, but it has some good discussions. You can also search past issues of the mailing list for previously discussed topics.

If your name is Thomas Jefferson, you would subscribe to the mailing list by sending a message like this one:

```
To: Listserv@listserv.msn.com
Subject:
subscribe VBScript Thomas Jefferson
```

If your name isn't Thomas Jefferson, be sure to insert your own name when you send the message. Also, be sure to leave the Subject line blank. After you send the message, you receive a reply that asks you to confirm your request to join. Follow the instructions to confirm your request, and you're on board. If you like to get just a few mail messages a day, forget about this list. If you don't mind a little e-mail traffic, however, you should join, even if only to read the list.

You don't have to be on the mailing list to browse (or search) through the mailing list archives. You can find past mailing list traffic at this address: `http://microsoft.ease.lsoft.com/archives/vbscript.html`.

Buy a Copy of Microsoft Visual Basic

If you plan to do lots of scripting with VBScript, you should consider investing in the full-blown version of Visual Basic (preferably the Professional Edition, which has lots of extra controls). Because VBScript is a strict subset of Visual Basic, you can do all your VBScript work in the Visual Basic environment, which is much better than cycling continuously from the Microsoft Control Pad to Script Wizard to Internet Explorer and back to Control Pad.

When you splurge and buy Visual Basic, you get lots of extra controls that you can use in your pages but aren't available from the Microsoft Web site. You also receive special tools for creating your own controls, which are included in Visual Basic 5.0. (You don't have to write your own controls because Microsoft is distributing Visual Basic Control Creation Edition for free at its Web site (`http://www.microsoft.com`).

Stop by VBPJ on the Web

The *Visual Basic Programmer's Journal* is a treasure trove of information about Visual Basic. Although the journal is clearly targeted toward the bigger sibling of VBScript, the *VBPJ* editors can see what's coming as well as the rest of us can: ActiveX and VBScript have received a great deal of coverage during the past several months. You can pick up the latest issue at your local newsstand or take a look at the Web site at `http://www.windx.com`.

Litter Your Scripts with Comments

When most people think of great literature, VBScript programs usually don't leap to mind — but you can change that. If your scripts are easy to read, you'll be even happier about it several months from now. If someone else has to pick up where your scripts left off, you can make a friend or two by leaving a legacy of well-commented code. You should follow a few guidelines when you're *commenting* your code (it's so important that it's actually a verb):

✔ Sprinkle comments throughout your code by using either Rem statements or the comment symbol (').

✔ Use sensible variable names: FahrenheitTemp is much clearer than x.

✔ Ditto for procedure names: It's easier to figure out what InchesToCms( ) does than to guess what Convert( ) converts.

✔ Join the crusade: Harangue friends and coworkers to comment their code.

Use the Option Explicit Statement

Always start your scripts with the Option Explicit statement, which must appear before any procedures:

```
<SCRIPT LANGUAGE = "VBScript">
Option Explicit    'Force declaration of all variables
   :
</SCRIPT>
```

The Option Explicit statement can help you in two ways: You avoid spelling mistakes, and you always know whether variables are local or global.

Win the VBScript spelling bee

With VBScript, it's too easy to create a new variable. Usually anything you type where VBScript expects to see a variable name becomes a new variable, including misspellings of previously defined variables. Suppose that you create a new function, InchesToMeters():

```
Function InchesToMeters(inches)
    cm = InchesToCms(inchs)
    InchesToMeters = cm / 100
end function
```

Here's what happens:

1. You have misspelled the function's parameter (inches) as "inchs" in the body of the function.

2. VBScript doesn't know that "inchs" is a misspelled version of "inches." Rather than say, "Hey, you misspelled inches!," VBScript just creates a new variable, called inchs.

3. Because all new numeric variables are set to 0, inchs is set to 0.

4. The value 0 is passed to the function InchesToCms() in the first line of the function InchesToMeters(). If you convert 0 inches to centimeters, you get 0 centimeters every time.

5. Because 0 divided by 100 — in the second line of InchesToMeters() — is always 0, the function InchesToMeters() always returns 0.

Here's the bottom line: One slip of the keyboard, and your new function always returns 0. If you had always used Option Explicit, VBScript would have complained that you never declared (using Dim) the misspelled variable inchs, and you would have caught the mistake before you began converting inches to 0 meters.

Global or local?

If you don't declare a procedure-level variable, you can't tell from looking at the procedure whether you wanted to use a local variable or whether a global variable of the same name was defined somewhere else:

```
<SCRIPT LANGUAGE = "VBScript">
    :

Function CalculatePay(EmployeeNum)
    EmployeeName = NumberToName(EmployeeNum)
```

```
      Salary = GetSalary(EmployeeName)
         :
end function

</SCRIPT>
```

Quick — is EmployeeName a local or global variable? If you always used Option Explicit, you would know that it must be global. How can you tell? If Employee-Name were supposed to be local, VBScript would complain that EmployeeName had not been declared (assuming that you used Option Explicit). If no error occurs when the script runs (and you have used Option Explicit), the reason must be that a global variable was already defined somewhere else. The Option Explicit statement guarantees that you don't have to worry about misspelled variable names or the occasional confusion between global and local variables.

Make Your Arrays As Dynamic As Your Pages

As long as you're going to have dynamic Web pages, you might as well have dynamic arrays to go along with them. You can use the VBScript ReDim statement to change the size of an array and add or subtract elements from the array. To create a *dynamic array* (an array that can be resized), you define it with the Dim statement, just as you would do for a normal array, except that you leave the parentheses empty:

```
Dim DynamicArray()
```

Later, when you know how large you want the array to be, use the ReDim statement:

```
ReDim DynamicArray(9)
```

This line creates a dynamic array of ten elements. If ten turns out to be too small, you can make the array larger without erasing any of the current elements:

```
ReDim Preserve DynamicArray(12)
```

If you use the ReDim statement without the Preserve keyword, your array is still resized but all the elements in the original array are erased. Also, if you shrink an array by "ReDimming" to a smaller size, you erase the values that were at the end of the array. Suppose that you begin with an array of 11 used cars:

1. Create an array of used cars:

```
Dim UsedCars(10)    'Create an array of 11 used cars
UsedCars(0) = "1977 Dodge Dart"
UsedCars(1) = "1987 Nissan Sentra"
     :
UsedCars(10) = "1993 Toyota Camry"
```

2. **After a few lean months of car sales, your program decides to move to a smaller car lot, which can hold only eight cars. You have to cut back, therefore, on your array of used cars:**

```
ReDim Preserve UsedCars(7)    'Inventory reduction
```

3. **Poof — your last three cars are gone for good! If sales pick up and you move back to the larger car lot, you can extend your arrays of used cars with this statement:**

```
ReDim UsedCars(10)    'Inventory expansion
```

Even though you have enlarged the same array, your last three cars are still gone. After you shrank your inventory in Step 3, VBScript tossed out the elements at the end of the array. If you want to sell that lovely '93 Camry (which was originally `UsedCars(10)`), you have to add it back to the array.

You can also use ReDim with multidimensional arrays; if you want to protect the data that's already there (using the Preserve keyword), however, you can change only the size of the last dimension:

```
ReDim MultiDynamicArray(10, 10, 10)
     :
'Can only change the last dimension
ReDim Preserve MultiDynamicArray(10, 10, 15)
```

Run a Script When a User Clicks a Link

One nice effect you can achieve with VBScript is to have something happen when a user clicks a link. With VBScript and Internet Explorer, you can attach a script to a link in two ways:

✔ Embed any script commands directly into the HTML link:

```
<A HREF="http://www.microsoft.com" language=VBScript
       onclick="InputBox 'Where would you like to go
       today?'">
Microsoft Home Page
</A>
```

✔ If you prefer the indirect method, you can name a procedure to be called within the link. In this example, the procedure DisplaySlackerMessage() is called when a user clicks the link (both methods still take the user to the link that was clicked, but each method runs a little script first):

```
<A HREF="http://www.microsoft.com" onclick =
        "DisplaySlackerMessage">
Click here to go somewhere today!
</a>
<SCRIPT Language = "VBScript">
<!--
SUB DisplaySlackerMessage()
   MsgBox "I don't know about you, but I don't want to go
        anywhere today!"
end sub
-->
</SCRIPT>
```

Write Fresh HTML in VBScript

You can use the Document object's write methods (Write() and WriteLn()) to write HTML to a page and create new pages at *run time* (the point at which your scripts are run — as opposed to *design time,* which is when you develop the scripts). The following sample script shows you how to write text to the browser window from an HTML file:

```
<HTML>
<HEAD>
<TITLE>Writing Fresh HTML</TITLE>

<SCRIPT LANGUAGE="VBScript">
<!--
OPTION EXPLICIT    'Always a good idea
Dim Language
Language = "Spanish"

Select Case Language
   Case "English"
      Document.Write "Hello."
   Case "Southern"
      Document.Write "Howdy, y'all."
```

(continued)

(continued)

```
    Case "German"
        Document.Write "Hallo."
    Case "Spanish"
        Document.Write "Hola."
End Select
-->
</SCRIPT>
</HEAD>

<BODY>
<p>This is a sample document</p>
</BODY>

</HTML>
```

The output of this script is shown in Figure 15-1, which displays the output of the Write() method (in this case, "Hola.") followed by the body of the HTML document.

Figure 15-1:
The string
Hola. has
been written
to the
Document
object,
which then
displays
the text
included in
the body of
the file.

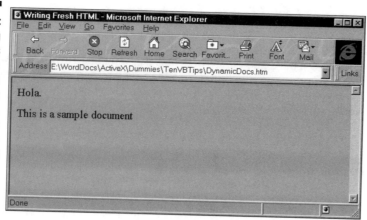

The browser ignores line breaks and spaces in the text you write, just as it does in an HTML file. If you want to insert a line break, you have to include the HTML code for it, as shown in this example:

```
Document.Write "Hello!<BR>I'm the <B>Microsoft Internet
        Explorer</B>."
```

This line writes "Hello!" and then "I'm the Microsoft Internet Explorer." on the next line.

Appendix

About the CD-ROM

*B*ecause ActiveX technologies are so new, related tools and products are still being developed. On this CD-ROM, you get not only sample code and examples to accompany the book but also a guide to the many ActiveX resources in the online world.

To get started, pop the CD-ROM into your CD-ROM drive, and open it just like any other CD-ROM. You see a bunch of folders and a few files. One of those files is index.htm, which is your gateway to the world of ActiveX. Load the index.htm file into your Web browser, and you're ready to explore the world of ActiveX.

The index.htm file has pointers to three different areas on the CD-ROM:

- **ActiveX Resource Guide:** Includes listings and descriptions of ActiveX-related products and information. If you're looking for an ActiveX control to do a job, this is a great place to start.
- **Sample code and explanations:** The code from the book, organized by chapter.
- **Dummies Web site:** A link to the book's section of the *...For Dummies* Web site (http://www.dummies.com), with updates and examples based on the book.

What You Need and What You Will Want

The CD-ROM is designed to work with as many systems as possible, so you can use most of it no matter what kind of computer you have. Because ActiveX is still relatively new, however, only a few systems can take full advantage of it today. At the least, you will need:

- Windows 3.1, Windows 95 or NT, or a Macintosh
- A Web browser with support for frames
- A CD-ROM drive (you probably guessed that one)

If you have enough RAM for your Web browser, you probably have enough for the CD-ROM. Although your browser doesn't have to support Java, you must have support for frames. *Frames* enable designers to split a browser's window into panes, which then can show different pages in each pane. Although frames aren't officially a part of HTML, most browsers support them. The most recent versions of Netscape Navigator, Microsoft Internet Explorer, and NCSA Mosaic all support frames. If you really want to play with ActiveX and get the most from the examples on the CD-ROM, you should have Internet Explorer Version 3.0 (or better) for Windows and Microsoft Control Pad. Here are the system requirements for Internet Explorer 3.01:

Windows 95:

- ✔ A computer with a 386DX (or better) processor
- ✔ 8MB RAM
- ✔ 5–10MB available hard disk space

Windows NT:

- ✔ A computer with a 486 (or better) processor
- ✔ 12MB of RAM
- ✔ 5–10MB available hard disk space

The system requirements for Control Pad are similar and also require Windows:

- ✔ A computer running a 486 (or better) processor
- ✔ Microsoft Windows 95 or Windows NT 4.0 Beta 2 (or later)
- ✔ 12MB of RAM
- ✔ 10MB available hard disk space
- ✔ Internet Explorer 3.0 final release (not the beta version)

"What about me? I have a Mac!"

Microsoft has a beta release of the ActiveX Software Development Kit (SDK, for short) for Power Macintosh, which should give most Mac users what they need to get started with ActiveX. You can download the SDK from the Microsoft Site Builder Workshop Web site, at `http://www.microsoft.com/intdev/sdk/mac/macdownl.htm`.

As you may have guessed from the term "Power Macintosh," only Power Mac users can enjoy this particular SDK. Microsoft has promised an SDK for Mac users with the original 680x0 processor class. In addition to code samples, the SDK includes a Netscape Navigator-type plug-in and a Mac system extension that you must install on your Mac. To properly install these support items, be sure to read the documentation included with the SDK.

Because this SDK is still in the beta stage, don't expect a great deal of stability, particularly if you want to use a Web browser other than Internet Explorer. Keep in mind that Internet Explorer uses different controls from its Windows counterparts, so you may not be able to view most of the examples included on the CD-ROM.

Here are the system requirements for the ActiveX SDK beta:

- Any PowerPC Macintosh or compatible
- Microsoft Internet Explorer 2.1 or higher (Internet Explorer 3.0, available as a beta version at the time of this writing, also works)
- MacOS System 7.5.3 or higher
- Metrowerks CodeWarrior 10 (necessary if you want to build ActiveX controls yourself)

The Internet connection

You don't have to have a connection to the Internet to use the CD-ROM, but it helps. The sample code and explanations on the CD-ROM are self-contained, so you can browse through them without being online. Many ActiveX resources are available on the Web, however, and you need an Internet connection to take advantage of them. If following a link would take you off the CD-ROM to a Web site, you see a small Web graphic just before the link appears. (The exception is the ActiveX Resource Guide, which doesn't include the Web graphic because all the links are to sites off the CD-ROM.)

Index

& (ampersand) as VBScript concatenation operator, 257
+ (plus sign) for list box, 74
16-bit processing, 20
32-bit processing, 20
<!- -...- -> as HTML comment tags, 249
<> (angle brackets) delimiting HTML tags, 4
' (single quote) as VBScript comment symbol, 353
[] (square brackets) for optional items in VBScript procedure syntax, 268
/ (forward slash) in Web pathnames, 32, 33
– (minus sign) as expanded list box indicator, 74
\ (backward slash) in Web pathnames, 32

• A •

<A>...</A> (anchor) tags, 31, 33
  for links to image files, 42
AboutBox() method, 123, 133, 140, 153, 154, 166, 194
absolute and relative pathnames, 33–34
absolute and relative positioning, 91
Accelerator property
  of display controls, 102, 105
  of form controls, 180
Acrobat Reader control, 345, 346
Action property of Form object, 333
active links, 85
ActiveMovie control, 120
ActiveX
  background to development of, 1, 11
  compared to Java, 21
  as cross-platform system, 13, 21–22
  Java Virtual Machine, 16
  requirements for this book's exercises, 6
  technologies involved in, 11
  See also sample scripts/code
ActiveX controls. See controls; form controls
ActiveX documents, 14–15
  See also forms; HTML files
ActiveX editors. See Microsoft Control Pad
ActiveX Scripting
  described, 2, 20
  See also scripting; VBScript
ActiveX Server Framework, 15, 16

AddItem() form control method, 194
  with Popup Menu control, 225
addresses of Web pages, 31–33
Adobe Acrobat Reader control, 345, 346
AfterUpdate event, 277
Alert() method of Window object, 311
ALIGN attribute
  of <CAPTION> tag, 43
  of <OBJECT> tag, 56–57
  of <IMG SRC> inline image tag, 41
aligning objects
  in HTML Layouts with Control Pad, 92–96
  to lines in HTML, 57
Alignment property
  of form controls, 180, 182–183
  of Label control, 149
aLinkColor property of Document object, 317, 318
Alpha (for Macs) with HTML add-on, 31
ALT attribute of <IMG SRC> inline image tag, 41
.ALX extensions, 90, 98
Anchor object, 331
  as property of Document object, 317
anchor tags (<A>...</A>), 31, 33
Anchors property of Document object, 317, 318
Animated Button control, 119–124
animations, popularity on Web sites, 9, 10, 155, 242
AppCodeName property of Navigator object, 337, 338
Apple computers. See Macintosh
applications
  applets, 15, 21
  helper, 14
AppName property of Navigator object, 337, 338
AppVersion property of Navigator object, 337, 338
arguments of methods, ordered and named, 146–147
arguments of VBScript procedures, 247, 268–269
arithmetic operators, VBScript, 264, 265, 266
arrays
  dynamic, 355–356
  VBScript, 255–256
As keyword, caution on use in VBScript, 275
aspect ratio, 143–144

.AU extensions, 157
audio. *See* RealAudio; sound effects
AutoGotoURL property of RealAudio ActiveX
    control, 161, 165–166, 173
AutoSize property
    of display controls, 102, 106
    of form controls, 180
AutoStart property of RealAudio ActiveX
    control, 161, 162
AutoTab property of form controls, 180, 183
AutoWordSelect property of form controls,
    180, 184
AVI (Audio Video Interleave) files, 119–120

• *B* •

Back() method of History object, 341
BackColor property
    of display controls, 102, 106
    of form controls, 180
    of Gauge control, 134
BACKGROUND attribute of <BODY> tag, 40,
    42–43
background image tags in HTML, 42–43
BackStyle property
    of display controls, 102, 106–108
    of form controls, 180
BASELINE value of ALIGN attribute of
    <OBJECT> tag, 57
BBEdit (for Macs), with HTML add-on, 31
BeforeDragOver event, 280–283
BeforeDropOrPaste event, 283–284
BeforeUpdate event, 277–278
bgColor property of Document object, 317,
    318–319
<BGSOUND> tag, 156–157
blank lines, creating onscreen in HTML, 35, 358
.BMP extensions, 141, 154
<BODY> tags
    described, 30
    not used with frames, 47
    used with floating frames, 50
<BOLD>...</BOLD> physical tags for
    boldface, 38
boldface
    as Font object, 110
    as notation convention, 5
    for text with Label control, 152
Boolean values in VBScript, 254
BORDER attribute
    of <OBJECT> tag, 58
    of <TABLE> tag, 43

BorderColor property
    of display controls, 102, 108
    of form controls, 180
borders, for setting off linked objects, 58
BorderStyle property
    of display controls, 102, 108–109
    of form controls, 180
BotPoints property of Label control, 149–151
BOTTOM value of VALIGN attribute
    (<CAPTION> table tag), 43
BotXY property of Label control, 149–151
BoundColumn property of ListBox form
    control, 209–211
boxes for objects, inner and outer, 61–62

 blank line tag, 35, 358
browsers. *See* Web browsers
bulleted list tags in HTML, 34–35, 36
ByVal keyword in VBScript, 275

• *C* •

Calendar control, 346–347
Call statements in VBScript, 270
CanPlayPause() method of RealAudio ActiveX
    control, 166, 167
CanStop() method of RealAudio ActiveX
    control, 166, 167
<CAPTION> table title tag, 43
Caption property
    of display controls, 102, 109
    of form controls, 180
cascading style sheets, 25
CD-ROM accompanying this book
    ActiveMovie control, 120
    ChangeLabelColor.htm, 78
    commercially developed controls, 274
    Microsoft Control Pad, 67
CENTER value of ALIGN attribute
    of <OBJECT> tag, 57
    of <TABLE> tag, 43
centimeters as units of measurement, 61
CGI (Common Gateway Interface) scripts, 21
Change event, 277, 278–279
ChangeLabelColor.htm, 77, 78
Chart control, 124–133
    example, 65
ChartType property of ActiveX Chart control,
    125–127
CheckBox form control, 178, 179, 198–199, 200
<CITE>...</CITE> logical tags for citations, 37
classes, 58
CLASSID attribute, of <OBJECT> tag, 58–59

Clear() method
  of Document object, 323, 324
  for form controls, 194, 195
  with Popup Menu control, 225
ClearTimeout() method of Window object, 311
Click event, 288, 290
  of Popup Menu form control, 225
client/server computing, 18
clients, as computers requesting services, 15
client-side maps/image maps, 64, 65
Clock control, 347, 348
Close() method
  of Document object, 323, 324
  of Window object, 311–312
clsid sequences, 58, 59
code
  source versus machine, 248
  See also sample scripts/code
<CODE>...</CODE> logical tags for code, 37
CODEBASE attribute of <OBJECT> tag, 59
CodeBase property
  of display controls, 102, 109
  of form controls, 180
CODETYPE attribute of <OBJECT> tag, 63–64
collections, 100
colors
  for Document objects, 84–85
  script for color-change-on-button-click
    example, 73–77
  setting with ActiveX control properties, 102,
    106, 112
ColorScheme property of ActiveX Chart
    control, 127–128
COLSPAN attribute for table tags, 43
Column property of ListBox form control, 211
ColumnCount property of ListBox form
    control, 211–212
ColumnHeads property of ListBox form
    control, 212
ColumnIndex property of ActiveX Chart
    control, 128
ColumnName property of ActiveX Chart
    control, 128
Columns property of ActiveX Chart control, 128
ColumnWidths property of ListBox form
    control, 212
COM (Component Object Model), 20
  clsid sequences, 58–59
ComboBox form control, 200–206, 207
CommandButton control, generating events
    for mouse actions, 287
comments in VBScript, 249, 272, 353
comparison operators in VBScript, 264, 265, 267

compilers, 248
compression of sound files, 156, 159
Confirm() method of Window object, 312
Console property of RealAudio ActiveX
    control, 161, 163–165
constants
  global variables as, 81
  predefined in VBScript, 252–253
containers, 305
context menus, 91
Control Pad. *See* Microsoft Control Pad
control properties
  altering for purchased controls, 101
  assigning custom values or constants,
    104–105
  changing from Microsoft Control Pad, 70–72
  common to display controls, 102
  described, 54, 65
  naming, 66
  syntax, 103–104
  understanding in HTML form, 103
  See also individual properties by name
controls
  adding to HTML Layouts, 91–92
  attribute types, 54
  for charts, 124–133
  described, 1–2, 11–13, 53
  for displaying, 102–119
  drag-and-drop toggle, 180
  fitting purchased, 101
  for forms. *See* form controls
  for "gauges," 133–140
  for gradients, 137–140
  hot keys/shortcut keys for, 102, 105, 180
  for images, 140–147
  for IME mode, 181
  intrinsic, 103, 118
  for labels, 147–153
  for mouse icon and pointer appearance, 102,
    113–115
  for new Web page items, 153–154
  nicknames for, 102, 112
  for NULL state handling, 182, 193, 199
  as objects, 53
  providing information about, 102, 109, 180
  for RealAudio Player, 157, 160–173
  refusing focus to, 102, 109–110, 180, 199
Controls property of RealAudio ActiveX
    control, 161, 162
Cookie property of Document object, 317,
    319–320
cookies, 319–320
Copy() form control method, 194, 195

cropped images, 143
cross-platform systems
  ActiveX, 13, 21–22
  described, 13
  Java, 16
CurLine property of TextBox form control, 231
Cut() form control method, 194, 195

• D •

DATA attribute of <OBJECT> tag, 60
data packets, 169
Data property of ActiveX Chart control, 128–129
DataItem property of ActiveX Chart control, 129–130
Date property of New Item control, 154
DblClick event, 288, 290–291
DECLARE attribute of <OBJECT> tag, 60
declaring VBScript variables, 250–251
decompression of sound files, 156
DefaultStatus property of Window object, 306–307
Delay property of SpinButton form control, 227–228
desktop, integration of Windows and Internet, 19
<DFN>...</DFN> logical tags for definitions, 37
dialog boxes, modal and nonmodal, 55
dictionary list tags in HTML, 35, 36
DIM statement in VBScript, 250–251, 255–256
  dynamic arrays, 355–356
dimensions of objects. *See* HEIGHT attribute; WIDTH attribute
Direction property of Gradient control, 138–139
Directories parameter of Open method, 314
DisplayLegend property of ActiveX Chart control, 130
<DL>...</DL> dictionary list tags, 35
Do loops in VBScript, 261–263
Document object
  described, 83
  in Internet Explorer Object Model, 316–326
  Link, Form, and Anchor objects as properties of, 317
  as property of Window object, 305
  Referrer property, 86–87, 322
documents
  as pages on Web sites, 10
  See also ActiveX documents
DoGotoURL() method of RealAudio ActiveX control, 166, 167, 173

DoNextItem() method of RealAudio ActiveX control, 166, 167
DoPlayPause() method of RealAudio ActiveX control, 166, 167
DoPrevItem() method of RealAudio ActiveX control, 166, 167
DoStop() method of RealAudio ActiveX control, 166, 167
DragBehavior property of form controls, 180, 184–185
DrawBuffer property of HTML Layout control, 99
drop buttons, 205
DropButtonClick event, 207
DropButtonStyle property of ComboBox form control, 203–204
drop-down lists, 203
DropDown() method of ComboBox control, 207
<DT><DD> dictionary term/definition tag pairs, 35
dynamic arrays, 355–356

• E •

EarthTime control, 349, 350
EditPreferences() method of RealAudio ActiveX control, 166, 168
elements
  intrinsic, 333
  in VBScript arrays, 255
Elements property of Form object, 333–334
<EM>...</EM> logical tags for emphasis, 37
Enabled property
  of display controls, 102, 109–110
  of form controls, 180, 199
encoding, 334
Encoding property of Form object, 333, 334
EndColor property of Gradient control, 139
EndPoint property of Gradient control, 139
Enter event, 277, 279
EnterFieldBehavior property of form controls, 180, 185
Envoy Viewer control, 349
Error event, 296–297
event handlers
  advantages of Script Wizard for writing, 275
  described, 54, 274
  on CD-ROM accompanying this book, 274, 276
  writing, 276
event-driven programming, 54, 55, 273

events
  control value changes, 276–279
  described, 54–55, 273
  keyboard activity, 285–287
  mouse clicks or movement, 287–296
  mouse drag-and-drop activity, 280–284
  scripting for, 273–276
  for synchronized multimedia, 174
  URL, 172
Exit event, 277, 279
extensions
  .ALX, 90, 98
  .AU, 157
  .BMP, 141, 154
  .GIF, 40, 140, 141
  .HTM or .HTML, 30
  .JPEG, 40, 140, 141
  .OCX, 20
  .PDF, 345
  .RA, 174
  .RAE, 174
  .RAM, 175
  .VBX, 20
  .WAV, 157
  .XBM, 40
external image tags in HTML, 42

• *F* •

Fax Plus control, 347–348
FFOs (form filler-outers), defined, 178
fgColor property of Document object, 317, 321
files
  specifying sources of data with DATA
      attribute, 60
  See also HTML files
FillStyle property of Label control, 151–152
floating frames, 49
flow of control in VBScript, 258–264
focus
  for Animated Button control, 121, 122–123
  refusing to controls, 102, 109–110
  switching on forms, 196
  in Windows, UNIX, and on Macs, 123
Font objects, 102, 110–111
  on form controls, 180
FontBold property of Label control, 152
FontItalic property of Label control, 152
FontName property of Label control, 152
FontSize property of Label control, 152
FontStrikeout property of Label control, 152
FontUnderline property of Label control, 152
For...Next loops in VBScript, 259–263

For Dummies Web site, 4
ForeColor property
  of display controls, 102, 112
  of form controls, 180
  of Gauge control, 134
form controls
  CheckBox, 178, 179, 198–200
  ComboBox, 178, 200–207
  for cycling through response possibilities, 179
  ListBox, 178, 208–219
  methods common to, 194
  OptionButton, 178, 179, 219–221
  Popup Menu, 179, 221–226
  SpinButton, 179, 226–229
  TextBox, 179, 230–233
  ToggleButton, 178, 179, 233–234
  for yes–no/true–false responses, 178
Form object, 331–336
  as property of Document object, 317
forms
  described, 16, 21, 331
  importance of user-friendliness, 177–178
  interactive, 242–243
  specifying URL for data submitted on, with
      NAME attribute, 62–63
Forms property of Document object, 317, 321
Forward() method of History object, 341
<FRAME> frame tag, 45
Frame object, 83, 305
  as property of Window object, 305
frame tags in HTML, 45–50
frames
  floating, 49
  separate, for RealAudio Player and slide
      shows, 173
  in Web browser windows, 170
<FRAMESET> frame tag, 45
framesets, 46
FrontPage HTML editor, 31, 89
FTP control (in Microsoft Internet Control
      Pack), 349
Function procedures in VBScript, 269–271

• *G* •

games, 244
Gauge controls, 133–137
  adding to Control Pad Toolbox, 96
.GIF extensions, 40, 140, 141
global variables
  with Script Wizard, 80–82
  in VBScript, 251–252, 354–355
GNU emacs (for UNIX) for HTML, 31
Go() method of History object, 341–342

Go To Page action in Script Wizard, 78–79
Gradient control, 137–139, 140
graphs. *See* charts
grid
  placing on charts, 130
  snapping to, 92
GridPlacement property of ActiveX Chart
    control, 130
GroupName property of OptionButton form
    control, 220

• *H* •

<H#>...</H#> Heading tags, 34, 35
hardware platforms, 13
Hash property of Link Object, 327
HasNextItem() method of RealAudio ActiveX
    control, 166, 167
HasPrevItem() method of RealAudio ActiveX
    control, 166, 167
<HEAD> tags, 30
heading tags <H#>...</H#>, 34, 35
HEIGHT attribute
  of <IMG> inline image tag, 41, 42
  of <OBJECT> tag, 60–61
Height parameter of Open method, 314
Height property
  of display controls, 102, 112
  of form controls, 180
"Hello World!" sample script, 246–247
Help from *For Dummies* Web site, 4
helper applications, 14
HideSelection property of form controls,
    181, 186
HideShowStatistics() method of RealAudio
    ActiveX control, 166, 168
history lists, 340
History object, 83, 340–342
  as property of Window object, 305
HorizontalGrid property of ActiveX Chart
    control, 130
Host property of Link Object, 327, 328
Hostname property of Link Object, 327, 328
HoTMetaL Pro HTML editor, 31, 89
HotSpot control, 345–346
HREF attribute of <A> anchor tag for external
    image references, 40, 42
Href property of Link Object, 327, 328
HSPACE attribute, of <OBJECT> tag, 61–62
.HTM or .HTML extension, 30
HTML control (in Microsoft Internet Control
    Pack), 349

HTML files
  comments in, 249
  creating from word processors, 31
  frame tags, 45–50
  image tags, 40–43
  inserting HTML Layouts into, 90, 97–98
  list tags, 34–35, 36
  logical style tags, 36–38, 39
  physical style tags, 36, 38, 40
  structure tags, 34–36
  table tags, 43–45
  validation services and editors, 30–31
  writing to browser window at runtime,
    357–358
  writing to browser window from, 357–358
  See also scripting
HTML For Dummies, 3, 25
HTML (HyperText Markup Language)
  continuing development, 29
  described, 2, 26, 29
HTML Layout Control
  for display of Layout file, 98
  DrawBuffer property, 99
  Item() method, 100
  onLoad event, 99
  setting properties, 98–99
HTML Layouts
  adding controls, 91–92
  automatic updating of, 90
  for controlling object positions in browser
    windows, 89
  formatting, 92–96
  inserting into HTML files, 90, 97–98
  using as template, 90
http://www. prefix for Web addresses, 31–33
HTTP control (in Microsoft Internet Control
    Pack), 349
HTTP (HyperText Transfer protocol)
  described, 27, 28
  problem of statelessness, 320
hypertext, 31
  See also links (hypertext)

• *I* •

<I>...</I> physical tags for italics, 38
icons used in this book, 5
ID attribute, of <OBJECT> tag, 62
ID property
  of display controls, 102, 112
  of form controls, 181
If...Then...Else if...Else statements (flow of
    control), VBScript, 258–259

<IFRAME> floating frame tag, 45, 49–50
Image control, 140–147
Image property of New Item control, 154
image tags in HTML, 40–43
images
  control for, 140–147
  cropped, 143
  including in HTML, 40–43
  inline, 40–42, 140–141
  scaling, avoiding distortion, 61
  using as clickable maps with USEMAP
    attribute, 64
IME (Input Method Editor) mode, 181, 186
IMEMode property of form controls, 181, 186
<IMG> inline image tag, 40–42
inches as units of measurement, 61
inner boxes for objects, 61–62
InnerBottom property of Gauge control, 135
InnerLeft property of Gauge control, 135
InnerRight property of Gauge control, 135
InnerTop property of Gauge control, 135
IntegralHeight property of form controls,
  181, 186
interactive forms, 242–243
Internet
  compared to World Wide Web, 10, 26
  described, 10
  See also Web (World Wide Web)
Internet Explorer
  background sound support, 156
  File⇨Open, 77
  notification of receipt of cookies, 320
  as popular Web browser, 10, 27
  requirement for this book's exercises, 6
  scripting language support, 240
  starting multiple instances of, 305
  testing color-change-on-button-click sample
    script, 77
  VBScript support, 240, 248
Internet Explorer control, 301
Internet Explorer Object Model for Scripting
  described, 299–301
  example changing background color of
    browser and Internet Explorer control,
    301 304
  hierarchical organization, 300–301, 304
Internet Information Server, 15
Internet Media Types, 64
interpreted languages, 240, 248
interpreters, 248
intranets, 2, 10–11
intrinsic controls, 103, 118
intrinsic elements, 333

IsStatisticsVisible() method of RealAudio
  ActiveX control, 166, 168
italics
  as Font object, 110
  as notation convention, 5
  for text with Label control, 152
Item() method of HTML Layout Control, 100
ItemCount property of Popup Menu form
  control, 224

•J•

Java, 16, 21
Java Virtual Machine (VM), 16
JavaScript, 77, 240
.JPEG extensions, 40, 140, 141
JScript, 240

•K•

<KBD>...</KBD> logical tags for keyboard-style
  (fixed-width) font, 37
KeyDown event, 285–286
KeyPress event, 285, 286–287
KeyUp event, 285–286
keywords in VBScript, 268
  caution on use of As and Private, 275

•L•

Label control, 147–153
  generating events for mouse actions, 287
Label object, 147
languages
  compiled, 248
  interpreted, 240, 248
  macro, 240
  markup, 29
  scripting, 237, 238, 240–241
  VRML (Virtual Reality Modeling
    Language), 242
LastModified property of Document object,
  317, 321
Left property
  of display controls, 102, 112–113
  of form controls, 181
LEFT value of ALIGN attribute
  of <OBJECT> tag, 57
  of <TABLE> tag, 43
Length property of History object, 341
<LI> list item tags, 34, 35

LineCount property of TextBox form control, 231
Link object, 326–331
  as property of Document object, 317
LinkColor property of Document object, 317, 321–322
links (hypertext)
  attaching script to, 356–357
  in original versions of HTML, 55
  to other Web sites and pages, 10, 31
  relative and absolute pathnames, 33–34
  visited and active, 84, 85, 323
Links property of Document object, 317, 322
List property of ListBox form control, 212
list tags, 34–35, 36
ListBox form control, 178, 208–219
ListIndex property of ListBox form control, 213
ListRows property of ComboBox form control, 204
lists, drop-down style, 203
ListStyle property of ListBox form control, 213–214
ListWidth property of ComboBox form control, 205
local variables
  with Script Wizard, 79–80
  in VBScript, 251–252, 354–355
Location object, 83
  as property of Window object, 305
Location parameter of Open method, 314
Location property of Document object, 317, 322
Locked property of form controls, 181, 186–187
logical operators in VBScript, 264, 265, 267
logical tags in HTML
  descriptions and list, 36–38
  examples of output, 39
LOOP attribute of <BGSOUND> tag, 157
loops in VBScript
  Do While, 261–263
  For...Next, 259–263
lossy compression algorithms, 156

• M •

machine code, 248
Macintosh
  HTML file creation, 31
  Internet Explorer and Control Pad availability for, 6
  support for ActiveX, 13
  support for RealAudio Players, 159
macro languages, 240

maps
  client-side and server-side images, 65
  images as, 64
margins around objects, 61–62
markup languages, 29
MatchEntry property of ListBox form control, 214–215
MatchRequired property of ComboBox form control, 205–206
Max property
  of Gauge control, 135
  of SpinButton form control, 228
MaxLength property of form controls, 181, 187
measurement by standard units, 60–61
Menubar parameter of Open method, 314
MenuItem property of Popup Menu form control, 224
menus, context, 91
Method property of Form object, 333, 334–335
methods
  as attribute of controls, 54
  See also methods by individual names
MicroHelp Calendar control, 346–347
MicroHelp Clock control, 347, 348
MicroHelp Fax Plus control, 347–348
Microsoft Control Pad
  caution on direct editing of HTML files, 70
  changing properties of controls, 70–72
  described, 67
  Edit⇨Insert ActiveX Control, 68
  Edit⇨Insert HTML Layout, 97–99
  File⇨New HTML Layout, 90
  Format menu commands, 92–96
  HotSpot control free with, 345–346
  for HTML Layouts, 89, 90
  inserting controls into HTML files, 68–70
  obtaining, 67
  requirement for this book's exercises, 6
  Toolbox, 91
  Toolbox enhancements, 96–97
  Tools⇨Script Wizard, 73
  See also HTML Layouts; Script Wizard
Microsoft Forms Label, 147
Microsoft FrontPage HTML editor, 31, 89
Microsoft Internet Control Pack, 348–349
Microsoft Internet Explorer. *See* Internet Explorer
Microsoft Internet Information Server, 15
Microsoft Network, The, home page, 156
Microsoft Web site, 67
MIDDLE value of ALIGN attribute (<OBJECT> tag), 57
MIDDLE value of VALIGN attribute (<CAPTION> table tag), 43

MIDI format sounds, 157
MIME (Multipurpose Internet Mail
    Extensions), 334
Min property
    of Gauge control, 135
    of SpinButton form control, 228
modal and nonmodal dialog boxes, 55
Mode property of Label control, 152
MORE HTML For Dummies, 25
mouse drag-and-drop behavior, 180, 184–185
mouse events with HotSpot control, 345–346
MouseDown event, 288, 291–294
MouseEnter event, 288
MouseExit event, 288
MouseIcon property
    of display controls, 102, 113
    of form controls, 181
MouseMove event, 288, 294–296
MousePointer property
    of display controls, 102, 113–115
    of form controls, 181
MouseUp event, 288, 291–294
Move() method of Image control, 146–147
Mozilla, 338
MsgBox() procedure, 247
MSN (The Microsoft Network) home page, 156
MultiLine property of TextBox form
    control, 231
multimedia, synchronized, 157, 172, 173–176
MultiSelect property of ListBox form control,
    215–216

• N •

NAME attribute
    of <FRAME> tag, 48
    of <OBJECT> tag, 62–63
Name property of Window object, 307
named arguments of methods, 146–147
Navigate() method of Window object, 312
Navigator. *See* Netscape Navigator
Navigator object, 83, 336–340
    as property of Window object, 305
NeedleWidth property of Gauge control, 136
nested framesets, 46
Netscape Navigator
    built-in HTML editor, 31
    notification of receipt of cookies, 320
    plug-in architecture, 159
    plug-in required for ActiveX support, 6
    as popular Web browser, 10, 27
    VBScript support, 240

New Item control, 153–154
    method, 154
newlines, 325–326

 blank line tag, 35, 358
news pages, 244
NNTP control (in Microsoft Internet Control
    Pack), 349
NoLabels property of RealAudio ActiveX
    control, 161, 165
nonmodal dialog boxes, 55
notation conventions for this book, 4–5
Notepad
    drawbacks for Web page layout, 89
    for HTML file editing, 31
NOWRAP attribute for table tags, 43
NULL state handling, 182, 193, 199

• O •

<OBJECT> tag, 55–65
Object Model. *See* Internet Explorer Object
    Model for Scripting
objects
    aligning, 56–57
    allowing margins around, 61–62
    borders around, 58
    class identification, 58–59
    described, 53–54
    naming with ID attribute, 62
    providing information with CODEBASE
        attribute, 59
    specifying type before downloading with
        TYPE/CODETYPE attributes, 63–64
    See also controls
.OCX extensions, 20
OCXs (OLE custom controls), 20, 52
    See also controls
<OL>...</OL> numbered list tags, 34
OLE, 20
OLE custom controls (OCXs), 20
onClick event of Link object, 330
OnClipClosed event of RealAudio ActiveX
    control, 169, 170
OnClipOpen event of RealAudio ActiveX
    control, 169, 170–171
OnGotoURL event of RealAudio ActiveX
    control, 169, 171–173
onLoad event
    of HTML Layout Control, 99
    of Window object, 83, 87, 99, 310
onMouseMove event of Link object, 330
onMouseOver event of Link object, 330

OnShowStatus event of RealAudio ActiveX
    control, 169, 171
onSubmit event of Form object, 335–336
onUnLoad event of Window object, 83, 87,
    88, 310
opaque controls, 102, 106–108
Open() method of Document object, 323, 324
Open() method of Window object, 312–314
Opener property of Window object, 308
Option Explicit statement in VBScript, 251, 353
OptionButton form control, 219, 220, 221
ordered arguments of methods, 146–147
Orientation property of SpinButton form
    control, 228–229
OS/2 support for RealAudio Players, 159
outer boxes for objects, 61–62
outline structure with heading tags for HTML,
    33, 35

• *P* •

<P>...</P> paragraph tags, 34, 35
packets of data, 169
PageGen utility, 152
pages on Web, 10, 28
    See also Web sites/pages
paragraphs, creating onscreen in HTML, 35
<PARAM> tag, 65–66
Parent property of Window object, 308
parsing, 99
Part of Tens
    cool ActiveX controls, 345–350
    VBScript tips, 351–358
PasswordChar property of TextBox form
    control, 231–232
Paste() form control method, 194, 195
Pathname property of Link Object, 327, 328
pathnames
    absolute and relative, 33–34
    as addresses on Web, 31–33
.PDF extensions, 345
performance considerations
    image display, 42, 60
    inline images, 42, 140–141
    "Please stand by" messages with STANDBY
        attribute, 63
    sound file size, 155, 156
physical tags in HTML
    descriptions and list, 36, 38
    examples of output, 40
picas as units of measurement, 61

Picture property
    of display controls, 102, 115
    of form controls, 181
    of Gauge control, 136
PictureAlignment property of Image control,
    141–142
PicturePath property of Image control, 142
PicturePosition property of form controls,
    181, 188
pictures, *See also* images
PictureSizeMode property of Image control,
    142–144
PictureTiling property of Image control,
    145–146
pixels as units of measurement, 61
placeholders with DECLARE attribute, 60
platforms
    Macintosh, 6, 13, 31, 159
    porting of programs between, 13, 241
    UNIX, 13, 31, 159
    Windows, 13, 159
    See also Macintosh
plug-ins for Web browsers, 14
points as units of measurement, 61
polygons, specifying with SHAPES attribute, 63
PopUp() form control method, 225
Popup Menu form control, 179, 221–222,
    224–226
    example, 222–224
port numbers, 32–33
Port property of Link Object, 327, 328–329
porting of programs from one platform to
    another, 13, 241
positional control of objects on Web pages, 90
    with HTML Layouts, 91
<PRE>...</PRE> tags for preformatted text,
    38, 326
presentations (slide shows), 157, 173–176
Preserve keyword, 355, 356
Private keyword, caution on use in
    VBScript, 275
procedures
    advantages of reusing, 82
    calling, 247
    definition in VBScript, 271
    described, 267
    Function in VBScript, 269–271
    prototype, 275
    Sub in VBScript, 268, 270, 274
progress bars, 96
Progressive Network RealAudio
    Web site, 158
    See also RealAudio

Prompt() method of Window object, 314–315
properties of controls. *See* control properties
Protocol property of Link Object, 327, 329
prototype procedures in VBScript, 275
prototyping of new applications, 240
pulling requested documents from servers, 59
pushing unasked-for documents to clients, 59

• R •

.RA extensions, 174
.RAE extensions, 174
.RAM extensions, 175
RealAudio
   creating files, 158, 160
   described, 157
   transmission statistics display, 168
RealAudio Content Creation Guide, 159, 165
RealAudio Encoder, 159
RealAudio home page, 160
RealAudio metafiles, 158, 165
RealAudio Personal Server, 159
RealAudio Player, 159
   embedding with RealAudio Player ActiveX
      control, 160–166
   preferences files, 168
RealAudio Player ActiveX control
   for embedding RealAudio Player inline,
      160–166
   events, 169–173
   methods, 166–169
   properties, 160, 161–166
   for streamed audio, 157
   for synchronized multimedia, 172, 173–176
   uses, 160
RealAudio Server, 158–159
real-time sound, 155
ReDIM statement in VBScript, 355–356
reference variables in VBScript, 256–257
Referrer property of Document object, 86–87,
   317, 322
Refresh() method, 137
relative and absolute pathnames, 33–34
RemoveItem() form control method, 194,
   196, 225
reserved words in VBScript, 249, 268
Reset property of RealAudio ActiveX
   control, 161
Resizeable parameter of Open method, 314
RGB color values, 321
RIGHT value of ALIGN attribute
   of <OBJECT> tag, 57
   of <TABLE> tag, 43

RowIndex property of ActiveX Chart
   control, 131
RowName property of ActiveX Chart
   control, 131
ROWS attribute of <FRAMESET> tag, 47–48
Rows property of ActiveX Chart control, 131
ROWSPAN attribute for table tags, 43

• S •

<SAMP>...</SAMP> logical tags for literal
   sequences in fixed-width font, 38
sample scripts/code
   Animated Button control, 124
   attaching script to links, 356–357
   background changes for browser and
      Internet Explorer control, 301–304
   background or link color changes, 80, 316
   calling VBScripts function on load of page, 310
   charts, 56, 129
   charts with ChartType property, 132
   command button, 69
   confirming hard disk erasure, 312
   cookie creation, 319–320
   drag-and-drop events, 280, 283
   Elements array creation within Form object,
      333–334
   floating frame creation, 49–50
   font specification in ToggleBox control, 111
   forecolor changes, 76
   frame creation, 46–47
   "Hello, world!", 246–247
   HTML layout insertion into HTML file, 98
   If...Then...Else if...Else statements in VBScript,
      258–259
   inches-to-centimeters conversion,
      269–270, 271
   label creation, 103
   listbox creation, 209–210
   listbox with preselected items, 217
   loops in VBScript, 259–264
   menu creation, 222–223
   mouse event handling, 288–290
   Navigator object properties display, 339–340
   procedure calls in VBScript, 270
   procedure-level and script-level variables, 252
   RealAudio Player shared Console value,
      163–164
   running procedure upon window content
      loading, 309
   Shockwave movie, 60
   Sub procedure use of form name and index
      value, 331–332

sample scripts/code *(continued)*
  table creation, 44–45
  text box updates upon spin button clicks, 227
  TextBox with Change event and
    SpinButton, 278
  variables assignment, 256
  varying color label display, 238–239, 272
  writing strings to document stream, 323,
    324–326
  writing to browser window from HTML file,
    357–358
Scale property of ActiveX Chart control, 131
scaling images with HEIGHT and WIDTH
    attributes, 42, 60
scope of VBScript variables, 251–252
screens, width considerations for users, 91
<SCRIPT>. . . </SCRIPT> tags, 247, 248–249
Script object, 83
  as property of Window object, 305
Script Wizard
  advantages for writing event handlers, 275
  caution on bug in Color button processing, 79
  choosing events to script, 74, 87–88
  creating global variables, 80–82
  described, 72–73
  Go To Page action, 78–79
  for scripting onLoad events, 99
  specifying actions to take upon events, 75–77
  specifying colors for Document objects,
    84–85
  starting, 73
  testing scripts with Internet Explorer, 77
  tracking sources of site visitors with Referrer
    property, 86–87
  using procedures, 82
  Window object, 82–84
scripting
  advantages, 2, 15, 73, 237–238, 241–244,
    245–246
  background color change example, 80
  for clients versus servers, 15, 16, 23
  color-change-on-button-click example, 73–77
  listbox with preselected items example, 217
  variable color label display example, 238–239
  See also ActiveX Scripting; Internet Explorer
    Object Model for Scripting; Script Wizard;
    VBScript
scripting languages, 237, 238, 240–241
scroll bars
  appearing automatically, 48
  specifying hidden, 48

scroll boxes, 189
Scrollbars parameter of Open method, 314
ScrollBars property of form controls, 181, 189
  TextBox control, 232
SCROLLING attribute of <FRAME> tag, 47, 48
Search property of Link Object, 327, 329
security considerations, of
  plug-ins for Web browsers, 14
  tools in Server Framework, 15
Select Case statements, VBScript, 263–264
Selected property of ListBox form control,
    216–217
SelectionMargin property of form controls,
    181, 190
Self property of Window object, 308
SelLength property of form controls, 181, 190
SelStart property of form controls, 181,
    190–191
SelText property of form controls, 181, 191
servers. *See* Web servers
server-side image maps, 65
SetFocus() form control method, 194, 196
SetTimeOut() method of Window object,
    315–316
SGML (Standardized General Markup Lan-
    guage), 29
SHAPES attribute, of <OBJECT> tag, 63
ShowDropButtonWhen property of ComboBox
    form control, 206
slide shows, 157, 173–176
SmallChange property of SpinButton form
    control, 229
SMTP/POP3 control (in Microsoft Internet
    Control Pack), 349
snapping to grid, 92
SoftQuad HoTMetaL Pro HTML editor, 31, 89
sound effects
  large file size of, 155, 156
  popularity of, on Web sites, 9, 10, 155
  streaming audio, 157, 158
  tips for enhancing, 160
source code, 248
SpecialEffect property
  of display controls, 102, 115–117
  of form controls, 181
spell checking with Option Explicit statement,
    251, 353
SpinButton form control, 179, 226–229
  with Change event, 278–279
SpinDown event of SpinButton form
    control, 229
SpinUp event of SpinButton form control, 229

SRC attribute
  of <FRAME> tag, 48
  of <IMG> inline image tag, 40–42
SRC property of RealAudio ActiveX control, 161, 162
standard units of measurement, 60–61
STANDBY attribute of <OBJECT> tag, 63
Starfish Software EarthTime control, 349, 350
StartColor property of Gradient control, 139
StartPoint property of Gradient control, 139
states
  for Animated Button, 121–122
  as attributes of controls, 54
Status parameter of Open method, 314
Status property of Window object, 308–309
streaming audio, 157, 158
streams, 323, 324
strikethrough
  as Font object, 110
  for text with Label control, 152
strings in VBScript, 254, 257–258
stroke weight as Font objects, 111
<STRONG>...</STRONG> logical tags for strong emphasis in boldface, 38
structure tags with heading levels for HTML, 34–36
Style property
  of ComboBox form control, 206
  of Gauge control, 136
style sheets in HTML, 25
style tags in HTML, 36–40
Sub procedures in VBScript, 268, 270, 274
Submit() method of Form object, 335–336
synchronized multimedia, 157
  with RealAudio Player ActiveX control, 168, 172, 173–176

● *T* ●

TabIndex property
  of display controls, 102, 117
  of form controls, 181
TabKeyBehavior property of form controls, 181, 192
<TABLE> tag, 43
table tags in HTML, 43–45
TabStop property
  of display controls, 102, 117
  of form controls, 181
tags in HTML. *See under* HTML files; *See also individual tags*

TARGET attribute
  of <A> tag, 31, 33
  of Open method, 314
Target property
  of Form object, 333, 335
  of Link Object, 327, 329
TCP/IP (Transmission Control Protocol/ Internet Protocol), 10, 26
<TD> table data cell tag, 43
text
  aligning, 57
  aligning in labels, 149
  curving in labels, 150–151
  in outline or solid characters, 151–152
  rotating in labels, 149
  selected, 190
  typefaces in labels, 152
  writing from Document object, 323, 324–325, 357, 358
  See also Label control
Text property
  of form controls, 181, 192
  of ListBox form control, 218
TextAlign property of form controls, 181, 192
TEXTBOTTOM value of ALIGN attribute of <OBJECT> tag, 57
TextBox form control, 179, 230–233
  with Change event and SpinButton control, 278
  generating events for mouse actions, 287
TextColumn property of ListBox form control, 209–211, 218
TEXTMIDDLE value of ALIGN attribute of <OBJECT> tag, 57
TEXTTOP value of ALIGN attribute of <OBJECT> tag, 57
<TH> table header cell tag, 43
Timeline Editor, 173, 175
timer setting, 315–316
<TITLE> tags, 30
Title property of Document object, 317, 323
ToggleButton form control, 178, 179, 233–234
Toolbar parameter of Open method, 314
Top property
  of display controls, 103, 118
  of form controls, 182
  of Window object, 309
TOP value
  of ALIGN attribute (<OBJECT> tag), 57
  of VALIGN attribute (<CAPTION> table tag), 43
TopIndex property of ListBox form control, 218
TopPoints property of Label control, 149–151
TopXY property of Label control, 149–151

<TR> table row tag, 43
transparent controls, 102, 106–108
TripleState property of form controls, 182, 193
<TT>...</TT> physical tags for typewriter (fixed-width) font, 38
Tumbleweed Envoy Viewer control, 349
TYPE attribute of <OBJECT> tag, 63–64
typefaces, 111

● *U* ●

<UL>...</UL> unnumbered list tags, 34
underlines
  as Font object, 111
  for text with Label control, 152
units of measurement, 60–61
UNIX
  HTML file creation, 31
  support for ActiveX, 13
  support for RealAudio Players, 159
URL events, 172
URL property of ActiveX Chart control, 131–133
URLs (Uniform Resource Locators)
  described, 31–33
  pointing to, as RealAudio sources, 161, 170
  specifying in CODEBASE attribute, 59
  specifying in DATA attributes, 60
  specifying in Navigate method, 312
  specifying in Open method, 313
  tracking sources of site visitors with Referrer property, 86–87
USEMAP attribute of <OBJECT> tag, 64
UserAgent property of Navigator object, 337, 338
utilities, PageGen, 152

● *V* ●

VALIGN attribute for table tags, 43
Value property
  of display controls, 103, 118
  of form controls, 182
<VAR>...</VAR> logical tags for variable values in italics, 38
variables
  global, 80–82, 251–252, 354–355
  local, 79–80, 251–252, 354–355
  reference, 256–257
  scope in VBScript, 251–252
  types and subtypes in VBScript, 253–255
  VBScript, 249–252

VarType() function of VBScript, 255
VBA (Visual Basic for Applications), 240
VBScript
  arithmetic operators, 264, 265, 266
  arrays, 255–256
  Call statements, 270
  caution on Private and As keywords, 275
  comments in, 249, 272, 353
  comparison operators, 264, 265, 267
  concatenation operator (&), 257
  constants, predefined, 252–253
  described, 2, 19, 20, 240, 241, 246
  DIM statement, 250–251, 255–256
  Do loops, 261–263
  For...Next loops, 259–263
  Function procedures, 269–271
  in HTML files with identifying tags, 248–249
  If...Then...Else if...Else statements (flow of control), 258–259
  logical operators, 264, 265, 267
  mailing list, 352
  multiple possible value tests (Select Case statement), 263–264
  Option Explicit statement, 251
  procedures as public, 275
  procedures definition, 271
  reference documentation site, 351
  reference variables, 256–257
  reserved words, 249, 268
  source of samples, 351–352
  spell checking with Option Explicit statement, 251, 353
  string handling, 257–258
  Sub procedures, 268, 270, 274
  syntax conventions, 250, 268, 269
  top ten tips for, 351–358
  variables, 249–252
    scope, 251–252
    types and subtypes, 253–255
  See also scripting
VBScript For Dummies, 352
.VBX extensions, 20
VBXs (Visual Basic controls), 20
version information with CODEBASE attribute, 59
VerticalGrid property of ActiveX Chart control, 133
video clips, popularity on Web sites, 9, 10, 155
viewers as external file handlers for Web browsers, 155
Visible property
  of display controls, 103, 118
  of form controls, 180, 182

visited links, 84, 323
Visual Basic Programmer's Journal, 353
Visual Basic (VB)
    availability for various architectures, 241
    described, 240
    new editions featuring ActiveX, 19
    overview of programming in, 20
    popularity of, 18
    Professional Edition, 352
    See also VBScript
vLinkColor property of Document object,
    317, 323
VREAM WIRL control, 350
VRML (Virtual Reality Modeling Language), 242
VSPACE attribute of <OBJECT> tag, 61–62

• *W* •

.WAV extensions, 157
Web browsers
    described, 10, 27–28
    frames as windows, 170
    helper applications for, 14
    history lists, 340
    sound file support lacking, 155
Web page design
    advantages of ActiveX for, 9, 16, 17–23
    See also HTML files; HTML Layouts
Web servers
    clients as customers, 27
    as computers offering services, 15, 26–27
    installing RealAudio capability, 158
Web sites/pages
    advantages of ActiveX for creating, 3
    described, 1
    games, 244
    highlighting (and expiration-date-marking)
        new items, 153–154
    as intranet pages, 2
    scripting/activating with ActiveX, 238–239
    viewing HTML code and scripts, 276
Web (World Wide Web)
    compared to Internet, 10, 26
    described, 10
    popularity of, 26
    See also Internet
WIDTH attribute
    of <IMG SRC> inline image tag, 41, 42
    of <OBJECT> tag, 60–61
    of <TABLE> tag, 45

Width parameter of Open method, 314
Width property
    of display controls, 103, 118
    of form controls, 182
Window object
    in Internet Explorer Object Model, 305–316
    in Script Wizard, 82
Windows 3.1, support for RealAudio
        Players, 159
Windows 95
    support for ActiveX, 13
    support for RealAudio Players, 159
windows, sending to front or back of
        z-order, 196
Windows desktop, 19
Windows Notepad. *See* Notepad
Windows NT
    support for ActiveX, 13
    support for RealAudio Players, 159
Winsock control (in Microsoft Internet Control
        Pack), 349
Wizards, Script. *See* Script Wizard
WordWrap property
    of display controls, 103, 119
    of form controls, 182
    of TextBox form control, 230
World Wide Web. *See* Web
World Wide Web Consortium (W3C), setting
        standards, 60–61
Write() method of Document object, 323,
        324–325, 357, 358
WriteLn() method of Document object, 323,
        325–326, 357

• *X* •

.XBM extensions, 40

• *Z* •

ZOrder() form control method, 194, 196–197

IDG BOOKS WORLDWIDE, INC.
END-USER LICENSE AGREEMENT

Read This. You should carefully read these terms and conditions before opening the software packet(s) included with this book ("Book"). This is a license agreement ("Agreement") between you and IDG Books Worldwide, Inc. ("IDGB"). By opening the accompanying software packet(s), you acknowledge that you have read and accept the following terms and conditions. If you do not agree and do not want to be bound by such terms and conditions, promptly return the Book and the unopened software packet(s) to the place you obtained them for a full refund.

1. **License Grant.** IDGB grants to you (either an individual or entity) a nonexclusive license to use one copy of the enclosed software program(s) (collectively, the "Software") solely for your own personal or business purposes on a single computer (whether a standard computer or a workstation component of a multiuser network). The Software is in use on a computer when it is loaded into temporary memory (i.e., RAM) or installed into permanent memory (e.g., hard disk, CD-ROM, or other storage device). IDGB reserves all rights not expressly granted herein.

2. **Ownership.** IDGB is the owner of all right, title, and interest, including copyright, in and to the compilation of the Software recorded on the disk(s)/CD-ROM. Copyright to the individual programs on the disk(s)/CD-ROM is owned by the author or other authorized copyright owner of each program. Ownership of the Software and all proprietary rights relating thereto remain with IDGB and its licensors.

3. **Restrictions on Use and Transfer.**

   (a) You may only (i) make one copy of the Software for backup or archival purposes, or (ii) transfer the Software to a single hard disk, provided that you keep the original for backup or archival purposes. You may not (i) rent or lease the Software, (ii) copy or reproduce the Software through a LAN or other network system or through any computer subscriber system or bulletin-board system, or (iii) modify, adapt, or create derivative works based on the Software.

   (b) You may not reverse engineer, decompile, or disassemble the Software. You may transfer the Software and user documentation on a permanent basis, provided that the transferee agrees to accept the terms and conditions of this Agreement and you retain no copies. If the Software is an update or has been updated, any transfer must include the most recent update and all prior versions.

4. **Restrictions on Use of Individual Programs.** You must follow the individual requirements and restrictions detailed for each individual program in the Introduction of this Book. These limitations are contained in the individual license agreements recorded on the disk(s)/CD-ROM. These restrictions may include a requirement that after using the program for the period of time specified in its text, the user must pay a registration fee or discontinue use. By opening the Software packet(s), you will be agreeing to abide by the licenses and restrictions for these individual programs. None of the material on the disk(s)/CD-ROM or listed in this Book may ever be distributed, in original or modified form, for commercial purposes.

5. **Limited Warranty.**

   (a) IDGB warrants that the Software and disk(s)/CD-ROM are free from defects in materials and workmanship under normal use for a period of sixty (60) days from the date of purchase of this Book. If IDGB receives notification within the warranty period of defects in materials or workmanship, IDGB will replace the defective disk(s)/CD-ROM.

   (b) **IDGB AND THE AUTHOR OF THE BOOK DISCLAIM ALL OTHER WARRAN-TIES, EXPRESS OR IMPLIED, INCLUDING WITHOUT LIMITATION IMPLIED WARRANTIES OF MERCHANTABILITY AND FITNESS FOR A PARTICULAR PURPOSE, WITH RESPECT TO THE SOFTWARE, THE PROGRAMS, THE SOURCE CODE CONTAINED THEREIN, AND/OR THE TECHNIQUES DE-SCRIBED IN THIS BOOK. IDGB DOES NOT WARRANT THAT THE FUNC-TIONS CONTAINED IN THE SOFTWARE WILL MEET YOUR REQUIREMENTS OR THAT THE OPERATION OF THE SOFTWARE WILL BE ERROR FREE.**

   (c) This limited warranty gives you specific legal rights, and you may have other rights which vary from jurisdiction to jurisdiction.

6. **Remedies.**

   (a) IDGB's entire liability and your exclusive remedy for defects in materials and workmanship shall be limited to replacement of the Software, which may be returned to IDGB with a copy of your receipt at the following address: Disk Fulfillment Department, Attn: ActiveX For Dummies, IDG Books Worldwide, Inc., 7260 Shadeland Station, Ste. 100, Indianapolis, IN 46256, or call 1-800-762-2974. Please allow 3–4 weeks for delivery. This Limited Warranty is void if failure of the Software has resulted from accident, abuse, or misapplication. Any replacement Software will be warranted for the remainder of the original warranty period or thirty (30) days, whichever is longer.

   (b) In no event shall IDGB or the author be liable for any damages whatsoever (including without limitation damages for loss of business profits, business interruption, loss of business information, or any other pecuniary loss) arising from the use of or inability to use the Book or the Software, even if IDGB has been advised of the possibility of such damages.

   (c) Because some jurisdictions do not allow the exclusion or limitation of liability for consequential or incidental damages, the above limitation or exclusion may not apply to you.

7. **U.S. Government Restricted Rights.** Use, duplication, or disclosure of the Software by the U.S. Government is subject to restrictions stated in paragraph (c) (1) (ii) of the Rights in Technical Data and Computer Software clause of DFARS 252.227-7013, and in subparagraphs (a) through (d) of the Commercial Computer—Restricted Rights clause at FAR 52.227-19, and in similar clauses in the NASA FAR supplement, when applicable.

8. **General.** This Agreement constitutes the entire understanding of the parties and revokes and supersedes all prior agreements, oral or written, between them and may not be modified or amended except in a writing signed by both parties hereto which specifically refers to this Agreement. This Agreement shall take precedence over any other documents that may be in conflict herewith. If any one or more provisions contained in this Agreement are held by any court or tribunal to be invalid, illegal, or otherwise unenforceable, each and every other provision shall remain in full force and effect.

Installation Instructions:
How to Use the CD-ROM

● ●

*H*ere are the instructions for installing the accompanying CD-ROM. (For more details about the CD-ROM and what's on it, see the Appendix, "About the CD-ROM," or the readme.txt file on the CD-ROM.)

Windows 95

1. **Insert the CD-ROM into the computer's CD-ROM drive.**

2. **Double-click the My Computer icon on the desktop.**

3. **Double-click the icon for your CD-ROM drive (usually drive D:).**

4. **Double-click the index.htm file on the CD-ROM.**

    For more details about the CD-ROM and what's on it, see the readme.txt file on the CD-ROM.

Windows 3.1

1. **Insert the CD-ROM into the computer's CD-ROM drive.**

2. **Double-click the File Manager icon.**

3. **Double-click the icon for your CD-ROM drive (usually drive D:).**

4. **Double-click the index.htm file on the CD-ROM.**

 **YES!**

Please keep me informed about IDG Books Worldwide's World of Computer Knowledge. Send me your latest catalog.

NO POSTAGE
NECESSARY
IF MAILED
IN THE
UNITED STATES

BUSINESS REPLY MAIL

FIRST CLASS MAIL   PERMIT NO. 2605   FOSTER CITY, CALIFORNIA

IDG Books Worldwide
919 E Hillsdale Blvd, Ste 400
Foster City, CA 94404-9691